FOURTH EDITION

THE
SOCIAL
DIMENSION
OF WESTERN CIVILIZATION
VOLUME 2

Readings from
THE SIXTEENTH CENTURY
TO THE PRESENT

FOURTH EDITION

THE SOCIAL DIMENSION

OF WESTERN CIVILIZATION

VOLUME 2

Readings from
THE SIXTEENTH CENTURY
TO THE PRESENT

RICHARD M. GOLDEN
University of North Texas

BEDFORD/ST. MARTIN'S
Boston/New York

For Bedford/St. Martin's

History Editor: Katherine E. Kurzman
Developmental Editor: Charisse Kiino
Associate Production Editor: Jessica Zorn
Production Supervisor: Scott Lavelle and Dennis J. Conroy
Marketing Manager: Charles Cavaliere
Art Director: Lucy Krikorian
Text Design: Anna George/Dorothy Bungert
Copy Editor: Judy Voss
Cover Design: Ann Gallager
Cover Art: St. James's Fair, Bristol by Samuel Colman (1780–1845) City of Bristol Museum and Art Gallery, Avon, UK/Bridgeman Art Library, London/New York
Composition: ComCom
Printing and Binding: Haddon Craftsmen

President: Charles H. Christensen
Editorial Director: Joan E. Feinberg
Director of Editing, Design, and Production: Marcia Cohen
Managing Editor: Erica T. Appel

Library of Congress Catalog Card Number: 98-86770

Manufactured in the United States of America.

4 3 2 1 0 9
f e d c b a

For information, write: Bedford/St. Martin's, 75 Arlington Street, Boston, MA 02116
(617-426-7440)

ISBN: 0-312-18253-8

Acknowledgments

PREFACE

The Social Dimension of Western Civilization, Fourth Edition (previously entitled *Social History of Western Civilization*), is a two-volume reader for Western Civilization courses. The essays in each volume deal with social history because I believe that the most original and significant work of the past three decades has been done in this area and because some Western Civilization textbooks tend to slight social history in favor of the more traditional political, intellectual, and cultural history, though this bias is changing.

Throughout the past twenty years in the classroom, I have used a number of anthologies, but the selections often assume a degree of background knowledge that the typical student does not possess. To make *The Social Dimension* better suited to students, I have sifted through hundreds of essays to find those that are both challenging and accessible, interesting and significant. To enhance the readability of the selected articles, I have included more than four hundred gloss notes that translate foreign words or identify individuals and terms that students might not recognize. All the footnotes are therefore my own unless otherwise indicated. Based on my classroom experience, gloss notes are invaluable to students using anthologies.

A Western Civilization anthology cannot be all things to all instructors and students, but I have consciously tried to make these two volumes flexible enough to work in a wide variety of Western Civilization courses. The fourth edition's broader range of themes and its expanded notion of Europe should meet more instructors' needs in that the coverage is now more tightly correlated to survey texts. Some historians argue that Western civilization began with the Greeks, but I have included in Volume One a section on Mesopotamia, Israel, and Egypt for the courses that begin there. In addition, both volumes contain material on the sixteenth and seventeenth centuries because instructors and institutions divide Western Civilization courses differently.

In this fourth edition, certain elements have been retained and strengthened, while new features have been added. It is my hope that instructors will find this edition not only more flexible but also more helpful in sparking class discussion and making thematic comparisons among the essays.

New Readings. In preparing this edition, there always seemed to be some-where a more attractive article on every topic, as is the case every time I revise. While maintaining a balance between classical pieces in social history with those on the cutting edge of recent scholarship, I have changed twelve of this volume's twenty-five essays. I have based the substitutions not only on my own searches but also on feedback from those who have used previous editions. The new read-ings, on themes such as interracial marriage, urban poverty, pregnancy, smell, working-class marriage, and the execution of criminals, reflect the active nature of historical scholarship today.

Thoroughly Revised Apparatus. In this fourth edition, I have extensively re-vised the part introductions as well as the selection headnotes, incorporating per-tinent prereading questions to guide students through the essays and to encour-age active reading about the problems and issues raised.

Social History Emphasis. Throughout the introductory and headnote ma-terial, I discuss the practice of social history — its growth and importance as well as its goals within the discipline. For each selection, I mention the types of sources the author used, in order to show students how social historians compile evi-dence.

Making Connections Questions. Four themes — in this volume, violence, disease and death, women and the family, and work — have been singled out, with an article on each theme in every part. New Making Connections questions at the end of particular selections link these themes over historical periods, en-couraging students to think about change over time while comparing various cultures and peoples.

Topical Table of Contents. This alternate table of contents groups all the se-lections under the topics they discuss, enabling instructors and students to com-pare articles according to theme.

Instructor's Manual. Prepared by Denis Paz, who has used this anthology in class since 1988, *Teaching Suggestions: THE SOCIAL DIMENSION OF WESTERN CIVILIZA-TION* includes discussion questions, topics for term papers, and student exercises. The manual also has useful handouts that show students how to underline and annotate a reading and a correlation chart that relates each essay to a relevant chapter in the major Western Civilization textbooks currently on the market.

Acknowledgments

Many people suggested essays to me, critiqued what I wrote, and helped in other ways as well. I thank Ove Anderson, Jay Crawford, Fara Driver, Patricia Easley, Phillip Garland, Laurie Glover, Tully Hunter, Christopher Koontz, John Leonard, Laurie McDowell, and James Sanchez. Especially generous with their time and comments on the first three editions were Philip Adler, Kathryn Babayan, William Beik, Robert Bireley, Richard Bulliet, Elizabeth D. Carney, Edward Coomes,

Suzanne A. Desan, Lawrence Estaville, Hilda Golden, Leonard Greenspoon, Alan Grubb, Christopher Guthrie, Sarah Hanley, George Huppert, Thomas Kuehn, Charles Lippy, Donald McKale, Steven Marks, Victor Matthews, John A. Mears, William Murnane, David Nicholas, Thomas F. X. Noble, James Sack, Carol Thomas, and Roy Vice. Steven D. Cooley, Charles T. Evans, Anita Guerrini, Benjamin Hudson, Jonathan Katz, Donna T. McCaffrey, Maureen Melody, Kathryn E. Meyer, Lohr E. Miller, Gerald M. Schnabel, Paul Teverow, Sara W. Tucker, and Lindsay Wilson reviewed the third edition or responded to questionnaires for preparing this edition. Edward Coomes, Henry Eaton, Lee Huddleston, Marilyn Morris, Laura Stern, and Harold Tanner provided generous assistance with the fourth edition.

The following historians gave helpful feedback via questionnaires or reviews for *The Social Dimension:* Ann T. Allen, University of Louisville; David Burns, Moraine Valley Community College; Leslie Derfler, Florida Atlantic University; John E. Dreifort, Wichita State University; Amanda Eurich, Western Washington University; William J. Everts Jr., Champlain College; Marie T. Gingras, University of Colorado at Denver; Christopher E. Guthrie, Tarleton State University; Carla Hay, Marquette University; Daniel W. Hollis III, Jacksonville State University; John Hunt, Joseph College; Katharine D. Kennedy, Agnes Scott College; Thomas Kuehn, Clemson University; Joyce M. Mastboom, Cleveland State University; John McCole, University of Oregon; David Nicholas, Clemson University; Philip Otterness, Warren Wilson College; Catherine Patterson, University of Houston; Denis Paz, University of North Texas; Dolores Davidson Peterson, Foothill College (Ph.D. candidate at University of Illinois at Chicago); Lowell Satre, Youngstown State University; Stephanie Sherwell, Charles County Community College; Malcolm Smuts, University of Massachusetts at Boston; Larissa Taylor, Colby College; Michael C. Weber, Northern Essex Community College; Michael Wolfe, Pennsylvania State University — Altoona; Anne York, Youngstown State University; and Ronald Zupko, Marquette University.

I have been fortunate in working with publishers and editors who show wonderful empathy for history and for historians. My experiences have been completely positive, and I thank all of the good people at Bedford/St. Martin's: the publishers, Chuck Christensen and Joan Feinberg, who have a feeling and appreciation for both books and the book market; Molly Kalkstein and Tom Pierce, Editorial Assistants, who have always been professional and efficient; Charisse Kiino, who as Developmental Editor did an absolutely superb job in helping me with a rather thorough revision; and Katherine Kurzman, Sponsoring Editor, who expertly and gently helped guide the project over a two-year period. Erica Appel, Jessica Zorn, and Judy Voss handled expertly production and copy editing, while Donna Dennison designed the new book covers and Fred Courtright handled permissions. Denis Paz, an eminent social historian who is more familiar with this anthology than anyone else, has given me for all four editions his perspectives as a historian and a professor. His help has been invaluable. Finally, I have been blessed with the support of my wife, Hilda, and my three children — Davina, Irene, and Jeremy. They have sharpened my perception of social life and have always given me their love. I dedicate this book to them.

CONTENTS

PART ONE

THE OLD RÉGIME

PART TWO

THE NINETEENTH CENTURY

PART THREE

THE TWENTIETH CENTURY

"Death, so omnipresent in the past that it was familiar, would be effaced, would disappear. It would become shameful and forbidden."

"Club Med was ultimately packaging the care of the self and its recuperation through play, relaxation, and pleasure. Physical health and physical beauty were central to this vision."

"Swedish society is endowed not just with material or political content but with philosophical or even moral significance, with 'the good life.'"

TOPICAL TABLE OF CONTENTS

CRIME

DISEASE AND DEATH

MARRIAGE AND THE FAMILY

COLLECTIVE ATTITUDES AND BELIEFS

RELIGION

RURAL LIFE

SEXUALITY

URBAN LIFE

WAR, TERRORISM, AND VIOLENCE

WOMEN

WORK AND ECONOMIC LIFE

INTRODUCTION

The selections in this volume deal with the social history of Western civilization from the sixteenth century to the present. Social history encompasses the study of *groups* of people rather than focusing on prominent individuals, such as kings, intellectual giants, and military leaders. Over the last three decades, social historians have examined a host of topics, many of which are included here: the family, women, sex, disease, everyday life, death, social groups (such as the peasantry and nobility), entertainment, work, leisure, popular religion and politics, criminality, the experience of soldiers in war, economic conditions, and collective mentality (the attitudes, beliefs, and assumptions held by a population). Social history, then, sheds light both on previously neglected areas of human experience and on forgotten and nameless people, including minorities and those at the bottom of the social scale. Indeed, some recent historians, perhaps a bit too optimistically, endeavor to write "total history," to include all aspects of people's lives.

Social historians take an analytical approach instead of the narrative and chronological approach generally used by biographers and traditional political historians. Social historians do not attempt to celebrate the heroes and heroines of a nation's history, although that is precisely the type of "feel good" history that many in the public wish to read and to see taught in school systems. They do not glorify any Alamos. Instead, their goal is to re-create and make known the lives of ordinary people. In taking this approach, social historians have expanded their research beyond diaries, personal and government correspondence, and court documents to include such sources as police reports, tax rolls, census schedules, writings by people in the lower classes, conscription lists, parish registers, marriage contracts, wills, church records, government commissions, records of small businesses, newspapers and magazines, popular literature, oral histories, songs, and material artifacts. By using such a variety of sources, social historians are able to reveal the private and public lives of people in all social groups. The head-notes to the articles in this volume mention some of the types of sources historians have consulted as they strive to explain the social past. Some students may, of course, choose to seek out primary sources and other evidence to research some of the topics covered here, and they may indeed arrive at different conclusions from those of the historians.

Many of the articles treat similar themes, as shown in the Topical Table of Contents. For four of these themes (violence, disease and death, women and the family, and work), I have developed Making Connections questions, which link readings to each other so students can begin to make comparisons among countries, cultures, and time periods. These questions will also help students make connections to material in their textbooks and in lectures. It is important to make such comparisons in order to place subjects in perspective and to discern causality and change over time.

Unlike traditional political history, social history rarely begins or ends with specific dates. The problem of periodization, always a thorny one, is especially difficult for social historians, who often study topics that can be understood only as long-term developments. Thus, infanticide, though surely declining in frequency in the late-nineteenth century, cannot be understood without looking back to antiquity and to the Middle Ages. Another such topic is human sexuality. Any discussion of the sexual practices of the Victorian Age must be set against the durable sexual relations that, in significant ways, changed little in the course of millennia. In social history, then, what has not changed is often more important than what has changed, making it difficult for the social historian to decide where to divide, cut off, or end a subject.

As a way out of this difficulty, social historians have come to favor a simple division between premodern (or traditional or preindustrial) society and the modern (or industrial) world. This split has several advantages. First, it clearly indicates that the Industrial Revolution constituted a watershed, affecting lifestyles and human relationships throughout society. The Industrial Revolution raised new problems and new questions involving workers' movements, nationalism, mass democracy, and women's emancipation, to name just a few topics. In the industrial era, developments occurred more rapidly than in preindustrial society, where dietary habits, family relationships, and work patterns, for instance, had changed more slowly over time. Second, the terms *traditional* and *premodern,* on the one hand, and *modern,* on the other hand, are general enough to permit historians to use the words while disagreeing about their meanings. What, exactly, does it mean to be *modern?* What is the process of modernization? Were people in the nineteenth century modern?

I am sympathetic to the division between premodern and modern, but for the sake of convenience I have grouped the selections in this volume into three parts. Part One, The Old Régime, concerns traditional Europe. The essays focus on the sixteenth, seventeenth, and eighteenth centuries. Part Two, The Nineteenth Century, begins with the Industrial Revolution. But because the Industrial Revolution actually began in England in the late-eighteenth century, a few of the articles start there. Some of the selections discuss much earlier material as they trace developments that reached fruition or ended in the nineteenth century. Part Three, The Twentieth Century, treats the Great War as a great divide. Here again, some essays go back in time to discuss the prior century and traditional Europe. In sum, historians impose periods on history that are always debatable and sometimes capricious but certainly essential in providing some order to the study of the past.

In any case, well-researched and well-written social history should convey excitement, for it makes us vividly aware of the daily lives, habits, and beliefs of our ancestors. In some ways, their patterns of behavior and thought will seem similar to ours, but in other ways our predecessors' actions and values may appear quite different, if not barbaric or alien. It is important to keep in mind that the living conditions and attitudes that exist in the present are not necessarily superior to those of the distant or recent past. Social history does not teach progress. Rather than drawing facile lessons from the daily lives of those who came before us, we might, as historians, attempt to immerse ourselves in their cultures and understand why they lived and acted as they did.

FOURTH EDITION

THE
SOCIAL
DIMENSION
OF WESTERN CIVILIZATION
VOLUME 2

Readings from
THE SIXTEENTH CENTURY
TO THE PRESENT

PART ONE

THE OLD RÉGIME

Richard van Dülmen
Christopher R. Friedrichs
Jacques Gélis
John McManners
Robert Darnton
Olwen Hufton
Albert Soboul
Keith Wrightson

Politically, the Old Régime was the Age of Absolutism, the era before the French Revolution; intellectually, it encompassed the Scientific Revolution and the Enlightenment; artistically, the Baroque and Rococo styles set the tone. The seventeenth and eighteenth centuries saw the nobility as preeminent over other social groups. Most people were poor physical specimens who worked hard, suffered from vitamin deficiency and malnutrition, and lived short lives. Although it is often difficult to read the minds of people who left few records of their feelings, one can suppose that happiness and enjoyment seemed out of the reach of the majority of Europe's population, save for that happiness that accompanies survival or the brief interlude of an exceptional occasion, such as a religious feast, a wedding, or some small victory extracted from a harsh and severe world.

All the essays in this section on the Old Régime convey the violence, uncertainty, and desperation that marked the lives of most Europeans. Richard van Dülmen's article points to the brutalization of life as evidenced in severe and public executions. Early modern cities, Christopher Friedrichs argues, could never cope sufficiently with the problem of poverty, which was exacerbated by the influx of immigrants who swelled the numbers of vagrants, beggars, prostitutes, and the laboring poor. Jacques Gélis's analysis of the fear of pregnancy explores the range of expedients, both physical and spiritual, that women put their faith in because of the dangers and pain accompanying the birthing process. Keith Wrightson's survey of infanticide throughout Europe reveals that some women believed they had little choice but to murder their infants because of the infamy associated with illegitimate births. Judges, exclusively male, did not exercise undo mercy toward women convicted of infanticide, a crime linked always to mothers, never to fathers.

As a rule, early modern Europeans revered unity and hierarchy, and abhorred dissent and pluralism. Although there were, to be sure, some outside the Christian fold — Jews, Muslims, and a sprinkling of atheists — nearly all Europeans in the Old Régime were Christians. After the Protestant Reformation had torn apart a relatively united Christendom in western Europe in the sixteenth century (the Eastern Orthodox Church had split from western Christianity in 1054), most states maintained an established church and discriminated legally against Christians who belonged to other denominations. Christians venerated order and authority, and they found them in a church, in the pope, or in scripture. The body politic likewise signified harmony and obedience. Monarchy was the model, a government that mirrored god's supremacy over the cosmos. Few were the religious and political visionaries who dared to consider an alternative to monarchical rule.

Deference and order characterized the social structure as well. Kings governed subjects, lords dominated peasants, men ruled women, and parents regulated their children's lives. Rank in the Old Régime was everything, and it certainly had its privileges. If men of commerce and industry rose in stature — in Great Britain and the United Provinces, for example — this social mobility in no way weakened the belief that hierarchy provided the ideal basis for society. Throughout most of Europe, the aristocracy stood at the pinnacle of the social pyramid, and in many places — some as far apart as France and Russia — the nobles experienced a resurgence of power and prestige. The aristocratic ethos offered a standard of behavior and a set of values that few non-nobles could emulate. Again, only a small number of individuals, primarily intellectuals or those on the fringes of society, dreamed of a democratic revolution that would sweep the aristocracy and their perquisites into the dustbin of history.

The Old Régime therefore possessed a certain unity in the midst of great diversity, a unity grounded in the respect, even glorification, of religious, political, and social order. Though changing, the Old Régime signified a stability that accompanied faith in respected institutions. The preferred form of change was individual change, a modest improvement in one's personal fortunes or those of one's family. Such alterations of status, however, did little to dispel the terrible and brutal conditions of daily existence that faced the vast majority of Europe's population.

The print-shop workers in eighteenth-century Paris could engage in an ephemeral revolt — a massacre of cats — against their boss, as Robert Darnton shows, but those workers had little hope of improving their social position. Working-class women had an active role in the economy, but Olwen Hufton concludes that their toil was unrelenting and their prospects for financial security dim, especially if they were single or widowed. In his essay, "Death's Arbitrary Empire," John McManners paints a riveting picture of the prevalence of disease, of the wracked condition of bodies, and of the vulnerability of most people to the vagaries of food production, weather, war, and the lack of healthy living conditions. Perhaps the greatest privileges of the wealthy were security from hunger and a diet that offered them better resistance to disease.

During the Middle Ages and the early modern period, Europeans had looked to the past for inspiration — religiously to the time of early Christianity and culturally to classical antiquity — and had grown accustomed to gradual change. The Industrial Revolution, however, increased dramatically the pace of change and brought the expectation of future improvement in social and economic life. Furthermore, the French Revolution put Europeans on notice that anything was possible, that the political and social order could be altered fundamentally according to human effort and will. The Parisian workers, craftsmen, and petty shopkeepers that Albert Soboul describes influenced greatly the course of politics during the French Revolution; no similar non-elite urban group had exercised such power in the preceding millennium. This relatively small number of politically committed workers provided a model for other groups that likewise had previously been excluded from political and social power.

Between them, the deluge of the Industrial and French Revolutions helped create a new régime in which modern technology ushered in the idea of progress and where political and social experimentation could occur.

RITUALS OF EXECUTION
IN EARLY MODERN GERMANY
Richard van Dülmen

Basing his study on the court records of major German cities, Richard van Dül-men describes a society that, lacking a police force and a prison system, imposed social control by means of rituals of torture and grisly public executions. A ver-itable "theatre of horror" (the title of the book from which this selection is drawn) maintained social order. Governments ordered corporal punishments — such as mutilation, branding, flogging — and the pillory that meant public dis-grace. The criminal's public confession, which courts demanded, legitimized the sentence and execution and offered a moral lesson to the audience. There were also ecclesiastical punishments, which emphasized public shame, but sec-ular court systems eventually incorporated these as early modern states sought to limit the ability of churches to act with any independence. Medieval legal sys-tems had stressed the public nature of trials. Early modern courts, however, re-moved the public from the process of determining guilt and instead insisted on the public spectacle of execution and on the ritual of social purification. Courts even ordered the execution of the corpses of criminals, thus underscoring the ne-cessity of the execution ritual and the accompanying cleansing of society.

The poor suffered more than the elite from the system of punishments; the latter's social status elicited more humane methods of execution. German courts, reflecting the anti-Semitism that pervaded early modern society, likewise treated Jews more brutally than Christians. Men and women often experienced differ-ent forms of execution (the latter being burned, drowned, or buried alive). Why does van Dülmen refer to these practices as rituals of purification? Why did courts demand such severe retribution?

The number of executions and the harshness of punishment peaked in the sixteenth century, in part owing to the Protestant and Catholic religions' new concern for the purification of morals. Why do you think horrific methods of ex-ecution, although they continued to exist, began to lose favor in the seventeenth and eighteenth centuries?

Richard van Dülmen, *Theatre of Horror: Crime and Punishment in Early Modern Germany,* trans. Elisabeth Neu (Cambridge: Polity Press, 1990), 88–97, 99, 101–106.

Do you think that brutal and public executions were justified because they brought the community together by reinforcing contemporary morality and social standards? To what extent do you believe such executions acted as an effective deterrent to criminals?

The traditional rituals of execution were burning, drowning and burying alive. Documented abundantly for the sixteenth century, and in part also practised in the early seventeenth century, they subsequently lost their significance. In so far as their objective was the radical extermination and annihilation of a malefactor of whom no trace — either memory or grave — must remain, these forms of execution can be viewed as society's rituals of purification. Society cleansed itself of crimes, especially of those that violated the religious and moral order in a way that brought fear of harm to the community if they were not punished accordingly. These punishments were mainly inflicted upon women. Death was not brought about by the executioner's hand, but without bloodshed by forces of nature, through fire, water or earth, to which specially destructive or purifying powers were attributed. To a certain extent hanging can be included, as the delinquent was abandoned to the power of air — that is, to the weather and the birds. With the authorities' increasing control over penal practice and executions designed for theatricality, intimidation and moral edification, "purificatory" rituals became more and more disfunctional in the eyes of the authorities and were substituted for the main part by the "deterrent" punishment of the sword.

Being buried alive was deemed a particularly horrific and severe punishment for a variety of sexual offences such as adultery, murder of one's spouse and infanticide, but it also punished cases of grand larceny. It was used mainly as a punishment for women, as a counterpart to breaking on the wheel for men. The delinquent was generally undressed and laid on her back in a pit beneath the gallows, bound, covered with thorns and buried from the feet upwards. This was often combined with impalement — that is, a pale was driven from above through the heart, navel or chest. This might be carried out before or after burial. The symbolism is not completely clear; obviously a return was to be rendered impossible and at the same time impalement prevented slow suffocation. One of the last and most famous cases of a delinquent being buried alive is documented for Frankfurt in 1585. A woman had killed her husband in bed, stabbing him sixty-four times. Burying her alive and driving "a long, pointed spike through her body" was considered the most appropriate punishment for her crime. Burying alive was practised frequently in the fifteenth and early sixteenth centuries, but is considerably less often documented than burning or drowning. It was deemed a particularly horrific punishment which occasionally resulted in pitiful scenes and it was therefore — often through the executioner's initiative — abandoned early on. In 1497 a woman in Nuremberg was buried alive beneath the gallows for grand larceny. "But the poor creature showed herself to be so resilient during the burying that her skin on hands and feet gashed open so that she aroused great pity in the people." She had obviously defended herself vigorously. After this, the council decided no longer to bury women alive, but rather to drown them, "and so it happened afterwards that those who had stolen in this way, had their ears cut off or were drowned." Despite this note in the records, burying alive continued to be carried out in Nuremberg. A last case is documented as late as 1522: a woman who had poisoned her husband and granddaughter was "chained to a cart at the hands and neck, led outside and pinched with red-hot tongs, then a spike was driven through her heart and afterwards she was buried alive under the gallows."

The far more widespread punishment of drowning was likewise mainly inflicted upon women. But occasionally men also were put to death in this way. Predominantly offenders who violated moral norms or the order of the church were drowned; child murderers, adulterers and heretics. Many Anabaptists[1] had to suffer this death. But if there was no river in the vicinity, drowning was replaced by other punishments. Besides the idea of annihilation, the purificatory power of water symbolizing the washing away of guilt played a significant role. There was a preference for running water. The courts made use of drowning throughout the sixteenth century. Although gradually abandoned in the seventeenth century, it was once more increasingly employed in Prussia and Saxony, mainly in the struggle against infanticide. Drowning was also considered a horrific punishment which — because of the relatively uncertain outcome — still retained many elements of a trial by ordeal.[2] The execution was generally carried out on a bridge. The malefactress was partially undressed, forced to squat so that a stick could be put through the hollows of her knees and then her hands and feet were tied together behind the stick. She was thrown into the water and an assistant of the executioner pushed her underneath the surface with long poles. There were other variations: for instance the so-called "sacking," originating in Roman law. The condemned person was put into a sack together with three or four animals. Justice required that these should be a dog, a cockerel,[3] a snake and a monkey. But since monkeys were hard to come by here and snakes were also rarely at hand, instead of the monkey a cat, and for the snake a painted image of a snake, were put into the sack. The meaning of these additions is not altogether clear. Perhaps they signified a refinement of the punishment or served to indicate especial shame. . . .

Another variation strongly reminiscent of trial by ordeal was found mainly in Switzerland. The executioner drew the malefactress into the water by means of a rope and pulled her out on the other shore. If she survived, she was free. Sources speak of "drifting downstream." Another variation consisted of the malefactress

---

[1] Radical Protestants who denied the doctrine of the Trinity, believed that only adults should be baptised, and refused to cooperate with the government.

[2] Used in the Middle Ages, a method of determining guilt by making the suspect undergo a test such as carrying a red-hot iron bar.

[3] Young rooster.

being bound and thrown into the water without a rope and left to drift. If the fetters loosened in the water and she could swim to the shore, she was also pardoned. We read in a document of 1521 from Elbing: "So she was carried along to the red fisherman's hut and thrown onto the shore still alive. The hangman's assistant wanted to push her into the river again, but the spectators, who had followed, rescued the woman from his hands and freed her from her bonds as they had seen the clear proof of her innocence." It was a tacit rule that a punishment that had been properly carried out, but failed to kill the delinquent, should not be repeated. The people wished to see this right retained, whereas the judicial authorities were increasingly successful in insisting on a repetition of the punishment.

The third, and in a sense most complete, form of punishment by annihilation and purification was burning. Predominantly those convicted of witchcraft, heresy, brewing poison, sodomy and forgery were burned. The punishment was inflicted upon men and women alike. Burning was most frequent during the sixteenth century, the time of the Counter-Reformation and the rigid enforcement of church morals. Afterwards, in so far as burnings continued to take place, the malefactor was strangled beforehand or a little sachet of gunpowder was put around his or her neck so that death would occur before fire consumed the body. Burning, especially if the fire was set badly, could last for a very long time and be extremely painful. It was always an intricate ritual of punishment. Usually, a post was rammed into the ground and bundles of brushwood, straw and wood piled round it. The condemned person was fastened to the post with an iron chain round neck or trunk. He or she could either be placed on the pyre or be set on a stool. The fire burned as long as it took to reduce everything to ashes. If the bones did not burn, they were eventually ground to powder. Then either all remains were buried underneath the gallows or thrown into a river. The killing was to result in total extermination and annihilation "so that the memory of this shameful deed may for ever be eradicated," as it is phrased in the sentence, or "so that the wrath of God and His punishment may be averted from the town and the land."

In 1659 in Nuremberg a young shepherd, "a cruel and abhorrent sodomite had to sit on the pyre made for this purpose and be burnt alive by fire and sent from life to death and executed, for him a well-deserved punishment, and since this horrible vice is strongly increasing and becoming more widespread, as a warning, abhorrence and example for others to beware all the more of such shameful misdeeds and reprovable crimes." A witness tells us that the shepherd died an extremely "pitiful and cruel" death because "not only the bonds and ropes burnt down along his hands and feet, but also when the fire cracked open his hands, feet and body, he was still alive." In cases of sodomy the animal was also burnt. Although burning was considered a death penalty with a secure, predictable outcome, as with burying alive or drowning, unexpected events could occur which would result in a "frightful and pitiful death" for the delinquent. It is understandable that the executioner, who had to prepare the fire, wished to see this punishment replaced by others, as he could be held responsible for a failed burning. Hence prior strangulation or the little sachet of gunpowder round the delinquent's neck was not only based on humane considerations, but also on the wish for a smooth execution.

Breaking on the wheel, quartering and dismemberment were also among the traditional execution rituals. These bloody butcherings fulfilled no purifying function, but translated *par excellence* the idea of retaliation into action and therefore corresponded to the older punishments of mutilation. They were predominantly inflicted upon men, but there were cases when they were also suffered by women. Severe crimes, such as multiple murder or treason, were punished by the wheel or by quartering. Although often threatened, quartering was rarely carried out in Germany and hardly ever inflicted from the sixteenth century onwards. But if it took place, the effect on the public was all the greater. Breaking on the wheel, however, remained a fairly widespread punishment for murder until well into the nineteenth century. However, the delinquent was often beheaded or strangled before being tied to the wheel.

Only a few instances of quartering are documented, but their descriptions are all the more vivid. Quartering was considered the cruellest punishment, and imposed mainly on traitors and regicides. . . . In the cases we know of, . . . the executioner and his assistants put the delinquent naked onto a wooden bed — often on a large scaffold in the middle of the town — and tied up all his limbs. The executioner then cut the chest from below with a large knife designed especially for this purpose, removed all the entrails together with the heart, lungs and liver and "all the contents of the body," "hurled them unto the mouth" of the culprit and subsequently buried the organs. The man was then put on a table, bench or block, his head struck off with a special axe and the body hacked into four pieces which were later nailed to oak columns or gibbets standing along the main roads.

Of the cases known to us, the execution of the noble conspirator Grumbach[4] in 1567 is the most instructive. The event was nothing more than butchery, witnessed by "a horribly large number of people, of princes, counts, noblemen, men of war, citizens and peasants." Six executioners erected a large scaffold in the market-place in Gotha, described in contemporary sources as a wooden bridge of blood or a shambles.[5] Many accounts circulated in public afterwards. The entire procedure of the execution of Grumbach and his five fellow conspirators lasted two hours. Two troops of soldiers surrounded the scaffold. The imperial provost with cavalry and trumpeteers led the condemned conspirators one by one from the town hall — Grumbach himself was brought from the castle. As Grumbach suffered from gout, eight gaoler's assistants had to carry him on a stool. The execution was staged as a sovereign act. Each convict was read his sentence by the clerk of the criminal court, sitting high upon his horse. The confessions followed

---

[4] Wilhelm von Grumbach (1503–1567), German knight who led a revolt in Saxony against the Holy Roman Emperor.

[5] Butcher shops.

just as solemnly. Grumbach admitted his guilt and asked everyone he had harmed to forgive him. . . . He was then undressed, bound and his heart cut out and hurled by the executioner at Grumbach's mouth with the words "Behold, Grumbach, your false heart!" The executioner then hacked his body into four pieces. Grumbach's chancellor Brück suffered the same fate. He had come to his execution in a black cloak of mourning, with a black ribbon on his black hat. His sentence was also read aloud. He too apologized and asked everyone for forgiveness. As his heart was cut out and slapped many times across his mouth, he is reported to have screamed "horribly and for a very long time." The other four conspirators suffered "more lenient" punishments which illustrate the complete range of possible executions. The first was decapitated and then quartered; the second had also been sentenced to death, but subsequently had his sentence commuted to incarceration, the third was decapitated in "magnificent" clothes and the last was hanged. After the execution, those who had been quartered were thrown onto a cart and their limbs [were] nailed to twelve pillars on the four roads leading to the gates of the city. . . .

Breaking on the wheel was considered a horrific, severe and disgraceful punishment. It was practised almost exclusively on men and predominantly served to punish robbery with murder or the murder of one's spouse. But from the seventeenth century delinquents were often beheaded or strangled beforehand. This act of mercy did not minimize the effect of deterrence. The public rarely knew anything of the strangling. No other punishment was as effective as a deterrent as breaking on the wheel. . . . Usually the condemned person was tied naked on the ground on spikes and a heavy wheel was thrust onto his limbs or he was put on a wheel-shaped base and his limbs were crushed either from the feet up or the head down. If a malefactor had not been strangled beforehand, a *coup de grâce*[6] might be administered if he so wished. The wheel had to be unused. A display of the wheel on which the dying malefactor was bound formed part of the ritual. Like that of those hanging on the gibbet, the corpse was now left to the birds. In St. Gallen a murderer and robber murderer was sentenced to death by the wheel in 1596. He was dragged head down on a hurdle[7] to the place of execution. There he was tied to a wooden bed and each of his four limbs was broken twice with the wheel, i.e. above and below the knees and elbows. A *coup de grâce* by the knife, which he begged of the executioner, ended his torments. Finally the corpse was bound to the wheel in an upright position "so that the birds may fly below and above the wheel." The number of thrusts was precisely laid down in the sentence and often corresponded to the number of offences committed.

Like every ritual of execution, breaking on the wheel might be intensified by additional punishments. It might be preceded by dragging the delinquent to the place of execution, by pinching him with red-hot tongs, or followed by behead-

---

[6] A deathblow administered as an act of mercy.

[7] Rectangular wooden frame on which traitors were dragged to execution.

ing and burning. Here the head was stuck on a pole above the wheel or the entire body was burnt. The boundary between quartering and breaking on the wheel was reached when the delinquent's limbs were not only broken, but subsequently torn from the body and displayed individually; this might be combined with removing the entrails, but this variation is rarely documented. These cases present not so much a refinement of punishments as already forms of cumulative punishments. If, for instance, a malefactor was accused and convicted of murder as well as of grand larceny and incest, an attempt was made to express this in the ritual of punishment in the way that breaking on the wheel was combined with hanging or burning. Either a gibbet was constructed above the wheel or the crushed body was burnt afterwards. Criminal courts in Switzerland were especially inventive in this respect. A criminal convicted of church robbery, murder, arson and rape — he had buried women alive after raping them — was punished in St. Gallen in 1600 as follows: he was dragged to the town hall on a hurdle and there pinched with red-hot tongs once on his chest and six times on each arm. The same procedure was repeated on his thighs in the market-place. At the place of execution he was put on a wooden plank, his arms and legs were crushed above and below the joints and he was tied to the wheel so that his head was in the gallows' noose without strangling him. Finally the wheel was displayed and everything burnt to ashes. At times special emphasis was put on burning the delinquent very slowly. . . . Such spectacles of execution were consciously staged by the authorities and attracted many spectators from far and near. Broadsheets ensured that news of the event was well publicized. Only a few representatives of the enlightened intelligentsia condemned these spectacles, but not because of the severity of the punishment. Their concern was rather the brutalization of the people through these spectacles and at the same time they disputed the value of such executions to the state. . . .

Hanging and beheading were the most frequent capital punishments. They had always existed, but gained dominance in the seventeenth century when the authorities became the sole organizer of executions. The most common offences, larceny and murder, were punished by the sword or by the rope.

The capital punishment most frequently carried out, at least in early times, was by hanging from the gallows. It was usually a punishment for grand larceny and fraud and was mainly designated for men. Because of its disgraceful character, hanging was replaced from the seventeenth century by beheading. Hanging was the most disgraceful punishment: it not only took the life and honour of the delinquent, but also put his entire family in disgrace. So relatives often sought commutation of the punishment to execution by the sword. In later times especially, residents and members of the upper strata of society were granted this relief. Hanging was deemed an indelible disgrace; moreover — and this was no less devastating at the time — exposure of the corpse to the birds meant that the delinquent was refused burial and his soul would not be granted peace. In this respect there was a correspondence between hanging and breaking on the wheel, where the body was left to decompose on the wheel. . . . Hanging was carried out in a variety of ways, but two methods prevailed. Either a delinquent, bound, had to mount the ladder backwards, the hangman put a noose round his neck and then pushed him off the ladder. Or the condemned person was pulled up by means of a strap by the hangman's assistants, the noose put round his neck before he was pushed down. . . .

According to the gravity of the offence, variations might be introduced into the process of hanging. It was, for instance, stipulated precisely how long an offender had to remain on the gallows. If the time was too long, there was a danger that the body might fall down or be stolen — or that at least several of the limbs would be removed. Although this was often done by those who placed great hopes in the healing powers of parts of the body, it was mainly family members who stole the entire corpse to wipe out the shame and grant their relative peace for the soul through burial. Moreover, the position on the gallows or the height of the gallows might be stipulated. Being hanged from the middle of the cross beam of the gallows was deemed especially disgraceful, as was being hanged very high. "The higher anyone was hanged, the more humiliating was the punishment."

The execution of the Jew Süss Oppenheimer[8] in Stuttgart in 1738 was a spectacle of a particular kind. Convicted of treason, fraud, incest and other crimes, Süss was hanged not only from unusually high gallows but also in a large cage which projected over the gallows. During the trial he had stated: "You cannot hang me higher than the gallows." The court had spared no cost in answering this challenge and succeeded in hanging Süss higher than the gallows before a large crowd of spectators. . . . A large number of soldiers marched in and many boxes had been especially erected for cavaliers and their ladies. Booths offered wine and beer. Street traders sold broadsheets with a picture of Jew Süss and derisory verses. It was an exciting, festive scene when Süss, who had stubbornly resisted both the court and the repeated attempts of Protestant ministers to convert him, put up a last desperate resistance to the hangmen when they tried to slip the noose round his neck. The convict had been driven through the city to the place of execution on a high knacker's[9] cart. He was clad in a scarlet mantle and had been allowed to keep a precious, conspicuous ring. As he was pulled up, the vicar of the city shouted at the dying man: "The devil take you, stubborn knave and Jew"; while Jews who had accompanied Süss prayed aloud "Jahve Adonai[10] is one God and eternal."

Occasionally a malefactor sentenced to hanging had to wear a placard round his or her neck on which either the stolen object was depicted or the offence proclaimed. The punishment was refined by the hand being struck off and stuck onto

---

[8] Joseph Süss Oppenheimer (1698–1738), financial advisor to the Duke of Württemberg; the Nazis made an influential anti-Semitic film, *Jud Süss* (1940), about his life.

[9] Dealer in horse carcasses.

[10] Lord Yahweh, the Jewish god.

a pole. Hanging might also qualify as an accumulation of punishments, as in the examples above. Subsequent burning is frequently documented.

The execution of Jews was a special ritual. They were hanged by the feet, flanked by two dogs. Often death did not occur for a number of days. These executions were mostly carried out in an open field on three- or four-legged gallows.

Although hanging may appear simple at first sight, it demanded great concentration on the executioner's part. If the rope was too short, painful strangulation ensued, which could lead to arguments between executioner and spectators. These might likewise occur if the rope was too long and therefore broke when the delinquent was pushed down, which meant that the execution had to be repeated. If an execution failed, an accusation of cruelty was voiced by the spectators and by the convicted person's family, who could then insist on mercy.

From the seventeenth century the predominant form of execution was beheading by the sword, the least severe and most acceptable form of capital punishment. As a rule, members of the nobility and persons of rank were beheaded. As before a hanging, the delinquent was blindfolded, his or her hands were tied behind and the neck bared so that the blow could be aimed with precision. The delinquent awaited beheading either standing, kneeling or sitting on a stool. Most delinquents wanted to be beheaded as it was the least painful way of dying. Yet to sever the head in one single blow was not an easy task. The audience was satisfied when blood gushed forth and the head fell after the first blow. But the delinquent might suddenly move his or her head, and therefore the executioner tried to gain the condemned person's assent beforehand. If the executioner's attempt was unsuccessful, his life was at risk, while a "masterly" stroke was met with appreciation by authorities and people. . . .

Criminals convicted of manslaughter, robbery, incest, infanticide (from the seventeenth century) and severe fraud were beheaded. Whether a delinquent was buried beneath the gallows after decapitation, handed over to the anatomists . . . or granted burial in a church yard often depended upon the verdict, or rather the mitigation of the verdict. It was deemed a special mercy if a delinquent could be buried by his or her friends and family immediately after the beheading. After a Franconian nobleman was executed for murder in Frankfurt in 1618 "on a particular scaffold on a black cloth by the sword, from life to death," he was placed in a coffin by soldiers "and carried in the customary funeral procession headed by a cross into the church of St. Niclas: there he lay until the following Sunday when he was fetched by his family who took him away." It was likewise deemed a great mercy if the delinquent was spared the executioner's touch. But not only were there various means of commuting punishments; equally numerous were combinations of punishments, whether enforced as refinements or as part of other forms of execution. The head that had been struck off might be stuck onto a pole or the gallows, the body might be put on the wheel or buried beneath the gallows. But this was generally the fate of delinquents who had been reprieved from death on the wheel. A normal case may illustrate this: a city messenger had insulted the council and citizens of Frankfurt in 1607. As a punishment, the two fingers of his right hand with which he had sworn were cut off in front of the town hall, then his head was struck off and together with the two fingers stuck on a pole "and the head had its face turned towards the street and then the dead body was buried beneath the gallows." Many kinds of combinations existed, yet they frequently bore traces of the intention of mirroring the crime in the punishment.

Alongside these forms of execution with their individual refinement or accumulation of punishments, there were execution practices that, although they were unique and comprehensible only in the context of the crime, bore characteristic traits of the penal practice of the early modern age. Two cases might be mentioned here. Both date from the sixteenth century, the century showing the most resourceful inventiveness in forms of punishment. Our examples pertain to executions immediately after the Peasants' War[11] and the collapse of the Anabaptists' revolt in Münster,[12] but remain atypical of the steps taken by the authorities against leaders of the peasants and Anabaptists, who on the whole were punished far more leniently than the average robber murderer or blasphemer.

Jäcklein Rohrbach, the leader of the Neckar revolt,[13] and the piper Melchior Nonnenmacher were arrested, Nonnenmacher because as a former piper to the nobility he had piped them to their death, Rohrbach for forcing noblemen to run the gauntlet.[14] Both were sentenced to death by burning. They were chained to a tree so that they were allowed some freedom of movement. Wood was piled round the tree. The convicted men could move within the ring of fire, but their chains were too short to allow them to curtail their agonies by jumping into the fire. Noblemen themselves set the fire, which slowly burned Rohrbach and Nonnenmacher to death. This execution was clearly an act of revenge on the part of the noblemen. Another special case, full of symbolism, is the execution of the Anabaptist leaders Jan van Leiden,[15] Bernd Knipperdolling[16] and Bernd Krechting[17] in 1536 in Münster. The Bishop of Münster ordered a large stage to be constructed in front of the town hall to which all three Baptists and rebels were chained by iron collars. The executioner pinched them with red-hot tongs "on all the fleshy and veined parts" of their bodies "so that from each part touched by the tongs, a flame blazed out and such a stench filled the air that nearly everyone standing in the market-place was unable to bear it in their noses." After this lengthy torture — which they survived — their tongues were torn out with red-hot tongs and a long dagger thrust deep into their heart "so that the seat of life was

---

[11] A massive rural uprising in 1525 that threatened the social order.

[12] A group of Anabaptists took over the city government of Münster in 1534 and attempted to establish a theocracy.

[13] Jäcklein Rohrbach, an innkeeper, led the peasants of the Neckar Valley in revolt in 1525.

[14] A military punishment whereby the victim was forced to run between two rows of men who beat him as he passed.

[15] A Dutch tailor who became the leader of the Münster Anabaptist revolt (1509–1536).

[16] Wealthy cloth merchant and Jan van Leiden's prime minister (ca. 1490–1536).

[17] Prominent supporter of Jan van Leiden.

wounded and they would lose the very thing all the more quickly." Finally the bloody corpses were locked into cages especially constructed for the occasion and hung high from the spire of St. Lamberti to be seen as a warning from far away.

But it is not only these special cases, which do not correspond to any pattern, that should be mentioned. We must finally consider the phenomenon of executing corpses. This does not mean executions in which a delinquent was beheaded or strangled before being put on the wheel, burnt or quartered and the entire procedure of torture exerted on the dead body, but rather those cases in which delinquents who were already dead were put on trial or the punishment to which the court had sentenced them before death was executed after their demise. . . . In 1690 an entire gang of church robbers was tried. When during his execution the Jew Jonas Meyer, "to the greatest annoyance of the bystanders and other Christians delivered very shameful and blasphemous speeches against our Saviour and Redeemer Jesus Christ," a second trial was instigated against him — or rather against his corpse. The sentence commended the tearing out and burning of his tongue and a second hanging, this time head down, next to a dog.

There are many more cases of criminals who before their apprehension or when already incarcerated committed suicide and the intended sentence was subsequently enforced on their bodies. Suicide in itself was deemed a crime and as a rule the offender was either burnt by the executioner, stuffed into a barrel and thrown into the river or buried beneath the gallows. But a prisoner who committed suicide might face a much more severe punishment. Some examples from Frankfurt may illustrate this. In 1685 a man who had often lived in disharmony with his wife had murdered her and then wounded himself so badly in his house that he died in the main watch house. The sentence prescribed that his corpse should be dragged publicly to the place of execution. There his head was struck off and stuck onto a pole while his body was put on the wheel. This was the punishment for murdering one's wife. A maid who, after killing her child, jumped into a well and drowned suffered the same fate in Frankfurt in 1690. The great procession leading to the execution of a footpad and citizen of Frankfurt in 1690 was arranged on purpose as a gruesome spectacle. While in prison, he had taken his life "intentionally." As punishment, he was dragged past his house to the place of execution. There his head was struck off with an axe, stuck onto a pole and his body put on the wheel for general abhorrence. Until the eighteenth century suicide was considered "one of the most severe and dangerous kinds of manslaughter since by committing it one shamefully depraves body and soul." If a sentence had been passed before the delinquent's suicide, "the very one must be executed, as far as possible, on the dead body, serving as a deterrent to others." We read this in the enlightened Prussian *Allgemeines Landrecht* of 1794.[18]

Although the original, cruel methods of execution such as quartering, burning, burying alive and breaking on the wheel were carried out, they do not entirely define the penal practice of the early modern age, not even that of the sixteenth

---

[18] Prussian code of criminal and civil law.

century. The same applies to commuted punishments carried out upon delinquents already beheaded or strangled. By the sixteenth century, and certainly in
the eighteenth century, hanging and beheading became the prevailing forms of execution. Cruel methods did not disappear altogether, and existed in the eighteenth century, but more in theory. They were, however, frequently threatened. Yet
everyone could easily witness a hanging or a beheading in their lifetime. Both
forms served predominantly as a more or less disgraceful liquidation without torture, but might be intensified by torments or defilement before or after death. . . .

We should not deduce from this that the intention of fitting the punishment
to the crime — which was obviously achieved best in the cruel variations — was
completely abandoned with the decrease in horrific methods and the increase of
hanging and beheading. It was only the character of the punishment fitting the
crime that altered. Despite all restraint, there were plenty of opportunities to emphasize traces of traditional rituals of punishment through refinement or diverse
combinations of punishments. Hanging might be combined with fixing placards,
or even the burning of the delinquent's corpse. Beheading did not exclude the possibilities of the head being stuck onto a pole or the hand being cut off. Although
traditional penal forms were increasingly obscured, important traces of the old
system survived until the end of the eighteenth, and even into the early nineteenth, century.

A third, instructive fact survived in the criminal penal system. Punishments
were inflicted not only upon the living, but also — and consciously — upon the
dead body. We have to differentiate between two dimensions. When hanging a
delinquent, it was decisive for how long he or she remained on the gallows, which
was of no importance to the dead offender, but considered a part of the punishment in legal practice and by the public. Equally, torture continued whether or
not the convicted person died with the first thrust of the wheel. The corpse was
crushed further, then put on the wheel or gutted and beheaded. In these cases torture before or after execution was an integral part of the punishment. Obviously
the aim was not only to kill the delinquent, but to exercise on him or her a punishment that corresponded to the offence, but bore no direct relation to the individual criminal. Moreover, it made no difference whether the punishment was inflicted upon the living or upon the dead body. Punishments were designed to
create a horror of the crime as well as to provide examples of the penalties for a
crime.

In whatever different ways the corpse might be included in the execution ritual, for a long time no clear distinction was made between living and dead. The
idea that a person and his or her criminal activities could still be punished by inflicting torture upon the corpse lasted up to the nineteenth century.

MAKING CONNECTIONS: VIOLENCE

1.   It would be difficult to determine which civilization has been the most violent, but
one can readily defend the proposition that Western civilization has been rhythmically
punctuated by violence, both in daily life and through warfare. Early modern Euro-

peans were accustomed to violence and brutality, as van Dülmen shows in his graphic portrayal of German rituals of execution. Discuss whether the callous disregard for pain inflicted on others has been a constant in Western civilization, or whether that attitude is peculiar to certain centuries or regions or social groups. How much of the brutality in sixteenth- and seventeenth-century German executions was due to German law and culture, or was that ferocity simply a natural part of the human condition that you have seen elsewhere in your study of history? Explain.

2. Was crueler violence inflicted on women than on men? On lower social groups rather than on the elite? Explain. What role did retaliation play in determining the method of punishment? What does van Dülmen mean when he describes some forms of execution as a purifying process?

3. What rituals of execution do we have today? To what extent are our punishments of criminals retaliatory? Are we less cruel than the early modern Germans, or is our cruelty, perchance, directed elsewhere rather than toward criminals? Why are executions in the United States private, whereas early modern German executions took place in public? Why did that society punish the dead as well as the living, and why do we not do so today?

POVERTY AND MARGINALITY
IN THE EARLY MODERN CITY
Christopher R. Friedrichs

Jesus said, "The poor ye have always with you." Some of his followers interpreted this remark to mean that there is no point in trying to eliminate poverty — it is simply part of life. Nevertheless, many individuals, groups, and governments have tried to help the poor, or at least some of the poor, often in the name of Christian charity and good will.

Christopher Friedrichs, a historian of the Reformation at the University of British Columbia, observes that Christianity long has commanded charity. Theologians held that the rich should give some of their surplus to the poor. Because Jesus denounced wealth, praised the poor in his Sermon on the Mount, and lived a life bereft of riches, Christians believed that poverty could be next to godliness. Poverty, for instance, was one of the vows that monks took. St. Francis of Assisi gave away his possessions and raised poverty to an ideal lifestyle that he and his new religious order of the Franciscans followed. There are many other such examples of Christian commitment to a life of poverty in medieval and early modern Europe. But this ideal soon clashed with reality as large numbers of poor poured into cities.

Poverty, Friedrichs says, was both a religious challenge and a social problem. Early modern cities had to balance a religious duty to help the poor with the fear that poverty and vagrancy would overwhelm urban resources. How did cities deal with the problem of poverty? What were the causes of urban poverty? What were the different types of "poor"? Which urban groups attempted to cope with the growing presence and problems the poor represented? To what extent were cities successful in dealing with the unemployed, beggars, and vagrants?

Christina Bobingerin was desperate. She was 19 years old in the summer of 1601, a peasant girl from the village of Göggingen just outside the walls of Augs-

Christopher R. Friedrichs, *The Early Modern City, 1450–1750* (New York: Longman Publishing, 1995), 214–229, 234–235.

burg. One day in June she sneaked into the city, trying to locate the soldier with whom she had been living some months earlier. He had long since abandoned her, but she had heard that he was in Augsburg and she thought if she found him he would have to take her back. As soon as she got into the city, however, Christina was arrested and jailed. Two days later she was interrogated.

This was not the first time Christina had been detained as an unwelcome visitor to Augsburg. At least half a dozen times before she had been arrested, whipped, led to the city gate and warned never to return. Knowing that she was unwanted, why did she insist on coming back? "Do you really think," the authorities asked her gravely, "that we should have to suffer such defiance from you?"

Christina's answer was simple. Sheer need had driven her to sneak into the city. No, she was not a prostitute, nor was she a thief. She had simply come to find her soldier or, failing that, to beg. But she was allowed to do neither. Once again she was banished from the city.

Christina's story was repeated not hundreds but thousands of times in European cities of the early modern era. Every city had its share of male and female beggars and vagrants who were desperately trying to make a living while eluding the authorities. Almost every city also had its beadles and beggar-wardens whose job was to apprehend vagrants and lock them up, kick them out, or — occasionally — permit them to carry on with their activities. Yet public begging was, in turn, only part of a vastly greater structural problem of urban poverty in early modern Europe. For countless people in the early modern city, life was not a struggle for power or prestige nor even for economic security: it was simply a struggle to survive from day to day.

"Countless" is said advisedly, for the numerical dimensions of urban poverty in early modern Europe can never be determined. Many of the poor, after all, belonged to the least systematically documented members of urban society. We may know how many households a city had, how many families paid taxes, how many people took communion, how many were born or died. Sometimes we even know how many families received welfare payments or how many beds were occupied in civic institutions. But we can never know for sure how many vagrants were living furtively in cellars or sleeping in sheds or huddled outside the city walls hoping to slip inside when the gates were opened. Nor did the size of this floating population remain constant. In times of distress — especially during wars or famine — the number of vagrants ballooned as outsiders flooded into the city in search of food or money.

Nor could the permanent residents of the city be divided with certainty into those who were poor and those who were not. Poverty itself is always difficult to define. Certainly a family which could not support its members without sustained recourse to private or public assistance would always be included among the poor. To some analysts, however, this group — the truly indigent — represented only the most extreme form of poverty; the urban poor can also be said to have included many householding families who, in normal times, seemed to be economically independent. For often these people were able to support themselves and their families only so long as they — and the local economy — remained in good health; they were liable to slip over the edge into destitution as soon as they faced some unmasterable catastrophe — a sudden collapse in the market for the goods they made, a sudden rise in the price of bread, the onset of a disabling illness, the death of a provider, or the birth of yet another dependant. In late fifteenth-century Nuremberg a city ordinance required that labourers in the building industry be given their daily wages in the morning, so that they could bring the money to their wives when they went home for a midday snack. People like this obviously lived perilously close to the margins of poverty; even when they were able to support themselves, they were bound to be conscious of indigence as a constant, looming threat.

Yet members of even the most modest householding families in the early modern city did have some resources with which to cope with the fear or fact of poverty. Every such family belonged to a network of institutions and relations which could be drawn upon for assistance. The best strategy, of course, was to anticipate and minimize economic distress in advance. Here the guilds[1] played a central role, by protecting the right of each member to earn a living and fighting to preserve traditional markets and monopolies. In addition to this, guilds often provided short-term assistance to distressed members or their widows. Sometimes confraternities[2] played this role, for often the strongest charitable impulses within the brotherhood were directed towards its own members. There were certainly cases in which poor citizens joined confraternities chiefly as a form of social insurance, knowing that in cases of illness or unemployment they would have the first claim on assistance from the richer brethren. Family relations provided another resource: in times of need, people borrowed from their relatives, or moved in with them. Only social custom could reinforce a sense of obligation between siblings or cousins, but the law often imposed an obligation among closer relatives. In some communities, for example, adult children were required to support indigent parents.

On top of all this, cities had long-established systems of private, church and municipal charity to which poor people could turn in times of need. Both the organization and the philosophy of urban charity underwent significant changes during the early modern period, but certain principles remained unchanged. Charity could take different forms, involving the distribution of food, clothing, firewood or money. But whenever possible, established residents were to be supported in their own homes. If householders were ashamed to let their neighbours know that they had become dependent on charity, discreet means of providing as-

---

[1] Economic and social associations of people who plied a specific craft or trade; they regulated the quality and output of goods and limited competition in order to maintain prices and so guarantee their members a secure living.

[2] Religious associations of laymen, often from the same occupation, that provided for the religious well-being of their members.

sistance were often arranged. Only in extreme cases would a person be removed from his or her own home to be looked after in a hospital or other institution.

In every city it was understood that recognized members of the community had a legitimate claim on the community's resources. This view of things owed much to the teachings of the church, but it was reinforced by the communal philosophy that lay behind the organization of the guilds and the very concept of citizenship. In fact the various forms of organized charity which had developed in European cities by the end of the middle ages would almost certainly have been sufficient to alleviate poverty without undue strain on local resources if cities had maintained a closed, stable population. But this was never the case. Urban poverty was always a serious social problem, and there is every indication that it became steadily more acute in the course of the early modern era. In city after city, the number of poor people and the desperation of their circumstances seemed to be growing. New measures to deal with poverty were constantly being devised and some of them were actually implemented. But they were never adequate, for the problem always ran far ahead of the solution.

The reason for this was simple: immigration. Not all of the poor were immigrants, and not all immigrants were poor. But immigration and poverty were always linked. Every community recognized that some immigration was inevitable and immigrants were often a valuable resource. Many male immigrants did well in the city, arriving as apprentices or journeymen and moving successfully into the ranks of householding artisans. Some even ascended into the urban elite. Many female immigrants also prospered: arriving in most cases as servants, they acquired husbands and founded stable households. Even immigrants with less promising prospects could still fill important niches in the urban economy as long-term servants or unskilled labourers. But the supply of immigrants always exceeded the city's capacity to absorb them effectively into the urban economy.

Immigration flows were never constant. The overall volume of migration to cities probably increased substantially in the sixteenth century, when the population of Europe as a whole was rapidly growing. It may have dropped somewhat during parts of the seventeenth century when the rate of demographic growth declined. But municipal authorities were little aware of any long-term trends. They were far more conscious of seasonal shifts or sudden increases in the migration rate during times of crisis. And they always felt, year after year, that far too many immigrants were turning up.

In theory only immigrants with the requisite wealth or skills would be allowed to stay in the community and settle down as permanent residents. In practice this was impossible to enforce, for the distinction between temporary and permanent residents was often blurred. This was especially the case in the rapidly expanding metropolitan centres with their sprawling outer districts — the suburbs and *faubourgs*[3] outside the walls where work and residence patterns were par-

---

[3] Outskirts; suburbs.

ticularly hard to control. Unlicensed artisans and unskilled workers abounded in these outer neighbourhoods, where overlarge parishes and underdeveloped institutions made it difficult to keep track of exactly who lived there. But even within the city walls, municipal governments found it hard to keep a close grip on the number of inhabitants. Every market-day, every seasonal fair brought a host of travellers. Not all of them left again. Innkeepers and citizens were constantly warned not to provide accommodation to visitors without notifying the authorities. It never helped. There always seemed to be more and more people in the city — and many of them, far from contributing to the urban economy, were in desperate need of help.

When all else fails, people beg. There had always been beggars in the European city, and what they did was powerfully sanctioned by medieval theology and social practice. To give alms to a beggar was the classic good work, as beneficial to the soul of the giver as it was to the body of the recipient. But the beggar did something good too: not only did his prayers aid the donor, but also his very existence gave donors the opportunity to do good by giving alms. In addition, the presence of mendicant religious orders,[4] whose members were supposed to support themselves by seeking alms, powerfully legitimized begging as a social activity. Nobody really imagined that all beggars were tinged with holiness and every act of giving sanctified the donor; people of the late middle ages were robust realists who knew that not every intimidating beggar who demanded a handout would ever remember the benefactor in his prayers. Occasional legislation condemning the idleness of vagrants and beggars can be traced back to the fourteenth century. Until the sixteenth century, however, such laws were largely ignored. For even when the recipient was not worthy, the act of giving was. And begging itself was still a legitimate enterprise in many communities. . . .

As long as begging remained socially and spiritually acceptable, every random act of almsgiving was regarded as commendable. But much charity was also given in the form of bequests after death, for this too, could help speed the donor's soul heavenward. Clothing, food or cash could be distributed at the deceased's funeral. Yet other, more lasting forms of posthumous charity were also common. Testaments often included bequests to support existing institutions in their work of charity or to establish new ones. Many of these institutions were of course religious, but it was by no means uncommon to bypass the church and establish a private charity to be administered by the secular authorities. By the start of the sixteenth century, every sizeable European city had a hodgepodge of hospitals, leper-houses, pilgrim hospices and other philanthropic institutions, supported largely by rents or other forms of income bequeathed by the faithful in their wills. Nobody had to restrict his or her bequest to existing institutions; any sincere gift would be equally commendable. In the early sixteenth century,

---

[4] The Franciscans and Dominicans, founded in the 1200s, who practiced strict rules of poverty.

for example, the Frankfurt merchant Jacob Heller bequeathed funds for the establishment of a public warming-house in the city. Every year from November to February this house was to be open from dawn to dusk, with a two-hour closure at midday, as a place where beggars and other poor people could find relief from the chills of a German winter. Where the visitors would spend the night was not considered; this was a day-time facility, not an attempt to deal with poverty on a structural level. But it was a classic act of traditional Christian charity.

Poverty, then, was a religious challenge. But it was also a social problem. Its dimensions could be masked by almsgiving and charity, but whenever a sudden crisis occurred the full extent of human need became glaringly apparent. In the late 1520s, for example, all over northern Italy a cycle of severe famines compounded by the disruptions of warfare drove huge masses of peasants into the cities in search of succour. A patrician of Vicenza described the situation in 1528:

> Give alms to two hundred people, and as many again will appear; you cannot walk down the street or stop in a square or church without multitudes surrounding you to beg for charity: you see hunger written on their faces, their eyes like gemless rings, the wretchedness of their bodies with the skins shaped by bones. . . . Certainly all the citizens are doing their duty with charity — but it cannot suffice.

Indeed it could not. Yet it was in exactly these years, beginning in the 1520s, that all over Europe a sudden burst of interest in the reform of poor relief became apparent. This movement began in cities, but it engendered widespread discussion among thinkers and policymakers and in some countries contributed to the enactment of new legislation on the national level. The details differed from one community to the next, but municipal leaders avidly followed what was happening in other cities, and the reforms had much in common. The most fundamental principle, reiterated in almost every community that drafted new poverty legislation, was the prohibition of indiscriminate public begging. The scattered complaints about dishonest beggars and occasional laws against public begging were consolidated into a universal condemnation of the practice. Everyone understood, of course, that some people were driven by desperate need to engage in begging. But the beggar would no longer be regarded as a universal category. Instead, each case would be assessed on an individual basis. Those who were entitled to assistance would receive it. Those who were not would not.

To implement this principle required new administrative arrangements. Commissions were appointed to distinguish between those who deserved aid and those who did not. The deserving poor were identified and listed; in many communities they were required to wear badges so that all could know who they were. They would no longer have to beg, for they and their needs were now clearly recognized, and they could wait at home for food or money to be delivered. The undeserving were also identified. Once they were, they might also be marked — generally with a whipping — before they were sent back to their home towns or simply led to the city gates with a warning never to return.

The commitment to support all the deserving poor called for a higher level of coordination than had formerly been the case. The money previously handed to individual beggars was now to be deposited in poor-boxes and offering plates or collected by officials who went from house to house. The money thus gathered would then be distributed to the deserving poor according to their needs. This often required the establishment of a new municipal agency. In addition, many city governments set up systems of inspection and supervision to ensure that existing charitable institutions were fulfilling their responsibilities in a fiscally sound manner. Sometimes the municipal government went even further, taking over existing charities to consolidate them into larger, more efficient units under the direct control of the city council.

In many cities of central Europe, the reform of poor-relief systems went hand in hand with the introduction of the Protestant Reformation. Certainly Protestant theology, with its rejection of salvation by works, saw no spiritual benefit in the act of giving alms to a beggar — and a rationally organized welfare system corresponded closely to the Protestant vision of the godly community whose members obeyed God's commands not in hopes of grace to come but in gratitude for blessings already received. There were practical reasons, too, why so many Protestant communities reorganized their welfare systems: when monasteries, convents and other church institutions were disbanded, it was only natural for municipal governments to take over some of their functions along with all of their revenues. But there was nothing inherently "Protestant" about the wave of welfare reforms which swept across Europe beginning in the 1520s. In Protestant cities they were often part of a larger package of ambitious social, political and educational reforms associated with the optimistic mood of the early Reformation. But in Catholic cities very similar welfare reforms were often enacted in response to a specific social or economic crisis — typically a severe famine which drove up food prices for the inhabitants while simultaneously flooding the city with refugees. One of the most characteristic manifestations of the new approach, for example, was the famous Aumône-Générale[5] established by the predominantly Catholic leaders of Lyon in the 1530s. This municipal agency was set up to receive charitable donations in lieu of the alms formerly given directly to beggars. Once a week, the Aumône-Générale distributed bread and money to the city's deserving poor, who were listed on the basis of careful house-to-house surveys.

Unlike Protestants, Catholic theologians were deeply divided over the issue of begging: some insisted that the spontaneous relationship between almsgiver and recipient must be retained, while others held that a less personal but more effective gift was equally meritorious. Virtually all Catholic theologians would have agreed, however, that alms must be given voluntarily. The idea of a compulsory poor-rate[6] imposed on all prosperous householders — as was implemented in England by the end of the sixteenth century — would not have appealed to

---

[5] Literally, "General Charity."

[6] A local property tax that funded welfare for the poor.

Catholic thinkers. But heavy moral suasion to pressure donors to give something was acceptable. In any case there were certainly enough Catholic theologians who favoured the thrust of the new approach to inspire or at least endorse the efforts of municipal leaders intent on welfare reform in cities like Lyon. . . .

. . . Much attention was focused on hospitals: old ones were reformed and new ones founded. Traditionally hospitals had served a variety of different purposes, in most cases reflecting the wishes of their original founders or subsequent benefactors. Some hospitals took in the sick of every description, others accepted only victims of a specific disease. Some were primarily rest-houses for travellers, some functioned as homes for aged paupers, some took in well-to-do widows or widowers who paid for their room and board. But before the sixteenth century, nobody expected hospitals to do more than relieve distress on an incidental basis. Now some reformers saw in hospitals a potential solution to broad social problems. If banishing beggars did not work, perhaps confining them to hospitals would. In 1581 a beggars' hospital was founded in Toledo. Public begging was forbidden and beggars were ordered to check into the new institution where all their needs would be met. Many chose to leave the city instead — and wisely so. Funding for the new hospital never lived up to expectations, and within a few years the project collapsed.

But the idea of confining the unstable elements of society survived. In the course of the seventeenth century, increasingly many institutional solutions to the problem of poverty were advanced. Workhouses were introduced. A hospital merely succoured the beggar; in the workhouse he or she would be taught some skill and, it was hoped, be habituated to a more industrious way of life. Closely linked in spirit to the workhouse was the orphanage, where the child who lacked parents would be introduced to good work habits before being put out as a servant or apprentice. Some workhouses even accommodated children whose parents were still living but could not afford to raise them. In the English town of Salisbury the tiny workhouse established to confine twelve adults in 1602 was expanded two decades later to include lodgings for poor children who would be taught the rudiments of a trade before being bound over as apprentices. At the same time, the city financed a programme under which masters in the textile trades would put poor people to work in their own shops, keeping them occupied with relatively unskilled tasks like spinning and knitting. But it soon became apparent that both funds and employment opportunities were too limited to make the programme a success; the workhouse survived, but the training programmes collapsed.

All such schemes turned out to be inadequate to the need. Yet in city after city, a new generation of municipal leaders would tackle the problem with a fresh burst of optimism. The vision of a comprehensive institution to combine confinement and training was particularly powerful in French towns in the seventeenth century. This normally took the form of an *hôpital-général*[7] which would en-

---

[7] General hospital; a refuge for those who were terminally ill, destitute, homeless, or aged.

close the ill, the aged, the orphaned, the insane and the idle all at once, providing palliative care or disciplined training as appropriate to each category. Many such institutions were proposed and quite a few were actually founded in the course of the seventeenth century. The *Hôpital-Général* of Paris, which was launched in 1657 with a spectacular round-up of beggars from the streets of the city, may have housed close to 10,000 inmates at a time. Smaller but similar institutions were founded in many provincial cities, often in the hope that systematic confinement would finally eliminate social disorder and wipe out habits of idleness among the poor. But even so it was never more than a small fraction of the rootless poor who were effectively confined. The costs were too high and the potential clients, in many cases, preferred the risk of remaining free to the punitive security of institutional confinement.

Begging could not be eliminated. No matter how many vagrants were banished or confined, desperate people still found their way on to the streets of the city, determined to collect whatever they could while staying out of the beadle's[8] sight. Catholic town-dwellers continued to believe that handing alms directly to a beggar was a work of mercy; even in Protestant cities it was hard for inhabitants to resist the insistent appeal of the outstretched palm. Completely consistent policies were impossible to enforce. Even communities which tried to maintain a general policy of expelling or confining beggars often made exceptions for special cases, for example by granting crippled or blind vagrants permission to beg in the streets. But the real problem was that no amount of charity, private or public, would ever be sufficient to cope with the dimensions of poverty.

Everyone agreed that scarce resources should be directed primarily to the deserving poor. But establishing exactly who was "deserving" was not a simple matter. Three intersecting systems of categorization were involved. One category was geographical: the local person — especially someone actually born in the community — was always more deserving of support than the outsider. A second category was physical: the person unable to work due to illness, youth or age was more deserving of aid than the person who had the physical capacity to earn a living. The third category was moral: the person who was willing to work was more deserving than the shirker. The "sturdy beggar" — the healthy person who was able to work but unwilling to do so — was a popular target of fierce moralizing and repressive legislation. In fact everyone knew, or could have known, that many such people were idle not by choice but by circumstance. But this was often ignored. For there was little that could be done even for paupers who were willing and able to work. Occasionally the physically able beggars were commandeered for public works projects such as rebuilding or reinforcing the city fortifications. But such undertakings and the funds to support them were usually short-lived. Nor was it easy to arrange private employment for the poor. Even when the law provided that local orphans were to be put out as apprentices, the guilds some-

---

[8] A minor parish officer responsible for keeping order and for dealing with petty offenders.

times raised objections. The likelihood that outside beggars could be converted to productive workers with an accepted niche in the local economy was always slight. It was altogether easier to act on the premise that beggars were deliberate shirkers, constitutionally unwilling to submit to the discipline of labour. Vagrants were depersonalized, seen not as distressed individuals but as a collective threat to the city's well-being. The city had to protect itself against the "plague of beggars" by quarantine measures not unlike those which were applied in the case of contagious illnesses. In actual fact, beggars were as hard to stop as infectious diseases. Many a gate-keeper or beadle found it convenient or even lucrative to let a beggar elude his notice. But whenever the authorities found the beggars too bothersome, it was easy to solve the problem: with a little effort, the current crop of beggars could always be apprehended, whipped, banished and forgotten.

The local poor, by contrast, could be neither removed nor ignored. The social obligation to meet their needs was conceded by all. But cities did everything they could to restrict their number. In many German towns, anyone who applied for citizenship or even just for local residence rights had to give evidence of an adequate degree of wealth before being accepted. Sometimes the applicant also had to promise to make no claim on the city's welfare institutions for a specific number of years. In England, where poor-rates were collected and distributed on the parish level, there were even obstacles to moving from one parish to another within the same city. Newcomers were often asked to post a bond to cover the initial costs of any poor-relief they might incur; if they failed to do so, they could be sent back to their original parish. In seventeenth-century Southwark, just south of London Bridge, a parish "searcher" promptly visited every new arrival who took up residence in the district. Anyone who lacked obvious means of support or refused to post a bond was quickly evicted by the constable.

Even in the face of such measures, however, every European city had an irreducible core of impoverished inhabitants — the "house poor" or "parish poor" who enjoyed an undisputed right to live in the community yet could not support themselves without assistance. How many people belonged to this category? Naturally the proportion varied enormously from town to town, and it could rise or fall drastically within a given community as economic conditions changed. A few examples can, however, give some evidence of the extent of poverty.

Start with the well-recorded case of Augsburg. For the year 1558 the tax register recorded a total of 8,770 citizen households. Of these, a total of 4,161 households — about 47 per cent — were listed as "have-nots." This was a tax category, not an indication of total destitution — but it does show that almost half the householders in Augsburg lacked any property worth taxing and lived almost entirely off their income. Many of them could not break even: in the same year exactly 404 households, containing a total of 1,038 men, women and children, received regular support in the form of bread, lard, firewood and other supplies from the city alms office. Thus, in 1558 about one out of every twenty citizen households were living in definite poverty. . . .

In every town, in fact, there would have been a similar difference between the number of "structural" poor who were permanently dependent on relief and those who needed assistance only in times of famine or other crisis. This was vividly apparent, for example, in the English town of Warwick. In 1582 St. Mary's parish, which encompassed most of the town, had a total of 373 families. Of these, only 42 families, or 11 per cent, actually received poor-relief. But another 68 families were said to be at risk of decaying into poverty. Precisely this happened to many of them five years later when a drastic famine hit the town, for in 1587 a total of 93 families in St. Mary's parish — close to a quarter of the total — stood in urgent need of assistance. A number of London neighbourhoods in the same era showed a similar pattern, with 5–10 per cent of the parish families regularly receiving relief and a second group, perhaps twice as large, needing assistance in times of crisis. Much the same applies to late sixteenth-century Lyon: it has been estimated that in normal years 6–8 per cent of the city's population needed poor relief, but in times of famine 15–20 per cent of the inhabitants required support. . . .

Early in the year 1635, the authorities in Salisbury undertook — not for the first time — a survey of the poor in each parish of the city. In one parish, St. Martin's, the enumerators even distinguished between two levels of poverty. Thirty-three households were listed as regularly receiving alms. One was headed by a man, three were headed by married couples, and fully twenty-nine were headed by women — widows, spinsters or wives whose husbands had abandoned them. Among the much larger group of 174 parish households which, though poor, did not need regular alms, 105 were headed by married couples. Among the rest, 48 were headed by women and only 21 by bachelors and widowers.

. . . Women were, by and large, less mobile than men — and more economically vulnerable. An unmarried man was more likely than an unmarried woman to leave his home town, whether as a journeyman, a soldier, a sailor or even a vagabond. Among married couples, husbands abandoned their families far more often than wives. But above all, the poor widow was a much more common phenomenon than the poor widower. A man's chances of remarrying were normally greater, and even if he did not remarry his economic resources were normally larger. It is true that among the social elite, widowhood could open up opportunities for a woman to deploy her property independently and find a new marriage partner of her own choosing. Among the poor, however, widowhood was always a disaster. The paltry dowry a poor woman had brought into her marriage — if it was even intact — offered no economic security, and her opportunities to continue to earn a living were always circumscribed. Even if the law guaranteed a widow the right to continue operating her husband's shop, in practice most poor women lacked the capital and the contacts to do so effectively.

Yet the "house poor" widow may still have been regarded with envy by some other women in the community. She at least had a recognized claim on a modest degree of social assistance. Women who had never established a household in the first place were often even more vulnerable. Among these were servants. To be sure, not all servants, male or female, were ill-treated. Some worked for patriarchal masters who recognized an obligation to care for those who had loyally served them. But mistreatment of servants was no less common, and female servants ran the additional risk of being subjected to sexual exploitation. In early modern Bordeaux many a last will included bequests for servants, often with a specific reference to the recipients' faithful service. But evidence from the same city also illustrates the risks that female servants faced. In the 1620s about thirty babies were abandoned by their mothers every year, to be taken in by the Jesuit[9] foundling hospital.[10] Generally, of course, babies were abandoned in secret, but occasionally the hospital staff was able to identify the parents. Looking after foundlings was an expensive proposition — in each case a willing wet-nurse had to be found and paid — and whenever possible the authorities hoped to pin the expenses on the responsible party. The fathers who were traced came from every social level — but ten of the eleven mothers whose circumstances were recorded were listed as domestic servants. In most such cases, a master had made his servant pregnant and then fobbed her off with a promise of regular child support — and when the payments eventually tapered off, the mother could see no other recourse than giving up the baby. . . .

One of the most famous of William Hogarth's[11] "progresses" was the set of twelve engravings issued in 1747 under the title "Industry and Idleness." This series compares the careers of two imaginary apprentices of London: the industrious Francis Goodchild, whose hard work and good conduct result in economic success and political eminence, and Tom Idle, whose laziness and irreligion lead via petty crime and underworld activity to the scaffold at Tyburn.[12] The whole series, like most of Hogarth's work, is didactic, moralistic and ironic all at once. The contrast between the careers is unrealistically extreme. Yet the point Hogarth made was a valid one: that for any young person arriving in London, or indeed in any city of early modern Europe, many options were still open. Whether the newcomer would eventually rise into the more secure world of the established householders or would sink into permanent marginalization was, in many cases, determined by economic factors far beyond his or her control. But personal conduct could make a difference. Parents, church, school and guilds all promoted values of hard work, deference and sexual morality which are easy to interpret as instruments of social control. But these were also values which helped the young adult to maximize his or her chances of securing a foothold on the social ladder — and by doing so to climb into the circle of established householders who formed the core of every urban community. . . .

---

[9] The Society of Jesus, a Roman Catholic religious order established in 1540.

[10] Orphanage.

[11] English painter (1697–1764) known for satirical pictures of eighteenth-century lowlife.

[12] Field in London where public executions were held until 1868.

THE EXPERIENCE OF PREGNANCY
Jacques Gélis

Pregnancy was a dangerous condition for both mother and child in medieval and early modern Europe. Pregnancy and delivery regularly resulted in the death of the mother and in the birth of a stillborn, deformed, or sickly child. It is no wonder that pregnant women sought to alleviate their fears in every way imaginable.

University of Paris historian Jacques Gélis probes the beliefs and customs concerning pregnancy in seventeenth- and eighteenth-century France. We should bear in mind that Gélis reconstructs the experiences of pregnancy primarily from the writings of male physicians and from folklore, for there are only a few accounts composed by women (midwives, for example).

Note the many and varied precautions pregnant women took to safeguard themselves and their children as well as the help Christianity and medical science offered. To what extent, if at all, is it possible to determine the effectiveness of the strategies women employed? In what specific ways were these precautions tied to religious ideas and practices (saints, statues, holy water, and superstitions, for example)?

Jacques Gélis examines society's attitudes toward pregnancy as well as mothers' fears. How did the early modern French view pregnancy and birth? Many historians believe that more people began to marry for affection, if not love, in the eighteenth century. Does Gélis's account show that early modern people (especially husbands) felt much sentiment toward pregnant women besides the desire to have a healthy male baby? It is interesting to compare the early modern French ideas of the proper steps necessary to ensure a good birth, of a husband's relations with his pregnant wife, of the role of diet, medicine, and religion in pregnancy, and of the ideal baby to similar attitudes in the West today. What differences and similarities do you find?

The evidence . . . allows us to guess at the pride women felt in being pregnant, but it is seldom expressed directly. Women expecting babies were discreet, . . .

Jacques Gélis, *History of Childbirth: Fertility, Pregnancy, and Birth in Early Modern Europe*, trans. Rosemary Morris (Boston: Northeastern University Press, 1991), 66–89.

even ashamed of it; they concealed their state as best they could. Being pregnant means losing one's freedom of body and mind: every gesture, every word spoken, every movement of a pregnant woman also involves the child. . . . [S]he has to ensure that her offspring is protected from every harmful influence, whatever its source. She has to think, calculate, keep herself under close supervision and constraint.

FEARS OF THE PREGNANT WOMAN

A pregnant woman lives in . . . constant fear of tripping on a stair, spraining a knee or an ankle, or falling heavily; her abdomen could bump against a table-edge; . . . to be jostled in the crowd on market-day or to fall over could have the gravest consequences . . . miscarriage. Fairground charlatans and chapbooks[1] sold or recommended lotions and poultices which were supposed to save a woman's baby after she had "hurt herself." . . .

. . . As is well known, pregnancy often causes loss of calcium, which affects the teeth. Caries[2] and toothache seemed to call for an extraction, but the doctors sometimes refused to perform it: better to let the woman suffer than to endanger the foetus and be blamed for it later!

However the accident happens, the woman knows that she will always be held responsible: . . . A premature birth, a deformed child, will set her asking what rashness, what error she has committed during her pregnancy. . . .

To safeguard her child and herself, a pregnant woman was banned from certain attitudes and actions, most often those which could complicate the birth or cause physical harm to the baby. The mother-to-be had to "avoid sitting without her feet touching the ground, or with her legs crossed, because it made children deformed and lengthened labour." Nothing on her body must constrict or enclose: no unnecessary ties or necklaces. . . . Fear of strangulation by the "circles of the cord" was universal. A pregnant woman had to avoid anything to do with movement in circles. . . .

. . . [I]t was not a good idea for a woman to work on the baby's layette during her pregnancy, as she would be anticipating the time of the birth, which was dangerous and might cause it to turn out badly.

A pregnant woman kept away from death and anything symbolical of death. . . . In the Valdaine region (Dauphiné) she must not see a dead child, "for her own child would be born as pale as a corpse." It was not only a corpse which could raise fears of evil influences: any "doubling" of the woman's situation could be equally malefic. Around Cambrai, "a pregnant woman should not be a godmother, or the child she is to bear will die." . . .

---

[1] Small books or pamphlets.

[2] Dental decay, cavities.

All these fears and forbidden actions go to explain why outside help was considered so important, why women constantly sought protective measures which would ease them through this difficult time.

HELPFUL AND PROTECTIVE MEASURES

Prayers and vows were used by the pregnant woman in an attempt to reassure herself and protect her fruit. If forbidden actions and dangers were numerous, so were the measures which could be taken against them. Some of these practices fitted in with the rituals of the reformed Catholic Church, which accorded a special importance to the Virgin; but others betray the survival of ancient beliefs based on the idea of the body's closeness to nature.

Pregnant women often carried a symbolic object which was supposed to ward off accidents and bad luck. Certain gemstones, such as agate, were much sought after, particularly those whose "flesh" bears brownish or reddish lines strangely reminiscent of the shape and colour of a foetus. . . . Since Antiquity, however, the favourite amulet had been the eagle-stone, known as the "pregnant stone" because inside it rattled a concretion which made one think of the foetus within the womb. It was simple to use: it was tied round the neck, against the skin, on a thong, ribbon or necklace; it could also go on the left arm. Carried on the upper part of the woman's body, rather than on the abdomen, it helped to hold back the child from being born before the proper time. Like all amulets, the eagle-stone had a purely psychological effect: a magic object made one feel safer, it was reassuring. Up to the end of the seventeenth century doctors made no attempt to cast doubt on the virtues which women assigned to such topical remedies, though they feared the excessive trust put in them and railed against the rash actions which women might consequently take. . . .

In the seventeenth and eighteenth centuries there were still some practices around which had a strong overtone of paganism, as is shown by the pastoral visitations of certain bishops. The Church tried more and more to channel superstitions and limit their excess, but it was extremely difficult to eliminate centuries-old practices rooted in everyday life and passed on from woman to woman with the complicity of the midwives: "old wives' tales" were a many-headed hydra which was always deforming and turning aside the belief-systems of peoples who were supposed to be thoroughly Christian. For a pregnant woman will do anything to overcome her tormenting anxiety and to avoid pain during the birth — even if the Church does condemn what she herself sees as a saving precaution. . . .

It is no new thing for mothers-to-be to entrust themselves to the Virgin: they often did this back in the Middle Ages. Some of her shrines had a miraculous image which was supposed to guarantee a trouble-free pregnancy and the birth of a healthy child. One of the most famous of these, the "underground Virgin" in the crypt of Chartres, was invoked by women in this dual hope.

The emphasis on Mariology, the cult of the Virgin Mother, in the seventeenth century tended to make the Mother of Christ into the pattern for all mothers. She was first and foremost the protectress and helper, Our Lady of All Succour or Our Lady of Good Help. She never failed to answer those who called on her. Sometimes the image itself was symbolic of her role as protectress: the Virgin of Good Help which was famous in and around Nancy in the seventeenth and eighteenth centuries was shown sheltering people under her mantle. But what the pregnant woman fears above all, to the point of obsession, is the end of her pregnancy, the birth itself: it was only natural to ask the Virgin for a happy outcome, since she was the mother above all mothers, and gave birth without pain. . . .

These big regional shrines presented certain problems to women with child, especially that of distance. The time of year had to be taken into account, and also the woman's condition: the more difficult the pregnancy, the more important the pilgrimage, and it was then that women could be imprudent. Obstetric textbooks have much to say about indispositions, often serious, caused by the fatigues of the journey and long hours spent standing up in a damp, chilly church. Thus some women preferred to rely on a "travelling girl" who would make the trip on their behalf; or they would vow to go and give thanks to the relevant virgin or saint after the birth, and with the baby.

In the hierarchy of saints helpful in pregnancy, Saint Margaret[3] held a special place: her cult covered the whole of Western Christendom, where she had displaced the Illythias, Dianas and Lucinas[4] of Antiquity. . . . She was very popular in Paris: her girdle, kept at the abbey of Saint-Germain-des-Prés, generated a cult which remained vigorous until the Revolution. In the seventeenth century Thomas Platter[5] reported that every year a great feast was celebrated, "during which, to make barren women fertile or to aid those who have difficult births, the priest drapes a girdle round their shoulders and body; this ceremony," he adds, "is carried out with the greatest fervour." . . .

The theme of virginity is a feature of the lives of most of the female saints invoked during pregnancy: it is almost always connected with their martyrdom, for they die in order to defend their virginity. In the *Golden Legend*[6] Jacopa da Voragine[7] explains that ". . . Margaret was white in her virginity, precious in her humility, and full of virtues by reason of her miracles." So as to remain a virgin she refused the marriage forced on her by the Prefect Olibrius; she was tortured by the Devil in the form of a hideous dragon, but held to her vow. Saint Foy[8] was likewise martyred because she refused to surrender her virginity. And the virgin girdles of these two saints played an important part in the devotions of pregnant women. . . .

---

[3] A fictional saint who was swallowed by the devil and beheaded rather than lose her virginity.

[4] Greek and Roman goddesses who were patron deities of women.

[5] Swiss printer, schoolmaster, and humanist (1499–1582).

[6] Collection of saints' lives popular during the Middle Ages.

[7] Medieval biographer of saints (ca. 1230–ca. 1298).

[8] A popular tale held that the Romans executed Saint Faith (Foy, or Fides), a twelve-year-old Christian girl in what is today southern France, for refusing to worship an image of the emperor.

Both in learned works and in popular belief, the preservation of virginity was closely associated with a healthy pregnancy. Women who had given their lives in defence of their honour seemed best equipped to protect the fruit of the marital union. But only the Virgin, the chosen mother of God,[9] had achieved the impossible and conceived, carried and given birth to a child without having known a man. . . . No wonder, then, if the Virgin outstripped all other intercessors to become the great protectress of women in pregnancy and in childbirth. . . .

The favourite image for pregnancy was that of the womb as a container for the "fruit": thus a "miraculous statue" was often itself shown to be pregnant, with a stomach protruding so emphatically that there could be no mistaking it. Saint Margaret, despite her reputation for virginity, was shown pregnant at Collorec and Bannalec. Even, astonishingly, the Virgin herself was subject to this symbolism of the pregnant body. There are statues and pictures painted on wood or stone which show the Mother of God as being with child. In sixteenth-century "images" she is often alone. . . .

The scene of the Visitation may be pictured in exactly the same way. In this case there are two characters: the Virgin and Elizabeth,[10] both pregnant, greet each other with a reverence or with the kiss of peace. The painter or sculptor will leave an opening in Elizabeth's robe to show the infant Saint John[11] bowing before the Jesus, shown in the Virgin's womb, his right hand raised in blessing. . . .

In a final model for the "pregnant Virgin," Saint Anne[12] also appears. Here, two or three generations are seen, as it were, one within the other: Saint Anne and the Virgin, or Saint Anne, the Virgin and the infant Jesus. . . .

These representations of the Virgin constitute a type for pregnancy whose origins must be very ancient. The stone statue of the "Quinipily Venus," in Morbihan . . . represents some ancient pagan goddess. . . . [T]his statue . . . was the object of an impressively continuous cult going back at least to the medieval period. Pregnant women from the country round would come to put themselves under her protection. . . .

Pregnant women often made their way to a sanctuary at some special moment in the liturgical year. On the particular saint's day, or on the great feast days of the Virgin, . . . expectant mothers would congregate — so long as their condition would permit it. A woman was not always able to wait for such a special day; in that case, . . . she would make at a suitable time the pilgrimage. . . .

. . . Breton women from the Finistère region were assured of a trouble-free pregnancy and birth if they went to Collorec and

> walked three times round the tower of the chapel of Saint Margaret before sunrise or after sunset. Each time round, they must go into the chapel and recite five

---

[9] Mary, the mother of Jesus.

[10] In Christian legend, the mother of John the Baptist.

[11] John the Baptist; in Christian legend, Jesus' cousin.

[12] In Christian legend, Jesus' grandmother.

Paternosters[13] and five Aves.[14] This having been done, they must touch their naked navel against the statue of the saint (shown as being pregnant), make their confession, and leave an offering.

. . . [T]ouching was an essential part of the ritual. Pregnancy relates to the abdomen, so it was by contact with this part of the body that the virtues of the protecting statue must act. The Church struggled to suppress such practices, which took place in public and which it considered to be indecent. . . .

Thus women normally had to be content with brushing the saint's robe with their hands; sometimes they were allowed to kiss the wooden or stone body of the protecting saint. They would depart happy in the conviction that they would carry their child to full term and have an easy birth. Sometimes they would bring the linen they intended to use during labour. By having it blessed, or even better, by bringing it into contact with the wonder-working image, they were convinced that they would be safely delivered when the time came. . . .

Often the pregnant woman would bring a "cord" back with her: a piece of ribbon which (as she had taken care to ensure) had touched the holy relic. Tied round her waist, it would give permanent protection during her pregnancy, and be a material token of that protection. The link with the miraculous girdle could sometimes be kept up in a more subtle way: until the dawn of the present century the women who came to call upon Our Lady Of Deliverance at Neufchâtel-en-Bray used to tie half of a ribbon to the statue and keep the other half on their persons until the birth. . . .

There were some "blessed springs" which were endowed with the same beneficent powers as saints' images or girdles of the Virgin. . . . Normally the women did no more than drink water from the spring, thinking that this would keep the foetus in good health and give it the strength to be born safely. Sometimes, however, they also washed themselves.

Pregnant women bathing in a spring was part of an ancient ritual which it was always hard to extirpate. When in 1660 the Bishop of Vannes decided to put an end to the cult, . . . he was largely influenced by the scandalous aspect (as he saw it) of what used to happen by the statue: naked women bathing in a sarcophagus fed by the spring. . . .

HYGIENE DURING PREGNANCY

A woman had to make sure that the child she carried had "the strength and good constitution which he will need to withstand the efforts he must make, and endure, in order to escape from his strait prison and make his appearance in a new world." Eighteenth-century doctors were interested in "the regulation of the life of pregnant women," and were free with advice and criticism. In particular they

---

[13] The Lord's Prayer.

[14] The Hail Mary.

came out against the latest fashions, which, it seemed to them, endangered the health both of the mother and of the unborn child, especially in towns; no less violent were their denunciations of "popular misconceptions" which were unworthy of an enlightened age. People must, they said, get rid of prejudices and stay close to nature — a nature which, however, was still little known, ill-defined and idealized.

Moreover, practitioners did not, on the whole, take account of differences in social condition: their advice was addressed primarily to their better-off clients in the towns, to women who had the means to "govern themselves well." How could an ordinary lower-class woman go in for a "regulation of life" which required some resources and some free time? Could she take walks, take a rest, turn her house into a "well-aired and agreeable dwelling place," avoid unhealthy food, "partake of nourishment in moderation" . . . ? Was that all?! Poor women compelled to work right up to the end of their pregnancies, never knowing today what would become of them tomorrow, could hardly benefit from suchlike advice. The choices made by the professional doctors, and the contradictions they fell into, are nowhere better illustrated than by the way they tackled the question of hygiene in pregnancy.

In the seventeenth century, and more especially in the eighteenth, doctors often drew attention to the hygiene of particular places, creating a sort of medical topography of town and country; they took particular care to mention the quality of the air, and would declare that in a certain parish the soil did not everywhere offer the same assurances of health to a pregnant woman. Thus they advised avoiding riverbanks and marshy areas, because the miasmas which issued from them were supposed to provoke miscarriage. Town slums presented the same dangers, added to those consequent on a shortage of sunshine. Everybody knew this to be true — the people who lived in such places knew it for a start — but what could they do about it if their home and jobs were there?

Expectant mothers had to be wary of the wind: winds blowing from the south were, it seems, exceedingly dangerous because they could bring a pregnancy to an abrupt end — just as they could make a green fruit, scarcely yet formed, wither on the tree. The north wind was no less to be feared: it caused coughs and could, again, bring about the loss of a baby; moreover, it often brought "bad smells and mists" which were most injurious to the health of pregnant women.

It was not only winds which had to be attended to. Day by day women were under threat from "harsh and nauseating smells": textbooks, following Aristotle,[15] warned that "the smell of the smoke from an extinguished candle can cause abortion." . . .

"Pregnant women must take exercise." Indeed it was customary for women to remain as inactive as possible during early pregnancy, when the foetus's hold on life was so fragile. In any case, observation of nature confirmed the idea: a fruit

---

[15] Greek philosopher and scientist (384–322 B.C.) whose writings were influential in late medieval and early modern Christian thought.

is never in greater peril than when it is forming or when the tree is in flower; a sharp shower of rain, a late frost, an ill-timed shaking of the trunk, and the hopes of a whole year can be endangered in a few minutes.

In the early stages of her pregnancy a woman was supposed not to travel by carriage and not to tire herself unnecessarily. Such was Madame de Sévigné's[16] advice to her pregnant daughter when the former heard that the latter was to accompany her husband, Monsieur de Grignan, on a tiring journey across Provence. "Do not agitate yourself at this early stage by a journey to Marseilles," wrote Madame de Sévigné; "let things become more settled; think of your delicate condition."

All doctors agreed that walking was by far the best exercise. "If a woman wishes to keep in good health during her pregnancy and know the inexpressible joy of bringing a thriving child into the world, she should go on foot. . . . Pedestrian travel is the most fitting for pregnant women; it is the most useful to their health." Dancing, on the other hand, was the worst kind of rashness; how many newly wedded wives had had the cruel experience of a miscarriage after an evening's entertainment? Was that not the reason why "we see so few dancing girls carry a child to the normal term of pregnancy"? It was necessary to "refrain from extremes, either too much or too little."

Total immobility was not to be recommended either. Well-off women from noble or bourgeois families in the towns took too much care of themselves; they lived without stirring themselves at all and so were in danger from the slightest stumble. Why not do as the village women did? Work got the body moving and was an aid to health!

> Country women do not cease working even if they know that they have conceived; being accustomed to hard work, they are safe from mishaps incident on idleness; their sinews are stronger, more elastic, more resistant to fatigue than those of wealthy women who, lying voluptuously on soft beds, find it hard to believe that healthy babies can come into the world upon straw, or even on bare earth.

Here we find a gathering of all the images cherished by the "ruralism" of the Enlightenment: an idealized vision of country life; the virtues of hard work; the happiness of the poor.

The documents rarely mention the toilette of pregnant women; even the doctors often pass in silence over the topic of day-to-day cleanliness.

Mothers-to-be took no more thought for bodily hygiene than they used to do during menstruation. It is not sufficient explanation to talk about the shortage of water supplies in towns and in some country districts. We are in fact talking about a society in which daily ablutions tended to be extremely sketchy in any case. Why should expectant mothers be any different? Until the mid-nineteenth

---

[16] Famous writer of letters (1626–1696).

century, personal hygiene was considered rather suspect from a moral viewpoint; only "women of pleasure" washed and bathed with any frequency!

But people thought equally badly of a pregnant woman who took a bath, for they were suspicious of her motives. Bathing was supposed to dilate and relax the muscles; it might bring about an abortion. And "The first doctors to propose bathing as a way of aiding the development of the womb during pregnancy . . . were looked upon as murderers out to kill both mothers and children" — so said a doctor from the end of the seventeenth century.

The dirty and neglected aspect of country women was sometimes remarked upon by practitioners: Doctor Nicolas, he of the sensitive nose, made special mention, in speaking of the women of the Dauphiné, of "the smell which issues from each and every one of them, because of the dirtiness of their bodies or their clothes." True, they did live in astonishingly crowded conditions and had no access to the scented toilet waters used so abundantly by their better-off sisters in the towns.

At every social level the most important part of the toilet was the coiffure. Combing and styling one's hair was a necessity: it got rid of vermin. But . . . in the doctors' opinion, . . . "their toilet was a dangerous thing." "I have known women who spent two or three hours doing their hair," declares one such doctor. "This task, so 'important' for women with any social ambition, is excellently suited to provoking abortion." Once again we note the fear of losing the fruit of the womb.

Pregnant women may have taken little thought for cleanliness, but they did take care of their bodies, and in a surprising way. They made generous use of "oils and liniments" intended to make the flesh of the bosom and the abdomen more elastic during pregnancy. These ointments were supposed to act over time so as to prepare the belly for labour and the breasts for suckling the child; all of them were white in colour.

Bourgeois ladies of Paris anxious to keep their abdomens in good shape used to anoint themselves with "pomades," which they prepared themselves or got their maidservants to prepare for them. Alongside the "pomade of melted pork fat purified with rose-water" favoured by Louise Bourgeois[17] there were others made from "calves'-foot marrow, the caul of a kid, the grease from a fat chicken, goose, linseed oil, almonds, marshmallow and March stocks, also very good." As for Flemish ladies, they "never use anything but oil of lilies, and so preserve their bellies very well so that they are not spoilt." Through the sixteenth and seventeenth centuries this growing anxiety to preserve the abdomen probably had something to do with the changing attitudes of better-off women towards pregnancy and towards children: a point to which we shall return.

Regular use of liniments of animal or vegetable origin could profitably be supplemented by bandaging: wide linen bandages helped to hold up an abdomen

---

[17] Midwife to Marie de Medici, wife of King Henry IV (1589–1610); the first midwife to write about her practice (ca. 1563–1636).

which in the last months of pregnancy would have become as fat and heavy as a stuffed sack.

Women also held up their abdomens by means of a pregnancy girdle made of dogskin, "or some other skin suitable for making gloves." . . .

Bandages and girdles held up the abdomen and made the burden less hard to bear; moreover, they prevented some infections of the urinary tract, as a doctor pointed out at the end of the seventeenth century: "If the belly falls too low, as often happens; if the bladder is compressed and the flow of urine constricted, this discomfort can be stopped by holding up the lower part of the abdomen with bandages and draw-sheets, which any woman can make, and so increase her comfort." Fear of a "fall of the womb" haunted all pregnant women of modest means who often had to work hard right up to the end of their pregnancy.

Bandaging the abdomen, and sometimes also the bosom, was the only notable change made to one's attire. Doctors were generous with their advice on clothing for a pregnant woman, but they were seldom listened to. They advised the expectant mother to "dress in light rather than heavy clothes," to wear "sober but widely fitting," "free and easy" garments. Dress, they said, must not impede "the expansion of the womb, and in consequence, of the foetus." Some maintained that the fastenings of the dress should be modified "by holding up the skirts by means of cords passing over the shoulders." Thus, they said, "one could get rid of the harm caused by the tightness of fastenings round the loins." Practitioners condemned with one voice "shoes with excessively high heels which disturb the balance of the body and cause sprains." When they speak of the right clothes and shoes to wear during pregnancy, the doctors are evidently addressing women of the wealthier classes: ordinary women could do nothing to change their manner of dress, and just had to adapt their poor everyday garment to the exigencies of their new state, in particular by adjusting the stitching at the waist. And they went on walking about in their clumsy sabots[18] — if they had even those.

A pregnant woman must "seek repose and take it when necessary." All the textbooks for midwives and obstetricians counsel prudence and emphasize this need for rest: good sleep means a successful pregnancy. . . .

. . . Late nights must be avoided because they "overheat the blood and attack the nervous system." Above all, mothers to be must not act like "great ladies, who turn day into night and night into day." They must realize that an ill-regulated kind of life would have immediate consequences for their offspring. Late nights produced "indigestion and illnesses which produce stunted children instead of large and beautiful ones."

Constipation was one of the scourges of past ages, due to the diet: so many "retaining" foods were eaten that it was necessary to have occasional recourse to purges or enemas. . . . Pregnancy predisposed women to be "hard in the bowels, unable to go to stool save with great discomfort and infrequency." Thence came

---

[18] Cheap wooden shoes worn by peasants and workers.

colics, aches and pains, and headaches. Constipation was all the more serious, for a mother-to-be, in that she feared the consequences for the fruit of her womb: retaining waste matter for too long could bring on premature labour, for "by bearing down for a long time and with violence in order to do what she must, ligaments can relax, or some vein might open and cause an effusion of blood."

Obstetricians, having witnessed such unfortunate outcomes, gave helpful advice to pregnant women. Jacques Guillemeau[19] (early seventeenth century) advised taking "some suppositories, not too harsh," or "clysters[20] made of [the liquid from] a calf's [or] sheep's head, with a little aniseed or fennel, in which has been dissolved red sugar or violet oil." Eighteenth-century practitioners, however, counselled prudence, saying that they feared the way that some women in towns overused enemas. It was quite otherwise in the country: "There is a prejudice against enemas during pregnancy." Women were afraid that the foetus might be dislodged by the enema and drawn out, expelled, at the same time as the waste matter. They also distrusted strong purgatives, thinking that they might "dislodge the child" and push it out of the mother's womb. So they turned to gentler purgatives: in Lorraine, to "relaxing substances, such as leeks, spinach, lettuce, fresh butter, veal, honey and cooked prunes," or, again, "senna leaves dipped in damson sauce"; or, in the Ile de France, to a brew made from "borage,[21] bugloss,[22] lettuce, purslane,[23] dock[24] and a little mercury."

In truth, according to the doctors, the only effective way to combat constipation was to prevent it by a regular, well-balanced diet — often no more than a pious hope in a world at the mercy of bad harvests and of famine.

"It is only in recent times that pregnant women have paid careful attention to their diet." In the seventeenth century, and especially in the eighteenth, the medical fraternity certainly made recommendations on diet during pregnancy and drew attention to certain dishes which they considered dangerous, but they had little effect on people's behaviour, except in some sections of urban society. But is it all that surprising?

It is commonly believed that what the mother ingests has a direct influence on the foetus: a pregnant woman shares her meals with the child she is carrying, which, like a parasite encysted in her womb, extracts what it needs; it is even the main beneficiary of the nourishment: "the first morsel goes to the child," according to an old proverb. Pregnant women yielded to the conviction that they had to "do their best to eat a lot," even if they were not "urged thereto by hunger." In short, they had to "eat for two." Doctors protested against the depraved appetite

---

[19] Surgeon and medical writer (1550–1613).

[20] Enemas.

[21] A plant with blue flowers and leaves used for flavoring.

[22] A bristly plant related to borage.

[23] A plant with green or golden leaves used as an herb and salad vegetable.

[24] A weedy plant of the buckwheat family.

of women who ate too much, and seemed to be "pregnant right up to the throat"! But the reason why pregnant women ate a lot was that they always feared "weakness," and so, to "keep their strength up," they ate more than usual and unhesitatingly partook of "spiritous liquors." This, declared the doctors, was a "destructive preconception," for such a "heat-engendering method" could not but lead to accidents; pregnant women must desist from ingesting too much "hot and dessicating" food and drink, which were always likely to produce thick and melancholy blood: such foods were . . . beef, hare, eel and other similar things, especially if salted and spiced: venison pâté, saveloys,[25] Mainz ham and so on. Also undesirable were vegetables, cheese, garlic, onions, quinces both wild and cultivated, hazelnuts, walnuts, medlars[26] and hard-boiled eggs. . . .

From the sixteenth century to the eighteenth, doctors continued to fight against popular patterns of behaviour and tried to define the ideal diet for a pregnant woman. Their recommendations — eat plenty of healthy, cooling foods at regular intervals, drink claret and sometimes red wine, in "reasonable" quantities — give us some idea of the gulf which then existed between medical theory and the day-to-day existence of the majority of women. However judicious, the medical men's advice seems singularly ill-adapted to actual conditions at the time.

The diet of pregnant women in olden times was mainly characterized by monotony, insufficient protein and seasonal variation. "Eating for two"? It was rather a case of sharing an already meagre repast. How could the child benefit if the mother could not get enough to eat? . . . In such cases the quality of what they ate was of secondary importance: what mattered was getting enough to eat. In the supply gap just before the harvest, when barns and purses were both empty, orchard fruits could be a boon; but while green fruit could satisfy hunger, it was highly dangerous to women who ate too much of it, without taking the precaution of cooking it first! "Fluxes"[27] were always to be feared; it was in summer that miscarriages were most frequent.

A pregnant woman, said the doctors, was not always able to control her feelings — which was not good either for her or for the child. "She is naturally inclined to anger and bad temper, more so than at other times," as the obstetrician Deleurye insisted in about 1770; consequently, anything which could provoke such passions must be avoided. All excess was dangerous: "immoderate shouting and laughing is bad for her." She must also beware of "loud sounds and noises, such as thunder, artillery and loud bells." Pregnant women had been known to die of fright on hearing thunder.

"These mental passions" were always bad for the child, for they "often cause miscarriage." . . . Fortunately the outcome was not always so dramatic: the mother must not, however, forget that passions "are perceptibly communicated to the foe-

---

[25] Pork sausages.

[26] Fruit similar to crab apples.

[27] Abnormal discharges of bodily fluids.

tus. It is very common to see children stained from birth with a thousand defects that they have brought from the womb of a dejected, quick-tempered, capricious or intemperate mother." . . .

THE PREGNANT WOMAN AND OTHER PEOPLE

Nowadays, a woman expecting a child is the object of consideration: as far as possible she is spared fatigue and annoyance; she is not expected to do tiring work; people willingly make way for her. In former times, nothing really changed for a woman who became pregnant, and among working people, where her life was always rather hard, she had no-one to rely on but herself. However, in the eighteenth century voices were raised in favour of a more considerate treatment.

Society in those days was harsh for everybody. Each and every member of the family took risks in the course of his or her daily round, from the shepherd-boy sleeping amidst his flock under the threat of attack by wolves to the grown man thatching a roof, risking his life without any insurance; or venturing onto a lake although he could not swim. There was a constant danger of accident or attack. It was the destiny of a woman to be pregnant; why should she have escaped the general rule? Her state, however "interesting" it may have been, did not free her from the necessity of earning a living — which could mean risking her life. Many are the descriptions of women at an advanced stage of pregnancy helping with hay-making or the harvest, winnowing the corn or carrying heavy baskets. Doctors and country priests sometimes complained bitterly about the consequences of such overwork; but what hope had they of being listened to when for a working woman, a day-labourer, work was the very condition of her survival?

Women did help one another; they did so without extravagant words or gestures, mother helping daughter, or friends helping out at the place of work, the communal wash-place or the public well. Someone would carry the pregnant woman's heavy burden, or go shopping for her.

Men, on the other hand, did not always behave towards their wives as might have been wished; in the eighteenth century, priests sometimes took their somewhat uncultivated parishioners severely to task for forgetting their duties towards "the carrier of so precious a burden." In 1769 Froger, priest of Mayet in the diocese of Le Mans, asked them to pay their wives a little more attention and help them in the hardest tasks. Most to be feared were quick-tempered husbands who threatened readily and sometimes lashed out. One brandished a sabre over the head of his wife when she was near her time; another laid into her with a stick, and caused premature labour and the death of the child, which was born with the back of its head flattened and bloody! The grief-stricken mother told the story to Louise Bourgeois: "She told me that six weeks before the birth her husband had struck her three blows on the lower back with a big stick from his bundle of faggots; to which she attributes the cause of this deformity." No doubt such were extreme cases.

The husband's "approaches" to his wife during pregnancy drew various comments from the doctors; but such approaches certainly took place, as is shown by the pages devoted to sexual relations during pregnancy in diverse textbooks of midwifery. The husband's desire to continue enjoying his wife is sufficient to explain the persistence of such relations, but the cultural reasons for such conduct should not be underestimated: was it not in this way that the husband helped to fashion the child? The shapeless mass within the mould of the womb thus received the stamp of the father.

Up to the beginning of the eighteenth century, most practitioners remained fairly tolerant of sexual relations during pregnancy; many of them also thought that coitus helped to shape the child. In any case, was it not behaviour which made a difference between men and beasts? "Some women being pregnant," wrote Guillemeau, "disdain the company of their husbands; which could be said of brute beasts when they are in whelp, the like of which ordinarily flee from the male." And Laurent Joubert emphasizes the sexual appetite of the woman during pregnancy: "Pregnant up to the bosom, [she] will often be more eager, indeed more hungry than if she were not pregnant at all." However, the doctors, while not proscribing "conjugal relations," considered that they ought not to be "made too frequent, because the womb can be damaged thereby." Guillemeau emphasizes that the woman should avoid "making the beast with two backs" during the first four months of pregnancy, "for fear of dislodging the fruit." Some, in fact, explained "superfetation," i.e. the simultaneous presence in the womb of children of differing ages, by a fresh conception on the part of an already pregnant woman.

The change of tone which appears in medical discourse during the second half of the eighteenth century can be explained by "populationist" ideas. On behalf of the future of the kingdom, doctors went into battle against anything which seemed likely to slow the increase in population. They fulminated against sexual relations in pregnancy as a threat to the survival of the foetus. And during the French Revolution, when the production of a "healthy and vigorous generation" was urged as a condition for the regeneration of the State, they appealed to the father's conscience, as the obstetrician Nicolas Saucerotte does here:

> As soon as there are signs of pregnancy, take care not to imperil, in the mother's womb, the existence of the fruit of your love. Husbands, be temperate in every way necessary for the state of an individual who, one might say, has two lives, that is her own, and that of the creature which she is to bring into the world.

The Church, for its part, insisted throughout the eighteenth century on the moral implications of the sexual act in pregnancy. To the Church, a husband who took his pleasure at such a time was a brute doing outrage to his wife, a "human monster whom everyone regarded with horror and who should be banished from society." The heated tone corresponds to the seriousness with which such an act was regarded — and to its relative frequency in the countryside up to the nineteenth century.

THE LONGED-FOR CHILD

Until the birth, the womb held a secret: what would it be like, this child who grew day by day away from all curious eyes? Reverie fed on mystery. How could you know? How could you find out in advance?

For centuries, if not for millennia, Western society kept to the same archetype of the ideal child; it was still very present to the minds of countrywomen over almost the whole of France until a few decades ago. . . . Girl or boy? Nowadays, echography and the testing of the amniotic fluid can give us the answer. There is no more room for reverie: we have to know; we are incessantly in quest of further certainty.

If the womb was an oven, the child that one wanted to see come forth from it was "done to a turn," neither undercooked nor overcooked. An "overcooked" child was one which had dull skin, a leaden grey complexion and a lot of black hair: such a child had been too long in the womb — unless the mother's temperament was too strong and the cooking had been too quick, or the water of the bath into which the newborn child had been plunged had been too hot. In contrast, the premature child was too pale, too small, too thin, like dough which had been baked at the wrong temperature and so had not risen properly. Between the two was the pink, hale, "blond, curly-haired" child of every expectant mother's dreams.

A curly-haired child is mentioned in the fertility and pregnancy rites of Burgundy, Bresse, Brittany and Touraine. Places visited by women desirous of bearing a handsome child on this model often have a fertility-spring under the patronage of some saint. Thus, the women of Bresse went to the spring of Saint-Jean-des-Eaux, near Tournus, to call on the aid of John the Baptist. But at the chapel of Beaumont-en-Dombes, which was near a famous spring, it was a miraculous virgin, Notre-Dame-des-Mouches, which received the women's prayers. . . .

But it is possible that "curly simply meant 'strong.'" This is indicated by the kind of prayers addressed to Saint Greluchon[28] or similar saints at certain sacred springs. Women came to pray to "the good saint" for fine children, and girls asked for a faithful and vigorous (in the amatory sense) husband. This allows us to construe this quest for a fine child as a response to the deep-seated anxiety of a mother: a sickly, weakly, not quite "human" child was perhaps a sort of evil enchantment, like the piece of sympathetic magic known as the *aiguillette* (whereby an ill-wisher rendered the husband impotent by tying a symbolical knot in a cord) which must be feared and guarded against.

Facial beauty was also a cause of concern. A woman always hopes that her child will have a good complexion. That is the only explanation for some food taboos in pregnancy and for certain fertility rites. In Lorraine the newborn baby's

---

[28] Legendary Celtic saint.

face would actually be rubbed with the placenta or cord, "so as to give it a clear complexion, and if it has any blemishes on its skin, to get rid of them." It was also believed that if the cord was drawn three times across the baby's eyes this would give it better eyesight. Eyes, and in particular their expression, were very important. Deep-set eyes were not popular: they "said" something about the father. According to Laurent Joubert, "Those who have deep-set eyes were engendered by an old man"; or, again, "a child will have more deeply set eyes, and also its whole body will be frailer and less plump, if such has been its father." But the colour of the eyes was also important: in Alsace, where black eyes were preferred, pregnant women were quite sure that if they swallowed *Kirchwasser*[29] during the first months of pregnancy, they would get what they wanted.

It is true that everywhere, in the seventeenth and eighteenth centuries, there was some belief in the use of liqueurs and wine to help the arrival of a fine offspring. Drinking brandy before the birth apparently helped to "ungrease" the child, to free it from the sebaceous covering of cheese-like material which was commonly believed to come from the father's sperm. It was widely believed that stimulants like coffee, tea or chocolate also made babies healthy and strong, though not everyone had the same confidence in chocolate. . . . One had to be wary of anything which could "taint" the foetus.

But why should not the mother, who helped to form her child by what she ate, try to act on it by eating particular things of proven virtue? It was not always greedy to gorge oneself with delicious firm, pink, quince jelly, as Primerose[30] remarked towards the end of the seventeenth century: "There are worthy women who, during their pregnancy, eat a great deal of marmalade, which, they say, is so that their children should be clever, having perhaps heard that it strengthens the retentive capacity of the brain by drying it out, because being yet tender like soft wax, it easily receives the impression and the virtue of the jelly."

Is it a boy or a girl? The mother-to-be could not fail to ask herself that question. However, it was seldom the mother who initiated the rite of divination; as a participant in the development of the foetus, she was not qualified to judge. It was the people around her who conducted the inquiry on her body.

The pregnant body, jealous of its secret, nevertheless had to reveal the sex of the child to those who know how to make the correct observations and deductions. The mask of pregnancy was the best known, because the most easily accessible, indication: in Brittany or Touraine a "marked face" or "spots" invariably meant a girl. The shape of the womb was also taken into consideration. A pointed womb meant a girl, a wide one a boy. But the essential criterion had to do with the two sides of the body. The right was always considered to be the noble, strong, positive side: it symbolized the masculine element; the left or "sinister" side was weak, negative, which is as much as to say feminine. If the woman was carrying

---

[29] In Christian belief, holy water said to have magical powers.

[30] Seventeenth-century alchemist and physician (died ca. 1660).

to the right she would have a boy; if to the left, a girl. But a part of the body could "speak" for the whole: in Morbihan, towards the end of the nineteenth century, one heard about women who were sure to have a boy if their right leg swelled up during the pregnancy.

Since observation was not always sufficient in itself, the body would be tested, made to react. If the woman, when told to move, set off on the right foot, she would have a boy; if she was made to sit on the ground, and used her left hand as a support when getting up, she would have a girl. One could also try the key test. A key was thrown to the ground, and the woman picked it up, unthinkingly using one hand or the other. . . .

Sometimes the sex would be determined by the toss of a coin. The coin was habitually put into the top of the woman's bodice, between her breasts: if it fell tails it foretold a girl; if it was heads, a boy. . . .

The last-born could also show the sex of the next child by its speech. According to whether its first word was "papa" or "mamma," it was telling its parents that it would have a little brother or sister. Normally the connection between the word and the sex was analogous, but it could also be inverse, so that "papa" foretold a girl and "mamma" a boy. The phases of the moon at the time of a birth also had an important part to play in determining the sex of the next child. If the new moon appeared in the course of the six days immediately following the birth, the next child would be of the same sex; otherwise it would be different. In Touraine, if the new moon appeared within nine days, the child to be would *not* be of the same sex; in the contrary case, it would be. . . .

These regional variations in interpretation should not obscure the essential fact: everyone was seeking a rule for "reading" the signs. Since the moon was thought to have an essential role in conception, it was only natural that it should be the preferred instrument for the divination of the sex. Here we find the temporal aspect intervening once again. Indeed, the "time of the pregnancy" was also taken into account; the beginning and end of pregnancy were useful indications. A particularly close eye was kept on the mother's behaviour during the first month: if she was sick during this time she would have a boy — which was perfectly logical, because it was believed at the time that only the male embryo was formed at that stage. A pregnancy which went beyond the expected term also meant a boy: did this mean that the "cooking" of a male child took longer?

Many other divinatory procedures were also tried. In one place, women went around the blessed springs and threw in two little garments, one for a boy, one for a girl; the one which floated longer showed the sex. . . .

MAKING CONNECTIONS: WOMEN AND THE FAMILY

1. Families formed in early modern Europe for several purposes, which might differ according to social group, location (rural or urban, for example), or time, but reproduction was invariably a reason for marriage among couples of child-bearing age. Un-

fortunately, pregnancy was dangerous and painful for women, and for babies as well, with high mortality rates for both mother and child. No wonder, then, that pregnant women did anything possible (and even impossible!) to ensure a safe pregnancy. To what extent are the constant fears of the women Jacques Gélis describes similar to those of other historical periods and societies in Western civilization? Which safeguards for pregnancy, both religious and medical, were peculiar to seventeenth-century French society?

2. In what ways were pregnant women's practices of bodily hygiene and diet effective? How did family members help (or hinder) pregnant women? What was the attitude of seventeenth-century husbands toward their pregnant wives? What type of a child did mothers and fathers want? Discuss whether the early modern family was more or less child-centered than the contemporary family.

3. Historians, like other people today, often err in labeling as superstitious beliefs and practices that do not seem to be based on empirical evidence and that seem to contradict modern science. Gélis describes many religious behaviors and medical practices that seem at odds with what we know — or think we know — about the natural world. Yet, certainly, it is unfair to label early modern French beliefs as superstitious. How did pregnant women's recourse to religious, magical, and medical panaceas reflect a coherent view of the universe? That is, why were the advice and practices surrounding pregnancy logical to the people of the seventeenth century? What specific precautions regarding pregnancy do women follow today?

DEATH'S ARBITRARY EMPIRE
John McManners

The eighteenth century is known as the Enlightenment, the Age of Reason, or the Age of Voltaire. John McManners, an Anglican priest and former Regius Professor of Ecclesiastical History at Oxford University, reveals the underside of that epoch of cultural achievement, a world where, for most people, death triumphed early. Observers who lived during that era, including physicians, give vivid accounts of the deplorable physical condition of the French populace. When McManners reviews the history of eighteenth-century France in terms of medicine, disease, and mortality, he finds ill-health, violence, and misery to have been as characteristic of the age as enlightened reason and Voltairian wit.

During the eighteenth century, the high rate of infant mortality was the primary reason for a low life expectancy. Why did so many infants and children die? What, if anything, could people have done to improve their children's health and longevity? Orphans were less likely to survive childhood than any other group. The presence of orphanages, however, suggests that society attempted to care for orphans. If that is true, why did so many die so young?

McManners paints a bleak picture of physicians and their ability to treat illness and disease. Why were medical doctors so ineffective? Surely we cannot place all of the blame on physicians, because their patients, even in the best of times, were models of poor health. The living conditions in towns (such as overcrowding and the lack of sanitation), an insufficient and poor diet, the dangers of the workplace, the vagaries of the weather, even the clothing — all made people easy prey for disease. And where could one be safe? Not in an institution, for hospitals, army barracks, and asylums were dangerous places. The economic elite, healthier because of a better diet, certainly fared better than most, but even the rich suffered from disease and illness to an extent scarcely imaginable to us in our era of antibiotics and long life expectancy. In the eighteenth century, death's empire was whimsically arbitrary.

Nothing, not even youth and robust health, could give security from suffering or early death, for eighteenth-century France was a violent society. Highwaymen, domestic violence, wild animals, and rural conflicts were omnipresent.

John McManners, *Death and the Enlightenment: Changing Attitudes to Death among Christians and Unbelievers in Eighteenth-Century France* (New York: Oxford University Press, 1981), 5–23.

Often hungry, cold, sick, and frightened by forces seemingly beyond their control, the overwhelming majority of people had little time to marvel at Voltaire's wit.

In eighteenth-century France, "death was at the centre of life as the graveyard was at the centre of the village." Speaking in averages, and confounding in one the diversity of the whole country and the fortunes of all classes, we find that something like a quarter of all babies born in the early years of the century died before reaching their first birthday, and another quarter before reaching the age of eight. Of every 1,000 infants, only 200 would go on to the age of fifty, and only 100 to the age of seventy. A man who had beaten the odds and reached his half-century would, we may imagine, have seen both his parents die, have buried half his children and, like as not, his wife as well, together with numerous uncles, aunts, cousins, nephews, nieces, and friends. If he got to seventy, he would have no relations and friends of his own generation left to share his memories. If this is a description of the average, what can we say of the unfortunates whose sombre ill luck weights down the figures to this mean? . . .

A new understanding of the eighteenth century comes to us when we review its history in terms of disease and mortality. In narrow fetid streets and airless tenements, in filthy windowless hovels, in middens and privies, in undrained pools and steaming marshes, in contaminated wells and streams — and, for that matter, in the gilded corridors of Versailles, where excrement accumulated — infections of every kind lurked. The files of the administrators, more especially those of the Royal Society of Medicine at the end of the *ancien régime*,[1] are full of information sent in by medical experts about local epidemics and peculiar illnesses, but it is often difficult to deduce from their accounts what the specific diseases were. They spoke essentially of symptoms. Fevers were "bilious," "putrid," "autumnal," "red," "purple," "intermittent," "malignant," "inflammatory." The spitting of blood so often mentioned could have been the result of cancer of lungs or larynx, infection of the trachea, or pulmonary tuberculosis; their "scurvy," deduced from bleeding gums and painful joints, could include arthritis and pyorrhoea. An autopsy frequently produced a report of "worms" in lungs or stomach, without any other evidence to bring precision. . . . "With their bodies assaulted on all sides, these people were carried off before the more subtle disorders had a chance to strike." The main killers were influenza and pulmonary infections, malaria, typhoid, typhus, dysentery, and smallpox, striking in waves across a debilitating pattern of routine afflictions — mange, skin disorders, gout, epilepsy. The grimmest scourge of all was smallpox, which seems to have become a more common and more virulent disease from the late seventeenth century. A doctor of Montpellier in 1756 described it as being "everywhere," as it were "naturalized" and "domes-

---

[1] Old Régime, the two centuries before the French Revolution of 1789.

ticated," especially at Paris, "where it never relaxes its grip." . . . Not surprisingly, then, the army records on new recruits continually speak of marked faces. . . . This was, indeed, a disease which destroyed the beauty of so many of those it did not slay. . . .

. . . There were two seasons when mortality was at its highest, winter and early spring on one hand, and autumn, especially the month of September, on the other. In some places, winter was the cruellest season, in others autumn. From December to March, pneumonia and pulmonary afflictions abounded, and the sheer cold took its toll of those who were ill-clothed and lacked the means to keep warm. And these were numerous. Wood was in short supply in the cereal-growing plains and in the cities. Heating arrangements were rudimentary; even in Versailles, wine froze at the royal table in winter, and the heavily padded and decorated coats of courtiers were not just for display. Clothing passed from upper to lower classes and from older to younger generations, getting more and more threadbare on its journey. The poorer streets of cities were a motley pageant of rags, anonymous or with prestigious social origins. There were peasants who never changed their linen, and when they discarded it, it was too worn to be sent to the paper-mills. Even the more prosperous peasants . . . made do with two shirts and two coats a year, and a cloak every five. There was not much in the wardrobe to keep them warm and dry in the snow or rain of winter. In August, September, and October, dysentery would strike, and before illnesses encouraged by the excessive heat had declined, there would come the onset of those which flourished in the ensuing dampness. . . . These were fevers — malaria (coming, as contemporaries noted, with the floods), typhoid, and "purple fever" which was often confused with the ubiquitous scarlatina or measles. Generally, it was adults, especially the aged, who succumbed in winter, and the younger children in the autumn — though there were exceptions: the cold in some places carried off more babies under the age of one than the intestinal infections of the hotter weather. Superimposed upon this yearly cycle of menace was the arbitrary onslaught of great epidemics, sometimes driving the death rate up to double and treble the monthly average; there was the dysentery in Anjou in 1707 and 1779, highly infectious and lethal within two or three days, the influenza in the same province which caused devastation in 1740, the typhoid and enteric fever in Brittany from 1758 onwards which was largely responsible for reducing the population of that province by 4 per cent; there were more localized outbreaks, like the military fever in Pamiers in 1782 which killed 800 people.

Being born was a hazardous business for both mother and child. "Don't get pregnant and don't catch smallpox" was Mme. de Sévigné's[2] advice to her married daughter . . . although she had only simple ideas of how to avoid either. The proverbial pride in pregnancy of primitive societies was overwhelmed, in eighteenth-century France, by fear. Medical manuals considered a pregnant

---

[2] Famous writer of letters (1626–1696).

woman to be suffering from an illness, and even cited Scripture in ascribing the pains of childbirth to the transgression of Eve. Many women, especially those of the poorer classes, came to their ordeal in wretched health, and the prevalence of rickets caused deformities which made delivery difficult. There were hardly any hygienic precautions, the technique for arresting haemorrhages was not yet developed, and the manipulation of forceps (supposed to be limited to qualified surgeons alone) was clumsy. Until the reign of Louis XVI, there was hardly any attempt to train midwives. In reporting to their bishops or to the secular authorities, parish priests described how the office of midwife came to be filled in their parish. . . . A curé[3]—"the diocese of Boulogne in 1725 said that his midwife inherited the job from her mother — "the women have a reasonable amount of confidence in her." Another curé said that "ours has worked here for thirty years: she took up the office of her own accord, the women of the parish accepted her, and it has not been thought fitting to oblige her to undergo further training." Horror stories about midwives abound — beating on the stomach to "hasten delivery," cutting the umbilical cord too close or failing to tie it, forgetting the placenta, crippling babies by rough handling, and — even — showing off by turning the infant round so that the feet emerged first. Louis XIV made a clean break with tradition when he called in a man, the surgeon Jacques Clément, to the accouchement[4] of the Dauphine in 1686. . . . But were surgeons much more use than midwives? Clément bled his patient, wrapped her in the skin of a newly flayed sheep, and kept her in a dark room for nine days without so much as a single candle. And how good was the gynaecologist whose advertisement in Paris has been preserved as a curiosity?—"Montodon, ci-devant pâtisseur, boulevard Bonne Nouvelle, est actuellement chirurgien et accoucher."[5] In fact, there was little that even the most expert practitioner could do if things went wrong. If the baby's head stuck, there would be a week of agony and the vileness of gangrene before inevitable death. The Caesarian section without anaesthetics left one chance in a thousand for the women. . . . Many babies were stillborn, or died within a few days, or were maimed for life. A memoir to an intendant in 1773 describes young people coming out of a parish mass, marked by inexpert deliveries — atrophied, hunchbacked, deaf, blind, one-eyed, bandy-legged, bloodshot of eye, lame and twisted, hare-lipped, "almost useless to society and fated for a premature end." Many women too were killed, or crippled, or mentally scarred; a curé blames the rise of contraceptive practices in his parish on the neurotic determination of so many women never to undergo the experience of childbirth again.

. . . Between 20 and 30 per cent of babies born died in their first year: in a particularly wretched hamlet in the early part of the century, over 32 per cent died

---

[3] Chief parish priest.

[4] Parturition.

[5] "Montodon, former pastry cook, boulevard Bonne Nouvelle, is currently a surgeon and obstetrician."

in their first year and over 22 per cent in their second. There were, of course, healthy and unhealthy areas, depending on the peculiar combination of advantages and disadvantages in food supplies, geographical features, and climate. The national average in the eighteenth century for children surviving to the age of ten was, roughly, 55 per cent; at Crulai in Normandy it was 65 per cent; in poverty-stricken villages amidst the stagnant malarial pools of the Sologne or of the Mediterranean littoral, it was 40 per cent. . . . The deadly season of the year for infants was early autumn, when heat, humidity and flies, and unhygienic ways of living brought the intestinal infections for which no remedy was known. These visitations were facilitated by the custom, prevalent among richer people and town dwellers, of sending infants away to be nursed by foster mothers. Towards the end of the century, of the 21,000 babies born each year in Paris, only 1,000 were fed by their mothers, another 1,000 by wet-nurses brought into the home, 2,000 to 3,000 were sent to places near the city, and the rest to more distant localities — concentric circles within which the proportion of deaths became higher as the distance from home increased. . . . For families of the urban working class, like small shopkeepers or the silk workers of Lyon, it was an economic necessity to get the wife back to counter or loom quickly. For the leisured class, a satisfactory explanation is harder to find; a certain harshness of mind, an unwillingness to become too attached to a pathetic bundle whose chances of survival were so limited, the desire to resume sexual relationships as soon as possible, the belief that loss of milk diluted the quality of the blood of the mother, a reliance on the therapeutic qualities of country air to give the baby a good start or (very doubtfully) some subconscious reaction against an infant's "oral sadism" — whatever the reasons, a compelling social custom had arisen. In 1774, a reformer, appealing to have children "brought up in the order of Nature," described the sensation when a mother declares her intention of breast-feeding her first child: protests from her parents, and all the ladies lamenting to see her risking her life for a new-fashioned theory. Given the demand, around the cities a wet-nursing "industry" had arisen. In some villages near Limoges, girls married earlier to qualify. Such glimpses as we get of this peculiar interchange between town and country show an unfeeling and mercenary world — women who take on two or three babies in addition to their own, knowing that there will be competition for survival, who go on drawing their pay when they know their milk is drying up and their client's infant will have no chance. . . . These practitioners are preying on legitimate children, with parents to look after their interests and hoping against hope that they will be trundled back home in nine months' time. What then of the illegitimate ones, the multitude of foundlings, the *enfants trouvés?*[6]

The fate of these unhappy infants throws a harsh, cold light on the cruel underside of the century of crystalline wit and rococo delicacy. Increasing numbers

---

[6] Orphans, foundlings.

of children were being abandoned. An average of 2,000 a year came to the Enfants Trouvés of Paris in the 1720s, rising to a record total of 7,676 in 1772; thereafter, royal edicts forbade the bringing-in of foundlings from the provinces, and the Parisian total stabilized at about 5,800 a year. In Bordeaux at the mid-century, there were about 300 admissions annually; in Metz, in the winter of 1776, no less than 900. . . . These numbers swamped the organizational abilities of the *ancien régime*, . . . and the hopeless problem they presented deadened the charitable instincts of those who cared. A Genevan doctor reports a nun of the Parisian foundling hospital taking refuge in the reflection that these innocent souls would go straight to eternal bliss, since the revenues of her institution could not feed any more of them anyway. There was a prejudice against making immoral conduct easier by spending money on those "unhappy fruits of debauchery" (though it is true that some children were abandoned by married parents who were too poor to maintain them). Many illegitimate children were doomed before ever they reached the shelter of an institution — physically impaired by the mother's attempts to conceal her pregnancy or to produce an abortion, infected with venereal disease, or hopelessly weakened by a journey from some distant place, crowded in baskets on the back of a donkey, or of a porter travelling on foot, or jolting in a wagon. The infants who got through the crucial first week in which so many died had to survive the grim and crowded conditions in the hospital, and the rigours of the system of putting out to nurse (with private families paying more to preempt the healthiest and most reliable foster mothers). Only one foundling in ten lived to reach the age of ten: nine had perished. Such survivors as there were would live gloomily learning a trade in some institution full of prostitutes, layabouts, and madmen, or in some ruthlessly disciplined orphanage; a very few might be found again by their parents or left with some sympathetic country family — but the chances of a decent existence were infinitesimal. One who did get through the hazards and succeeded was the *philosophe* and mathematician d'Alembert,[7] left as an infant on the steps of the church of Saint-Jean-la-Ronde. An expert on the calculus of probabilities, he must often have reflected on the odds that he had beaten.

Driven to despair by poverty, some parents abandoned their children: there were suspicions that others did not strive officiously to keep them alive. The synodal statutes of various dioceses ordered the *curés* to warn their flocks against the dangerous practice of putting children to sleep in the beds of their parents, where so often they were suffocated. . . . A surgeon described the injuries suffered by babies in the vineyard country around Reims: while their mothers toiled among the vines they were sometimes attacked by animals — eyes pecked by turkeys, hands eaten off by pigs. And for the healthy grown-up, the ordinary routines of life were precarious. Society was ill-policed, unable to take effective measures to suppress

---

[7] Jean le Rond d'Alembert (1713–1783).

highwaymen and discipline vagabonds. Rural life was violent. Wife-beating was common. Unpopular *curés* were kept awake by nocturnal *tapages*[8] which could degenerate into riots. There were affrays with cudgels and clubs at fairs. In Languedoc, where the hunting rights of the lords had been bought off, peasants went around with guns; poachers returned the fire of gamekeepers; and pot-shots were taken at *seigneurs*[9] and other unpopular local worthies. The youths of villages were organized, quasi-officially, into bands, the *"garçons de paroisse,"*[10] who fought pitched battles with those from other places at fairs, marriages, and the draw for the *milice,*[11] or when communities quarrelled over boundaries or grazing rights. . . . In towns, the police force was inadequate to maintain order at festivals or to organize precautions against accidents. A panic at the fireworks in Paris for the marriage of the Dauphin in 1770 led to more than 1,000 being trampled to death; two years later, the great fire at the Hôtel-Dieu claimed many victims. There were, indeed, few precautions against fire — for long the only Parisian fire brigade was the Capuchin friars, swarming into action in frocks and cowls, with axes and ladders. Narrow streets, ramshackle buildings, and an abundance of wooden construction made the old parts of cities hopelessly vulnerable, tinder dry in summer, and underpinned with extra fuel in winter when the cellars of the rich were crammed with firewood and grain. . . . Buildings, especially the parish churches for whose maintenance a local rate had to be levied, were often left unrepaired and dangerous; every year there were floods from unbanked rivers, wreaking devastation and leaving legacies of fever. In the streets and in the countryside, savage dogs, some with rabies, wandered; in remote areas wolf packs hunted — there was a government bounty for each one killed, the parish priest to issue a certificate on the production of the ears; in 1750, 126 were killed in the province of Anjou alone. Our modern concept of "accident" as some technical failure — burnt-out wire, slipping flange, broken lever — obtruding into wellorganized habitual comfort, was almost unknown in the eighteenth century. Life was hazardous throughout. . . .

Up to the last two decades of the *ancien régime,* hardly anything was done to regulate dangerous trades or to prevent industrial accidents. . . . Even so, though nothing was being done, contemporaries were becoming aware of the terrifying hardships which crippled industrial workers and abbreviated their lives. . . . Conditions in French mines were grim enough: twelve hours a day underground, in continual danger from explosions (because fires were burning to suck air along the galleries) and from flooding (if the horse-turned pumps failed). The workers who polished mirrors, their feet continually in water and hands continually getting cut, were worn out by the interminable pushing to and fro of the heavy

---

[8] Rows.

[9] Lords.

[10] Boys of the parish.

[11] Militia.

weight; printers received fractures and bruises from the levers of their presses; candle makers stifled in the heat around the furnaces; hemp crushers invariably got asthma; gilders became dizzy within a few months from the mercurial fumes which eventually poisoned them; workers who handled unwashed wool were recognizable by their pale and leaden countenances, upon which would be superimposed the permanent stains of the colours used in dyeing. Alarming examples of the effect of bad conditions of working and living on mortality rates can be studied in the armed forces. In war, few sailors were killed by cannon-balls. The seventy-four-gun ship *Ajax* patrolled in the Atlantic and Indian Oceans from February 1780 to June 1784; during that period 228 of her crew of 430 died. Battle accounted for only thirty (and of these half perished from the explosion of one of the ship's own cannon); nine were drowned . . . ; no less than 185 were killed by diseases: scurvy, dysentery, malaria — infections that ran riot among men cooped below decks for most of their time afloat, and living on food lacking in indispensable vitamins. . . . It could be said that war killed soldiers, but essentially indirectly. The mortality rate in a particular regiment from 1716 to 1749 was five times higher in war years than in those of peace, but the deaths occurred principally from December to April, when the troops were in winter quarters. In the barracks built in the eighteenth century (always at the expense of the local authorities, not of the Crown), the standard size for a room was 16 by 18 feet, to contain thirteen to fifteen men crammed into four or five beds. These stifling conditions, rampant epidemics, the cold outside, and venereal disease killed many more in winter quarters than the shot and steel of the enemy in the summer campaigning season. It was a rule under the *ancien régime* that life in State institutions was abbreviated. When *dépôts de mendicité*[12] were set up in 1767 to clear vagabonds off the roads, the inmates died off rapidly. . . . At Rennes, of 600 initially arrested, 137 died within a year, though it is true there were a lot of infections about at the time. At Saint-Denis, the death rate in the *dépôt* was consistently double that for the town, not excepting the high infant mortality from the latter total.

. . . [D]eath was not without deference to rank and possessions, to the well-to-do with their log fires, warm clothing, protein diet, and spacious houses. . . . True, in this age of multitudinous servants, it was difficult to erect effective barriers of unofficial quarantine — in the last resort, infections got through. . . . No doubt there were special afflictions to descend upon the self-indulgent; moralists (with some injustice to the sufferers) liked to instance apoplexy, paralysis, and gout. Cynics would add the dangers from the medical profession; the peasant, who distrusted blood-letting and could not afford to pay the surgeon to do it, was at least free from his attentions. Even so, the life expectancy of the rich was much better than that of the poor, and the men of the eighteenth century knew it. In statistical terms, we might guess that the advantage was something like ten years above the average and seventeen years above that of the very poor. Peasants, liv-

---

[12] Workhouses.

ing crowded together in single-roomed cottages, were very vulnerable, and even more so were the poor of the towns, whose debilitating conditions of working were allied to crowded, insanitary accommodation. Disease spread quickly where there was only one bed for a family. A doctor in the countryside complained of the way in which people "occupy the beds of those who are dead of the malady [typhoid] on the same day the corpse is taken out of it," and it was well known that the communal bed was one of the reasons why the great plague of 1720 in Provence so often swept off a whole family. . . . The church-wardens of the poverty-stricken parish of Saint-Sauveur in Lille complained that the death rate of their parishioners in the epidemic of 1772–3 had been much higher than in the wealthy parish of Saint-André. "The higher numbers here," they said, "can only be because the inhabitants are poor, more numerous and crowded into little houses, often occupied by many families, and situated in very narrow streets called alleyways . . . , they breathe the less pure air here, and because of the dirt which is virtually inseparable from poverty, they propagate all the diseases which catch a hold among them." In Lyon, the silk workers lived twelve to fifteen in a garret, forty to fifty families in a house in the tall buildings around sunless courts, stinking of the chickens, pigs, and rabbits that they reared, and of latrines. . . .

When the Royal Council on 29 April 1776 set up its commission to investigate epidemic diseases in the provinces, one of the questions it posed was: "Why do epidemics sometimes seem to spare a particular class of citizens?" Probably, the intention was not to look at the obvious overcrowding of the slums, but at the food and water supplies and at the dietary habits of the different classes. Seventy years earlier, during the misery at the end of the reign of Louis XIV, the economist Boisguilbert, in a burning tirade, had censured the maldistribution of food supplies which cut short so many lives. There are men, he said, who sweat blood in their toil, with no food other than bread and water, in the midst of a land of abundance, who "perish when only half their course is run," and whose children are "stifled in their cradles." . . . Estimates . . . — at Arles in 1750, by the agricultural society of La Rochelle in 1763, by the owner of a carpet factory in Abbeville in 1764 — show that the poorer peasants and urban workers, though far from being reduced to bread and water, lived all their lives on the margins of danger: any loss of working days had to be paid for by starvation later. There was a cycle of illness, debt, and hunger which made death almost certain on the next round of visitation, and it was not unusual for wretches who had struggled fiercely against starvation to give up on hearing that they had caught some disease, knowing that the future had little hope.

Most people in France lived on cereals, because this was what they could afford. A modern attempt to work out a typical budget for a family of the poor majority in an ordinary year, suggests 50 per cent of expenditure on bread, 16 per cent on fats and wine, 13 per cent on clothing, and 5 per cent on heating. So far as the proportion on bread is concerned, eighteenth-century estimates studied more recently confirm the generalization. The ration in hospitals was one and a half livres a day, and this was the amount an employer generally allowed to a servant in Paris. . . . Judged on the scale of calories, in a fair year, the workers of France were fed efficiently, so far as potential energy was concerned, but, as more than 90 per cent of these calories came from cereals (including maize porridge in the south and beer in the north), the dietary deficiencies are obvious. The food consumption of the inmates of the hospital of Caen (bread, and the unusual advantage of plenty of Norman cider), of the conscripts doing guard duty at the citadel of Saint-Malo in the mid-century (unimaginative bread, biscuits, and salt meat, with none of the coastal fish which ought to have diversified their diet), of the peasants of Périgord (chestnuts and maize in fearful stews kept simmering all day), of the peasants of Basse-Auvergne (bread, soup of nut oil, and water tinctured with wine) — all show the same deficiencies: a lack of meat, fish, dairy produce, and fresh vegetables. That meant a deficiency of vitamins, animal fats, calcium, and trace elements, leaving the way open for rickets, scurvy, skin eruptions, loss of teeth, the breaking down of the natural power of resistance to cold, and the stunting of growth, both physical and mental. It was a matter for wonder that men from mountain areas (where the pastures offered milk and meat) were so tall — as in Auvergne, where they towered over the puny inhabitants of the cereal-growing plain. . . . The ill effects of the inevitable deficiencies were increased by ignorance. . . . [T]here was little knowledge of what constituted a balanced diet. Even the rich did not know what was good for them. They ate a large amount of meat. . . . But an analysis of the meals eaten by a magistrate of Toulouse and of the pupils at a boarding-school for young nobles shows, even so, a lack of calcium and some vitamins. The food available to ordinary people was not always wisely used. The regulation stew-pot of the peasants boiled away the vitamins. . . . Fresh bread was unusual, since for economy, huge loaves which lasted for two or three months were baked in communal ovens. The oft-recorded obstinacy of peasants in refusing to eat unusual food like potatoes, even when starving, is paralleled by the refusal of the Parisians to accept the government economy bread of wheat, rye, and barley, invented during the dearth of 1767. And of course, the people were spendthrift; living on crusts and onions all week, they would go to drinking booths on Sunday night, or swig a tot of *eau-de-vie*[13] on their way to work in the mornings. But statistics of vitamin, calcium, and trace-element deficiencies can prove too much. Like the analysis of wages in eighteenth-century France, they go to show that half the population ought not to have been alive at all. Life, for these people, was "an economy of makeshifts," patching up a living by all sorts of incongruous combinations of earnings; no doubt they supplemented their food supplies by tilling odd corners, keeping animals in hutches, gleaning in hedgerow and common, begging, poaching, and pilfering. That was why it was so dangerous to become institutionalized, whether shut up in a *dépôt de mendicité*, a hospital, a madhouse, or on shipboard. Survival became difficult when there was no scope for enterprise.

Whatever mysterious and useless medicines they prescribed, the doctors of eighteenth-century France knew the primary importance of sound nourishment

---

[13] Brandy.

to aid the sick to recovery. Meat soup was the standard prescription for all con-
valescents. . . . "Remedies and advice are useless unless there is a foundation of
solid nourishment," said a physician called in to investigate the outbreak of dysentery in Anjou in 1707, and he asked for "bouillons" to be dispatched daily to all
who had been afflicted. "Bread, wine, and blankets" were the prescriptions of the
doctors of Anjou who dealt with epidemics of dysentery in 1768 and typhus in
1774. In times of dearth, the poor were driven to eat contaminated or unripened
grain, and were poisoned in consequence. . . . Officials in Brittany in 1769 and
1771 reported diseases (one called them of an "epileptic" kind) which were
sweeping the provinces because the crop failures had driven the people to eat
grain that had been damp when stored and had fermented and grown musty. . . .
In the Sologne, there were outbreaks from time to time of ergotism caused by infected grain — the disease was called "St. Anthony's fire" and "dry gangrene": it
led to the loss of fingers, noses, or whole limbs, and eventually to madness. And
the greatest killer of all was contaminated water. Springs and wells would become
infected as they dried up or floods overflowed them from dubious catchment
areas, or were permanently dangerous because of defective masonry in cisterns,
or because animals had access to them. Typical complaints concern effluent from
flax-crushing or animal manure getting into drinking supplies, or froth from the
oxen's mouths still floating on the top of buckets brought in for domestic consumption. In some villages without a well, water was collected in shallow holes
dug here and there and had to be filtered through linen. And any Parisian who
gave a thought to where his water supply came from would confine himself to
drinking wine always — if he could afford it.

Certain seasons of the year brought the shadow of food shortages. There
were the dangerous months . . . from April to July, when the previous year's
grain was being used up, and before the new crop was harvested. There was a
danger period too in winter, especially for townspeople, for freezing weather
might ice up the canals along which the supply barges came, or stop the water-
mills from grinding the flour. And, worst of all, the crop might fail, damaged by
unseasonable cold or rain or hail; rumour would race ahead of truth, encouraging the hoarding which transformed fear into the first instalment of grim reality.

It is generally said that the era of great famines ended in 1709; thereafter came
shortages, serious indeed, but not deadly. . . . "In the seventeenth century people
died of hunger: in the eighteenth they suffered from it." This is true so far as dying
as a direct result of starvation is concerned, though local historians can always find
a catastrophic year to form an exception worthy to qualify as the last of the
crises. . . . A common-sense review of the probabilities of dying might suggest a
logical sequence: famine, hunger weakening the resistance of the population, the
resort to contaminated food causing illness, the onset of some killing disease,
and the starving poor forced into vagabondage acting as carriers for the infection.
In practice, in the eighteenth century this proposed pattern of death's operations
is only occasionally borne out by comparisons of the graphs of corn prices, illness,
and mortality. At Dijon in the 1740s, it seems clear that famine must have been

the essential cause of the increase in the number of deaths, though an epidemic could strike at a particular place with an overwhelming impact only explainable by its own virulence. . . .

It has been argued, with eighteenth-century England as the example, that malnutrition does not weaken resistance to disease, except in the case of afflictions arising directly from deficiencies of diet, and tuberculosis and dysentery. A historian who has never known what it is to be hungry for very long instinctively feels inclined to doubt this assertion. True, studies of the Third World today show how deprived peoples can sometimes maintain themselves in calorific and protein balance on a diet that would mean starvation to the inhabitants of advanced countries. While bodily size and appearance are affected by the food supply, the same does not necessarily apply to resistance to infection. But there is a distinction to be made. While the nutrition taken by individuals seems not to have much effect on their chance of becoming infected with most diseases, it is of the utmost importance in deciding what their ultimate fate will be. "Malnutrition does not particularly favour or impede the acquisition of infection, but it goes a long way to determine the course of the resulting disease." The relationship between dearth and epidemic among the poorer classes of eighteenth-century France is not so much a short-term correspondence, but a general pattern of attrition by the alternations and the accumulated onslaughts of hunger and disease. The point may be taken, however, that pathogenic bacteria and viruses do not need to wait to find a human population weakened by famine before they strike; some apparently hopeless human groups may have built up an immunity, while some apparently flourishing ones may be unprotected. One disease may fade out, leaving the weak as predestinate victims for another; thus the plague vanished from Languedoc after 1655, and malaria took over, its victims forming a new reservoir of infection to pass on to future generations. We may picture death as vigilant but unhurried and patient. Sometimes hunger served its purposes, as in the terrible dearth in the spring of 1740 in Auvergne, where a *curé* reported that the women let their children die so that the adults could live, and the men, to avoid conceiving children, resorted to unnatural practices with animals. Sometimes some overwhelming contagion, like the plague of Marseille, swept away all human defences. It could be, in these disasters, that the swift succumbing of the physically weak was a precondition for a widespread pattern of infection which trapped the rich, who might otherwise have escaped. . . . More often, the continuing cycle of disease, hunger, renewed disease, and despair brought life to an end. There is a story of Louis XV encountering a funeral procession and asking what the man had died from. "Starvation, Sire." It was an indictment of his government, and the answer would have been true, indirectly, of many other deaths from infections and accidents. "C'est de misère que l'on meurt au dix-septième siècle."[14] . . . Though the situation was changing in the eighteenth century, this grim generalization was

---

[14] "It was destitution that brought on death in the seventeenth century."

still broadly applicable. Particular diseases were the indispensable infantry in Death's dark armies, but his generals were Cold and Hunger.

MAKING CONNECTIONS:
DISEASE AND DEATH

1. John McManners paints a dark picture of life in eighteenth-century France. Shorn of the facade of Enlightenment, society seemed mired in wretchedness — deplorable living conditions, malnutrition, and high infant mortality. To what extent is McManners's bleak description of social life — and death — applicable to previous centuries? Were most people in the Middle Ages and in early modern Europe doomed to ill-health, low life expectancy, and the daily fear that accompanies economic insecurity? To what extent did a person's gender or socioeconomic status affect the ability to fend off misery and postpone death?

2. How would the twentieth century fit into the model of social deprivation that McManners details? That is, in what areas of life have conditions improved and where in Western civilization do we find life to be as bleak as in eighteenth-century France?

THE GREAT CAT MASSACRE
Robert Darnton

Princeton University cultural historian Robert Darnton examines a slice of eighteenth-century daily life as seen through the eyes of Parisian workers. Although the history of humor and insult remains to be written, Darnton's essay suggests how rich, varied, and important that subject is. Darnton uncovered a bizarre incident in which a Parisian printer's apprentices and journeymen massacred cats. He wondered why those workers thought the slaughter hilarious and what else lay behind their deed besides a morbid sense of humor. This incident reveals the strained relationship between workers and their employer. Darnton also analyzes the importance of cats as historical symbols of sexuality and explores the economic and social divisions that separated artisanal workers from the bourgeois establishment. Darnton thus links humor to popular culture, labor conflict, and the relationships between different social groups and animals. He brings the reader face-to-face with the thinking and actions of eighteenth-century people, which are quite different from our own.

What sexual meanings and symbolism infused the workers' massacre of the cats? Why did popular culture tolerate the torture of animals? Why do you think the print-shop workers found the torture and killing of the cats to be gleeful? Why did the print-shop owner and his wife feel humiliated by the cat massacre?

The funniest thing that ever happened in the printing shop of Jacques Vincent, according to a worker who witnessed it, was a riotous massacre of cats. The worker, Nicolas Contat, told the story in an account of his apprenticeship in the shop, rue Saint-Séverin, Paris, during the late 1730s. Life as an apprentice was hard, he explained. There were two of them: Jerome, the somewhat fictionalized version of Contat himself, and Léveillé. They slept in a filthy, freezing room, rose before dawn, ran errands all day while dodging insults from the journeymen and abuse from the master, and received nothing but slops to eat. They found the food especially galling. Instead of dining at the master's table, they had to eat scraps

Robert Darnton, *The Great Cat Massacre and Other Episodes in French Cultural History* (New York: Basic Books, 1984), 75–83, 85, 89–92, 94–101.

from his plate in the kitchen. Worse still, the cook secretly sold the leftovers and gave the boys cat food — old, rotten bits of meat that they could not stomach and so passed on to the cats, who refused it.

This last injustice brought Contat to the theme of cats. They occupied a special place in his narrative and in the household of the rue Saint-Séverin. The master's wife adored them, especially *la grise* (the gray), her favorite. A passion for cats seemed to have swept through the printing trade, at least at the level of the masters, or *bourgeois* as the workers called them. One bourgeois kept twenty-five cats. He had their portraits painted and fed them on roast fowl. Meanwhile, the apprentices were trying to cope with a profusion of alley cats who also thrived in the printing district and made the boys' lives miserable. The cats howled all night on the roof over the apprentices' dingy bedroom, making it impossible to get a full night's sleep. As Jerome and Léveillé had to stagger out of bed at four or five in the morning to open the gate for the earliest arrivals among the journeymen, they began the day in a state of exhaustion while the bourgeois slept late. The master did not even work with the men, just as he did not eat with them. He let the foreman run the shop and rarely appeared in it, except to vent his violent temper, usually at the expense of the apprentices.

One night the boys resolved to right this inequitable state of affairs. Léveillé, who had an extraordinary talent for mimickry, crawled along the roof until he reached a section near the master's bedroom, and then he took to howling and meowing so horribly that the bourgeois and his wife did not sleep a wink. After several nights of this treatment, they decided they were being bewitched. But instead of calling the curé[1] — the master was exceptionally devout and the mistress exceptionally attached to her confessor — they commanded the apprentices to get rid of the cats. The mistress gave the order, enjoining the boys above all to avoid frightening her *grise*.

Gleefully Jerome and Léveillé set to work, aided by the journeymen. Armed with broom handles, bars of the press, and other tools of their trade, they went after every cat they could find, beginning with *la grise*. Léveillé smashed its spine with an iron bar and Jerome finished it off. Then they stashed it in a gutter while the journeymen drove the other cats across the rooftops, bludgeoning every one within reach and trapping those who tried to escape in strategically placed sacks. They dumped sackloads of half-dead cats in the courtyard. Then the entire workshop gathered round and staged a mock trial, complete with guards, a confessor, and a public executioner. After pronouncing the animals guilty and administering last rites, they strung them up on an improvised gallows. Roused by gales of laughter, the mistress arrived. She let out a shriek as soon as she saw a bloody cat dangling from a noose. Then she realized it might be *la grise*. Certainly not, the men assured her: they had too much respect for the house to do such a thing. At this point the master appeared. He flew into a rage at the general stoppage of

---

[1] Chief parish priest.

work, though his wife tried to explain that they were threatened by a more serious kind of insubordination. Then master and mistress withdrew, leaving the men delirious with "joy," "disorder," and "laughter."

The laughter did not end there. Léveillé reenacted the entire scene in mime at least twenty times during subsequent days when the printers wanted to knock off for some hilarity. Burlesque reenactments of incidents in the life of the shop, known as *copies* in printers' slang, provided a major form of entertainment for the men. The idea was to humiliate someone in the shop by satirizing his peculiarities. A successful *copie* would make the butt of the joke fume with rage — *prendre la chèvre* (take the goat) in the shop slang — while his mates razzed him with "rough music." They would run their composing sticks across the tops of the type cases, beat their mallets against the chases, pound on cupboards, and bleat like goats. The bleating (*bais* in the slang) stood for the humiliation heaped on the victims, as in English when someone "gets your goat." Contat emphasized that Léveillé produced the funniest *copies* anyone had ever known and elicited the greatest choruses of rough music. The whole episode, cat massacre compounded by *copies,* stood out as the most hilarious experience in Jerome's entire career.

Yet it strikes the modern reader as unfunny, if not downright repulsive. Where is the humor in a group of grown men bleating like goats and banging with their tools while an adolescent reenacts the ritual slaughter of a defenseless animal? Our own inability to get the joke is an indication of the distance that separates us from the workers of preindustrial Europe. The perception of that distance may serve as the starting point of an investigation, for anthropologists have found that the best points of entry in an attempt to penetrate an alien culture can be those where it seems to be most opaque. When you realize that you are not getting something — a joke, a proverb, a ceremony — that is particularly meaningful to the natives, you can see where to grasp a foreign system of meaning in order to unravel it. By getting the joke of the great cat massacre, it may be possible to "get" a basic ingredient of artisanal culture under the Old Regime.[2]

It should be explained at the outset that we cannot observe the killing of the cats at firsthand. We can study it only through Contat's narrative, written about twenty years after the event. There can be no doubt about the authenticity of Contat's quasi-fictional autobiography. . . . Because printers, or at least compositors,[3] had to be reasonably literate in order to do their work, they were among the few artisans who could give their own accounts of life in the working classes two, three, and four centuries ago. With all its misspellings and grammatical flaws, Contat's is perhaps the richest of these accounts. But it cannot be regarded as a mirror-image of what actually happened. It should be read as Contat's version of a happening, as his attempt to tell a story. Like all story telling, it sets the action in a frame of reference; it assumes a certain repertory of associations and re-

---

[2] Europe in the seventeenth and eighteenth centuries, before the French Revolution of 1789.

[3] Typesetters.

sponses on the part of its audience; and it provides meaningful shape to the raw stuff of experience. But since we are attempting to get at its meaning in the first place, we should not be put off by its fabricated character. On the contrary, by treating the narrative as fiction or meaningful fabrication we can use it to develop an ethnological *explication de texte*.[4]

The first explanation that probably would occur to most readers of Contat's story is that the cat massacre served as an oblique attack on the master and his wife. Contat set the event in the context of remarks about the disparity between the lot of workers and the bourgeois — a matter of the basic elements in life: work, food, and sleep. The injustice seemed especially flagrant in the case of the apprentices, who were treated like animals while the animals were promoted over their heads to the position the boys should have occupied, the place at the master's table. Although the apprentices seem most abused, the text makes it clear that the killing of the cats expressed a hatred for the bourgeois that had spread among all the workers: "The masters love cats; consequently [the workers] hate them." After masterminding the massacre, Léveillé became the hero of the shop, because "all the workers are in league against the masters. It is enough to speak badly of them [the masters] to be esteemed by the whole assembly of typographers."

Historians have tended to treat the era of artisanal manufacturing as an idyllic period before the onset of industrialization. Some even portray the workshop as a kind of extended family in which master and journeymen labored at the same tasks, ate at the same table, and sometimes slept under the same roof. Had anything happened to poison the atmosphere of the printing shops in Paris by 1740?

During the second half of the seventeenth century, the large printing houses, backed by the government, eliminated most of the smaller shops, and an oligarchy of masters seized control of the industry. At the same time, the situation of the journeymen deteriorated. Although estimates vary and statistics cannot be trusted, it seems that their number remained stable: approximately 335 in 1666, 339 in 1701, and 340 in 1721. Meanwhile the number of masters declined by more than half, from eighty-three to thirty-six, the limit fixed by an edict of 1686. That meant fewer shops with larger work forces, as one can see from statistics on the density of presses: in 1644 Paris had seventy-five printing shops with a total of 180 presses; in 1701 it had fifty-one shops with 195 presses. This trend made it virtually impossible for journeymen to rise into the ranks of the masters. About the only way for a worker to get ahead in the craft was to marry a master's widow, for masterships had become hereditary privileges, passed on from husband to wife and from father to son.

The journeymen also felt threatened from below because the masters tended increasingly to hire *alloués,* or underqualified printers, who had not undergone the apprenticeship that made a journeyman eligible, in principle, to advance to a

---

[4] A detailed analysis of a literary work.

mastership. The *alloués* were merely a source of cheap labor, excluded from the upper ranks of the trade and fixed, in their inferior status, by an edict of 1723. Their degradation stood out in their name: they were *à louer* (for hire), not *compagnons* (journeymen) of the master. They personified the tendency of labor to become a commodity instead of a partnership. Thus Contat served his apprenticeship and wrote his memoirs when times were hard for journeymen printers, when the men in the shop in the rue Saint-Séverin stood in danger of being cut off from the top of the trade and swamped from the bottom. . . .

Contat . . . began his description of Jerome's apprenticeship by invoking a golden age when printing was first invented and printers lived as free and equal members of a "republic," governed by its own laws and traditions in a spirit of fraternal "union and friendship." He claimed that the republic still survived in the form of the *chapelle* or workers' association in each shop. But the government had broken up general associations; the ranks had been thinned by *alloués;* the journeymen had been excluded from masterships; and the masters had withdrawn into a separate world of *haute cuisine*[5] and *grasses matinées.*[6] The master in the rue Saint-Séverin ate different food, kept different hours, and talked a different language. His wife and daughters dallied with worldly abbés.[7] They kept pets. Clearly, the bourgeois belonged to a different subculture — one which meant above all that he did not work. In introducing his account of the cat massacre, Contat made explicit the contrast between the worlds of worker and master that ran throughout the narrative: "Workers, apprentices, everyone works. Only the masters and mistresses enjoy the sweetness of sleep. That makes Jerome and Léveillé resentful. They resolve not to be the only wretched ones. They want their master and mistress as associates (*associés*)." That is, the boys wanted to restore a mythical past when masters and men worked in friendly association. They also may have had in mind the more recent extinction of the smaller printing shops. So they killed the cats.

But why cats? And why was the killing so funny? Those questions take us beyond the consideration of early modern labor relations and into the obscure subject of popular ceremonies and symbolism.

Folklorists have made historians familiar with the ceremonial cycles that marked off the calendar year for early modern man. The most important of these was the cycle of carnival and Lent,[8] a period of revelry followed by a period of abstinence. During carnival the common people suspended the normal rules of behavior and ceremoniously reversed the social order or turned it upside down in riotous procession. Carnival was a time for cutting up by youth groups, particularly apprentices, who organized themselves in "abbeys" ruled by a mock abbot

---

[5] Gourmet food.

[6] Sleeping in; getting up late.

[7] Abbots. *Abbé* was also a courtesy title given to all ecclesiastics.

[8] In the Christian calendar, forty days of fasting before Easter.

or king and who staged charivaris or burlesque processions with rough music in order to humiliate cuckolds,[9] husbands who had been beaten by their wives, brides who had married below their age group, or someone else who personified the infringement of traditional norms. Carnival was high season for hilarity, sexuality, and youth run riot — a time when young people tested social boundaries by limited outbursts of deviance, before being reassimilated in the world of order, submission, and Lentine seriousness. It came to an end on Shrove Tuesday or Mardi Gras,[10] when a straw mannequin, King Carnival or Caramantran, was given a ritual trial and execution. Cats played an important part in some charivaris. In Burgundy, the crowd incorporated cat torture into its rough music. While mocking a cuckold or some other victim, the youths passed around a cat, tearing its fur to make it howl. *Faire le chat,*[11] they called it. The Germans called charivaris *Katzenmusik,*[12] a term that may have been derived from the howls of tortured cats.

Cats also figured in the cycle of Saint John the Baptist,[13] which took place on June 24, at the time of the summer solstice. Crowds made bonfires, jumped over them, danced around them, and threw into them objects with magical power, hoping to avoid disaster and obtain good fortune during the rest of the year. A favorite object was cats — cats tied up in bags, cats suspended from ropes, or cats burned at the stake. Parisians liked to incinerate cats by the sackful, while the Courimauds (*cour à miaud* or cat chasers) of Saint Chamond preferred to chase a flaming cat through the streets. In parts of Burgundy and Lorraine they danced around a kind of burning May pole with a cat tied to it. In the Metz region they burned a dozen cats at a time in a basket on top of a bonfire. The ceremony took place with great pomp in Metz itself, until it was abolished in 1765. The town dignitaries arrived in procession at the Place du Grand-Saulcy, lit the pyre, and a ring of riflemen from the garrison fired off volleys while the cats disappeared screaming in the flames. Although the practice varied from place to place, the ingredients were everywhere the same: a *feu de joie* (bonfire), cats, and an aura of hilarious witch-hunting.

In addition to these general ceremonies, which involved entire communities, artisans celebrated ceremonies peculiar to their craft. Printers processed and feasted in honor of their patron, Saint John the Evangelist,[14] both on his saint's day, December 27, and on the anniversary of his martyrdom, May 6, the festival of

---

[9] Husbands whose wives are having affairs.

[10] In the Christian calendar, a festival the day before Lent.

[11] Playing games with cats.

[12] Cat music, caterwauling.

[13] In Christian legend, Jesus' cousin.

[14] Supposed author of the fourth Gospel and the Book of Revelation in the New Testament.

Saint Jean Porte Latine.[15] By the eighteenth century, the masters had excluded the journeymen from the confraternity[16] devoted to the saint, but the journeymen continued to hold ceremonies in their chapels. On Saint Martin's[17] day, November 11, they held a mock trial followed by a feast. Contat explained that the chapel was a tiny "republic," which governed itself according to its own code of conduct. When a worker violated the code, the foreman, who was the head of the chapel and not part of the management, entered a fine in a register. . . . On Saint Martin's, the foreman read out the fines and collected them. The workers sometimes appealed their cases before a burlesque tribunal composed of the chapel's "ancients,"[18] but in the end they had to pay up amidst more bleating, banging of tools, and riotous laughter. The fines went for food and drink in the chapel's favorite tavern, where the hell-raising continued until late in the night. . . .

So much for ceremonies. What about cats? It should be said at the outset that there is an indefinable *je ne sais quoi*[19] about cats, a mysterious something that has fascinated mankind since the time of the ancient Egyptians. One can sense a quasi-human intelligence behind a cat's eyes. One can mistake a cat's howl at night for a human scream, torn from some deep, visceral part of man's animal nature. . . .

This ambiguous ontological position, a straddling of conceptual categories, gives certain animals — pigs, dogs, and cassowaries[20] as well as cats — in certain cultures an occult power associated with the taboo. That is why Jews do not eat pigs . . . and why Englishmen can insult one another by saying "son-of-a-bitch" rather than "son-of-a-cow." . . . Certain animals are good for swearing. . . . I would add that others — cats in particular — are good for staging ceremonies. They have ritual value. You cannot make a charivari with a cow. You do it with cats: you decide to *faire le chat,* to make *Katzenmusik.*

The torture of animals, especially cats, was a popular amusement throughout early modern Europe. You have only to look at Hogarth's *Stages of Cruelty*[21] to see its importance, and once you start looking you see people torturing animals everywhere. Cat killings provided a common theme in literature, from *Don Quixote*[22]

---

[15] Feast commemorating the legend that the aged John the Evangelist was thrown into a boiling cauldron outside the Latin Gate at Rome, survived, and went into exile.

[16] Religious association of laymen, often from the same occupation, that provided for the religious well-being of its members.

[17] Bishop of Tours and a patron saint of France (d. 397).

[18] Workers with seniority.

[19] Something that cannot be explained fully.

[20] Large flightless birds related to the ostrich.

[21] English painter (1697–1764) known for satirical pictures of eighteenth-century lowlife. *Stages of Cruelty* (1751) tells the story of a sadist's progress from torturing animals to murder.

[22] The Spaniard Miguel de Cervantes's (1547–1616) satirical novel (1605).

in early seventeenth-century Spain to *Germinal*[23] in late nineteenth-century France. Far from being a sadistic fantasy on the part of a few half-crazed authors, the literary versions of cruelty to animals expressed a deep current of popular culture. . . . All sorts of ethnographic reports confirm that view. On the *dimanche des brandons*[24] in Semur, for example, children used to attach cats to poles and roast them over bonfires. In the *jeu du chat*[25] at the Fete-Dieu[26] in Aix-en-Provence, they threw cats high in the air and smashed them on the ground. They used expressions like "patient as a cat whose claws are being pulled out" or "patient as a cat whose paws are being grilled." The English were just as cruel. During the Reformation in London, a Protestant crowd shaved a cat to look like a priest, dressed it in mock vestments, and hanged it on the gallows at Cheapside. It would be possible to string out many other examples, but the point should be clear: there was nothing unusual about the ritual killing of cats. On the contrary, when Jerome and his fellow workers tried and hanged all the cats they could find in the rue Saint-Séverin, they drew on a common element in their culture. But what significance did that culture attribute to cats?

To get a grip on that question, one must rummage through collections of folktales, superstitions, proverbs, and popular medicine. The material is rich, varied, and vast but extremely hard to handle. Although much of it goes back to the Middle Ages, little can be dated. It was gathered for the most part by folklorists in the late nineteenth and early twentieth centuries, when sturdy strains of folklore still resisted the influence of the printed word. But the collections do not make it possible to claim that this or that practice existed in the printing houses of mid-eighteenth-century Paris. One can only assert that printers lived and breathed in an atmosphere of traditional customs and beliefs which permeated everything. . . .

First and foremost, cats suggested witchcraft. To cross one at night in virtually any corner of France was to risk running into the devil or one of his agents or a witch abroad on an evil errand. . . . Witches transformed themselves into cats in order to cast spells on their victims. Sometimes, especially on Mardi Gras, they gathered for hideous sabbaths at night. They howled, fought, and copulated horribly under the direction of the devil himself in the form of a huge tomcat. To protect yourself from sorcery by cats there was one, classic remedy: maim it. Cut its tail, clip its ears, smash one of its legs, tear or burn its fur, and you would break its malevolent power. A maimed cat could not attend a sabbath or wander abroad to cast spells. Peasants frequently cudgeled cats who crossed their paths at night and discovered the next day that bruises had appeared on women believed to be witches — or so it was said in the lore of their village. Villagers also told stories of farmers who found strange cats in barns and broke their limbs to save the cat-

---

[23] The French writer Émile Zola's (1840–1902) novel (1885) about a coal strike.

[24] Sunday of the firebrands.

[25] Cat play.

[26] The feast of Corpus Christi, a Christian holiday commemorating Holy Communion.

tle. Invariably a broken limb would appear on a suspicious woman the following morning.

Cats possessed occult power independently of their association with witchcraft and deviltry. They could prevent the bread from rising if they entered bakeries in Anjou. They could spoil the catch if they crossed the path of fishermen in Brittany. If buried alive in Béarn, they could clear a field of weeds. They figured as staple ingredients in all kinds of folk medicine aside from witches' brews. . . .

There was a specific field for the exercise of cat power: the household and particularly the person of the master or mistress of the house. Folktales like "Puss 'n Boots"[27] emphasized the identification of master and cat, and so did superstitions such as the practice of tying a black ribbon around the neck of a cat whose mistress had died. To kill a cat was to bring misfortune upon its owner or its house. If a cat left a house or stopped jumping on the sickbed of its master or mistress, the person was likely to die. But a cat lying on the bed of a dying man might be the devil, waiting to carry his soul off to hell. . . . Cats could harm a house. They often smothered babies. They understood gossip and would repeat it out of doors. But their power could be contained or turned to your advantage if you followed the right procedures, such as greasing their paws with butter or maiming them when they first arrived. To protect a new house, Frenchmen enclosed live cats within its walls — a very old rite, judging from cat skeletons that have been exhumed from the walls of medieval buildings.

Finally, the power of cats was concentrated on the most intimate aspect of domestic life: sex. *Le chat, la chatte, le minet* mean the same thing in French slang as "pussy" does in English, and they have served as obscenities for centuries. French folklore attaches special importance to the cat as a sexual metaphor or metonym. As far back as the fifteenth century, the petting of cats was recommended for success in courting women. Proverbial wisdom identified women with cats: "He who takes good care of cats will have a pretty wife." If a man loved cats, he would love women; and vice versa: "As he loves his cat, he loves his wife," went another proverb. If he did not care for his wife, you could say of him, "He has other cats to whip." A woman who wanted to get a man should avoid treading on a cat's tail. She might postpone marriage for a year — or for seven years in Quimper and for as many years as the cat meowed in parts of the Loire Valley. Cats connoted fertility and female sexuality everywhere. Girls were commonly said to be "in love like a cat"; and if they became pregnant, they had "let the cat go to the cheese." Eating cats could bring on pregnancy in itself. Girls who consumed them in stews gave birth to kittens in several folktales. Cats could even make diseased apple trees bear fruit, if buried in the correct manner in upper Brittany.

It was an easy jump from the sexuality of women to the cuckolding of men. Caterwauling could come from a satanic orgy, but it might just as well be toms howling defiance at each other when their mates were in heat. They did not call

[27] A children's story about a cat that dresses in his master's clothes.

as cats, however. They issued challenges in their masters' names, along with sexual taunts about their mistresses: "Reno! Francois!" "Où allez-vous? — Voir la femme à vous. — Voir la femme à moi! Rouah!" (Where are you going? — To see your wife. — To see my wife! Ha!) Then the toms would fly at each other like the cats of Kilkenny,[28] and their sabbath would end in a massacre. The dialogue differed according to the imaginations of the listeners and the onomatopoetic[29] power of their dialect, but it usually emphasized predatory sexuality. "At night all cats are gray," went the proverb, and the gloss in an eighteenth-century proverb collection made the sexual hint explicit: "That is to say that all women are beautiful enough at night." Enough for what? Seduction, rape, and murder echoed in the air when the cats howled at night in early modern France. Cat calls summoned up *Katzenmusik*, for charivaris often took the form of howling under a cuckold's window on the eve of Mardi Gras, the favorite time for cat sabbaths.

Witchcraft, orgy, cuckoldry, charivari, and massacre, the men of the Old Regime could hear a great deal in the wail of a cat. What the men of the rue Saint-Séverin actually heard is impossible to say. One can only assert that cats bore enormous symbolic weight in the folklore of France and that the lore was rich, ancient, and widespread enough to have penetrated the printing shop. In order to determine whether the printers actually drew on the ceremonial and symbolic themes available to them, it is necessary to take another look at Contat's text.

The text made the theme of sorcery explicit from the beginning. Jerome and Léveillé could not sleep because "some bedeviled cats make a sabbath all night long." After Léveillé added his cat calls to the general caterwauling, "the whole neighborhood is alarmed. It is decided that the cats must be agents of someone casting a spell." The master and mistress considered summoning the curé to exorcise the place. In deciding instead to commission the cat hunt, they fell back on the classic remedy for witchcraft: maiming. The bourgeois — a superstitious, priest-ridden fool — took the whole business seriously. To the apprentices it was a joke. . . . Not only did the apprentices exploit their master's superstition in order to run riot at his expense, but they also turned their rioting against their mistress. By bludgeoning her familiar, *la grise,* they in effect accused her of being the witch. The double joke would not be lost on anyone who could read the traditional language of gesture.

The theme of charivari provided an additional dimension to the fun. Although it never says so explicitly, the text indicates that the mistress was having an affair with her priest, a "lascivious youth," who had memorized obscene passages from the classics of pornography . . . and quoted them to her, while her husband droned on about his favorite subjects, money and religion. During a lavish dinner with the family, the priest defended the thesis "that it is a feat of wit to cuckold one's husband and that cuckolding is not a vice." Later, he and the wife

---

[28] A nursery rhyme about cats who fought so fiercely that one could not tell where one cat ended and the other began.

[29] Naming an action or thing by the sound associated with it.

spent the night together in a country house. They fit perfectly into the typical triangle of printing shops: a doddering old master, a middle-aged mistress, and her youthful lover. The intrigue cast the master in the role of a stock comic figure: the cuckold. So the revelry of the workers took the form of a charivari. The apprentices managed it, operating within the liminal area where novitiates traditionally mocked their superiors, and the journeymen responded to their antics in the traditional way, with rough music. A riotous, festival atmosphere runs through the whole episode, which Contat described as a *fête:*[30] "Léveillé and his comrade Jerome preside over the *fête,*" he wrote, as if they were kings of a carnival and the cat bashing corresponded to the torturing of cats on Mardi Gras or the *fête* of Saint John the Baptist.

As in many Mardi Gras, the carnival ended in a mock trial and execution. The burlesque legalism came naturally to the printers because they staged their own mock trials every year at the *fête* of Saint Martin, when the chapel squared accounts with its boss and succeeded spectacularly in getting his goat. The chapel could not condemn him explicitly without moving into open insubordination and risking dismissal. . . . So the workers tried the bourgeois in absentia, using a symbol that would let their meaning show through without being explicit enough to justify retaliation. They tried and hanged the cats. It would be going too far to hang *la grise* under the master's nose after being ordered to spare it; but they made the favorite pet of the house their first victim, and in doing so they knew they were attacking the house itself, in accordance with the traditions of cat lore. When the mistress accused them of killing *la grise,* they replied with mock deference that "nobody would be capable of such an outrage and that they have too much respect for that house." By executing the cats with such elaborate ceremony, they condemned the house and declared the bourgeois guilty — guilty of overworking and underfeeding his apprentices, guilty of living in luxury while his journeymen did all the work, guilty of withdrawing from the shop and swamping it with *alloués* instead of laboring and eating with the men, as masters were said to have done a generation or two earlier, or in the primitive "republic" that existed at the beginning of the printing industry. The guilt extended from the boss to the house to the whole system. Perhaps in trying, confessing, and hanging a collection of half-dead cats, the workers meant to ridicule the entire legal and social order. . . .

Cats as symbols conjured up sex as well as violence, a combination perfectly suited for an attack on the mistress. The narrative identified her with *la grise,* her *chatte favorite.*[31] In killing it, the boys struck at her: "It was a matter of consequence, a murder, which had to be hidden." The mistress reacted as if she had been assaulted: "They ravished from her a cat without an equal, a cat that she loved to madness." The text described her as lascivious and "impassioned for

<hr>

[30] Festival.

[31] Favorite pussy.

cats" as if she were a she-cat in heat during a wild cat's sabbath of howling, killing, and rape. An explicit reference to rape would violate the proprieties that were generally observed in eighteenth-century writing. Indeed, the symbolism would work only if it remained veiled — ambivalent enough to dupe the master and sharp enough to hit the mistress in the quick. But Contat used strong language. As soon as the mistress saw the cat execution she let out a scream. Then the scream was smothered in the realization that she had lost her *grise*. The workers assured her with feigned sincerity of their respect and the master arrived. "'Ah! the scoundrels,' he says. 'Instead of working they are killing cats.' Madame to Monsieur: 'These wicked men can't kill the masters; they have killed my cat.' . . . It seems to her that all the blood of the workers would not be sufficient to redeem the insult."

. . . By assaulting her pet, the workers ravished the mistress symbolically. At the same time, they delivered the supreme insult to their master. His wife was his most precious possession, just as her *chatte* was hers. In killing the cat, the men violated the most intimate treasure of the bourgeois household and escaped unharmed. That was the beauty of it. The symbolism disguised the insult well enough for them to get away with it. While the bourgeois fumed over the loss of work, his wife, less obtuse, virtually told him that the workers had attacked her sexually and would like to murder him. Then both left the scene in humiliation and defeat. . . .

. . . The question remains, however, what precisely was so funny about the cat massacre? There is no better way to ruin a joke than to analyze it or to overload it with social comment. But this joke cries out for commentary — not because one can use it to prove that artisans hated their bosses (a truism that may apply to all periods of labor history, although it has not been appreciated adequately by eighteenth-century historians), but because it can help one to see how workers made their experience meaningful by playing with themes of their culture. . . .

. . . [I]t seems clear that the workers found the massacre funny because it gave them a way to turn the tables on the bourgeois. By goading him with cat calls, they provoked him to authorize the massacre of cats, then they used the massacre to put him symbolically on trial for unjust management of the shop. They also used it as a witch hunt, which provided an excuse to kill his wife's familiar and to insinuate that she herself was the witch. Finally, they transformed it into a charivari, which served as a means to insult her sexually while mocking him as a cuckold. The bourgeois made an excellent butt of the joke. Not only did he become the victim of a procedure he himself had set in motion, he did not understand how badly he had been had. The men had subjected his wife to symbolic aggression of the most intimate kind, but he did not get it. He was too thick-headed, a classic cuckold. The printers ridiculed him in splendid Boccaccian[32] style and got off scot-free.

---

[32] Ribald and boisterous, from Giovanni Boccaccio's (1313–1375) collection of stories, the *Decameron*.

The joke worked so well because the workers played so skillfully with a repertory of ceremonies and symbols. Cats suited their purposes perfectly. By smashing the spine of *la grise* they called the master's wife a witch and a slut, while at the same time making the master into a cuckold and a fool. It was metonymic[33] insult, delivered by actions, not words, and it struck home because cats occupied a soft spot in the bourgeois way of life. Keeping pets was as alien to the workers as torturing animals was to the bourgeois. . . .

The workers also punned with ceremonies. They made a roundup of cats into a witch hunt, a festival, a charivari, a mock trial, and a dirty joke. Then they redid the whole thing in pantomime. Whenever they got tired of working, they transformed the shop into a theater and produced *copies* — their kind of copy, not the authors'. Shop theater and ritual punning suited the traditions of their craft. Although printers made books, they did not use written words to convey their meaning. They used gestures, drawing on the culture of their craft to inscribe statements in the air.

Insubstantial as it may seem today, this joking was a risky business in the eighteenth century. The risk was part of the joke, as in many forms of humor, which toy with violence and tease repressed passions. The workers pushed their symbolic horseplay to the brink of reification, the point at which the killing of cats would turn into an open rebellion. They played on ambiguities, using symbols that would hide their full meaning while letting enough of it show through to make a fool of the bourgeois without giving him a pretext to fire them. They tweaked his nose and prevented him from protesting against it. To pull off such a feat required great dexterity. It showed that workers could manipulate symbols in their idiom as effectively as poets did in print.

The boundaries within which this jesting had to be contained suggest the limits to working-class militancy under the Old Regime. The printers identified with their craft rather than their class. Although they organized in chapels, staged strikes, and sometimes forced up wages, they remained subordinate to the bourgeois. The master hired and fired men as casually as he ordered paper, and he turned them out into the road when he sniffed insubordination. So . . . they generally kept their protests on a symbolic level. A *copie*, like a carnival, helped to let off steam; but it also produced laughter, a vital ingredient in early artisanal culture and one that has been lost in labor history. By seeing the way a joke worked in the horseplay of a printing shop two centuries ago, we may be able to recapture that missing element — laughter, sheer laughter, the thigh-slapping, rib-cracking Rabelaisian[34] kind, rather than the Voltairian[35] smirk with which we are familiar.

---

[33] A figure of speech that uses the name of one thing for something else with which it is associated.

[34] Coarse satire and humor, as in the works of the French novelist François Rabelais (ca. 1494–ca. 1553).

[35] Characterized by sardonic humor, as in the works of Voltaire (1694–1778), the French philosopher.

WOMEN AND WORK
Olwen Hufton

The idea of equal pay for equal work did not exist in early modern Europe. Using autobiographies, letters, and quantifiable sources (such as demographic information), Olwen Hufton, a Harvard University historian, shows that European women had more difficulty finding employment than did men, that their work was often harder, and that their pay was always less. Women helped propel the economy, but their diligence did not relieve them of constant worry, long hours, and low wages. Moreover, the slightest economic downturn brought them less work and more suffering, for they inevitably lost their jobs before men did.

Although she explains the economic situations of aristocrats and women of middling families, Olwen Hufton concentrates on working-class women. On the one hand, she offers a depressing account of the wretched reality of their existence. For example, single women toiled for years to accumulate dowries and work skills so that they could attract husbands. On the other hand, resourcefulness pervaded women's lives as they attempted to cope with the labor market and their own circumstances, whether they were single, married, or widowed.

What employment opportunities were available to women in towns and in the countryside? How did social and economic developments, such as the population increase from the sixteenth through the eighteenth centuries, affect women's work? Do you think women fared better in farm work, in domestic service, or in industrial labor? Women made up most of the labor force in certain sections of the economy, as servants or in the silk and lace industries, for example. In other areas, women had fewer work options. What factors determined the employment opportunities for women?

Note how the work life of married women could vary significantly from that of single women and how marriage influenced women differently according to a husband's social status. Hufton states that economic considerations were the major factor in the choice of a marriage partner. In fact, marriage was a significant goal for single working women, whereas widowhood and spinsterhood often doomed women to poverty and economic insecurity. Hufton thus depicts

Olwen Hufton, "Women, Work, and Family," in *A History of Women in the West*, ed. Natalie Zemon Davis and Arlette Farge, vol. 3 of *Renaissance and Enlightenment Paradoxes* (Cambridge: Belknap Press of Harvard University Press, 1993), 15–34, 38–45.

bleak economic lives for most women in early modern Europe, despite their active engagement in the economy. Accordingly, the adage that "a woman's work is never done" rings true, for a woman, in addition to long hours of work outside the home, had other responsibilities, including helping a husband in his business and running a household.

W hen the essayist Richard Steele sought in 1710 to define woman, he did so in a terse but, by the standards of the day, fully acceptable manner: "A woman is a daughter, a sister, a wife and a mother, a mere appendage of the human race. . . ."

A good woman, one such as to merit the praise of men, might find herself commemorated as did the Elizabethan noblewoman Marie Dudley on her funeral monument in St. Margaret's Westminster:

> Here lyeth entombed Marie Dudley, daughter of William Howard of Effingham, in his time Lord High Admiral of England, Lord Chamberlain and Lord Privy Seal. She was grandchild to Thomas Duke of Norfolk . . . and Sister to Charles Howard, Earl of Nottingham, High Admiral of England by whose prosperous direction through the goodness of God in defending his lady Queen Elizabeth,[1] the whole fleet of Spain was defeated and discomforted.[2] She was first married to Edward Sutton, Lord Dudley and after to Richard Monpesson Esquire who in memory of his love erected this monument to her.

From the moment a girl was born in lawful wedlock, irrespective of her social origins she was defined by her relationship to a man. She was in turn the legal responsibility of her father and her husband, both of whom, it was recommended, she should honor and obey. Father or husband, it was assumed, served as a buffer between her and the harsh realities of the violent outside world. She was expected to be the economic dependent of the man who controlled her life. The duty of a father, according to the model, was to provide for his child until her marriage, when he, or someone on his behalf, negotiated a settlement for his daughter with a groom. A husband expected to be compensated at the outset of marriage for taking a particular woman to wife. Thereafter he was responsible for her well-being, but her contribution at the moment of marriage was critical in the establishment of the new household.

This model had rigorous application in upper- and middle-class society throughout the early modern period. Marriage settlements for children were interpreted, in the language of the day, as "the weightiest business" a family could undertake. Ideally, the money and resources that a female child took from her family purchased her future well-being and enhanced the standing of her kin through the new alliance. A woman's dependency was a closely negotiated item.

---

[1] Elizabeth I (1558–1603) established Anglicanism and led England to victory over Spain.

[2] Disheartened or sorrowful.

For most women, the model could not be so completely applied. Women of the working classes were expected to work to support themselves both when single and when married. . . .

Notwithstanding the obligation to labor in their own support, society did not envisage that women could or should live in total independence. Indeed, the independent woman was seen as unnatural and abhorrent. It was assumed that father and husband would provide her with a home and hence contribute in some degree to her maintenance. This assumption was reflected in customary female wages: a woman could be paid less for her labors because a man put a roof above her head. If a woman could not find work to keep her in her own home before marriage, a substitute protective environment must be sought for her. She must enter her employer's home. He would assume the role of protective male figure and be responsible for the costs of feeding and sheltering her and would stand *in loco parentis*[3] until she left to work elsewhere, to return home, or to marry. The wages he paid her would reflect the fact that she was fed and sheltered. Ideally, she would spend as little of these wages as possible, and her employer would save them for her and place them in her hands when she left his home.

The target of the single woman's working life was thus explicit: while sparing her own family the cost of feeding her, she was in the business of accumulating a dowry and work skills to attract a husband. When no more than a child, she was taught by her family and the society in which she lived that life was a struggle against grinding poverty and that for long-term survival she needed a husband to provide shelter and aid. Such realizations were what impelled about 80 percent of country girls to leave home at about age twelve — two years before their brothers did so — to begin equipping themselves for the time when they might hope to marry. From the moment of her departure, the average European girl began a ten- or twelve-year phase of her working life, upon the success of which her future depended. The prospect may have been daunting and frightening, and the pitfalls were known to be many. Childhood was brief for the daughters of the poor.

The female children of smallholders, agricultural laborers, or odd-job men commanded few skills beyond those transmitted by their mothers — perhaps no more than the ability to sew, spin, perform simple farm tasks, or care for younger children. Demand for work as a residential farm servant was very high, far outstripping the supply. Residential work for women in the agricultural sector was limited to large establishments, especially dairy farms, where milking and cheese and butter making were the work of women. There was great competition for farm jobs because they offered servant girls the chance to remain near their families and to avoid an abrupt change in their way of life. . . .

Throughout Europe, family contacts accounted for most placements in farm jobs. In some regions of France, such as Champagne, the spread of cottage industry led to an increase in the number of farm servants because it made possi-

---

[3] In the place of parents.

ble ancillary industrial labor that contributed to a girl's keep during the dead season. The availability of farm work thus varied from region to region. But overall, by the end of the eighteenth century this kind of work became increasingly scarce, in part as a result of demographic growth, in part as a result of the emergence of larger commercial farms and greater regional specialization. In other areas the overproliferation of smallholdings as a result of population growth reduced the keeping of livestock and the ability to maintain a female servant. When the cow was missing from the landscape, there were few female farm workers.

The girl who could not find farm work near home looked townward, although she did not necessarily have to go very far; the nearest town of five or six thousand might afford her work as a maidservant, ranging from the lowest resident drudge, who carried heavy loads of laundry to and from the local washplace or loads of vegetables from the market and emptied privies, to cook and cleaner. The demand for urban domestic service appears to have increased considerably throughout the early modern period, reflecting both growing affluence in some sectors of urban society and the cheapness of the labor on offer. Again, the best jobs came through family and village contacts.

The potential for local jobs was usually exhausted before a young girl ventured farther afield. When she did so, it was usually along a well-established route, and at her destination she would find neighbors' daughters and kinsfolk in the vicinity. In short, young girls were rarely pioneers. Sometimes they followed an established migratory flow set up by male seasonal migrants, like the girls of the Massif Central[4] who went down to Montpellier or Béziers to work as servants and whose brothers came down every year to the region to pick grapes; or those of South Wales who stayed in the London area as maidservants after accompanying their male relatives to work in the market gardens of Kent and who made contacts while ferrying fruit and vegetables to Covent Garden.[5]

Female servants constituted the largest occupational group in urban society, accounting for about 12 percent of the total population of any European town or city throughout the seventeenth and eighteenth centuries. . . .[I]n 1806 . . . London had as many as 200,000 servants of both sexes but . . . there were twice as many women as men. . . .

Types and conditions of service must have varied widely. Much depended upon the status of the employer. Servants were an indicator of social standing, and since female labor was cheap and abundant, it was one of the first luxuries even a modest family permitted itself. But although certain ducal families such as the House of Orleans[6] or the Dukes of Marlborough[7] counted their household servants in hundreds, it was unusual for even the most extensive aristocratic house-

---

[4] Large plateau in south central France.

[5] London's main fruit and vegetable market.

[6] Junior branch of the French royal family.

[7] Descendants of John Churchill (1650–1722), brilliant British general during the War of the Spanish Succession (1702–1714).

hold to employ more than thirty servants of both sexes. The gentry and affluent merchants in the great cities might have six or seven. Indeed, one definition of a poor noble throughout the period was someone who had only three servants. In seventeenth-century Amsterdam, however, which had more than its share of wealthy merchants, one or two servants was the norm; and this was perhaps the commonest urban model. The fewer the number of servants, the likelier it was that all the servants would be women.

In the hierarchy of employees of both sexes maintained by an aristocratic household — cooks, coachmen, footmen, butlers, ladies' maids, chambermaids, laundrymaids, grooms, scullery maids, and so on — women held many of the jobs at the bottom. Modest households employed a maid of all work — for which there is an equally cumbersome phrase in most European languages. Tradesmen might employ a girl both to work in the shop and to run errands delivering and picking up work; tavernkeepers employed girls as barmaids, waitresses, and washers up; busy housewives helping in family businesses such as cookshops and bakeries employed girls to do anything from turning a hand in commercial food production to taking the family's washing to the washplace, carrying or pumping water, or lighting and maintaining ovens and fires.

The best jobs were gained through contacts and by ascending the servant hierarchy as one acquired experience and skill. However, a great deal depended upon good fortune and the kind of qualifications one had at the outset. Employers were concerned that a girl have an honest background and would not open the door to a pack of thieving relatives or disappear into the night with the family silver. . . .

The girl who entered a multiple-servant household at the bottom could expect to come by a variety of skills in kitchen service and in laundry work, tending and repairing linen. After a few years of washing dishes and scrubbing floors, lighting fires, and fetching and carrying coal, water, and slops, if she maintained a neat air and had a degree of good looks and a trim figure, she might advance to parlormaid. With a measure of good luck, which might include resisting the advances of employer or, more probably, fellow servant, she might find her way upstairs to chambermaid or lady's maid.

However, at each stage of the upward journey, she faced competition or came up against the limited demands of the household of which she was a member. If she was ambitious she must move "for her preferment." Hence the intense mobility within the world of domestic service by the end of the eighteenth century and the fading image, much bemoaned and exaggerated by the affluent, of the long-term retainer. Mobility was made possible by contact and recommendation and, in Britain, the newspaper. However, competition at the upper end of the scale was intense; one advertisement for a lady's maid would bring scores of applicants.

There were many girls, however, who could not compete in the career structure of service, and the immiseration of certain regions as a result of demographic growth in the sixteenth and eighteenth centuries brought many from the countryside into the towns. These girls were chronically poor, undernourished, rickety, pockmarked, dirty, and lice-ridden. They lacked the training that fitted them for employment in even a modest household. Girls from entire regions — and, in the case of Ireland, from an entire nation — who arrived in British cities seeking work were automatically excluded by the very poverty of their backgrounds from anything approaching a respectable situation as a servant.

Service, then, embraced a vast range of conditions. For a small minority it had a career structure, and in her mid-twenties a maidservant who had managed to become a chambermaid or lady's maid would have a respectable capital sum, the amount depending upon her ability to accumulate without cutting into her wages to help her family or to cope with periods of illness or unemployment. At the other end of the scale were the vast majority of women whose work was wretched, volatile, dependent upon the honesty of the employer and upon staying constantly in work so that they did not eat into their reserves. A maidservant who became pregnant was simply dismissed. In the middle were those who by their mid-twenties might have fifty pounds to their names, a modest sum but a personal triumph.

In some industrial areas, which relied on a reservoir of cheap female labor, the domiciled servant was in fact the resident textile worker. Cheap female labor was critical in the development of European textile industries, such as the silk industry at Lyons. Silk was a costly delicate fabric intended for the wealthy and prepared from start to finish in urban workshops under the supervision of a master. Female labor was used to empty the silk cocoons, twist the thread, wind the shuttles, and draw them through the loom to achieve patterned effects of great complexity. The work of men was to set up and pull the loom. Every workshop included a minimum of three to four girls, a male apprentice, the master, and his wife. Over the industry as a whole, female workers outnumbered males by five to one. . . . Girls of twelve and fourteen started work in the lowest job, that of cocoon unwinder, sitting over basins of scalding water into which they plunged the cocoons to melt the sericine, the sticky substance binding the cocoon together. Their clothes were continually damp, their fingers lost sensitivity, and tuberculosis was rampant. Still, if she could survive without long periods of unemployment — during the frequent slumps, girls were unceremoniously shown the door — and advance to draw girl, then after about fourteen years a female silk worker had not only a sum of money but also a wide range of industrial skills. She was the ideal wife for the ambitious apprentice because she could provide him with the lump sum to pay for his mastership and contribute to the running of a new workshop.

The lace industry, too, could be organized on a resident basis to help young girls accumulate a dowry. From the purchase of raw thread through the actual fabrication to the sale of the finished product to the wholesaler, the lace industry tended to be entirely in the hands of women — an unusual state of affairs in European handicrafts. Lace was the costliest textile commodity in Europe. . . . The value lay entirely in the handiwork, and many years were required to learn the skill. Yet the remuneration was at the lowest level of female wages: in France a day's labor might provide a couple of pounds of bread. In lace areas tens of thousands of women were involved in production. In some of these areas, notably in Flanders, where the best lace was made, and in the Pays du Velay in France, philanthropic effort achieved the seemingly impossible and converted lace production into a small dowry-raising enterprise. In Flanders convents taught lacemaking to children for nothing and, when they were proficient, put aside a little of their wages to help them accumulate a small lump sum. When they married they could become outworkers or come to the convent workshops, where they did not have to pay lighting and heating costs. In the Velay there were no such convents, but groups of pious women called Béates,[8] backed by some philanthropic money, ran lace dormitories in the city of Le Puy free of charge and negotiated the sale of work with the merchants to see that the lacemakers got the best price. After a small deduction for food, they held onto the proceeds of the sale to help the girls accumulate their precious dowries. After marriage these young women could work at home, and the Béates, by invitation of the villages, ran communal houses where the village women could congregate and share lighting costs and a common soup pot.

Silk and lace production were thus tailored to bring girls into the towns, teach them a craft, and help them with their dowries. . . .

Except in a few industrial cities, a girl born of working-class parents in a town or city was unlikely to become either a domestic servant or a textile worker. Instead, as censuses make clear, she pursued one of a limited number of options in the garment trades (as seamstress, mantua maker,[9] milliner,[10] glove stitcher, embroiderer) or service trades (as washerwoman, street seller, stall operator). Or, perhaps most commonly, she contributed to a family business, working at home.

In most European towns girls' work options were limited by the restrictions of the guilds, which regulated the urban world of skilled work with varying comprehensiveness. The daughters and wives of tradesmen involved themselves in aspects of artisanal production, but most guilds resisted women's attempts to enter their specialties. Resistance to women in guild-regulated production often came less from the masters than from their workmen, who were afraid that women would work for less and hence undercut journeymen's wages. When work was plentiful and labor scarce, the guilds were relatively tolerant and turned a blind eye to women's activities in their sphere; but when times were hard, attitudes changed. . . .

By the late eighteenth century the guilds were fast disappearing in Britain and France. Even so, women existed most easily in newer trades such as millinery and mantua making, which had no medieval antecedents. During the eighteenth century work became more plentiful, particularly in the garment trades, but as the

---

[8] Blessed ones.

[9] Dressmaker.

[10] Maker of women's hats.

number of women seeking such employment increased, the work became identified as "women's work," and wages fell accordingly. *Campbell's Directory of London* in 1762 placed all the garment trades practiced by women in the category of pauper work, exposing the incumbent to dire necessity and providing the recruiting ground for prostitution.

At a somewhat lower level than that of the solid artisan family the mother was more likely than the father to shape the choice of a daughter's job. The washerwoman's daughter became a washerwoman, the seamstress' daughter a seamstress, and the innkeeper's daughter stayed at home and served the beer and victuals. The tendency of urban parents to absorb their female children into a work pattern perhaps explains the relatively small number of recorded formal apprenticeships for women. Indeed, those who sought such apprenticeships were likely to be either orphans, on whose behalf orphanages sought guaranteed work and protection, or girls whose parents were in work that could not absorb them and who lacked relatives such as a seamstress aunt who could provide structured help. These two categories sought formal apprenticeship not because the training would guarantee a girl a better job but because they needed assurance of continuous training leading to regular employment. . . .

Most women in fact married as the model insisted they should. Between 1550 and 1800 the proportion of women who died above the age of 50 in the celibate state varied from 5 to 25 percent. The highest levels occurred in the mid-1600s but fell dramatically over the next century; permanent spinsters constituted something under 10 percent of the population by the end of the eighteenth century. In the seventeenth century more French women married than English women, but thereafter the number of French spinsters began to rise, and by 1789 about 14 percent of those dying over the age of 50 had never married. In the seventeenth century, English women married on average at the age of 26, but by the end of the eighteenth century at just over 23. In France, women's average age at marriage at the beginning of the seventeenth century, 22, rose gradually to 26.5 on the eve of the Revolution. . . .

Whom one married depended upon one's class, in some instances upon birth position — the oldest daughter of an upper-class family usually had priority — and upon the size of one's dowry. Most women did not marry beneath themselves. An aristocratic heiress had the pick of the market. The daughters of clergymen, doctors, and lawyers married men in the same profession as their fathers and thus cemented business connections. Farm servants married farm laborers and hoped to set up with their accumulated resources on a small farm. Sometimes girls who had gone to work in town as servants returned home with their little sums and set up as smallholders' wives. But those who had emigrated to town from an area of large farms were unlikely to return to their native villages. . . .

Of the young people who did not return home to marry, a minority of servant girls married other servants, and of these a minority may have remained in service, although demand for a resident couple was limited. The logical course for a servant girl upon marriage was to use her portion and her husband's contribution to set up in business of some kind, running a drink shop or a café bar, or for the pair to go into the catering business. Often the maidservant's main social contacts with the opposite sex had been with apprentices delivering goods to the back door. Tavern servants married construction workers. Other servants married tradesmen and opened lodginghouses. In industrial areas, spinners married carders or weavers. The large unskilled and largely urban female work force of flower sellers, peddlers of haberdashery, load carriers, and the like who had no dowry on marriage, or those who had failed to amass a dowry because of illness or unemployment, were not precluded from finding a marriage partner; but, lacking capital or a substitute skill, they could expect to marry only a man in a similar position.

The evidence everywhere points to economic considerations as the main determinant in the choice of partner, although this fact need not have precluded romantic considerations as well. Marriage was interpreted as an institution designed to furnish succor and support to both parties, and a clear perception of economic imperatives was essential to survival.

Marriage was seen not merely as woman's natural destiny but also as a metamorphic agent, transforming her into a different social and economic being as part of a new household, the primary unit upon which all society was based. The husband's role was that of provider of shelter and sustenance. He paid taxes and represented the household in the community. The role of the wife was that of helpmate and mother. . . .

Generally, although the labors of a wife were deemed essential for the well-being of a family and an idle wife was seen as a curse upon her husband, her work was rarely estimated in monetary terms. Even in areas where countrywomen were able to work in domestic industry, in agriculture, or even on the roads for pay, they were seen not as generators of money but as providers of largely unremunerated support services within the family.

Married countrywomen with children and encumbered with the work of a holding did not take on more paid work than they regarded as strictly necessary to the subsistence of their families. They defined need by reference to an adequate diet, warmth, and the ability to ward off debt. In short, they sought outside work only when the family was in need. Otherwise the arduous, long, and physically unpleasant work related to family and holding was paramount. Women carried water to steep mountain terraces in areas where the terrain was difficult and water scarce. In many cases the terraces themselves had been constructed from earth carried there in buckets by women. They cut and dried turf, collected kelp, firewood, weeds by the roadside to feed rabbits. They milked cows and goats, grew vegetables, collected chestnuts and herbs. The commonest source of heating for British and some Irish and Dutch farmers was animal turds, which were gathered by hand by women and received their final drying out stacked near the family fire. Haymaking and harvesting involved heavy spells of work, and weeding had to be done in all weather. Small wonder that women liked spinning: it gave them the chance to sit down for a few hours while productively occupied.

By the end of the eighteenth century the work patterns of the countrywoman had changed in many areas. One reason was population growth, which reduced the number of available subsistence units, depressed wages in the agricultural sector, pushed up prices, and inspired commercially minded landlords to curtail commons and gleaning rights. Growing numbers of married women tried to become casual daylaborers, hoeing and weeding vegetables on large properties in the appropriate season. In Britain, however, the introduction of heavier farm tools curtailed their labors as harvesters. Everywhere a potential labor force of married women seems to have been anxious to perform industrial work, leaving the running of the smallholding to husbands and perhaps abandoning the keeping of livestock or time-consuming agricultural work. . . .

Generally, when farms in arid or mountainous regions could no longer feed a family, women assumed responsibility for the farming for months or even years while their husbands worked as seasonal laborers or even emigrated for a time. Sometimes the woman ran the farm only between planting and harvest, and when the man returned from his seasonal job as, say, a chimney sweep, he performed the more difficult chores. Occasionally migration occurred in winter: peasants from Auvergne, Savoy, Tuscany, the Pyrenees, or Ireland went to the city — Paris, Bordeaux, Saragossa, Valladolid, Livorno, or London according to the traditions of their region — and looked for work on the docks or hauled coal or wood. Others went off in the summertime, like those peasants of the Massif Central who traveled south to Mediterranean regions to help with the grape harvest. Sometimes they stayed away for several years. In Corrèze and Aveyron a considerable number of married men as well as bachelors walked to Spain to offer their services in the ports. Their wives took over all farm work. Irish peasants also left for long periods, but of course potato farming was work that could easily be done by women. The men's remittances would pay the rental on holdings and the return fare across the Irish Sea, but the work of the farm was done by women. Everywhere, women's activity was deemed needful to hold a farmstead together and feed the children.

The role of married townswomen in the family economy does not lend itself to easy generalization; much depended on the town and the potential it offered. There, too, however, most married women filled roles complementary to their husbands'. In a family business, such as a printing shop or a drapery, a woman might function as an organizer, a fellow worker (mixing ink, cleaning letters, measuring cloth or ribbon), or, more often, a bookkeeper. Many mercantile houses in cities such as Amsterdam and London drew on the bookkeeping services of the merchant's wife. . . . Lower down the social scale, women appear to have virtually monopolized the actual sale of objects made by their husbands. Or they operated in their own right as petty traders in the market or shop or merely on street corners. In many towns, married women were prevented through borough custom, guild regulations, or municipal laws from trading in their own right. . . . Nevertheless, women did the actual work of selling even though the shop or stall was leased in their husband's name. Hence the fishwives of Amsterdam, Marseilles, Paris, Glasgow, Edinburgh, and London dealt with customers in the market while the fishmongers handled the wholesale trade. While butchers were responsible for slaughtering cattle and preparing joints of meat, their wives and daughters were frequently involved in taking the money from customers and in selling tripe, sausage meat, and black puddings (blood sausages). Covent Garden and Les Halles[11] were packed with women selling all kinds of food, from eggs and cheese to fruit. They also played a role in the sale of grain and flour. . . .

One form of selling in which married women were preponderant and which was quite independent of the activities of their husbands was the secondhand clothes trade. The importance of this traffic in early modern Europe should not be underestimated. A substantial proportion of the population did not purchase new clothing. Children wore hand-me-downs or cut-down adult clothing. In times of hardship, the poor parted with their clothes (outerwear first) and acquired others from secondhand dealers when times improved. Paris in the 1760s had 268 registered secondhand clothes dealers, all of whom were married women or widows. The business needed little capital input and involved transactions primarily among women. Mothers exchanged children's clothing with appropriate compensation to a middlewoman; maidservants bartered employers' castoffs; the clothes of a deceased person were exchanged for money or other garments by the inheriting relatives. These businesswomen seldom encountered opposition from male guilds. . . .

Many married women in town and country were multioccupational, with no single aspect of their work occupying them full time. They might operate as saleswomen only on market days, or as washerwomen by arrangement with specific families only a few times a month. Other responsibilities always waited: caring for children, shopping, carrying water, and perhaps organizing older children into some kind of remunerative activity, such as selling pies or commodities made by the parents. Frequently entire families performed one set of tasks during the day and another in the evening — like the Spitalfields silkworkers who made fireworks when they went home or the silk seamstresses of the Leicester area who supplied fine condoms for Mrs. Phelp's[12] mail-order service. In the economy of expedients that characterized the way most families lived in early modern Europe, the woman was likely to be the pivotal figure. While her husband performed the single job of agricultural laborer or casual worker she might be engaged in very different tasks at different seasons. Unlike her husband's tasks, which were clearly demarcated and began and ended (unless at harvest) at a specific time and usually permitted him some leisure to spend in the tavern or village square, "a woman's work was never done." If her man fell ill, was suddenly unemployed, failed to return from his seasonal migrations, or died, her work must expand to cover the deficit created in the family economy. In his lifetime she may have been

---

[11] The central market in Paris.

[12] Eighteenth-century pornographer and brothel-keeper.

an ancillary worker, but she was nonetheless crucial to the survival of the family unit. . . .

If her child survived infancy, a mother assumed the role of educator, although what that meant varied with social class, time, and place. A mother taught her child to negotiate the world in which they both lived. Notwithstanding the battery of servants, nannies, nurserymaids, and governesses available in aristocratic households, memoirs of aristocratic mothers frequently reveal concern for the advancement of their daughters and for equipping them for the marriage market. A daughter's success reflected upon the mother: in addition to some acquaintance with vernacular literature she needed to know how to present herself, dress, manage a household of servants, dance, embroider, play a musical instrument, and speak French. Lady Mary Wortley Montagu[13] considered the upbringing of three daughters a full-time occupation. A middle-class girl accompanied her mother on charitable errands, learned how to keep household accounts, and knew about pickling, preserving, and other methods of food preparation appropriate to the season even if she herself was not the cook. A daughter reflected the image of the household. . . .

Along with cooking, a mother was expected to teach her daughter needle skills. Fine needlework marked a great lady. A woman, however high her rank, was expected to produce baby bonnets and layettes and embroidered waistcoats to offer at Christmas to her husband or brother. Lower down the social scale, the emphasis was on hemming, seaming, mending, and darning. Shirts, petticoats, children's garments, and smocks were all made by women at home. Girls were also taught all tasks designated as female around the home. They assisted in the care of younger children. They helped to prepare food for their brothers and stitched their clothing. . . .

At the lowest levels of society the expedients for maintaining a frail livelihood involved close cooperation among family members, but the partnership between mother and daughter in the work force was perhaps the most striking. Girls learned survival skills from their mothers. Mothers and young daughters together sold milk, crockery, and vegetables in the markets; they also begged together. The economy of the poor was invariably a delicate balancing act, and those who lost their footing and fell into the ranks of the destitute were numerous. Where to turn in hard times was valuable knowledge. . . .

. . . Every mother knew that her daughter needed material assets on marriage and that the more she had, the higher her standing would be in the community and in the eyes of her husband's family. To assist in the important process of dowry accumulation, mothers put aside some of their work profits when they could, perhaps from the sale of eggs, a pot of honey, or a fattened pig that had been

---

[13] English traveler and writer (1689–1762).

the runt of the litter, as a cumulative contribution. Or mother and daughter might rear rabbits on hand-picked weeds for the same purpose. Many mothers directed their young daughters' needlework toward making quilts and household articles either from scraps or from bits of raw wool picked from hedgerows and converted over the years into cloth. This collaboration in the accumulation of a dowry helped to cement the mother-daughter relationship and perhaps also helped it to survive physical distance. . . .

The loss of a husband in a society that defined a woman in terms of her relationship to a man was obviously an event that carried immense social, economic, and psychological consequences for a woman. The higher the social standing of the family, perhaps the less the upheaval. An aristocratic woman was, at least theoretically, in command of her jointure, the income guaranteed to her when she brought her dowry into the marriage to sustain her in her lifetime in the event of her husband's death. Furthermore, the aristocratic widow was usually delegated rights in the wardship of her children. Hence she passed into a directorial capacity and became arbiter of her own destiny, unrestrained by any tutelage. . . .

Most widows, however, were left in middle age with adolescent families and insufficient means to indulge their whims. Society expected the widow to bury her husband with decorum or honor; doing so might entail expenses that she could ill afford. . . .

No one ever assumed that a widow could do as well as her husband had done. Hence journeymen and servants to whom debts were due now demanded settlement, adding further to the widow's problems. Many had to default, and the most conspicuous sufferers were servant girls, who failed to realize their accumulated wages. Once debts had been paid, the widow had to decide at what scale she could continue to operate. . . . Taken overall, the need to make good the husband's labor by paying for a substitute probably stripped over 90 percent of artisans' widows of the ability to keep their husband's business fully functioning.

Best tailored to cope with the eventuality of a husband's death was the family economy that included a small business, especially a tavern, a café bar, a victualler's shop, cake, pie, or muffin production, or a lodginghouse. Most of these activities lay outside guild regulation. . . . [A] large number of taverns, cabarets, and refreshment stands were run by widows, with large numbers of widows' children selling hot pies and sweetmeats from trays in the street.

The widow thrown back on the work of her hands with children to support probably sank as low as it was possible to sink in the European economic hierarchy. She was heavily represented on poor lists and records of charities, and if charity was to be had — and there was nothing automatic about this — she was the most conspicuous candidate whose claims were universally acknowledged. . . .

Permanent spinsters were not much better off than widows unless they had family members to provide support. The low level of female wages precluded an independent existence. Many single women clustered in towns, sharing garrets and sparse lodgings and serving as support networks to one another. Their exiguous wages left them with little or nothing to buttress them during sickness, un-employment, or old age. Some might find shelter in a brother's dwelling or serve as mother substitute to a relative's orphaned family, but the prospects were bleak, even for those with more than a rudimentary education. . . .

MAKING CONNECTIONS: WORK

1. Nearly all people historically have worked; very few have lived lives of leisure. Many historians have argued that women have, as a rule, worked longer and harder than men and with less remuneration. Indeed, hard work, long hours, and difficult lives have marked women throughout history. If most men also did not eschew a life of work, they might find some solace in knowing that they had a better chance than women of having a modicum of power and leisure. According to Hufton, in what ways did the working lives of single women differ from those of married women? How did motherhood affect women and work? Why did women work?

2. Compare the types of work women did in the eighteenth century to those done by men. How did working women interact with men?

3. Distinguish the working women of the eighteenth century from those of today. What are the differences? What do they have in common?

THE SANS-CULOTTES
Albert Soboul

One of the great watersheds in history, the French Revolution signaled the passing of the Old Régime. Monarchy, hierarchy, and privilege — all pillars of the social order — came under attack, not only in France but through much of Europe. French armies crisscrossed the Continent, attempting to spread revolutionary ideals of "liberty, equality, and fraternity," and in the process they inadvertently awakened the most potent of nineteenth-century ideologies, nationalism. Historians have long debated the French Revolution, questioning, among other things, whether or not it was favorable to liberty, or to capitalism, and which social groups benefited the most from the Revolution.

Albert Soboul once held the chair of the history of the French Revolution at the Sorbonne. The selection here is from his doctoral dissertation on the *sans-culottes* movement in Paris from 1792 to 1794. As a Marxist historian, he argued that the Revolution opposed what was a feudal society, virtually destroying the old nobility, and so prepared the triumph of a capitalist economy. For Soboul, class conflict was an integral part of the Revolution. Soboul gained fame with his magisterial study of the Parisian *sans-culottes*, a fascinating, if ephemeral, social group that influenced political events in Paris and supported vociferously the Terror of 1793–1794.

The *sans-culottes* were workers, artisans, and shopkeepers distinguishable, according to Soboul, by their dress (pants and a red bonnet), behavior, and attitudes (political, economic, and social). The term *sans-culotte* means "without knee-breeches" and refers to urban workers who wore trousers rather than the aristocracy's knee-breeches. Why did the *sans-culottes* detest aristocrats, abhor wealthy merchants, and loathe the rich? What did the *sans-culottes* want from the Revolution? What political ideas did they espouse? Why did they favor executions as an instrument of state policy?

We should not romanticize the *sans-culottes* as virtuous workers out to rid society of an oppressive nobility, exploitative businessmen, and other enemies of the "people," for the *sans-culottes* often resorted to pillaging, frequently hailed violence, and cheered the guillotine as it lopped off thousands of heads. Ironi-

Albert Soboul, *The Sans-Culottes,* trans. Remy I. Hall (New York: Doubleday, 1972), 2–10, 13–20, 158–162.

cally, many of the *sans-culottes* themselves fell victim to the guillotine when their influence declined and the Right sought retribution.

Soboul's study is valuable not only as an example of Marxist historiography but as a thorough examination of the *sans-culottes* as well. He depicts their violent behavior and also analyzes what motivated them to indulge in it.

If we are to attempt to discern the social characteristics of the sans-culottes, it is important first to draw attention to the manner in which they defined themselves. . . .

Ostensibly, the sans-culottes were recognizable by their costume, which set them apart from the upper strata of the former Third Estate. Robespierre[1] used to differentiate between *golden breeches* and *sans-culottes*. The sans-culottes themselves made the same distinction. Noting the intrigues that undermined the Sceaux Committee of Surveillance, the observer Rousseville, in his report on 25 Messidor, year II,[2] stresses the antagonism between the "silk-stockings" and the sans-culottes. Conventions of dress also pitted sans-culottes against the *muscadins* [royalist sympathizers]. Arrested on 4 Prairial, year III, for having said that "the blasted muscadins'll soon have a spade up there . . ." and questioned as to what he meant by these words, Barack, a clockmaker's assistant of the *Lombards* section,[3] replied that "as far as he was concerned, muscadins were those who were well dressed." . . .

Costume was accompanied by particular social behavior. Again, on this subject, the sans-culottes declared their stand through opposition. In the year II, the manners of the ancien régime were no longer acceptable. The sans-culottes refused to adopt a subordinate position in social relations. Jean-Baptiste Gentil, timber merchant, arrested on 5 Pluviôse, year II, for not having fulfilled his duties toward the Republic, was reprimanded for his public demeanor: "One had to approach him with hat in hand, the word *sir* was still used in his household, he retains an air of superiority." . . . The principal charge against Gannal, iron merchant from the *Réunion* section, arrested on 7 Frimaire, was his "haughty manner toward his workers." . . .

The sans-culottes often estimated a person's worth by external appearance, deducing character from costume and political convictions from character; everything that jarred their sense of equality was suspect of being "aristocratic." It was difficult, therefore, for any person of the old regime to find favor in their eyes, even

---

[1] Maximilien Robespierre (1758–1794), leader of the most extreme political faction during the Terror of 1793–1794.

[2] The French Revolution introduced a new calendar on 5 October 1793 and dated the year I from 21 September 1792, the beginning of the Convention. There were new names for the months (such as Messidor, Prairial, etc.), each with thirty days. Five days were added at the end of the year (six in leap years).

[3] In June 1790, Paris was divided into forty-eight sections, which held regular meetings.

when there was no specific charge against him. "For such men are incapable of bringing themselves to the heights of our revolution; their hearts are always full of pride and we shall never forget their former grandeur and their domination over us."

. . . The sans-culottes tolerated neither pride nor disdain; those were aristocratic sentiments contrary to the spirit of fraternity that existed between equal citizens and implied a hostile political stand toward democracy as practiced by the sans-culottes in their general assemblies and in their popular societies. These character traits appeared frequently in reports justifying the arrest of suspects.

On September 17, 1793 (Fructidor, year I), the committee of the *Révolution-naire* section decided to arrest Etienne Gide, clock merchant, who had supported the Brissotins;[4] he was also accused of being haughty and proud and of often speaking *ironically*. On October 12, one bourgeois, a solicitor, was arrested by the revolutionary committee of *Réunion*: he had risen to support aristocrats in the general assemblies; more particularly, he demonstrated a "haughty manner toward the sans-culottes." . . .

Even more serious, according to the sans-culottes, than a haughty or disdainful manner toward themselves or straightforward indifference were statements referring to them as being of a lower social order. In its report of 8 Frimaire on Louis-Claude Cezeron, arrested for being a "suspect," the committee of the *Poissonnière* section made a particular case of a statement made during a meeting of the general assembly on the preceding May 31 (12 Prairial): "that the poor depended on the rich and that the sans-culottes were never any more than the lowest order possible." Bergeron, a skin merchant from *Lombards,* said that "although he understood that the sans-culottes were fulfilling their duty as citizens . . . it would be better for them to go about their work rather than meddle in politics." He was arrested on suspicion on 18 Pluviôse.

The sans-culottes refused to tolerate others taking advantage of their social or economic status to impose upon them. . . . Anthéaume, a former abbé, . . . was arrested on 16 Brumaire: he was reprimanded for "pride and intolerable pedagogy contrary to equality and the simplicity of a good republican."

The sans-culottes had an egalitarian conception of social relations. Their behavior also concealed realities which were more specific. To what extent were they seized upon and expressed?

The most clearly stated social friction in popular awareness was that which pitted aristocrat against sans-culotte: it was against the aristocrats that the sans-culottes addressed themselves from July 14[5] to August 10,[6] and against whom they continued to battle. The address of the sans-culottes society of Beaucaire before

---

[4] Followers of Jacques-Pierre Brissot de Warville, who in 1791 advocated that France go to war against European monarchies.

[5] 14 July 1789, fall of the Bastille in Paris.

[6] 10 August 1792, overthrow of the French monarchy.

the Convention[7] of September 8, 1793, is significant: "We are sans-culottes . . . poor and virtuous, we have formed a society of artisans and peasants . . . we know who our friends are: those who freed us from the clergy and from the nobility, from feudalism, from tithes, from royalty and from all the plagues that follow in its wake. . . ."

The nature of the class struggle was even more clearly stated in the address of the Dijon Popular Society on 27 Nivôse, year II: "We must be one people, and not two nations, opposed . . . all recognized aristocratic individuals without exception should be condemned to death by decree." According to mechanic Guyot . . . , "all the nobles, without exception, deserve to be guillotined."

At this point, the aristocracy was the main enemy of the sans-culottes. Ultimately, they managed to include in this term all their adversaries, although these might not necessarily belong to the quondam nobility, but to the upper echelons of the former Third Estate. In this way the role of the sans-culottes is imprinted upon the Revolution, and further demonstrates the autonomy of their action.

On July 25, 1792, the *Louvre* section announced the fall of the King, at the same time denouncing the hereditary aristocracy, "the ministerial, financial and bourgeois aristocrats, and particularly the hierarchy of recalcitrant priests." By the year II, the meaning of the word "aristocrat" was extended to embrace all the social classes against which the sans-culottes were struggling. . . . Hence the specifically popular definition, coined by an anonymous petitioner in the year II, which has both political and social connotations: the aristocrat was one who regretted the passing of the ancien régime and disapproved of the Revolution, did nothing to further its cause, did not swear his allegiance to it, did not enlist in the National Guard,[8] one who did not purchase expropriated land, although he might have had the means to do so; one who left land uncultivated without selling it at its true value, or leasing it, or giving a half share in the produce. The aristocrat was also he who did not give work to laborers or journeymen, although he might be in a position to do so, and "at a wage commensurate with food prices"; did not subscribe to contributions for the volunteers; and had done nothing to improve the lot of his poor and patriotic countrymen. The real patriot was he who took a contrary attitude on every possible occasion. The term aristocrat in the end, therefore, designated all the opponents of the sans-culottes, bourgeois as well as noble, those who formed "the class of citizens from whom one should take the billion we have to levy throughout the Republic." The most extreme sans-culottes did not use the term "aristocrat" for the old nobility, but for the bourgeoisie. On May 21, 1793, a popular orator from the *Mail* section declared that "aristocrats are all the people with money, all the fat merchants, all the monopolists, law students, bankers, pettifoggers and anyone who has something."

---

[7] Name of the governmental assembly that first met on 21 September 1792 and established a republic.

[8] Citizen militia organized in Paris after the fall of the Bastille.

The economic crisis had contributed to bringing social clashes to a head: to the fundamental hostility between sans-culotte and aristocrat was added that of the sans-culottes and the upper sectors of the Third Estate. . . . A note sent to the Public Safety Committee in Pluviôse, year II, pointed out the existence of two parties in the *Brutus* section: that of the people, the sans-culottes, and the other consisting of "bankers, money changers, rich people." An address delivered before the Convention on 27 Ventôse mentioned the brave sans-culottes, who were opposed not only to the clergy, the nobility, royal coalitions, but also to attorneys, lawyers, notaries and also all "those fat farmers, those egotists, and those fat, rich merchants: they're at war against us, and not against our tyrants."

Was this the "haves" against the "have-nots"? Not precisely. As far as the sans-culottes were concerned, artisans and shopkeepers belonged to the propertied classes. More particularly, the friction was between those who believed in the notion of limited and controlled ownership and the partisans of total ownership rights such as were proclaimed in 1789. Or the opposition between those who believed in controls and taxation, and those in favor of economic freedom; the opposition between consumer and producer.

Contemporary documents, over and beyond these basic reactions or distinctive statements, also allow us to explore the nuances of the social antagonisms expressed by the sans-culottes with some accuracy. They denounced "respectable people," meaning by this those who possessed, if not riches, then at least leisure and culture, the better-educated citizens, the better-dressed, those conscious if not proud of their leisure and their education. They denounced the propertied classes, that is to say, those who had unearned incomes. Finally, they denounced the rich in general, not only the propertied classes or the "haves," but also the "big men" as opposed to the "little men," which they were. The sans-culottes were not against property already owned by artisans and shopkeepers, and which journeymen aspired to possess, provided that it was limited.

The expression "respectable people" was first heard after June 2 (13 Prairial), when sans-culottes and moderates opposed one another on political and social platforms. The term was first applied to the bourgeoisie opposed to equality, but ended by having as wide a connotation as the term "aristocrat," and embracing all the enemies of the sans-culottes. . . . A certain Lamarre, lemonade vendor from the *Bon-Conseil* section, was arrested on 5 Prairial, year III; he consistently raised his voice against "respectable people," demanding before the assembly that they all be guillotined. As for washerwoman Rombaut, she stated that every single one of those so-called "respectable people" should be guillotined.

If the sans-culottes ironically called their adversaries "respectable people," the latter did not fail to treat them as rabble; thus, with two expressions, the lines for social clashes were drawn. On September 25, 1793 (4 Vendémiaire, year II), carpenter Bertout was arrested on the orders of the committee of the *République* section: he had declared a desire for "another government being established to oppose the rabble, because respectable people were lost." . . .

This opposition was further expressed in the animosity between the sans-culottes and those who possessed unearned incomes, a situation that came to a head during the autumn of 1793, when the economic crisis and the difficulties of daily living resulted in increased class antagonism. The fact of being independently wealthy gave cause for suspicion. On September 18, 1793 . . . , the revolutionary committee of *Mucius-Scaevola* ordered the arrest of Duval, first secretary of the Paris Police, on two counts: for contempt toward the assemblies of that section, and for enjoying an income of 2,000 livres. . . . On 2 Germinal, the revolutionary committee of the *Mont Blanc* section issued a warrant for the arrest of Jean-François Rivoire, formerly a colonist in Santo Domingo: he had not signed the Constitution, he had never contributed to the funds, nor had he served in the Guard. Further, he had an income of 16,000 livres. In one extreme case a certain Pierre Becquerel from *Guillaume-Tell* was arrested on 19 Ventôse during a raid by the police in the Gardens of Equality, simply for having said he had a private income. On the preceding 2 Frimaire, the *Lepeletier* popular society adopted a petition to exclude from all government posts not only former nobles, the sons of secretaries to the king, brokers and dealers, but also all persons known to possess incomes of more than 3,000 livres. Posts vacated by this measure would be reserved for sans-culottes. These latter were not therefore opposed to all forms of income from investments, but only to the very wealthy. . . .

The sans-culottes' hostility toward those with large private incomes was merely one particularly stressed aspect of their instinctive opposition to the rich. Extreme sans-culottes like Babeuf[9] in the year IV were not far from considering the Revolution as a declared war "between the rich and the poor." The nature of this clash to a large extent characterized Terrorist sentiments. . . . When sectional power was in the hands of the sans-culottes, full of animosity or hatred toward the rich, they did not fail to take discriminatory action against them. Wealth was often the motive for suspicion. Although wealth was rarely the only motive invoked, it often lent support to vague accusations. . . .

This deep-rooted tendency among the sans-culottes to speak against the rich was encouraged in the year II by the ruling politicians of the time. "Herein lies the revolution of the poor," wrote Michel Lepeletier in the National Education Project which Robespierre read before the Convention on July 12 and 29 of 1793 (Messidor/Thermidor, year I). . . . Saint-Just[10] said: "The unfortunate are the powerful on earth; they have the right to speak as masters to governments who neglect them." . . . The crisis of the Revolution from the spring to the autumn of 1793 made the popular alliance necessary: the sans-culottes formed the cadre that was to permit the most advanced faction of the bourgeoisie to quell the aristocracy and its allies. "The hidden danger," wrote Robespierre in his diary during the June 2 insurrection, "lies in the bourgeois; in order to conquer the bourgeois, it will be necessary to rally the people." . . . Those who did not belong to the government

---

[9] François Babeuf (1760–1797), firebrand who formed the "Conspiracy of Equals" and attempted to overthrow the government in 1797.

[10] Louis-Antoine Saint-Just (1767–1794), a revolutionary leader during the Terror.

openly exploited the antagonism between the rich and the sans-culottes for political ends. . . .

The differences between the sans-culottes and the rich were rounded out by
the former's hostility toward business enterprise, and this hostility constituted one
of the fundamental currents of popular opinion during the year II.

Being urban consumers, the Parisian sans-culottes were naturally against
those who controlled staple food supplies. Retailers, they blamed the wholesalers.
Artisans or journeymen, hardly workers in the actual meaning of the word, they
remained essentially small independent producers, hostile toward those who had
interests in commercial capital. The economic crisis and political struggles intensified this inherent antagonism among the sans-culottes. Scarcity and high prices
spiraled, and every merchant was soon suspect of being a monopolist or a shark.
The struggle against the Girondins[11] and subsequently, after May 31, against the
moderates, was often, at least on the sectional level, turned into a struggle against
the merchant bourgeoisie. The sans-culottes were insistent upon taxation and
controls, and the conflict deepened; to the extent that they defended freedom of
enterprise, the merchants became suspect. Henceforth, the sans-culottes included
with the noble aristocracy and the religious hierarchy the mercantile aristocracy
as well. . . .

In 1793 and in the year II, popular hostility against the merchants was
marked, in its moments of paroxysm, by violence and pillage. It was also marked
by a constant desire for repression. . . . In March of 1793 (Ventôse/Germinal, year
I), during the recruitment of troops for the Vendée campaign, collections for volunteers were often an occasion for the sans-culottes to confirm their hostility toward the merchants. In *Lombards,* Jean-Baptiste Larue, journeyman mason and
member of the revolutionary committee, declared that the volunteers were "idiots
if they left without each having a hundred pistoles[12] in their pockets, that we
should cut off the heads of all these buggers, those merchants, and that after this
operation, the sums of money required would soon be found."

Once popular power was on firm ground, the title of merchant alone was
often reason enough for suspicion on the part of revolutionary committees. They
were encouraged by the Commune,[13] whose arrests of the nineteenth of the first
month ranged among their suspects "those who felt sorry for needy farmers and
merchants, against whom the law must take measures." Certain committees had
not expected this encouragement. After September 14, the committee of *Lombards,*
where hostility toward the merchants was particularly strong, arrested a certain
Dussautoy; he was reprimanded simply for being a wholesale grocer. . . . In *Bon-
Conseil,* the committee justified the arrest on 25 Brumaire of Jean-Louis Lagrave,

---

[11] Name given to a group of moderate republican deputies. They were purged from the Convention in 1793.

[12] Gold coins.

[13] Government of the city of Paris, 1789–1795, divided into forty-eight sections and dominated
by radical factions.

wholesale grocer, merely because of his social behavior: "He spends his time among business people, snobs like himself, not consorting with any patriot . . . always flaunting his rank among the wholesalers, censuring and even molesting citizens, like most wholesalers." . . .

The hostility of the sans-culottes toward business was not restricted to measures against individuals; this was a war against an entire social class that, although it did not seek to eliminate that class from politics, at least sought to curb its powers, to put a halt to its prejudicial activities. . . .

The reaction set in finally after the year III, and the merchants made the most of their revenge against former Terrorists for the maltreatment to which they had been subjected. During Germinal and Prairial, a simple remark was sufficient motive for arrest. The food shortage, worse because the "maximum"[14] had been abolished, once again increased hostility toward commerce among the sans-culottes. The dossiers of the anti-Terrorist repression offer ample evidence, allowing us to determine the precise nature of public opinion on this subject; this varied, circumstances permitting, from a simple expression of hostility to a suppressed desire for the elimination of a social class.

For having said, in year II, "Neither the merchants nor the rich are worth sparing," Davelin, a feather dealer from *Amis-de-la-Patrie,* was disarmed on 5 Prairial, year III. Jacques Barbant, from *Arsenal,* was arrested: he had made certain vague derogatory remarks about merchants. . . .

From hostility toward commerce, the more aware or the more violent among the sans-culottes went on to justify pillage. . . .

During the upheavals of February 25 and 26, 1793 (Ventôse, year I), cobbler Servière, revolutionary commissar of the *Muséum* section in the year II declared before the general assembly, in what was formerly the Germain church, "that he thoroughly approved of pillage and would be very much against having to oppose it." . . . In *Bonne-Nouvelle,* water carrier Bergeron was arrested on 6 Pluviôse, in the year III, when "as a result of his provocations he incited the pillaging of the wood merchants." In some ways . . . , pillage corresponded to the fundamental egalitarianism of the sans-culottes: individual action was legitimated by the inequality of living conditions.

Beyond the offensive remarks or the exhortation to pillage, Terrorist exaltation and the desire for punitive measures show the deep-rooted hostility of the sans-culottes toward the commercial bourgeoisie. Many militants considered the threat of the guillotine in times of shortages an excellent remedy. To oblige farmers to sell their grain according to the official price, they insisted upon the creation of a revolutionary army. When this army was created, the sans-culottes constantly demanded that it be accompanied by a mobile guillotine, in order further to insure its efficaciousness. This outlook can be traced throughout all the Terrorists'

---

[14] Term applied to two laws in 1793 that set maximum levels for wages and prices. The ceiling on wages, but not that on prices, was stringently enforced. Thus the *sans-culottes* were not satisfied.

abusive remarks made in the year II against the merchants. Widow Barbau, from *Indivisibilité,* a veritable harridan according to her denunciators, had the habit of declaring "that until the snobbish merchants, the aristocrats, the rich, etc., are guillotined or dispatched en masse, nothing will work out properly." Widow Barbau quite naturally placed the merchants before the aristocrats. In *Unité,* a certain Roux asked for the erecting of guillotines "on every street corner in Paris, on the doorsteps of every merchant, so that, he said, we can have cheap merchandise." . . . In *Invalides,* the clockmaker Fagère declared that "when the aristocrats are finished, we'll take up with the merchant class again. . . ."

In the year III, shortages and misery still exacerbated sans-culottes' hatred of the merchants. Terrorist remarks abound in the dossiers of the repression. On 19 Ventôse, Jacques Rohait, a job printer from the *Panthéon-Français* section exasperated by the high cost of meat, said that "all those wretched merchants deserve to swing." . . .

During those Prairial days, frenzied offensive remarks were not unusual. Nicolas Barrucand, dyer, former revolutionary commissar of *Arsenal,* declared that on the feast day of Corpus Christi "the streets should be carpeted with the heads of merchants." . . .

The still vivid memories of the year II suggested to many sans-culottes the need for a return to organized terror in order to put an end to the merchants, as they had done to the aristocrats. Ferrier, a hatter from *Gardes-Françaises,* remembering the uprisings in Lyons, Marseilles and Bordeaux in 1793, and the repression which followed, declared that "the large communes composed entirely of merchants and the wealthy must be destroyed, their inhabitants humbled and put down." . . .

These texts reveal that the sans-culottes identified themselves by opposition to the aristocracy, riches, and to commerce — antagonisms that account for the imprecise nature of the social distinctions within the former Third Estate and the difficulty of defining the sans-culottes as a social class. The sans-culottes can be clearly defined only when compared to the aristocracy; when compared to the bourgeoisie, the distinction becomes less clear. Composed of many socially disparate elements, the sans-culottes were undermined by internal dissent, which explains both their inability to establish a coherent program and, in the last analysis, their political defeat. . . .

The sans-culottes considered violence to be the ultimate recourse against those who refused to answer the call of unity. This stand was one of the characteristics of their political behavior. Popular violence had allowed the bourgeoisie to carry out its first attacks against the ancien régime; indeed, the struggle against the aristocracy would not have been possible without it. In 1793 and in the year II, the sans-culottes used that violence not solely against the aristocrats, but also against the moderates who were opposed to the establishment of an egalitarian republic.

Doubtless we should at times seek the biological roots of this recourse to violence, of this exaltation. Temperament offers some explanation. The reports of Prairial, year III, on the former Terrorists often mention their irascible, passionate nature and their tendency to fits of rage; "Their outbursts were usually the result of being in a position to make malicious remarks without thinking of the consequences." Their reactions were the stronger because the sans-culottes were often frustrated, poor, uneducated, inflamed by awareness of their misery.

In the year III the reactionaries indiscriminately labeled all Terrorists drinkers of blood. Although one must be careful not to generalize and take denunciations and police reports literally, one must nevertheless concede that, for certain individuals, violence did mean the spilling of blood. . . . Bunou, from the *Champs-Elysées* section, who was arrested on 5 Prairial, demanded in the year II that a guillotine be erected in the section, "and that he would act as executioner if there was none to be found." Lesur, from the *Luxembourg* section, was arrested on 6 Prairial for having made a similar suggestion: "that the guillotine was not working fast enough, that there should be more bloodletting in the prisons, that if the executioner was tired, he himself would climb the scaffold with a quarter loaf to soak up the blood." In the *Gardes-Françaises* a certain Jayet was arrested on 6 Prairial for having declared in the year II, "that he would like to see rivers of blood, up to the ankles." On leaving the general assembly of the *République* section, another declared: "The guillotine is hungry, it's ages since she had something to eat." Women shared this Terrorist exaltation. A certain Baudray, a lemonade vendor from the *Lepeletier* section, was arrested on 8 Prairial for having said "she would like to eat the heart of anyone opposed to the sans-culottes"; she intended to raise her children on the same principles: "You hear them talk of nothing but cutting, chopping off heads, not enough blood is flowing."

Nevertheless, temperament alone does not sufficiently explain the fact that the majority of the popular militants approved of if they did not exalt violence and the use of the guillotine. For many, brute force seemed the supreme recourse when a crisis had reached its paroxysm. These same men, who did not hesitate to make blood flow, were more often than not ordinarily quite calm, good sons, good husbands and good fathers. Cobbler Duval from the *Arsenal* section was condemned to death on 11 Prairial, year II, for his role during the uprising of the first; his neighbors testified that he was a good father, good husband, good citizen, a *man of probity*. The feeling that the nation was threatened, the belief in the aristocratic plot, the atmosphere of turbulent days, the tocsin and the issuing of arms made these men beside themselves and created in them something like a second nature. According to the civil committee of the *Faubourg-du-Nord* section, Josef Morlot, a house painter, arrested on 5 Prairial, year III, was a man with two distinct personalities. "One of these, guided by his natural bent, was gentle, honest and generous. He has all the social virtues, which he practices in private. The other, subjugated by present threats, manifests itself in the bloody colors of all the conjoined plagues in their utmost virulence."

This violence was not gratuitous. It had a political aim and a class content; it was a weapon which the sans-culottes were forced to use in their resistance to the aristocracy. A teacher by the name of Moussard employed by the Executive Commission of Public Instruction, was arrested on 5 Prairial, year III. "Yes, I was carried away," he wrote in his defense. "Who wasn't during the Revolution? . . . They say I am fanatical: yes; passion burns within my breast, I am intoxicated with the idea of liberty and I shall always rage against the enemies of my country."

The guillotine was popular because the sans-culottes saw in it an instrument whereby they could avenge the nation. Hence the expressions *national cleaver, national ax;* the guillotine was also known as the *scythe of equality.* Class hatred of the aristocracy was heightened by the belief in an aristocratic plot which since 1789 had been one of the fundamental reasons behind popular violence. Foreign war and civil war further strengthened the popular notion that the aristocracy would only be exterminated by the Terror and that the guillotine was necessary for consolidating the Republic. Becq, a clerk in the Navy Department, a good father, a good husband and well thought of, but extraordinarily impassioned according to the civil committee of the *Butte-des-Moulins,* turned his impassioned nature against priests and noblemen, whom he *usually* recommended for assassination. Jean-Baptiste Mallais, cobbler and revolutionary commissar of the *Temple* section, was the same: he did not hesitate to use clubs when arguing with noblemen and priests considered enemies of the people; he spoke of arming the wives of patriots "so that they in turn can slit the throats of the wives of aristocrats." . . . Even more indicative of the political aims which the sans-culottes hoped to achieve through violence and through the Terror were the words recorded by the observer Perrière on 6 Ventôse, year II: "Is the guillotine working today?" asked a dandy. "Yes," replied an honest patriot, "there is always somebody betraying somebody or something."

During the year III violence became even more important for the sans-culottes. The Terror had also been an economic aspect of government; it had sanctioned the application of the "maximum," which had guaranteed the people their daily bread. Whereas the reaction coincided with the abolition of price-fixing and the worst shortages, certain among them came to identify the Terror with abundance, in the same way as they associated popular government with the Terror. Cobbler Clément from the *République* section was denounced on 2 Prairial for having declared "that the Republic cannot be built without blood flowing." . . . Mistress Chalandon from the *l'Homme-Armé* section declared, "Nothing will really work properly until permanent guillotines were erected at every street intersection in Paris." Carpenter Richer, from the *République* section, touched the heart of the matter when he said, on 1 Prairial: "There will be no bread unless we spill some blood; under the Terror we didn't go without."

Whatever specific aims the Parisian sans-culottes had in mind, the Terror and popular violence to a great extent swept away the remnants of feudalism and absolutism for the bourgeoisie. They nevertheless corresponded to a different form of behavior, in the same way as popular political practices, essentially characterized in 1793 and in the year II by voting by acclamation and by fraternity, expressed a concept of democracy that was fundamentally different from that of the bourgeoisie, even of the Jacobins.[15]

---

[15] Members of republican political clubs during the French Revolution. Originally moderates, the Jacobins became increasingly radical and dominated the government during the Terror.

Doubtless the revolutionary bourgeoisie, during the critical moments of its struggle against the aristocracy, also resorted to violence; they, too, made use of certain popular practices; for example, during the course of the Convention elections, in Paris, they used the roll-call vote. Events justified this departure from the usual concepts of liberal democracy, and also class interests. Once the revolutionary government was in power, neither these interests nor the events would allow these practices to continue. Although these practices were in accord with the popular temperament, they were incompatible with the behavior and political ideas of the bourgeoisie. They also threatened its sovereignty.

INFANTICIDE IN EUROPEAN HISTORY
Keith Wrightson

The practice of infanticide has existed throughout history in all civilizations. Ancient societies in western Asia as well as Greece and Rome condoned infanticide, although historians debate its frequency. In ancient western Asia, only the Hebrews condemned infanticide out of hand. Indeed, one could interpret the famous (or infamous) account in Genesis — wherein god ordered Abraham to sacrifice Isaac, his only son, before sending an angelic emissary to stop Abraham at the last moment from plunging his knife into his son — as a divine injunction against the murder of children. Christianity continued the Jewish custom of forbidding infanticide.

Keith Wrightson, an English social historian at the University of Cambridge, surveys the practice of infanticide and its legal history across Europe. In doing so, he uncovers the irony that although Christianity always condemned infanticide, Christian social morality nonetheless contributed to infanticide by preaching that a woman giving birth to an illegitimate child should be shunned and ostracized and by attaching a stigma to the illegitimate offspring. What other social and economic factors might have led women to infanticide, even though they knew that, if caught and convicted, they would in all likelihood suffer public humiliation and an excruciating death? Why did the Catholic and Protestant Reformations of the sixteenth and seventeenth centuries become more interested in the pursuit of infanticides than had the medieval Church?

Which women were most likely to practice infanticide, a "horror crime"? Wrightson points out that only a small minority of single women murdered their children. Of course, historians of crime must rely on court records of depositions and trials, and we therefore have no knowledge of people who committed infanticide undetected by the criminal justice system. Beginning in the late-eighteenth century, changes occurred that altered the public perception of the infanticidal mother. How did "infanticidal nursing" in the nineteenth century further modify the practice of infanticide? Finally, what factors contributed to the decline of infanticide by the end of that century?

Keith Wrightson, "Infanticide in European History," *Criminal Justice History: An International Annual* 3 (1982): 1–16.

On 5 April 1578, the burial of a child of one Marie Lyttell was recorded in the parish register of Great Hallingbury, Essex. Having borne an illegitimate child on 30 March 1578, the entry informs us, the mother "most unnaturalye by all cyrcystances murthered it, cast it in to a privie having before nyped it by the throte and sculle most lamentablie." This rare example of the parochial registration of a case of infanticide encapsulates the predominant attitude towards the crime of infanticide in early modern Europe: the deed was unnatural. The English moralist William Gouge[1] . . . described infanticidal mothers as "lewd and unnatural." The clergyman and gentleman who reported another Essex case to the authorities in 1645 wrote of it as "an unnatural and barbarous murther." Elsewhere in early modern Europe infanticide took its place among those crimes which were regarded with peculiar horror — witchcraft and heresy, parricide, incest, sodomy, arson, and murder (including infanticide); the . . . *heinous crimes* . . . which were "taken to constitute, *ipso facto*,[2] a challenge to the established political, religious or social order." So horrid did the crime of infanticide appear in the eyes of European jurists that it was frequently singled out as meriting especially appalling punishment. In late medieval France burning or burial alive, sometimes accompanied by additional torments, was the fate of convicted murderers of infants. In the Holy Roman Empire the criminal code published by the Emperor Charles V[3] in 1532 followed medieval German precedents in prescribing death by burial alive, drowning in a sack, or impaling, punishments which were replaced by decapitation after torture in the seventeenth century.

Such punishments reflect both horror at a crime deemed odious in the sight of God and a perceived need for exemplary retribution which would dissociate the Christian community from such wickedness and cleanse it of guilt. That a crime so unnatural might be the result of an unbalanced mind was also recognised, but it was long before this alternative explanation of infanticide prevailed over punitive severity in the courts of Europe. In fifteenth century France, mental disturbance was one of the grounds on which mercy might be granted to women convicted of infanticide, if only after long imprisonment. In the later sixteenth and seventeenth centuries, however, such clemency was actually more difficult to obtain for infanticide than for witchcraft. Similarly, in England, the law allowed that a person *non compos mentis*[4] should not be charged with felony for homicide, and cases survive in which such a defence was successful. Yet there are equally clear cases of the condemnation and execution of women who were almost certainly victims of severe psychological disturbance.

---

[1] English Puritan writer (1578–1653).

[2] By the very nature of the case.

[3] Holy Roman Emperor from 1519 to 1556.

[4] Not of sound mind.

Explanations of infanticide in terms of either human iniquity or psychiatric disorder turn upon the connected ideas of infanticide as an unnatural and irrational act. Within the cultural tradition of Christian Europe both responses may appear to have been appropriate. Yet they are not wholly adequate to the understanding of infanticide in European history, for there are situations in which social circumstances, coupled with the absence or relative weakness of cultural and legal restraints, may render infanticide both a natural and a rational response to the problem of the unwanted child. It is well established that infanticide has been extensively practiced in human societies as a form of population control or demographic selection. Among the Tikopia[5] of Polynesia population was carefully "measured according to the food" by the smothering of unwanted children at birth. In eighteenth century Japan, infanticide was employed not only "to thin out" populations pressing too heavily upon inadequate resources, but also as an element in what has been termed "household building strategy": a means of achieving the optimum size and sex composition of a family, a desired number of heirs, higher living standards and social prestige. Whether motivated by physical need and the pressures of a marginal existence or by social aspirations, infanticide has appeared a sensible and responsible solution to difficulties threatening the welfare of the larger group.

Nor were such circumstances unknown in the European past. It seems certain that the exposure of deformed, sickly and illegitimate children was not uncommon in the Europe of antiquity. In addition, Athenian families of middling and upper rank were prepared, on occasion, to expose supernumerary children once the continuance of the line was assured, while the evidence of Hellenistic[6] inscriptions suggests that some leading families were unwilling to raise more than one daughter. In Republican and early Imperial Rome,[7] the right of life and death exercised over his children by the *pater familias*[8] was enshrined in the ritual whereby he either recognised and raised up the newborn child laid before him or ordered its exposure. Among both wealthy families and peasant proprietors, preservation of the family patrimony from the burden of too many heirs appears to have been the principal motive governing such rites and actions.

In the light of such considerations, the emergence of infanticide as one of the classical horror crimes of Christian Europe and its subsequent history and eventual reappraisal in European law become problems of considerable interest. For the history of infanticide provides examples not only of the processes by which crime is defined and redefined, but also of the complex interrelationships between law and social, moral and communal values. . . .

---

[5] A people living on one of the Pacific Solomon Islands.

[6] Relating to Greece and western Asia from the reign of Alexander the Great to the Roman Empire, 323–31 B.C.

[7] Roman history from the eighth century B.C. to the third century A.D.

[8] Father of the family; head of the household.

The initial identification of infanticide as a sinful and unnatural act and the proscription of the practice by law are customarily and correctly attributed to the influence of the early Christian Church. From the outset, the tradition of Judaeo-Christian thought was uncompromisingly hostile to the taking of infant life. Infanticide was repeatedly condemned by the councils and synods of the early Church, and their hostility was gradually embodied in legislation following the formal Christianisation of the Roman Empire. . . .

This long-term shift in attitudes and values remains obscure and deserves further investigation. It seems probable, however, that the gradual triumph of Christianity did much to enhance the security of infant life. Though the restraining force of the teachings of the Church may have been slow to develop its full strength, it seems unlikely that the systematic exposure of legitimate children (if it had ever been commonplace) long survived the effective Christianisation of European societies and the enshrinement of Christian values in law and custom. Nevertheless, that process left in its wake a persistent tension between the ideals taught by the Church and the needs of particular families, needs which might on occasion prove sufficiently urgent to break the restraints of morality and law.

Awareness of this tension led the medieval Church to view with suspicion the apparently accidental deaths of children overlain by their parents during sleep. . . . Such cases were regarded by the Church as the result of culpable negligence and were seriously investigated, both parents usually being called to answer before an episcopal court. The extent to which they represent deliberate infanticide, however, is open to debate. . . .

Where unambiguous evidence of infanticide is available, in the records of the criminal courts of late medieval and early modern Europe, it relates much more narrowly to one kind: the killing of illegitimate children. Such evidence permits, for the first time in European history, a thorough investigation of infanticide. It also raises the disturbing possibility that if Christian social morality had done much to overcome the practice of infanticide motivated by considerations of communal or familial interest, it may have exacerbated resort to it to avoid the stigma of illegitimacy.

The need to conceal illegitimate births or dispose of illegitimate offspring had its place in the history of infanticide from the earliest times, but from medieval times these motives clearly predominate in surviving historical evidence. The first asylum for exposed children, established in eighth century Milan, was intended primarily for the relief of bastard children. The records of thirteenth century exposure and abandonment cases make it clear that most of the infants concerned were illegitimate. In Germany, France, England, Scotland, Sweden, Russia and the Netherlands, women tried for murdering their children between the fifteenth and the nineteenth centuries were overwhelmingly either single women or widows, and their children illegitimate. A series of remarkably similar laws was enacted in European states between the early sixteenth and the late seventeenth centuries for the suppression of the crime. Each laid down that mothers of bastard children who had concealed their pregnancy would be assumed, should their children be found dead after birth, to have killed them. . . .

Like the harsh laws intended to suppress the crime, the circumstances of the killings of bastard children by their mothers were remarkably similar across Europe and over time. The unmarried woman would conceal her pregnancy, helped by the ample nature of traditional female dress. She would give birth in secret and, having delivered the child herself, kill it and dispose of the corpse. Recorded cases generally arose from lack of success in either bearing the child secretly or concealing its body. A representative case was cited by the seventeenth century English obstetrician Percival Willughby.[9] A young woman of Hampton Ridway, Staffordshire, attempted to conceal her pregnancy although she shared a bed with her sister. She bore her child at night in an outhouse, killed and buried it and returned to bed. She was, however, "mistrusted by her neighbours" and a woman was sent to examine her, upon which she confessed. She was hanged at Stafford in March 1670.

What motivated these women? The answer is succinctly given in the English act of 1624, which speaks of their desire "to avoyd their shame and to escape Punishment." In most of Europe the consequences of bearing (as distinct from begetting) a base child were potentially, and often actually, socially disastrous. A bastard birth dishonored the individual mother and in some societies her family too. . . .

In addition to the possibility of rejection by family and friends, the pregnant single woman also faced the likelihood of public humiliation by the Church and sometimes further punishment by officers of the state. Both possibilities became likelier from the sixteenth century on, when, in the aftermath of the Reformation and Counter-Reformation, both Catholic and Protestant nations witnessed an intensification of social regulation aimed at the reformation of popular manners. In France from the sixteenth century *curés*[10] were expected to report illegitimate pregnancies to the authorities, leading to a searching interrogation, then to a public *déclaration de grossesse*.[11] In Germany unmarried mothers were automatically excommunicated and readmitted to the Christian community only after a humiliating penance. The Kirk Sessions[12] of Presbyterian Scotland and the archdeaconry courts[13] of Anglican England also enforced public penance for illegitimacy, while in the latter country Justices of the Peace[14] might in some instances order the corporal punishment of bastard-bearers or their incarceration in a House of Correction. If all this was not enough, the unmarried mother was likely to lose her livelihood (especially if, as was common, she was a servant), and since provision for

---

[9] English writer on obstetrics (1596–1685).

[10] Chief priests of parishes.

[11] Statement about the circumstances of pregnancy.

[12] The minister and elders of a Scottish Presbyterian congregation.

[13] The lowest courts in the Church of England.

[14] English local magistrates.

her was at best uncertain, she faced the prospects of poverty, isolation, vagrancy and perhaps prostitution.

These dangers, quite apart from the probability of further punishment, drove some women to kill their children, as they vividly testified. Jeanne Pion hid her pregnancy in 1450 "for fear, doubt and shame," being particularly apprehensive of the reactions of her mother, stepfather and brother. In 1473 Jeanne Hardouyn, aged 24, killed her child "fearing the shame and contempt of the world." Two centuries later an Essex servant girl hid her pregnancy and bore her child in silence in the room she shared with her mistress: "it would have been bine a griefe unto her freinds if she should have discovered it. And the other cause was that she feared she should not have bine relieved[15] if she had made it knowne that she was with child." To another English servant girl the discovery of her pregnancy in 1737 spelt "certain ruin to her for life."

These women cogently expressed their shame and anxiety but left unanswered the question of why only a small minority of pregnant single women chose to conceal their pregnancies and kill their children. . . . [W]omen formerly of excellent reputation, even possessed of unusual strength of will and determination, might be those most tempted to salvage what they could by concealment and infanticide. It is an intriguing possibility and may be true of those women who intended from the outset to dispose of their unwanted children. In most cases, however, a more satisfactory explanation may lie in the findings of a recent Swedish study which suggest that the infanticidal mother was more likely to be a person peculiarly isolated in society and bereft of any help or support in pregnancy or motherhood. For many there may have been a chain reaction set in motion by an initial concealment of pregnancy resulting more from confusion than decision. The final infanticidal impulse may have come only after an exhausting and emotionally devastating secret birth. Some may have been temporarily unbalanced by the experience, like the London girl hanged in 1688 despite her plea that at the time "she had not her Senses and was Light-headed." Others may have been forced at last to choose between abandonment of the child and infanticide and found the latter the more practical alternative.

Whatever the case, the records of this most conspicuous form of infanticide carry a significant implication. They suggest that the crime sprang not from the persistence of norms alien to the conventional morality of Christian Europe, but rather from the fact that those norms and the sanctions which upheld them made so deep an impression upon the minds of pregnant (and often servant) women, most of whom were scarcely moral delinquents. The popular culture of much of Europe allowed a degree of sexual contact during serious courtships, and bridal pregnancy was common enough. But license stopped short when mistaken trust, disappointed hopes, or foolishness turned a potential pregnant bride into an actual bastard-bearer. The known consequences were sufficiently disproportionate

---

[15] Received aid from the poor law.

to the offence to terrify some who faced unmarried motherhood alone into concealment and worse.

The best documented form of direct infanticide in Europe between the fifteenth and the nineteenth centuries can thus be attributed largely to the very strength of the social sanctions, informal and formal, which served to uphold conventional morality. How common were such cases? The records of the courts would suggest that they were surprisingly rare. . . . [There were] only two cases of infanticide among the records of over 4,000 late medieval coroners' inquests for four English counties. In sixteenth and seventeenth century Nuremburg, only 42 cases were reported to the city authorities. A study of homicide indictments in the English counties of Sussex and Hertfordshire between 1559 and 1625 produced only 50 infanticide trials. . . . The Parlement of Paris[16] dealt with some 2,000 appeals in infanticide cases in the years 1565–1640, a seemingly large number. Yet when we remember that this court exercised its appeal jurisdiction over a large part of the densely populated kingdom of France, including some 500 inferior court jurisdictions, the figure is less impressive. In eighteenth century England, infanticide cases in the areas so far studied (including London) scarcely averaged one case per year. In the *présidiaux*[17] of Brittany in the same period one or two cases a year was the norm, while in Amsterdam only some 24 to 30 cases were tried in the period 1680–1811.

Given the relatively small numbers of infanticide cases recoverable from criminal records, one might wonder why such an apparently infrequent crime attracted so much attention from contemporaries, and why indeed it was the object of such Draconian laws. There are several answers to this question. In the first place, infanticide had become established as a horror crime, akin to sodomy or witchcraft in the repulsion and loathing which it commonly evoked. It was a crime to be weighed rather than counted, and in consequence we should not expect any necessary relationship to exist between public concern with the crime and its actual incidence. Moreover, for the same reason, it was a crime which attracted publicity. The Essex clergyman Ralph Josselin[18] was aware of the full details of a case in a nearby village in 1655 within a day of the event and was sufficiently shocked to enter in his diary a prayer that "the lord keepe mee and mine from any such wickedness." In the eighteenth century, newspapers assiduously reported the details of cases to a public torn between horror and fascination, thereby stimulating public awareness.

Even before the advent of the popular press there were more dreadful means of publicity. Infanticide cases, though infrequent in absolute terms, might form a relatively high proportion of all homicide cases (though these in turn were a small

---

[16] A sovereign judicial court with jurisdiction over approximately one-half of France.

[17] Courts of appeal for minor civil and criminal cases.

[18] English clergyman and diarist (1616–1683).

component of the business of the courts). In sixteenth and early seventeenth century Essex, Sussex and Hertfordshire, infanticide accounted for between 18.6% and 21.7% of all extant homicide indictments, while in eighteenth century Staffordshire the figure was 25%. Given the ease with which guilt could be proved under the discriminatory concealment laws, infanticidal mothers also made up a substantial proportion of all persons publicly executed. In the late sixteenth and early seventeenth centuries some 10 to 20% of all executions ordered by the Parlement of Paris were for infanticide. In eighteenth century Sweden infanticide was only one of 68 capital crimes in the laws, yet in the years 1759–78 it accounted for 217 of 617 executions (35%). Frederick the Great[19] informed Voltaire[20] in 1777 that in the Kingdom of Prussia infanticide was the most common single cause of executions, some 14 or 15 a year.

In a period such as the sixteenth and seventeenth centuries, when the legislators of many European states were preoccupied with the suppression of ungodliness, it is easy to see why such an emotionally charged and widely publicised crime as infanticide was singled out again and again for special treatment. The very nature of the concealment laws then adopted, however, also demonstrates a persistent suspicion that many cases of infanticide escaped prosecution. Of all forms of homicide, infanticide was perhaps the easiest to conceal. The image of latrines, drains and rivers echoing to the cries of infants cast into them to hide their mothers' shame was a popular one with the preachers of early modern France. Nor was it without foundation in fact. When a drain was uncovered following the fire of 1721 in Rennes, over eighty infant skeletons were recovered. In eighteenth century Amsterdam the paucity of infanticide trials in the court records has been revealingly set against the discovery each year of the corpses of several newborn babies in the canals and public *secreten*.[21] The numbers of such corpses increased markedly in the later decades of the century, when illegitimacy rates rose rapidly throughout western Europe. The sight of infant corpses on the dunghills of eighteenth century London was yet further disturbing evidence of the extent of infanticide (though it has been argued that at least some of these were children who had died naturally, whose parents could not afford the costs of their interment). Many cases of infanticide may have escaped discovery and prosecution. Unmarried mothers could, as we have seen, bear their children in secret and with luck a well concealed corpse might remain undiscovered, or at least fail to be traced to the mother. This was perhaps more possible in great cities than in small country villages where the attentions and suspicions of neighbors were more easily aroused. How frequently this may have occurred it is simply impossible to say. Finally, in some areas sympathetic neighbors might even have turned from or condoned the dread solution.

---

[19] King of Prussia from 1740 to 1786.

[20] French philosopher (1694–1778).

[21] Public toilets.

However, it is also true that some of the women tried and condemned for the crime were innocent. The harsh laws of the early modern period not only failed to distinguish between premeditated infanticide and acts of unbalanced mothers, but also permitted the condemnation of women who, having concealed their pregnancies, gave birth to stillborn children. It is an established fact that illegitimate children are born prematurely with higher frequency as a result of inadequate prenatal care, and this alone significantly increases infant mortality. How much more might this have been so among mothers who concealed their pregnancy? The phenomenon of high rates of premature stillbirths among unmarried mothers was explored by one nineteenth century German doctor. Having considered the hypothesis that infanticide was being practiced, he rejected it and concluded that poor prenatal care and childbirth procedures were to blame. Such factors were rarely considered by the courts of early modern Europe. Percival Willughby recorded the case of a "Naturall foole" who miscarried her illegitimate child while alone. Despite his evidence at her trial, the judge insisted on the letter of the statute of 1624, the jury obediently found her guilty, and "she was, afterwards, hanged for not having a woman by her at her delivery." Some juries, however, were sympathetic to a woman's plight and refused to find her guilty. As the foreman of a Derby jury which acquitted a woman in 1647 remarked, "he thought it no reason that a woman should be hanged for a mistaken harsh word or two in the statute."

In order to avoid both judicial errors and contempt for the law, increasing emphasis came to be laid in infanticide trials upon tests to determine whether a child had been born alive, and upon evidence that its mother had intended it to live. If the lungs of the child failed to float in water, it might be concluded that it had never breathed. If its navel was tied, this was taken to be proof that there had been no murderous intention, while even the preparation of child-linen by a mother might serve to acquit her of criminal intentions. If the child's body was marked, however, this might be damning evidence that force had been used. The increasing weight given to such considerations in England and the gradual shift of public sympathy towards women accused under the concealment laws were such that whereas in early seventeenth century Essex only two-fifths of women tried for infanticide were acquitted, the acquittal rate in eighteenth century Middlesex and London had risen to approximately three-quarters of those tried.

Growing unease over the harshness of the law and concern for the plight of the infanticidal mother, from the later eighteenth century, set in motion the process of legal reform and fostered the conviction that temporary mental disturbance was the overriding cause of infanticide. From the 1770s, capital punishment for infanticide was gradually abolished in the major states of continental Europe. In Britain, where it was long retained, reprieve became virtually automatic for those convicted, the last execution for the crime taking place in 1849. Such shifts in social and judicial attitudes, however, did not affect the stubborn persistence of infanticide in its classical form wherever the social stigma of illegitimacy and the informal social sanctions against the unmarried mother retained their traditional force. The virtual elimination of infanticide in its classical form undoubtedly owes more to the gradual softening of attitudes towards illegitimacy, the availability of effective contraception and abortion, and the growth of welfare and adoptive institutions to ameliorate the position of the unmarried mother, than to changes in the attitude of the law.

From the mid-nineteenth century however, the attention of legislators was less upon the killing of illegitimate children by their mothers than upon a form of indirect infanticide which had long existed, yet had been little noticed by the law: the problem of what can be termed "infanticidal nursing." As early as the end of the twelfth century Thomas of Chobham[22] had included in his catalogue of infanticidal practices the refusal of mothers to nurse their own children. In his opinion, one frequently echoed by doctors and moralists in the early modern period, children throve best on their own mothers' milk. (This view has the support of modern evidence.) Children put out to nurse by their parents commonly suffered substantially higher rates of infant mortality than did children nursed by their mothers at home, partly as a result of inadequate child care, partly because "nurslings" were often hand- rather than breast-fed. The practice of employing nurses was, of course, common among prosperous families throughout medieval and early modern Europe, and continued to be frequent among French urban artisans well into the nineteenth century. Though mortality among "nurslings" remained disproportionately high, there is no reason to believe that the parents of these children deliberately sought their children's deaths by employing nurses. They simply conformed to a long-established custom, one found convenient for a variety of reasons and clearly expected among families of a certain rank.

The nursing industry, however, had a dark side. Parents of illegitimate or unwanted infants (and even loved ones) frequently chose, or were obliged by circumstances, to leave their children in the care of cheap "baby farmers," who at best provided poor nourishment and at worst tacitly guaranteed a child's early death. The case of a Rennes gardener's wife who in 1778 nursed seventeen bastard children, in 1779 ten and in 1780 a further three, all of whom died, is only an extreme example of a system of veiled infanticide which is well documented for early modern France and England. Indeed, the activities of baby farmers in England reached a peak only in the nineteenth century. It was the publicity given to a number of particularly scandalous cases of deliberate neglect of this kind which did much to prompt late nineteenth century legislation for the protection of infant life by the registration and control of nurses.

The number of children allowed to die as the result of the deliberate neglect of baby farmers can never be accurately assessed, though the most recent estimate attempted suggests that the annual figure for mid-Victorian England may have been a thousand or more. Whatever the actual figure, the fate of these infants reveals a marked ambivalence in attitudes towards the lives of unwanted, usually il-

---

[22] Medieval bishop and scholar (ca. 1255–1327).

legitimate, children. They were rarely directly killed, yet they were allowed, even encouraged, to die. The same attitudes are demonstrable on a much larger scale in the treatment of abandoned children left to the care of public charity. Though the total numbers of children abandoned might be small in relation to the total population, abandonment nonetheless constituted a serious problem. Between two and three hundred abandoned infants were found every year on the streets of mid-nineteenth century London, most of them dead or half-dead from exposure. In eighteenth century France the situation was far worse. One parish of Angers recorded 42 children abandoned in the years 1740–64, and as many as 467 in the years 1765–89. It has been estimated that perhaps 40,000 children were abandoned each year in France as a whole during the 1780s.

The reasons for abandonment on this scale are twofold. On the one hand, there were parents who could not afford to raise their legitimate offspring. On the other hand, there was the familiar motive of disposing of an illegitimate child. Examples of both forms of behavior can be found throughout the history of Europe, but can be examined in particular detail in the records of the foundling hospitals[23] of eighteenth century France. Study after study has revealed that short term fluctuations in the frequency of abandonment in France were closely linked to times of economic distress. When the price of bread rose, or employment became scarce, temporary peaks in the statistics of abandonment swiftly followed. The longer-term upward movement of abandonment figures, however, appears to be related above all to the dramatic upswing of illegitimacy experienced throughout Europe in the later eighteenth century.

This dual causation naturally raises the question of the relative proportions of legitimate and illegitimate children among the *enfants trouvés*.[24] In most cases it would appear that the origins of the foundlings were unknown. This led to most being assumed to be illegitimate, an assumption questioned by some scholars. Where better information is available, it appears that perhaps 20–30% of abandoned children were legitimate, often significantly older than their illegitimate counterparts, most of whom were abandoned at birth.

Abandonment must be distinguished to some degree from infanticide. The fact that it existed on such a large scale in France is in part a consequence of the widespread provision of foundling hospitals in that country. French foundlings were rarely actually exposed on the streets to die. More commonly they were either born in public institutions, brought in by midwives, or delivered anonymously at the gates of the foundling hospitals. Some were accompanied by notes, naming the child, explaining the mother's circumstances, sometimes expressing the hope that the child would eventually be reclaimed, though few such reclamations ever took place. For unmarried mothers the possibility of abandoning their children at the foundling hospitals may have provided an alternative to in-

---

[23] Orphanages.

[24] Orphaned or abandoned children.

fanticide as a way out of their predicament — one of the reasons for the foundation of these institutions in European cities. Yet in practice the distinction might mean little more than the shifting of responsibility from the individual parent to a public institution, for the mortality rate among abandoned children was appalling.

Bastards or not, the foundlings were treated in the manner usually reserved for illegitimate children; which is to say, they were not encouraged to live. The ghastly racket in which abandoned children were transported from the French provinces to the Paris foundling hospital prior to 1779, up to nine-tenths of the infants dying on the way, was only the most blatant example of such neglect. Foundlings were generally distributed as soon as possible to the cheapest rural nurses, with minimal supervision by the authorities. Of the women of one village where children from Rheims were put out to nurse, for example, those who took foundlings were a specialist group, distinguished by their poverty.

The mortality of foundlings, not surprisingly, was disproportionately high as compared with legitimate children placed with nurses. Of the 3,558 children abandoned in Rouen in the years 1782–9, as many as 3,076 died young. Nine-tenths of those abandoned at birth failed to survive one year — and this in a city where the normal rate of infant mortality was only 18–20% in the same period. The same depressing story could be told of the children maintained by the workhouses of eighteenth century London (many of whom were illegitimate), and of the infants admitted by the foundling hospitals of Imperial Russia (which were popularly known as "angel factories"). But the point is sufficiently made. Institutional neglect by well-intentioned but overburdened and under-financed charitable institutions made what was probably the largest single contribution to infanticide in modern Europe, one which long escaped public attention and legal intervention. As in the case of private baby farming, to which it was closely related, the problem persisted until the later nineteenth century, when public opinion and then national legislatures woke up to the need to regulate nursing and protect the lives of all children, whatever their origins.

The realities of infanticide by either commission or neglect retain their capacity to shock. Yet, as Marc Bloch[25] observed, "the historian's sole duty is to understand." In the light of the evidence reviewed here, several conclusions can be suggested concerning the problem of infanticide in European history. First, consideration of the circumstances underlying infanticide draws the historian into a morass of complexity. Infanticide is not, as has sometimes been assumed, a straightforward indicator of the psychological disposition of parents towards their children. The killing of infants might spring from callous indifference to the lives of unwanted children, from the anguish of mental disturbance, from the pressures exerted by marginal subsistence and the interests of the larger group, from coldly

---

[25] An influential medieval historian of the twentieth century; executed by the Nazis for membership in the French Resistance (1886–1944).

rational calculation of familial betterment, or from the fear of harsh social sanctions against breaches of the moral norms of society. These motives can all be found in some periods of the past, yet they varied also in their relative presence and strength. Second, it seems doubtful that infanticide was ever so commonplace in European societies as has been suggested by some historians of childhood. Though infanticide was neither morally nor legally proscribed in the ancient Mediterranean civilisations, the common assumption that it was frequent, even systematic, has been brought into question. Since early medieval times it seems unlikely that infanticide has played an important role in either population control or familial strategies. When short term crises dislocated family economies, abandonment was sometimes resorted to. Evidence of parental neglect can also be cited. Yet there is no conclusive evidence that such expedients were part of the norm of parental experience. Despite the deficiencies of the information available to us, it seems clear that direct infanticide in medieval and modern Europe has been largely confined to a small minority of illegitimate children, while indirect infanticide by negligent nursing was the fate of a substantially larger proportion of abandoned nurslings.

A third conclusion is that the evidence for shifts in attitudes toward infanticide suggests that change has come very largely after a series of periods of intensified public sensitivity to the problem, each of which requires explanation and deserves further study. The first of these periods, which was both the longest and the most obscure, embraced the Christianisation of the later Roman Empire and its successor kingdoms. . . . Christian teaching on the value of infant life, expressed in both moral exhortation and law, strove to establish a strong cultural inhibition on infanticide, identifying the practice as a crime of peculiar enormity. At the same time, however, the gradual institutionalisation of the Church's moral teaching had the effect of strengthening sanctions against sexual immorality, thereby contributing to infanticide motivated by the need to conceal illegitimate births or to dispose of illegitimate children. Thereafter, the history of infanticide has been punctuated by periods of augmented public concern with the crime, each of which bred legal responses appropriate to its time and helped to shape future developments: the concealment laws of the sixteenth and seventeenth centuries; the amelioration of those laws at the turn of the eighteenth and nineteenth centuries; the attempts to regulate nursing and protect infant life in the later nineteenth century.

The precise timing of such legislative initiatives varied from country to country, in consequence, no doubt, of particular national circumstances. Yet the existence of distinct periods of heightened concern of a pan-European nature seems clear and necessitates an attempt at explanation. The answer may lie in the enormous symbolic significance which infanticide had acquired in European Christian culture. Infanticide had been identified as an unnatural act; its very existence was therefore a perennial reminder of the fragility of the prevailing moral order. In times of relative social stability this peculiar resonance may have been muted. In times of significant change, when established values appeared to be threatened, a crime like infanticide might engage attention and elicit an emotional response out of all proportion to its actual incidence. Infanticide challenged a response from both the official moralists and the governors of Europe for the simple reason that attitudes toward the crime involved a judgement of the legitimacy of the prevailing moral and social order. The result could be a powerful reassertion of established norms, in which the upholding of fundamental values in the face of changing social realities might be seen to depend in part upon the repression or containment of such symbolically charged deviance.

It is perhaps for this reason that the later sixteenth and seventeenth centuries, fraught as they were with social, economic, religious and political instability, witnessed such an urgent preoccupation with the repression of the traditional horror crimes, notably witchcraft and infanticide. In the eighteenth century such concern was fading, though the crime of infanticide stubbornly persisted. The quickening pace of social change in the late eighteenth and nineteenth centuries, however, involving as it did massive population expansion, rural congestion, urbanisation, industrialisation, and all their attendant problems, again raised fears of the disintegration of the traditional social and moral order. Attention was once more focused upon infanticide; though the independent processes of change in judicial attitudes and social institutions meant that attempts were made to come to grips with the problem by other means, means more appropriate to new conditions and new perceptions of the circumstances that underlay a crime which retained its capacity to shock and challenge the public conscience.

The history of infanticide thus provides an example of the manner in which legal definitions and redefinitions of criminality are closely linked not only to the broad processes of social change, but also to persisting elements in the self-image of society. It was the established symbolic significance of infanticide in a time of change that provoked the harsh legislation of the sixteenth and seventeenth centuries as state after state was stirred to reaffirm its commitment to traditional values. Again, it was the persisting emotional resonance of the crime that finally drew the attention of social investigators, governors and legislators to the situation of the unmarried mother and her child, setting in motion the slow process of legal, administrative and institutional change which has sufficiently alleviated their position as to render infanticide by any other than a mentally disturbed parent rare and unlikely.

PART TWO

THE NINETEENTH CENTURY

Anna K. Clark
Sidney Pollard
K. H. Connell
F. M. L. Thompson
Richard J. Evans
Eugen Weber
Alain Corbin
Stephen P. Frank
Theresa M. McBride

Historians generally count the nineteenth century as lasting from the end of the Napoleonic Wars (1815) to the beginning of World War I in 1914. Nineteenth-century Europeans appeared to exhibit a confident optimism, if not arrogance, that rested on European scientific achievement, industrial advance, and imperial conquest. The great world fairs of the period — London, 1851; Paris, 1867; Paris, 1900 — that displayed the world's art and manufactures, and that asserted European superiority over the rest of the world, suggest how rich, powerful, self-assured, and nation-proud were the times. In short, the nineteenth century was an era of apparent greatness as Europe flexed its industrial and political muscles. Then, however, came World War I, the "war to end all wars," revealing the terrible consequences of modern technology coupled with rampant nationalism and militarism.

Not all Europeans, of course, shared or reveled in the power exercised by the leaders and the social elite of various nations. Power and wealth were not evenly distributed, and most people continued their never ending struggle for food, work, and a modicum of security.

The major socioeconomic development in this century was the Industrial Revolution, whose effects were felt throughout society. The factories and machines of the Industrial Revolution altered relations among social classes, gave rise to new types of work and workers' organizations, inspired original ideas about the reorganization of society, raised the standard of living, contributed to the formation of immense urban centers, and made change rather than stability the expected fact of life. The unequal distribution of the new riches helped to spawn class conflict, as evidenced in the programs of socialists, communists, and anarchists as well as in mass political parties that recruited the laboring classes.

One of the themes of nineteenth-century history is the development of worker consciousness (aided perhaps by growing literacy and the penny press) and the increasing politicization of the masses, who resented the lifestyles and power of the bourgeoisie. These changes occurred in the midst of the new urban landscape, transformed by technological wonders such as steel and electricity. Great new industries arose in chemicals, oil, and pharmaceuticals. At the same time, Europe's colonization of other societies was at its peak; this was the great age of European power. Textbooks sometimes stress nineteenth-century intellectual

116

and cultural movements such as Romanticism or political developments such as the unification of Italy and of Germany. These were all important in their own right, but they must be set against the background of rapid and unsettling change in the relationships, values, and beliefs of the vast majority of the population.

The essays in this section deal with the nineteenth century's profound social changes. Many historians have come to use gender as a tool of analysis in order to better understand these changes. For instance, during this era traditional male dominance sometimes clashed with socioeconomic developments. Anna K. Clark shows that the wages working-class wives earned gave them a certain independence their husbands resented, thus leading to marital conflict. Traditional patriarchal attitudes existed well into the twentieth century, as Theresa M. McBride illustrates in her analysis of the lives of female department-store clerks in Paris. Store owners thought they were obligated and entitled to regulate both the working and personal lives of female employees.

Social historians continue to uncover unattractive aspects of the Industrial Revolution. Sidney Pollard underscores the imposition of factory discipline on workers unaccustomed to such restrictions. K. H. Connell's account of the potato in Ireland points to economic causes of the great famine at mid-century that industrialized Great Britain did not prevent or alleviate. In England itself, heartland of nineteenth-century economic advance, the capital city, London, groaned and stank under the weight of horse refuse, as F. M. L. Thompson's essay shows. While urban centers grew exponentially, their problems did not diminish. Cities remained hotbeds of disease. In a careful study of cholera epidemics in Hamburg, Richard J. Evans explains the disastrous effects of bourgeois attitudes toward trade and the poor, which led city leaders to place the continuation of trade above all other concerns and to adopt medical explanations for cholera's spread that ignored the fetid conditions where Hamburg's down-and-out lived. Even the history of perfume, according to Alain Corbin, reveals the elites' identification of noxious smells with the poor and bourgeois disgust with the lifestyles and living conditions of those below them on the socioeconomic ladder. It might well be said that those who benefited from the Industrial Revolution kicked the ladder down behind them and tried to increase the distance between themselves and the poor, whether English factory workers, Irish peasants, or Hamburg port workers.

Some areas of nineteenth-century Europe seemingly were little affected by industrial or political change. Although the secularism and de-Christianization that had emerged in eighteenth-century France continued to turn many away from the Catholic Church, Eugen Weber details the resilience of the traditional religious beliefs and practices of French Catholics, attitudes and behavior little altered since medieval times. Stephen P. Frank's account of popular justice among the Russian peasantry reveals a seemingly immobile village culture, impervious to the rapid transformations we routinely ascribe to nineteenth-century Europe.

THE STRUGGLE FOR THE BREECHES: PLEBEIAN MARRIAGE
Anna K. Clark

In nineteenth-century Great Britain, as has been the case throughout Western civilization, husbands have dominated their wives, according to law and custom. In early modern England, for example, a wife who disobeyed her husband could be charged with the crime of petty treason, analogous to a subject committing high treason by disobeying the king. Anna K. Clark, a historian who has concentrated on sexual politics and the influence of gender in British history, examines here working-class marriages during the early Industrial Revolution.

The ability of wives to earn wages meant that plebeian (working people's) marriages were often business partnerships, with both spouses contributing to the maintenance of the home and family. Nevertheless, husbands demanded wifely submission and control of the household. According to Clark, the clash between the old patriarchal tradition and the new family economy led to conflicts over power and the command of family resources, that is, over the struggle for the breeches ("who wears the pants"). Given the independence that wage-earning fostered, a woman often chafed under her husband's yoke. How do the autobiographies of wives and husbands differ in describing their marriages? How did popular literature (including song) satirize marriage, especially through the image of the struggle for the breeches? Clark uses court records to describe the reality of plebeian marriages, including wife-beating and murder, control over earnings, and disputes arising because of men's leisure habits (such as drinking, gambling, and socializing with other men) and infidelities. Did the popular literature accurately reflect plebeian marital relations? How did different sectors of British society react to the abuse of wives? What factors inhibited marital equality?

Clark paints a dark picture of the effects of industrialization on working-class life and marriage. Previous historians have sometimes praised the growth of radical politics in late-eighteenth- and early-nineteenth-century Britain, the

Anna K. Clark, *The Struggle for the Breeches: Gender and the Making of the British Working Class* (Berkeley: University of California Press, 1995), 63–75, 77–85, 87.

birth of worker solidarity and consciousness, and the widening of democracy. Clark, however, asserts that the working-class culture of the era seems less harmonious and less admirable when viewed from the perspective of gender relations. Gender, she implies, should be included in any and every historical investigation of social and economic phenomena.

The life of David Love, a peripatetic ballad-writer and former collier,[1] did not follow the pattern of his name, for he found marital happiness difficult to attain. He married his second wife expecting a docile helpmeet, but their relationship soured as the shop they kept together failed and, in his words, she "strove to be master." As he continued in his autobiography, "I would not submit; but asserted my authority, which caused great contention." However, he eventually won her over:

> With her my ground could hardly stand,
> She strove to get the upper hand;
> 'Till eight years join'd in marriage band,
>   Chang'd was her life,
> She did submit to my command,
>   A loving wife.

In common with many religious and popular authorities, David Love believed marriage should be "patriarchal yet companionate." Contemporary moral authorities made it quite clear that husbands ought to rule — albeit with love. But they feared that submission was "directly contrary to women's inclinations, an order which could be sustained only by vigilant suppression of their unruly drives.". . . The Rev. William Secker[2] both advised husbands to love and respect their wives and stressed, "Our ribs were not ordained to be our rulers. . . . The wife may be a sovereign in her husband's absence, but she must be subject in her husband's presence." Secker warned, "Choose such a one as will be a subject to your dominion. Take heed of yoking yourselves with untamed heifers." John Stephens, a London preacher, declared that woman "is forbidden to aspire to rule, for her Maker designed her for a helper." Women must not brawl, he continued, but must submit themselves to their husbands, while men must not act bitterly or inhumanly toward their wives. The Rev. Mark Wilks, a radical Baptist minister, told men to "rule in love."

Yet as Love found, there was an essential contradiction between the patriarchal and companionate ideals. Plebeian[3] marriage was often a business partnership, for both spouses had to contribute to the family's maintenance. But wives

---

[1] Coalminer.

[2] Clergyman and religious writer (d. 1681?).

[3] One of the working people, small masters, or shopkeepers.

were not supposed to acquire equal authority thereby. The sense of independence wives gained by wage-earning clashed with husbands' desire to dominate, resulting in the "struggle for the breeches" satirized in comic popular literature and more tragically evident in court records of wife-beating.

To be sure, autobiographies reveal that many plebeian partnerships were happy and harmonious, especially when husbands demonstrated respect for their wives' contributions. J. B. Leno praised his wife as "a good mother, an affectionate partner, a wise counsellor, a model of industry." Whatever the faults of his second wife, David Love valued his first wife as "a blooming young woman . . . excellent at working, careful and industrious." Similarly, John O'Neill's wife helped him in his shoemaking business by binding shoes, and he remembered her upon her death during her thirteenth confinement[4] as "a mild, sober, industrious, generous-hearted woman, a good wife, an affectionate mother, a disinterested friend." The cooper William Hart, of London, tried to set up a little shop so that he and his "beloved dear" wife could support their children. . . .

In the relative poverty of Scotland, industrious wives were prized even more than in England. As one mother in a popular chapbook[5] advised her son, he shouldn't wed a thin girl who'll "di naething but prick and sew . . . an drink tea, but you maun get ane that can card and spin, and wirk in barn and byre." Indeed, Alexander Somerville, son of farm laborers in the mid Lowlands, remembered that his mother not only made clothes and engaged in other "domestic toil," but had to "add by outfield labor to the family income," carrying haystacks and performing other heavy farm work.

Weavers and other textile workers were especially likely to seek hardworking wives, for women's work in spinning was essential to the production process, and a weaving wife could contribute even more to the family's earnings. Joseph Gutteridge described his prospective wife as "kind, truthful, and industrious, gaining her living by weaving; in fact, she was just the kind of helpmeet I needed." Joseph Livesey, a Preston weaver, praised a good wife as "sober, affectionate and industrious." In Scotland, the "'slubber spinners' who 'drew long from the Flax on the rock,' producing uneven yarn, were less likely to find husbands than the fine spinners, who . . . were the object of the pragmatically-tinged affections of males who sought the best spinners as partners, and hence a higher standard of living." A young female weaver in Spitalfields could allure potential husbands by flaunting her "showy ribbons, the ear-drops, the red coral necklaces of four or five strings" she bought with her own wages, for a man would be "disposed to consider the earnings which she can make at her loom as far more advantageous to him than all she could gain or save by the use of a needle, or could benefit him by cooking dinners which his wages do not enable him to buy." . . .

---

[4] The time of a woman's giving birth.

[5] A small book or pamphlet.

Not only wives' industry but their wisdom was valued. "The Weavers' Garland, or a New School for Christian Patience," advises a hard-pressed weaver to abandon his drinking companions and seek solace in his wife's good counsel and industry. James Paterson, a Scottish printer, attended political meetings and holiday rambles with a cobbler and his wife who were "exemplary in conjugal felicity as they were in their habits of industry and sobriety." The Rev. Mark Wilks, a former buttonmaker, remembered of his wife that "never was an attachment founded on a greater equality of esteem, or a stronger reciprocity of friendship. . . . His wife was his companion, and his friend, and he never entered on any step without first availing himself of the benefit of her opinion."

However, wives had to ensure that their husbands did not perceive their advice as undermining patriarchal authority. David Gilmour recalled several types of overt or covert struggles for power within artisan marriages in a Baptist weaving community in Paisley, near Glasgow. Gilmour's neighbor Henry Buchan acknowledged that wives could rule their husbands through manipulation:

> In every case what maistry was contended for, the idea o' marriage in its proper sense is excluded; marriage involving the acknowledgement on the part of each that the ither had the richt to be consulted. . . . A true wife will aye see her highest wisdom in her husband's, an' a true husband will always rejoice in his wife's love o' his wisdom. Mairfortaken that love o' his wisdom gies her a pow'r tae rule owre him an' his household, which a true wife will do, while as the poet says, she 'seems to obey.'

However, this patriarchal partnership was not always so companionate. Gilmour also remembered another neighbor, a radical who "waxed eloquent now and then in defence of liberty and equality, but he was from constitutional tendencies a strong-willed aristocrat, and exercised his family headship, not as a responsibility for which he was accountable, but as an authority that ought and must be obeyed."

Most male autobiographers, unlike David Love, were reluctant to reveal marital misery. . . . [S]uch revelations would have been "undignified" for writers trying to depict self-improvement. However, children may have been able to be more critical of their parents' marriages. . . . [In] working-class autobiographies, "The father emerges almost as a stereotype — frequently a drunkard, often thoughtless and uncaring of his wife and children, bad-tempered and selfish, but occasionally over-generous and sentimental."

The very few plebeian women's autobiographies presented a different perspective from that of the men. In the examples I have found, women depict marriage as a pragmatic effort to survive. The Scottish Janet Bathgate described a youthful friendship to another girl in much more intense terms than she used for her later two marriages. Similarly, Mary Ashford remembered a strong attachment to a female fellow servant, but she expressed little emotion when describing her marriages. Ashford accepted her first husband's proposal because she had just lost a place as a servant. They promised to pool their savings and "act fair and candid toward each other." Although he had an irritable temper due to gout, he "exerted himself" on behalf of their family of six children. After her first husband died, she married the widower of a close friend, who said "he knew I should do my duty by him, and he could assist me in rearing his old comrade's children." When Mary Saxby, a peripatetic ballad-singer, left her lover for another man, she lamented, "Here I only exchanged one state of slavery for another." Ann Candler suffered in an unhappy marriage for forty years. Despite her "unbounded" affection for her husband, "he treated me in a very unbecoming manner." When she finally left him, he "wept most bitterly at parting; I was sensibly affected, but had suffered too severely to waver in my resolution." Her resolution may have been strengthened by the fact that her husband was not a good provider and drank away their money when he was not serving in the army. Candler was unusual only in that she wrote an autobiography; her experience of neglect and violence was very common among plebeian women.

Popular literature often admonished husbands and wives to respect each other and forget their quarrels, upholding the values of companionate, patriarchal marriage. "The Fair Sex Vindicated" asked,

> Who then is your constant affectionate friend?
> 'Tis no sottish companion, I'm sure, whose advice
> Has ruined your children, and cheers you in vice,
> But 'tis your best friend, your affectionate wife,
> Who values your health as she values her life.

. . . Yet publishers aimed not to inculcate morals but to sell songs. To do so, their productions had to speak to the realities, not just the aspirations, of plebeian life. The ideal marriage was rather difficult to attain, and was in any case not a source of satirical or tragic narrative. Even when songs and tales ended with promises of harmony, they almost always began with assumptions of conflict. Many plebeians felt stuck in unhappy marriages, or at least constantly overheard their neighbors' quarrels. Yet popular songs and chapbooks about marriage did not simply reflect marital misery, either, for dreary reality would not appeal to buyers any more than moralism would.

Instead, popular literature satirized marriage through a variety of rhetorical tropes[6] and ancient images — most notably the image of the "struggle for the breeches," an ancient motif in European popular culture. . . . "Breeches represent force, dominance, freedom," a crucial yet vulnerable symbol of manhood. A thinly veiled phallic symbol, the breeches symbolized male domination. However, unlike the phallus, they could easily be removed and worn by a woman. Popular culture's representations of wives wearing the breeches evoked male anxieties that women could easily undermine their rightful power, yet also excited laughter by their incongruity. Songs upheld husbandly domination by ridiculing men who were unable to enforce their will on their wives. For example, in a Scottish song, "Will the Weaver," the hero complains,

---

[6] Figures of speech.

Mother dear now I'm married,
I wish I had longer tarried
For my wife she does declare
That the breeches she will wear.

His mother admonishes him, "Loving son give her her due, Let me hear no more from you." Similarly, the wife comes off victorious in a song about marital quarrels over the respective costs of whisky and tea. The husband threatens,

You impudent jade[7] take care what you say,
You are bound by the laws of the land to obey,
And while I am able I vow and declare,
I will not allow you the breeches to wear.

But the song warns husbands,

For if you should flail [wives] from head to toe;
You may depend on it they'll have the last blow.

. . . [T]he image of the violent wife could be seen as humorous because it transgressed the passive, subordinate, female role — and rarely occurred in reality.

The motif of the struggle for the breeches could appeal to female readers and purchasers of popular literature as well as to disgruntled husbands. Chapbooks presented men as desiring patriarchal marriage while women dreamed of companionate unions. In the chapbook *The Jealous Man . . .* , the wife declares, "I am your yokefellow, but not your slave; your equal, but not your vassal," and her husband retorts, "I own this all to be true, and yet the breeches belong to me. Is not man lord of the creation? . . . I work for you by day, and drudge for you by night [an allusion to her sexual demands], and yet you are not contented, without superiority over me." In the popular *New and Diverting Dialogue Between a Husband and His Wife,* an impatient woman dragging her husband out of the alehouse threatens to cuckold him when he declares he'll beat her. He accuses her of rebelling against "her lord and Master," but she retorts that he is an "unnatural monster, cruel brute, tyrant," who does not remember "that husbands are to love and cherish their wives."

Many songs, especially those from the eighteenth century, vented female discontent but upheld the overall framework of husbandly dominance. But as female literacy increased in the early nineteenth century, publishers began to circulate songs that provided women with a newly defiant rhetoric against oppressive husbands. Perhaps women sang such tunes over washtubs or at their friendly society[8] meetings, egging each other on against brutal spouses. These rather bitter ballads advised women to fight back in the sex war, to "whack him with a rolling pin," a shovel, a poker, or even a chamberpot.

---

[7] A disreputable woman.

[8] An organization that collected weekly savings to protect workers from unemployment, illness, and a pauper's funeral.

What was new was that these songs drew upon a language of tyranny and slavery familiar from the political rhetoric of the time. The simple message of one song ran:

> I'll be no submissive wife,
> No, not I — no, not I;
> I'll not be a slave for life,
> No, not I — no, not I.

Publishers tried to increase sales by exposing the sexual antagonism of plebeian life, printing misogynist anti-marriage broadsheets[9] and indignant female responses. "A Woman That Is Plagued with a Man," a retort to "A Man That Is Plagued with a Woman," warned, "A woman had better be laid in her grave/Than suffer herself to be any man's slave." "The Woman That Wished She Never Got Married" seconded this warning, proclaiming, "While you ladies do single remain,/By a tyrant you'll never be hurried."

The counterparts to women's defiance were anti-marriage songs and caricatures that most likely found their audiences in the homosocial[10] worlds of plebeian culture, the pubs and clubs where men drank, sang, and caroused, the arenas where the bachelor culture of journeymen flourished. For example, the *Trades' Newspaper* reported one story about a shoemaker who sang "The Struggle for the Breeches" to a workmate who was so struck by its resemblance to his own marital woes that he dropped dead in a fit.

In song, bachelors vowed to avoid the burdens of matrimony — the expense of childbirth and childrearing, the "self-less" labor for a family, the risk of cuckoldry, and, above all, "those termagant[11] jades who'd still wear the breeches." Men should "kiss and cuddle girls," but when they're pregnant, it's "Time to Say No!" The records of the Foundling Hospital[12] and of the Glasgow kirk sessions[13] bear witness to the reality of the problem of seduction and desertion. In song, however, bachelors adamantly celebrated their state, pointing out that in marriage,

> There's scolding and fighting, while we're delighting
> Our selves with our freedom, while you have this strife.

If men stayed single, resources could be circulated among workmates rather than being saved for the home. "Advice to Sailors" declares,

> For we that are merry and free
> Carouse and merrily sing

---

[9] Large pieces of paper with information printed on one side only.

[10] Same-sex social groups, such as fraternities and sororities.

[11] Quarrelsome, shrewish.

[12] Orphanage in London, founded in the eighteenth century.

[13] The minister and elders of a Scottish Presbyterian congregation.

For we have no wives that will scold
We can both borrow and lend.

Nonetheless, most plebeians eventually married or cohabited, but the loyalty of many husbands to their drinking mates obviously caused tensions between husband and wife. Although these clashes did not necessarily lead to violence, the husbands of popular literature often required that their wives allow them to frequent the alehouse. In radical weaver Alexander Wilson's popular song "Watty and Meg, or the Wife Reformed," Watty complains to his mates in a pub of his unhappy marriage to a scolding wife:

See you, Mungo, when she'll clash [gossip] on
Wi' her everlasting clack [scolding],
Whyles I've had my nieve [fist], in passion,
Liftet up to break her back!

But his friend Mungo advises, "O, for gudesake, keep from cuffets, [blows]," and advises him that simply threatening to desert her will infallibly keep her in line.

Yet the "humorous" intention of popular literature allowed songs to both mock and condone wife-beating. By its title, the ambiguous "A Fool's Advice to Henpeck'd Husbands," one song ridiculed men who could not control their wives. But it also advised them,

When your wife for scolding finds pretences, oh
Take the handle of a broom,
Not much thicker than your thumb,
And thwack her till you bring her to her senses, oh.

And a misogynist streak within popular culture meant that some songs and caricatures celebrated the torture of wives as funny and as justified by their shrewishness. The early nineteenth-century Glasgow ballad-singer Hawkie drew crowds with his "Cure for Ill Wives," which advised the unhappy husband to "nail her tongue to a growing tree." Congregating outside the windows of print shops to see the latest caricatures was a favorite male recreation. One engraving, "Tameing a Shrew, or Petruchio's Patent Family Bedstead, Gags and Thumscrews [sic]" depicted a man stretching his recalcitrant wife on a rack. Another viciously portrayed "The Cobbler's Cure for a Scolding Wife" to be sewing up her mouth. . . . In the punchline to a late eighteenth-century "joke," the irate husband declares to his scolding wife, "By Gingo, I will break all the Bones in your Skin, but I'll have quiet."

The wife-beating cobbler — the protagonist of a whole genre of songs — may have appealed as an anti-hero, transgressing the patriarchal ideal of companionate partnership and instead simply celebrating the misogyny of the degraded artisan who married to obtain domestic services and insisted on retaining his bachelor freedoms. "The Bold Cobbler" declares,

I'll let the vixen know,
That I will be her Master;

When I to dine set down,
I'll no more bones picking,
I will have a bit of brown,
Or Ma'am she knaps a kicking,
All skittle grounds I'll see,
To play a cheerful rubber,
And if she follows me,
Dam'me but I'll drab her.[14]

The cobbler's popularity as a wife-beater in popular literature may, to be sure, be derived from the many puns on his trade; but the puns derived their humor from an acceptance of violence. For instance,

And when my wife began to strap
  Why I began to leather
  So where to take her down some pegs
  I drubb'd her neat and clever.

. . .

T'would break my heart to lose my awl,
To lose my wife's a trifle.

When we look at the incidence of wife-beating, we will see that the violent cobbler was not only a stereotype but a reality.

The image of the struggle for the breeches buttressed male dominance by presenting patriarchal authority as the natural state of things and a wife who refused to submit as aberrant. Even one magistrate described a woman who allegedly beat her husband as wearing the breeches. Police court reporters, who sometimes spiced up their accounts with satire, could use this metaphor to discredit abused wives, ridiculing them as pugnacious termagants. For instance, a *Weekly Dispatch* reporter buttressed George Parker's claim that his wife Mary beat him by describing her as a "stalwart dame who possessed the power of 'wearing breeches' and refused him his connubial rights." However, in this case, the magistrate found her more convincing and rejected Parker's charge. Similarly, when reporting a marital brawl the *Thistle's* police court reporter observed, "The wife showed marks of no slight description, which showed her husband to be of good pluck."

The image of the struggle for the breeches concealed the reality that men assaulted women in 78 to 95 percent of the domestic violence cases reported in the courts. Many wife-beaters seemed to feel they had a right to abuse their wives, and indeed until 1853 legal authorities equivocated as to whether wife-beating constituted legitimate correction or criminal assault. The alleged ruling of Francis Buller, "Judge Thumb," that a man could beat his wife with a stick no bigger than his thumb was never a legal precedent, but it entered folklore. For instance, the

---

[14] "The Bold Cobbler" states that he will give his wife a sharp kicking ("knaps a kicking") if she does not serve him beer ("a bit of brown"). If she intrudes upon his playing a game of ninepins (skittle), he will treat her as a whore ("drab her").

pornographic *Rambler's Magazine* cited it as a charter for wife-beaters. Even in the 1830s, at least one Glasgow magistrate did not take wife-beating very seriously. In a case in which a man had slashed his wife's face, the magistrate told him, "If he had so beaten any other person, than his wife, he would have been punished most severely, but as it was only his wife," he was bound over to keep the peace under a penalty of five pounds if he beat her again. The magistrate next fined a carter, who had whipped his horse till it bled, ten shillings and sixpence. . . .

Many abused women, however, did not accept their husbands' right to beat them. Sometimes women themselves used the language of popular literature's sex war to express their complaints. Elizabeth Cooney testified that she had been married to John Cooney for only a week "when he began to tyrannise over her." Similarly, the wife of Henry Stracey complained that "her husband was so tyrannical, she lived in constant fear of her life." At least one woman a week appeared before the Middlesex magistrates in the late eighteenth century to complain of her husband's violence. In a three-month period in 1824, fifty-six cases appeared before the Glasgow police court — more than four a week. . . .

The root cause of domestic violence, then as now, was that abusive men wanted to dominate their wives and used violence to do so. However, to put domestic violence into historical perspective requires an examination of the specific triggers for violence in a particular era. When did husbands believe their authority was being undermined, and what inspired wives to fight back and take violent spouses to court? . . . [M]id-nineteenth-century working-class couples fought over money, drink, and authority. In late eighteenth- and early nineteenth-century Glasgow and London, conflict between plebeian husbands and wives erupted over many of the same issues, but the contradictions between patriarchal ideals, the realities of the family economy, and the pull of plebeian sociability were particular to this earlier plebeian culture.

Wife-beating was not a deviant act caused by unusual pressures of poverty and unemployment, for wife-beaters could be found in all levels of plebeian society. In Old Bailey[15] sessions trials for murders and attempted murders of wives between 1780 and 1845, clerks, tradesmen, and small shopkeepers accounted for 19 percent of the 177 cases in which occupations were known. Laborers accounted for 40 percent of the cases, but their percentage of the London work force is difficult to establish. Skilled working men accounted for 41 percent of these cases in London, and this percentage approximately matches their proportion of the population of London. Only three weavers appeared, although they were the group hardest hit by unemployment. Five carpenters and four tailors were tried, a number roughly proportional to their numbers in the population, but shoemakers were overrepresented at fourteen cases, the largest single occupational group of wife-beaters. In Glasgow, they represented 6.2 percent (16 cases) of the police court domestic-violence cases, although they made up only 2.9 percent of

---

[15] Criminal court in London.

the occupied population. The discrepancy was less marked in Lancashire, where they composed 3.6 percent (7 cases) of the wife-beaters and 2.7 percent of the occupied population. In both Glasgow and Lancashire, artisans in traditional apprenticed trades were strikingly overrepresented as wife-beaters. . . .

As in London, textile workers, especially handloom weavers, accounted for many fewer of these cases than would be expected from their representation in the population. Some textile workers did beat their wives, to be sure, but it is again possible that the sexually cooperative culture of the textile industry diminished the incidence of such violence. When husbands needed their wives' skill at weaving or spinning, domestic violence could be seen to disrupt a profitable household economy. Conversely, artisans' domestic violence may have stemmed from tensions between loyalty to the family and loyalty to the hard-drinking world of journeymen's bachelor culture.

For families in all trades, the dual responsibilities of husbands and wives in the family economy could lead to productive partnerships — or to quarrels over the amount of work each performed and the allocation of resources. Proletarianization could increase these tensions, for both partners often brought in wages, but until later in the nineteenth century, when husbands often gave their wives a set amount for housekeeping, there was no clear pattern for which spouse controlled the family budget. Plebeians knew very well that husbands legally controlled their wives' earnings, but in practice women did not surrender their wages readily. The social investigator Sir Frederick Eden[16] commented in the 1790s that the legal right of husbands to claim their wives' wages deterred many industrious women from earning money, "from a thorough conviction that her mate would, too probably, strip her of every farthing which she had not the ingenuity to conceal." Hannah More[17] painted a vivid picture of a woman whose gambling husband took the pittance she earned: "She bore with patience her husband's spending all he got upon his own pleasures, and leaving her to shift for herself; but when he came home, and tore from her what she had worked so hard for, she could not help weeping and complaining."

Popular literature and witnesses in trials echoed the concerns of social investigators. From a husband's point of view, a comic broadside mandated in a mock statute that "every Washerwoman, or any Women going out to daily work, shall keep one half of her earnings, and the other shall be given to her Lord and Master, for drinking money." When "Watty" of Alexander Wilson's famous poem finally gains dominance over his wife, he makes her promise

> That ye'll ne'er, like Bessy Miller,
> Kick my shins or rug my hair,
> Lastly, I'm to keep the siller [silver];
> This upon your soul you swear?

---

[16] Political economist and social critic (1766–1809).

[17] Writer of religious tracts for the working classes (1745–1833).

Court records reveal real-life examples. When Daniel Heath set up his wife in a milk walk,[18] he allowed her the silver she earned but kept the gold for himself. Catherine Rolph complained that her husband, a shopkeeper, not only beat her but forced her to give him the money she had earned selling stock neckties.

Women whose small savings or skills gave them independence could be exploited by irresponsible husbands. When Margaret Evans left her husband Daniel Heath on account of his ill treatment, he allowed her only eight shillings a week, although, as we have seen, he had been taking the gold she earned in her milk walk. Similarly, Benjamin Blake had his new wife mind the coal shed he bought with her savings; meanwhile, he told her he worked as a carpenter, but in fact he was spending her earnings on another woman. Although Sarah Purryer and her common-law husband made and sold mats together, he beat her as well as refused to give her money to feed the children. Finally, one night after he had gotten drunk and thrown her down the stairs, she killed him with a mallet-blow to the head. Three years after she had served two months in Newgate for manslaughter, she had established herself in partnership, rather than common-law marriage, with William Umney, a Spitalfields matmaker, and was earning enough to keep a servant.

For women who had their own craft skills, small businesses, or inheritances, marriage could be disadvantageous, but at the same time their experience of public life may have given them the courage to protest against abusive husbands. The wife of John McDonach voiced a common complaint when she told the Glasgow police court in 1829 that she had to support him and the children since he refused to work, and all she had received in return were two black eyes. She assured the justices, "I am willing still to do so," to support the family, but she added, "I think if he does not contribute, he should be bound, at least, to keep the peace." The magistrate sympathized with her but feared that any fine would merely come out of her pocket; all he did, therefore, was to admonish the man, who "went away unconcerned."

Some women went to court because they resented loss of property and independence as well as their husbands' violence. Elizabeth Sims asked a magistrate for a separation because "in the absence of her husband, which frequently happened for some considerable time, she did very well, and got forward, but whenever he returned, he beat her, spent her money, and threatened her life." Similarly, Ann Casson deposed that "prior to her intermarriage . . . she kept a grocer's shop in Edgeware Road and was doing very well when she unfortunately became acquainted with and met her said husband who had little or no property at all." Phoebe Darwell, who kept a tobacconist's shop before she married, lamented, "I had respectability and some money, when I married him; but he has blasted my character, and he has done me every public and private injury." The wife of a dyer from Hume, near Salford, prayed the court to grant her an article of the peace

---

[18] A milk delivery route.

against her husband, who not only led an "idle and dissolute life" but beat her and forced her to spend her small inheritance from an uncle on his support. For such women, husbands represented more of a liability than an asset.

But most plebeian wives, working at charring,[19] washing, or hawking, were paid wages so low that their work could not serve as an avenue to independence. For them, work was only a bitter necessity, especially when a drunken husband contributed little to the family income. "The Drunkard's Wife" complained,

> *I am forc'd to get up in the morn,*
> *And labor and toil the whole day,*
> *Then at night I have supper to get,*
> *And the bairns to get out of the way,*
> *My husband to fetch from the alehouse*
> *And to put him to bed when I go* [sic]
> *A woman can ne'er be at rest,*
> *When once she is joined to a man.*

In a real-life version of this story, a man named Devon was arrested on suspicion of cutting the throat of his wife, "a sober and industrious woman, [who] dealt in fish, but had the misfortune to live very uncomfortably with her husband." Some wives had to trade support for violence. A laborer defended himself against a charge of wife-beating by claiming that "he was a well-doing man," for in the last week he had earned five shillings and had given four of them to his wife. . . .

Alcohol, of course, loosens inhibitions and aggravates any inclination toward violence. Forty percent of the domestic violence cases in the Old Bailey sessions involved drinking by the husband, the wife, or both. The percentage was even higher in Glasgow, where the availability of cheap whisky aggravated the problem. In the Gorbals police courts, 63 percent of the domestic violence cases in 1835–1836 involved a charge of drunk and disorderly. Twenty-six percent of the male assailants in the Old Bailey sessions cases were drunk at the time they committed the assault, as were 30 percent of the women. Fifteen percent of the men and 13 percent of the female assailants used their victims' drunkenness as an excuse. Men claimed that their wives were drunkards in order to excuse violence against them, and there were cases of apparently alcoholic women who assaulted their husbands and pawned all their possessions. This problem, too, seems to have been particularly acute in Scotland, where whisky could quickly intoxicate a small woman. If a man drank, his wife might still be able to hold the household together, but if the wife was an alcoholic as well the family was doomed. Working people and social reformers alike tended to see women's drinking as pathological while viewing men's as a normal, if unfortunate, part of plebeian culture. . . .

Drinking crystallized larger issues of competition over access to plebeian sociability and over control of resources. J. P. Malcolm observed of eighteenth-

---

[19] Housecleaning.

century journeymen and laborers that "their domestic amusements chiefly consist in disputes with a Wife, who finds herself and children sacrificed to the brutal propensities of Drinking and Idleness; and the scene of contention is intolerable, if the lady possesses a high spirit; so entirely so [to] the husband, that he fixes himself for the evening with a party at the public house." Both men and women participated in the free and easy world of libertine plebeian culture, but wives often found their highest priority was to feed the children, while artisan husbands retained their primary allegiance to the homosocial world of workshop and pub. The wife fetching her husband home from the alehouse was the subject of two of the most popular tales about marriage, "Watty and Meg" and "A New and Diverting Dialogue Between a Shoemaker and His Wife." Husbands resented what they perceived to be their wives' "nagging" about their main pleasure in life — drinking with their mates. Archibald M'Lean beat his wife with a poker when she asked him where he had spent the evening.

In turn, women resented the enjoyment their husbands found at pubs and clubs while they starved at home. Another wife defended herself against a charge of stabbing her husband, a butcher, by declaring that he beat her and "kept herself and family without decent clothes, while he went out to the play, dressed like a gentleman, smoking cigars, and stopping out most nights of the week." One printer's wife actually prosecuted a publican for keeping his tavern open too long, because her husband "spent all his earnings at the defendant's house and only brought her three farthings last Sunday." Women resented the freedom and conviviality men found in their pubs and clubs. One woman became so enraged when her husband forbade her to smoke at home although he was enjoying a pint and a pipe at his club, that she disguised herself in his coalheaver's work clothes and went to his pub. There, after imbibing a bit too much porter and tobacco, "with great volubility [she] commenced a discourse on the rights of women." The coalheavers who surrounded her, realizing she was a woman come to spy on them, hauled her to a police court, where her husband declared that "he'd larn her to vear [sic] his breeches again." . . .

The insecurity of marriage may have intensified jealousy, for 20 percent of the protagonists and witnesses in Old Bailey trials cited this emotion as a motive for violence. As the Poor Law records and bigamy trials reveal, men often deserted their wives for other women, and it was by no means uncommon for women to desert their husbands as well. Since common-law marriages were acceptable, at least in the "libertine" sections of plebeian culture, both men and women could readily seek more suitable partners if they were discontented with their first union. For instance, the wife of William King, a working ship's carpenter, left him after his drinking had "reduced his family to indigence," and she went to live with a prosperous hatter at Wapping, who established her in a snug little cottage. Jane Rogers endured the violence of John Dennet, the greengrocer she lived with, for eight years, but finally left him to marry a gardener. Although Dennet drank their health at the wedding, he eventually murdered her. . . .

The infidelity of husbands had serious economic consequences for wives, although it was much more difficult for them than for men to draw on the power of the law or popular justice to gain redress. Mary Taylor, for instance, accused her husband of treating her with "inhumanity" by spending all his money on "naughty women" and depriving her of the "necessities of life." The magistrate allowed her a separation and ordered John Taylor to pay her 3 shillings[20] a week, which was certainly not enough for subsistence. Husbands who patronized prostitutes could contract venereal disease and then transmit the disease to their wives. Thomas Dickers, for instance, "a wild debauched profligate," consorted with prostitutes and infected his wife with "the clap." Amelia Brazier fled her husband's syphilitic embraces and charged him before a magistrate with assault, but he told the judge that "he would beat and pox his wife whenever he thought proper."

British society viewed a wife's infidelity much more seriously than it did her husband's adultery. *Conjugal Infidelity,* a popular pamphlet, warned wives with the sad tale of Maria Stent, the unfaithful wife of a butcher who stabbed her in revenge. It painted a pathetic picture of the bleeding wife proclaiming, "You, my dear Henry, were the best of husbands, the most indulgent of men. I was very wicked; O may my fate prove a salutary warning to all bad wives." A husband who claimed that his wife had been unfaithful could sometimes escape punishment for beating her. In 1804 Francis Morris was found guilty of assaulting his wife, "but it appeared the Lady was not quite so pure as she held herself out to be, he was only sentenced to pay one shilling and be discharged.". . .

Neighbors sometimes assisted abused wives, but only if they screamed particularly loudly or the violence was unusually severe. The neighbors of William Carter, a shopkeeper, insisted that he be tried for murdering his long-suffering wife, whom they had found drowned in a water tub. Men sometimes tried to prevent husbands from assaulting wives, but it was much more likely that female neighbors would interfere. When John Simpson, a Shoreditch hairdresser, was tried for the murder of his wife, Eleanor Evans testified that she had told Mrs. Simpson to leave her husband and come live with her. Elizabeth Ernby warned Abraham Winter to stop abusing his common-law wife, Mary Ann Stone, telling him, "Do not use the woman so ill, for I know to my certain knowledge that she has been a wife to you, and a mother to your children." Unfortunately, he continued beating Mary Ann, and she finally defended herself by stabbing him. When John Ruddle beat his wife for telling him to get his own dinner, a female neighbor heard the commotion and alarmed Ann Baker, whose husband worked with Ruddle. She scolded him, "I am surprized at you, Ruddle, to get ill-using of your wife." Rebecca Bishop, their landlady, also heard the quarrel. She testified, "I asked him, why he made such a noise and such a piece of work in my house for; I asked him whether or no he was not ashamed to use a poor woman so ill?" He retorted that it was none of her business and threatened her. However, neighbors, whether male or female, did not always interfere in domestic matters, and their help could not always prevent domestic homicide. Instead of rescuing Mrs. Rud-

---

[20] A former unit of British currency; one-twentieth of a pound.

dle, Mrs. Bishop went back to her own room because she feared for the safety of her infant, and Ruddle proceeded to murder his wife. In another trial, Eleanor Burke failed to respond to cries for help from the wife of Edward Welch, a porter who had told Eleanor he would murder his wife, because "there were often such cries; I thought he was beating her, or pulling her hair." Similarly, Sarah Paskin heard Mary Stark cry out, but, as she testified, "it was nothing new to me, as I heard them cry out very often, I continued at my work." In one Scottish case, the plebeian neighbors of Charles Donaldson often heard him beat his wife, but said, "We paid no particular attention to his doing so, as it was his daily practice.". . .

One of the fault-lines of plebeian culture ran between husbands and wives and fissured the larger community as well. Whether expressed in physical or verbal violence, the contradiction between patriarchal ideals and the reality of the family economy resulted in a struggle for power, resources, and freedom within the family — the struggle for the breeches. Of course, husbands and wives had always struggled over these issues, if the popularity of this theme in songs is any indication, but new sources of tension arose in the late eighteenth and early nineteenth centuries. For all urban plebeians, the libertine pleasures of metropolitan life proved both tempting and perilous. Husbands and wives quarreled over who would spend money at the pub, and the increasing flexibility of plebeian morals could spark flares of jealousy and fears of abandonment. Artisans seemed particularly prone to wife-beating, a phenomenon that may have resulted from the clash between bachelor journeymen's culture and the needs of married life. Textile workers may have worked out more harmonious marriages based on partnership, but neither popular culture nor religion matched practice with an ethic of marital equality.

MAKING CONNECTIONS:
WOMEN AND THE FAMILY

1. Jacques Gélis, in "The Experience of Pregnancy," approaches the history of women and the family through the story of French mothers worried about the tribulations and dangers of the birthing process. In doing so, he discusses the attitudes of husbands toward their wives during pregnancy and thus uncovers the nature of seventeenth-century marriage. Anna Clark writes of wives who achieved a degree of independence that wage-earning could bring in industrializing Britain during the late-eighteenth and early-nineteenth centuries. Compare the marriages, approximately one century apart, that Gélis and Clark describe. Some historians believe that affection and sentiment began to bind wives and husbands more frequently in the eighteenth and nineteenth centuries and so began to replace the loveless marriage that was common in medieval and early modern Europe. Is love evident in the plebeian marriages that Clark evaluates? If so, where and in what circumstances? If not, does this lessen the effect of industrialization on the family, using English working-class marriages as evidence?

2. What circumstances and situations did working-class wives and husbands face that led them — unlike aristocratic or wealthy bourgeois spouses — to wage a "battle for the breeches"? Is there evidence of any battle for the breeches in the marriages Gélis depicts? Explain.

FACTORY DISCIPLINE
IN THE INDUSTRIAL REVOLUTION
Sidney Pollard

The nature of work and leisure time changed dramatically with the Industrial Revolution. Previously, workers could proceed at their own pace, deciding when to rest or to cease their labors for the day. After all, who would care if a woman at a loom in her own home suddenly decided to take a fifteen-minute break? Basing his research on investigative reports of parliamentary committees and royal commissions as well as on memoirs, correspondence, and business records, the English business and economic historian Sidney Pollard shows that early factory owners consciously tried to change the more relaxed work habits of preindustrial England in order to maximize productivity and profits. In the process, they aimed at nothing less than the reformation of the workers' morals and character.

What exactly was the new factory discipline, and how did it operate? The need to alter the employees' concept of work stemmed from the factories' machinery. In what ways did machinery make it imperative for workers to conform to factory discipline and to the concept of "time-thrift"?

It was not enough for the owners to demand factory discipline; they also had to force or cajole their workers to relinquish centuries-old patterns of behavior. The owners used three methods: the carrot, the stick, and "the attempt to create a new ethos of work order and obedience." How did each of these methods work, and how effective were they? Surely some of the problems of factory-operative behavior — problems from the owners' point of view, that is — still persist today. Child workers presented a special problem for the owners. Notice what methods helped ensure that the very young would become accustomed to factory discipline.

Pollard claims that the carrot, a method favored by enlightened factory owners, was successful but was not copied very much. What did the owners think of the workers' character, and why did the owners try to prohibit swearing and indecent language? Did they usually treat their workers with respect, or did they view them as mere cogs in the wheels of production?

Sidney Pollard, "Factory Discipline in the Industrial Revolution," *Economic History Review* 16 (December 1963): 254–271.

It is nowadays increasingly coming to be accepted that one of the most critical, and one of the most difficult, transformations required in an industrializing society is the adjustment of labour to the regularity and discipline of factory work. . . . [T]he first generation of factory workers will be examined, irrespective of its appearance at different times in different industries.

The worker who left the background of his domestic workshop or peasant holding for the factory, entered a new culture as well as a new sense of direction. It was not only that "the new economic order needed . . . part-humans: soulless, depersonalised, disembodied, who could become members, or little wheels rather, of a complex mechanism." It was also that men who were non-accumulative, non-acquisitive, accustomed to work for subsistence, not for maximization of income, had to be made obedient to the cash stimulus, and obedient in such a way as to react precisely to the stimuli provided.

The very recruitment to the uncongenial work was difficult, and it was made worse by the deliberate or accidental modelling of many works on workhouses and prisons, a fact well known to the working population. Even if they began work, there was no guarantee that the new hands would stay. "Labourers from agriculture or domestic industry do not at first take kindly to the monotony of factory life; and the pioneering employer not infrequently finds his most serious obstacle in the problem of building up a stable supply of efficient and willing labour." Many workers were "transient, marginal and deviant," or were described as "volatile." It was noted that there were few early manufactures in the seaport towns, as the population was too unsteady. . . . Thus it was not necessarily the better labourer, but the stable one who was worth the most to the manufacturer: often, indeed, the skilled apprenticed man was at a discount, because of the working habits acquired before entering a factory. . . .

. . . [I]n Scotland even the children found the discipline irksome: when the Catrine cotton mills were opened, one of the managers admitted, "the children were all newcomers, and were very much beat at first before they could be taught their business." At other mills, "on the first introduction of the business, the people were found very ill-disposed to submit to the long confinement and regular industry that is required from them." The highlander, it was said, "never sits at ease at a loom; it is like putting a deer in the plough."

In turn, the personal inclinations and group *mores* of such old-established industrial workers as handloom weavers and framework knitters were opposed to factory discipline. "I found the utmost distaste," one hosier reported, "on the part of the men, to any regular hours or regular habits. . . . The men themselves were considerably dissatisfied, because they could not go in and out as they pleased, and have what holidays they pleased, and go on just as they had been used to do. . . ."

As a result of this attitude, attendance was irregular, and the complaint of Edward Cave,[1] in the very earliest days of industrialization, was later re-echoed by

---

[1] Printer (1691–1754).

many others: "I have not half my people come to work to-day, and I have no great fascination in the prospect I have to put myself in the power of such people." Cotton spinners would stay away without notice and send for their wages at the end of the week, and one of the most enlightened firms, McConnel and Kennedy, regularly replaced spinners who had not turned up within two or three hours of starting time on Mondays, on the reasonable presumption that they had left the firm: their average labour turnover was 20 a week, i.e. about 100 per cent a year.

Matters were worse in a place like Dowlais, reputed to employ many runaways and criminals, or among northern mining companies which could not guarantee continuous work: "the major part of these two companies are as bad fellows as the worst of your pitmen baring their outside is not so black," one exasperated manager complained, after they had left the district without paying their debts. Elsewhere, ironworks labourers, copper and tin miners and engineering labourers deserted to bring in the harvest, or might return to agriculture for good if work was slack.

"St. Monday" and feast days, common traditions in domestic industry, were persistent problems. The weavers were used to "play frequently all day on Monday, and the greater part of Tuesday, and work very late on Thursday night, and frequently all night on Friday." Spinners, even as late as 1800, would be missing from the factories on Mondays and Tuesdays, and "when they did return, they would sometimes work desperately, night and day, to clear off their tavern score, and get more money to spend in dissipation," as a hostile critic observed. In South Wales it was estimated as late as the 1840's that the workers lost one week in five, and that in the fortnight after the monthly pay day, only two-thirds of the time was being worked.

As for the regular feasts, "our men will go to the Wakes," Josiah Wedgwood[2] complained in 1772, "if they were sure to go to the D — l the next. I have not spared them in threats and I would have thrash'd them right heartily if I could." . . .

Employers themselves, groping their way towards a new impersonal discipline, looked backwards sporadically to make use of feasts and holidays, typical of the old order in cementing personal relationships and breaking the monotony of the working year. . . . The Arkwrights and the Strutts, standing on the watershed between the old and the new, had feasts in Cromford in 1776, when 500 workers and their children took part, and annual balls at Cromford and Belper as late as 1781, whilst in 1772 the Hockley factory had an outing, led by the "head workman" clad in white cotton, to gather nuts, and be regaled to a plentiful supper afterwards.

Other examples from industries in their early transitional stages include Matthew Boulton's[3] feast for 700 when his son came of age, Wedgwood's feast for 120 when he moved into Etruria, . . . and the repast provided by the Herculaneum

---

[2] Owner of a pottery factory (1730–1795).

[3] Inventor (1728–1809), along with James Watt, of an efficient steam engine.

Pottery at the opening of its Liverpool warehouse in 1813. Conversely, the Amlwch miners organized an ox-roast in honour of the chief proprietor, the Marquis of Anglesea, when he passed through the island on his way to take up the Lord-Lieutenancy of Ireland. 600 workmen sat down to a roasted ox and plenty of liquor at the Duke of Bridgewater's expense to celebrate the opening of the canal at Runcorn, and feasts were usual thereafter at the opening of canals and railways, but within a generation it was the shareholders that were being feasted, not the workers, whose relationship with the employers had by then taken on an entirely different character.

Once at work it was necessary to break down the impulses of the workers, to introduce the notion of "time-thrift." The factory meant economy of time and . . . "enforced asceticism." Bad timekeeping was punished by severe fines, and it was common in mills such as Oldknow's or Braids' to lock the gates of the factory, even of the workrooms, excluding those who were only a minute or two late. "Whatever else the domestic system[4] was, however intermittent and sweated its labour, it did allow a man a degree of personal liberty to indulge himself, a command over his time, which he was not to enjoy again."

By contrast, in the factories, Arkwright,[5] for example, had the greatest difficulty "in training human beings to renounce their desultory habits of work, and identify themselves with the unvarying regularity of the complex automaton." He "had to train his workpeople to a precision and assiduity altogether unknown before, against which their listless and restive habits rose in continued rebellion," and it was his great achievement "to devise and administer a successful code of factory diligence." "Impatient of the slovenly habits of workpeople, he urged on their labours with a precision and vigilance unknown before." The reasons for the difference were clear to manufacturers: "When a mantua[6] maker chooses to rise from her seat and take the fresh air, her seam goes a little back, that is all; there are no other hands waiting on her," but "in cotton mills all the machinery is going on, which they must attend to." It was "machinery [which] ultimately forced the worker to accept the discipline of the factory."

Regular hours and application had to be combined with a new kind of order in the works. Wedgwood, for example, had to fight the old pottery traditions when introducing "the punctuality, the constant attendance, the fixed hours, the scrupulous standards of care and cleanliness, the avoidance of waste, the ban on drinking." . . .

Finally, "Discipline . . . was to produce the goods on time. It was also to prevent the workmen from stealing raw materials, putting in shoddy, or otherwise

---

[4] Also known as the putting-out system, whereby a merchant provided raw materials to workers, who then worked in their own homes.

[5] Richard Arkwright (1732–1792), inventor of the water-frame, a spinning machine that led to the creation of large cotton mills.

[6] A woman's loose gown.

getting the better of their employers." It allowed the employer to maintain a high quality of output. . . .

Works Rules, formalized, impersonal and occasionally printed, were symbolic of the new industrial relationships. Many rules dealt with disciplinary matters only, but quite a few laid down the organization of the firm itself. "So strict are the instructions," it was said of John Marshall's[7] flax mills in 1821, "that if an overseer of a room be found talking to any person in the mill during working hours he is dismissed immediately — two or more overseers are employed in each room, if one be found a yard out of his ground he is discharged . . . everyone, manager, overseers, mechanics, oilers, spreaders, spinners and reelers, have their particular duty pointed out to them, and if they transgress, they are instantly turned off as unfit for their situation."

While the domestic system had implied some measure of control, "it was . . . an essentially new thing for the capitalist to be a disciplinarian." "The capitalist employer became a supervisor of every detail of the work: without any change in the general character of the wage contract, the employer acquired new powers which were of great social significance." The concept of industrial discipline was new, and called for as much innovation as the technical inventions of the age.

Child work immeasurably increased the complexities of the problem. It had, as such, been common enough before, but the earlier work pattern had been based on the direct control of children and youths, in small numbers, by their parents or guardians. The new mass employment removed the incentive of learning a craft, alienated the children by its monotony and did this just at the moment when it undermined the authority of the family, and of the father in particular. It thus had to rely often on the unhappy method of indirect employment by untrained people whose incentive for driving the children was their own piece-rate payment.

In the predominantly youthful population of the time, the proportion of young workers was high. In the Cumberland mines, for example, children started work at the ages of five to seven, and as late as 1842, 200–250 of the 1,300–1,400 workers in the Lonsdale mines were under eighteen. At Alloa collieries,[8] 103 boys and girls of under seven were employed in 1780. In the light metal trades, the proportion was higher still. Josiah Wedgwood . . . had 30 per cent of his employees under eighteen, 3.3 per cent under ten years of age. The greatest problems, however, were encountered in the textile mills.

The silk mills were dependent almost exclusively on child labour, and there the children started particularly young, at the ages of six or seven, compared with nine or ten in the cotton mills. Typically from two-thirds to three-quarters of the hands were under eighteen but in some large mills, the proportion was much higher: at Tootal's for example, 78 per cent of the workers were under sixteen. Adults were thus in a small minority.

---

[7] Textile magnate.

[8] Coal mines, with associated buildings and equipment.

In the cotton industry the proportion of children and adolescents under eighteen was around 40–45 per cent. In some large firms the proportions were higher: thus Horrocks, Miller and Co. in 1816 had 13 per cent of their labour force under ten years of age, and 60 per cent between ten and eighteen, a total of 73 per cent. The proportion of children under ten was mostly much smaller than this, but in water mills employing large numbers of apprentices it might be greater: New Lanark, under David Dale in 1793, had 18 per cent of its labour force nine years old or younger.

In the flax and the woollen and worsted industries, the proportions of workers under eighteen were rather higher than in cotton, being around 50 per cent. Again individual large works show much higher figures. In John Marshall's Water Lane Mill in 1831, for example, 49.2 per cent were under fifteen, and 83.8 per cent altogether under twenty-one. Further, in all the textile branches the children were largely concentrated in certain sections, such as silk throwing and cotton spinning. In such departments, the difficulties of maintaining discipline were greatest.

These, then, were the problems of factory discipline facing the entrepreneurs in the early years of industrialization. Their methods of overcoming them may be grouped under three headings: the proverbial stick, the proverbial carrot, and, thirdly, the attempt to create a new ethos of work order and obedience.

Little new in the way of the "stick," or deterrent, was discovered by the early factory masters. Unsatisfactory work was punished by corporal punishment, by fines or by dismissal. Beatings clearly belonged to the older, personal relationships and were common with apprentices, against whom few other sanctions were possible, but they survived because of the large-scale employment of children. Since the beating of children became one of the main complaints against factory owners and a major point at issue before the various Factory Commissions,[9] the large amount of evidence available is not entirely trustworthy, but the picture is fairly clear in outline.

Some prominent factory owners . . . prohibited it outright, though the odd cuff for inattention was probably inevitable in any children's employment. More serious beatings were neither very widespread, nor very effective. . . . [L]arge employers frowned on beatings, though they might turn a blind eye on the overlookers' actions. "We beat only the lesser, up to thirteen or fourteen . . . we use a strap," stated Samuel Miller, manager of Wilson's mill in Nottingham, one of the few to admit to this to the Factory Commission, "I prefer fining to beating, if it answers . . . (but) fining does not answer. It does not keep the boys at their work." The most honest evidence, however, and the most significant, came from John Bolling, a cotton master. He could not stop his spinners beating the children, he stated, "for children require correction now and then, and the difficulty is to keep it from being excessive. . . . It never can be in the interest of the master that the children should be beaten. The other day there were three children run away; the

---

[9] Royal commissions established to investigate working conditions.

mother of one of them brought him back and asked us to beat him; that I could not permit; she asked us to take him again: at last I consented, and then she beat him."

Dismissal and the threat of dismissal, were in fact the main deterrent instruments of enforcing discipline in the factories. At times of labour shortage they were ineffective, but when a buyers' market in labour returned, a sigh of relief went through the ranks of the employers at the restoration of their power. Many abolished the apprenticeship system in order to gain it, and without it others were unable to keep any control whatsoever. Where there were no competing mill employers, as at Shrewsbury in the case of Marshall and Benyon's flax mills, it was a most effective threat.

In industries where skill and experience were at a premium, however, dismissals were resorted to only most reluctantly. . . .

Fines formed the third type of sanctions used, and were common both in industries employing skilled men, and in those employing mostly women and children. They figure prominently in all the sets of rules surviving, and appear to have been the most usual reaction to minor transgressions. Where the employer pocketed the fine there was an additional inducement to levy it freely, and in some cases, as in the deductions and penalties for sending small coal or stones up in the corves from the coal face, these became a major source of abuse and grievance.

Their general level was high and was meant to hurt. Typically, they were levied at 6d.[10] to 2s.[11] for ordinary offences or, say, two hours' to a day's wages. Wedgwood fined 2s. 6d. for throwing things or for leaving fires burning overnight, and that was also the penalty for being absent on Monday mornings in the Worsley mines. At Fernley's Stockport mill, swearing, singing or being drunk were punished by a fine of 5s. and so was stealing coal at Merthyr. Miners were fined even more heavily: average weekly deductions were alleged to be as high as 1s. or 2s. out of a wage of 13s.

Deterrence as a method of industrial discipline should, strictly, also include the actions taken against workers' organizations. . . . The law could usually be assumed to be at the service of the employer, and was called into service for two types of offence, breaches of contract and trade-union organization and rioting. Workmen's combinations were widely treated as criminal offences in employers' circles, even before the law made them explicitly such, and in turn, the legal disabilities turned trade disputes easily towards violence, particularly before the 1790's. In the Scottish mines, serfdom was only just being eradicated, and in the North-East the one-year contract, coupled with the character note, could be used also to impose conditions akin to serfdom; opposition, including the inevitable rioting, was met by transportation and the death penalty not only in the mines, but even in such advanced centres as Etruria as late as 1783.

---

[10] The abbreviation for *penny*.

[11] The abbreviation for *shilling*.

Where their powers permitted, employers met organization with immediate dismissal: "any hands forming conspiracies or unlawful combinations will be discharged without notice" read one rule as late as 1833. More widespread, however, was the use of blacklists against those who had aroused the employer's disfavour. Little was heard of them, even in contemporary complaints by workmen, but their importance should not be underrated: . . . it is increasingly obvious that they were a most important prop of that reign of terror which in so many works did duty for factory discipline.

By comparison with these commonly used examples of the "stick," more subtle or more finely graded deterrents were so rare as to be curious rather than significant. John Wood, the Bradford spinner, made the child guilty of a fault hold up a card with his offence written on it; for more serious offences, this punishment was increased to walking up and down with the card, then to having to tell everyone in the room, and, as the highest stage, confessing to workers in other rooms. Witts and Rodick, the Essex silk-mill owners, made their errant children wear degrading dress. These measures presuppose a general agreement with the factory code on the part of the other workmen which today few would take for granted. . . .

Employers were as conservative in the use of the carrot as they were in the use of the stick. For a generation driving its children to labour in the mills for twelve to fourteen hours a day, positive incentives must indeed have been hard to devise and, for the child workers at least, were used even less than for adults. Much better, as in the case of at least one flax mill, to give them snuff to keep them awake in the evenings. The extent of the predominance of the deterrent over the incentive in the case of the factory children is brought out in the returns of the 1833 Factory Commission, in replies to item 57 of the questionnaire sent out: "What are the means taken to enforce obedience on the part of the children employed in your works?" . . . Bearing in mind that most respondents were merely concerned to deny that they beat their children, and that many replied with the method they thought they ought to use, rather than the one actually in use, the following proportion may appear even more surprising:

Number of firms using different means to enforce obedience among factory children, 1833

Negative		Positive	
Dismissal	353	Kindness	2
Threat of dismissal	48	Promotion, or higher wages	9
Fines, deductions	101	Reward or premium	23
Corporal punishment	55		
Complaint to parents	13		
Confined to mill	2		
Degrading dress, badge	3		
Totals	575		34

The contrast is surely too strong to be fortuitous, especially since the bias was all the other way.

For adults, there were two positive methods which formed the stock-in-trade of management in this period. One was sub-contract, the transference of responsibility for making the workers industrious, to overseers, butty-men,[12] group leaders, first hands and sub-contractors of various types. But this solution, which raises, in any case, questions of its own, was not a method of creating factory discipline, but of evading it. The discipline was to be the older form of that of the supervisor of a small face-to-face group, maintained by someone who usually worked himself or was in direct daily contact with the workers.

The other method was some variant of payments by results. This provided the cash nexus symbolic for the new age. It was also a natural derivation from the methods used in earlier periods in such skilled and predominantly male trades as iron-smelting, mining, pottery or the production of metal goods. In 1833, of 67,819 cotton-mill workers in 225 mills, 47.1 per cent were on piece-work and 43.7 per cent were paid datally,[13] the method of payment for the remainder being unknown. Labourers, children and others under direct supervision of a skilled pieceworker, and some highly skilled trades in short supply, such as engineers and building craftsmen, did, however, remain on fixed datal pay.

In many enterprises the "discovery" of payment by results was greeted as an innovation of major significance, and at times the change-over does seem to have led to marked improvements in productivity. . . .

Many of the older systems of payment by results, as in copper or tin mines, or in sinking colliery shafts, consisted of group piece-work, in which the cohesion and ethos of the group was added to the incentive payment as such to create work discipline. The newly introduced systems, however, were typically aimed at individual effort. As such, they were less effective . . . and they were often badly constructed, particularly for times of rapid technological change. There were many examples of the usual problems of this type of payment, such as speed-up and rate cutting, as at Soho and Etruria, loss of quality, and friction over interpretation and deductions. Nevertheless, it represented the major change and forward step in the employer's attitude towards labour, not only because it used cash as such but more specifically because it marked the end of the belief that workers were looking for a fixed minimum income, and a rate of earnings beyond this would merely lead to absenteeism . . . and the beginning of the notion that the workers' efforts were elastic with respect to income over a wide range.

The rise in the belief in the efficacy of incentive piece payments coincided with a decline in the belief in the efficacy of long-term contracts. These contracts were largely a survival of the pre-industrial age, adopted by many employers even during the Industrial Revolution at times of acute shortages of labour. In the north-eastern coalfield, the one-year binding had become almost universal since

---

[12] Middlemen between proprietors of coal mines and workers.

[13] Daily.

the beginning of the eighteenth century and it had spread to salters, keelmen, file-workers and others. Ambrose Crowley[14] bound his men for six months, Arkwright for three months, . . . some potteries for seven years, some cotton mills for five up to twenty-one years and the Prestonpans chemical works for twenty-one years. But any hope that these indentures would ensure discipline and hard work was usually disappointed, and the system was quickly abandoned as a disciplinary method, though it might be continued for other reasons.

A few employers evolved incentive schemes with a considerable degree of sophistication. In their simplest form, overseers bribed children to work on for fourteen or fifteen hours and forgo their meal intervals, and John Wood[15] paid them a bonus of 1d. weekly if they worked well, but hung a notice of shame on them if they did not. At Backbarrow mill, apprentices received a "bounty" of 6d. or 1s., to be withdrawn if offences were committed, and in silk mills articles of clothing were given to the children as prizes for good work; at one silk mill, employing 300 children aged nine or less, a prize of bacon and three score of potatoes was given to the hardest working boy, and a doll to the hardest working girl, and their output then became the norm for the rest. Richard Arkwright, in his early years, also gave prizes to the best workers.

Later on, these bonuses were made conditional on a longer period of satisfactory work, or modified in other ways. In the early 1800's the Strutts introduced "quarterly gift money" — one-sixth of wages being held back over three months, and paid out at the end only after deductions for misconduct. At John Marshall's the best department received a bonus each quarter, amounting to £10 for the overlooker and a week's wage for the hands, and some Dowlais men, at least, also received a bonus of £2 every quarter, conditional upon satisfactory performance. At the Whitehaven collieries, the bonus to the foremen was annual and was tied to net profits: when these exceeded £30,000, the salary of the two viewers was nearly doubled, from £152 to £300, and those of the overmen raised in almost like proportion from a range of £52–82 to a range of £90–170 — a particularly effective and cheap means of inducing industry. In other coal mines, the ladder of promotion to overmen was used effectively as an incentive. . . .

Compared with the ubiquity of financial rewards, other direct incentives were rare and localized, though they were highly significant. Wedgwood at times appealed directly to his workers, in at least one case writing a pamphlet for them in which he stressed their common interests. . . . Arkwright gave distinguishing dresses to the best workers of both sexes and John Marshall fixed a card on each machine, showing its output. Best known of all were the "silent monitors" of Robert Owen.[16] He awarded four types of mark for the past day's work to each superintendent, and each of them, in turn, judged all his workers; the mark was

---

[14] Iron smelter who pioneered the large-scale importation of Swedish ores.

[15] A worsted manufacturer who began the movement for a ten-hour day.

[16] Industrialist and social reformer (1771–1858).

then translated into the colours black-blue-yellow-white, in ascending order of merit, painted on the four sides of a piece of wood mounted over the machine, and turned outward according to the worker's performance.

There is no doubt that Owen attached great importance to this system, entering all daily marks in a book as a permanent record, to be periodically inspected by him. There is equally no doubt that, naive as they might seem to-day, these methods were successful among all the leading manufacturers named, Robert Owen, in particular, running his mills, both in Manchester and in Scotland, at regular high annual profits largely because he gained the voluntary co-operation of his workers. Why, then, were these methods not copied as widely as the technological innovations?

The reasons may have been ignorance on the part of other masters, disbelief or a (partly justified) suspicion that the enlightened employers would have been successful with or without such methods, enjoying advantages of techniques, size or a well-established market; but to limit the reasons to these would be to ignore one of the most decisive social facts of the age. An approach like Owen's ran counter to the accepted beliefs and ideology of the employing class, which saw its own rise to wealth and power as due to merit, and the workman's subordinate position as due to his failings. He remained a workman, living at subsistence wages, because he was less well endowed with the essential qualities of industry, ambition, sobriety and thrift. As long as this was so, he could hardly be expected to rise to the baits of moral appeals or co-operation. Therefore, one would have to begin by indoctrinating him with the bourgeois values which he lacked, and this, essentially, was the third method used by employers.

In their attempts to prevent "Idleness, Extravagance, Waste and Immorality," employers were necessarily dealing with the workers both inside the factory and outside it. The efforts to reform the whole man were, therefore, particularly marked in factory towns and villages in which the total environment was under the control of a single employer.

The qualities of character which employers admired have, since Weber's[17] day, been to some extent associated with the Protestant ethic. To impart these qualities, with the one addition of obedience, to the working classes, could not but appear a formidable task. That it should have been attempted at all might seem to us incredible, unless we remember the background of the times which included the need to educate the first generation of factory workers to a new factory discipline, the widespread belief in human perfectibility, and the common assumption, by the employer, of functions which are today provided by the public authorities, like public safety, road building or education. . . . [O]ne of their consequences was the preoccupation with the character and morals of the working classes which are so marked a feature of the early stages of industrialization.

---

[17] Max Weber (1864–1920), German sociologist and author of *The Protestant Ethic and the Spirit of Capitalism.*

Some aspects of this are well known and easily understandable. Factory villages like New Lanark, Deanston, Busby, Ballindaloch, New Kilpatrick, Blantyre, and . . . Antrim, had special provisions, and in some cases full-time staff, to check the morals of their workers. Contemporaries tended to praise these actions most highly, and it was believed that firms laying stress on morals, and employing foremen who "suppress anything bad" would get the pick of the labour. Almost everywhere, churches, chapels and Sunday Schools were supported by employers, both to encourage moral education in its more usual sense, and to inculcate obedience. Drink and drunkenness became a major target of reform, with the short-term aim of increasing the usefulness of scarce skilled workers . . . who were often incapacitated by drink, and the long-term aim of spreading bourgeois virtues.

In this process much of the existing village culture came under attack. "Traditional social habits and customs seldom fitted into the new pattern of industrial life, and they had therefore to be discredited as hindrances to progress." Two campaigns here deserve special mention.

The first was the campaign against leisure on Saturdays and Sundays, as, no doubt, examples of immoral idleness. "The children are during the weekdays generally employed," the Bishop of Chester had declared solemnly in 1785, "and on Sunday are apt to be idle, mischievous and vitious." This was not easily tolerated. Thus Deanston had a Superintendent of streets to keep them clear of immorality, children and drink. Charles Wilkins of Tiverton formed an "Association for the Promotion of Order" in 1832 to round up the children and drive them to school on Sundays. All the hands at Strutt's and Arkwright's under twenty had to attend school for four hours on Saturday afternoons and on Sundays to "keep them out of mischief." Horrocks' employed a man "for many years, to see that the children do not loiter about the streets on Sundays." At Dowlais the chapel Sunday school teachers asked J.J. Guest in 1818 to order his employees to attend, otherwise there was the danger that they might spend the Sabbath "rambling and playing." Even Owen expressed similar sentiments: "if children [under ten] are not to be instructed, they had better be employed in any occupation that should keep them out of mischief," he asserted.

The second was the prohibition of bad language. At the beginning of the eighteenth century, Crowley's "Clerk for the Poor," or teacher, was to correct lying, swearing, "and suchlike horrid crimes"; while at the same time Sir Humphrey Mackworth, at Neath, fined "Swearing, Cursing, Quarrelling, being Drunk, or neglecting Divine Service on Sunday, one shilling," and the Quaker Lead Company, at Gadlis, also prohibited swearing in 1708. Later this became quite regular, wherever rules were made: at Darley Abbey, in 1795, the fine was 9d. or 1s.; at Mellor, 1s.; at Nenthead, 6d.; at Galloway's where "obscene and vulgar language" was prohibited, the men themselves levied the fines. At Marshall and Benyon's also, according to Rule 4 of 1785, a jury of seven was to judge the offence of striking, abusing or harming another workman.

Again, the rules of Thomas Fernley, Jr., Stockport, cotton mills, stated: "while at work . . . behaviour must be commendable avoiding all shouting, loud talk, whistling, calling foul names, all mean and vulgar language, and every kind of indecency." Swearing, singing, being drunk were fined 5s.; overlookers allowing drink in the mills were fined 10s. 6d. . . .

This preoccupation might seem to today's observer to be both impertinent and irrelevant to the worker's performance, but in fact it was critical, for unless the workmen *wished* to become "respectable" in the current sense, none of the other incentives would bite. Such opprobrious terms as "idle" or "dissolute" should be taken to mean strictly that the worker was indifferent to the employer's deterrents and incentives. According to contemporaries, "it was the irrationality of the poor, quite as much as their irreligion, that was distressing. They took no thought of the morrow. . . . The workers were by nature indolent, improvident, and self-indulgent."

The code of ethics on which employers concentrated was thus rather limited. Warnings against greed, selfishness, materialism or pride seldom played a large part, sexual morals rarely became an important issue to the factory disciplinarians (as distinct from outside moralists) and, by and large, they did not mind which God was worshipped, as long as the worshipper was under the influence of some respectable clergyman. The conclusion cannot be avoided that, with some honourable exceptions, the drive to raise the level of respectability and morality among the working classes was not undertaken for their own sakes but primarily, or even exclusively, as an aspect of building up a new factory discipline.

Any conclusions drawn from this brief survey must be tentative and hesitant, particularly if they are meant to apply to industrial revolutions in general.

First, the acclimatization of new workers to factory discipline is a task different in kind, at once more subtle and more violent, from that of maintaining discipline among a proletarian population of long standing. Employers in the British Industrial Revolution therefore used not only industrial means but a whole battery of extra-mural powers, including their control over the courts, their powers as landlords, and their own ideology, to impose the control they required.

Secondly, the maintenance of discipline, like the whole field of management itself, was not considered a fit subject for study, still less a science, but merely a matter of the employer's individual character and ability. No books were written on it before 1830, no teachers lectured on it, there were no entries about it in the technical encyclopaedias, no patents were taken out relating to it. As a result, employers did not learn from each other, except haphazardly and belatedly, new ideas did not have the cachet of a new technology and did not spread, and the crudest form of deterrents and incentives remained the rule. Robert Owen was exceptional in ensuring that his methods, at least, were widely known, but they were too closely meshed in with his social doctrines to be acceptable to other employers.

Lastly, the inevitable emphasis on reforming the moral character of the worker into a willing machine-minder led to a logical dilemma that contemporaries did not know how to escape. For if the employer had it in his power to reform the workers if he but tried hard enough, whose fault was it that most of them remained immoral, idle and rebellious? And if the workers could really be taught their employers' virtues, would they not all save and borrow and become entre-preneurs themselves, and who would then man the factories?

The Industrial Revolution happened too rapidly for these dilemmas, which involved the re-orientation of a whole class, to be solved, as it were, *en passant.*[18] The assimilation of the formerly independent worker to the needs of factory rou-tine took at least a further generation, and was accompanied by the help of tra-dition, by a sharply differentiated educational system, and new ideologies which were themselves the results of clashes of earlier systems of values, besides the forces operating before 1830. The search for a more scientific approach which would collaborate with and use, instead of seeking to destroy, the workers' own values, began later still, and may hardly be said to have advanced very far even today.

---

[18] Casually, in passing.

THE POTATO IN IRELAND
K. H. Connell

The Irish, unlike any other Western people, depended almost solely on the potato for a long time. Seldom has a single food, other than grain, so shaped a culture. K. H. Connell, a specialist in Irish economic and social history, sees the widespread use of the potato originating in the Irish landholding system and influencing, perhaps more than any other element, the fate of the Irish in the seventeenth, eighteenth, and nineteenth centuries. Connell bases his findings on census data, royal commissions, parliamentary committees, and reports of Poor Law inspectors.

Introduced to Europe from the New World in the sixteenth century, the potato became a staple crop in Ireland and, to a lesser extent, elsewhere in Europe. It is interesting that the potato's popularity had nothing to do with its taste or with the population's desire for that particular vegetable. The potato was the right food at the right time and situation. Connell blames the English for their rapacious presence in Ireland and for Ireland's dependence on a single crop. England's exploitation of the land and its people largely contributed to the great famine. To what extent, then, were the English responsible for Ireland's adoption of the potato and for the crop's failure? For Connell, the answers to these questions are fundamentally economic.

Nevertheless, the potato had certain qualities that other foodstuffs did not, attributes that convinced or compelled the Irish to grow it extensively and eat it nearly exclusively. Did the potato make the Irish a healthy people in comparison to the peasantry of western Europe?

Note how the potato affected population growth and the age of marriage in Ireland. Although the potato may have had beneficial effects, it proved to be a fragile prop to the millions of Irish in the nineteenth century. One wonders what the Irish could have done to ward off the disaster that took at least half a million lives.

How does Connell's discussion of the famine's causes differ from explanations contemporaries offered? Much of the populace returned to the potato after

K. H. Connell, "The Potato in Ireland," *Past and Present: A Journal of Historical Studies,* no. 23 (November 1962): 57–71.

the famine despite knowing that the potato might fail again. What finally motivated the Irish to vary their diet?

Connell begins this essay with landholding practices; he concludes by underlining the importance of land legislation in the late-nineteenth century. How did land acts affect the lives and foods of the peasantry?

According to Arthur Young,[1] writing in the 1770s, "The food of the common Irish [is] potatoes and milk." Many of the uncommon Irish of Ulster and parts of Leinster ate as much oaten bread or porridge as potatoes; they were familiar with the taste as well as the look of butter and eggs; and in good times they expected a daily meal with fish or bacon, even a weekly meal with meat. But for the greater part of the country, for a century before the Famine,[2] Young's generalization will serve: the great mass of the population had, in effect, a single solid foodstuff: stirabout, or an oatmeal loaf, was an occasional treat: weeks or months separated the red-letter occasions when meat was eaten: day after day, three times a day, people ate salted, boiled potatoes, probably washing them down with milk, flavouring them, if they were fortunate, with an onion or a bit of lard, with boiled seaweed or a scrap of salted fish.

No other western people, generation after generation, has starved or survived with the bounty of the potato: why did the Irish depend on it so long, and so nearly exclusively?

The tradition is that the first Irish potatoes were grown by Sir Walter Raleigh[3] in 1588: certainly, by the following decade, he or another had introduced this new crop and food. An agricultural community, isolated and backward, is likely to be conservative in both its farming and its eating. Nonetheless, when the potato reached Ireland the traditional foods were already being displaced — and by forces whose persistence made the potato almost inevitably their successor. Formerly, milk and its derivatives had bulked large in the Irish dietary. No other food may be as readily available to a nomadic, pastoral people; but a settled society, practising tillage, is likely to retain milk as its staple only while land is abundant. But land in the sixteenth century was made scarce by confiscation, the redistribution of population and the landlord's demands. Some alternative was needed to livestock produce, some foodstuff more economical of land. Traditionally, only grain had been available, and dairy produce had given way to oaten bread and porridge. But once the potato was known, not only milk, but grain also rapidly receded in the popular dietary. The potato, in much of the country, was a more rewarding crop than oats. An impoverished people, ill-provided with gra-

---

[1] Agriculturist and traveler (1741–1820).

[2] Of 1845–1849.

[3] English soldier and explorer (1554–1618).

naries, mills and ovens, welcomed a food that could be stored in earthen clamps and made edible simply by boiling. Troubled times, too, favoured the potato: it had a briefer growing season; it remained relatively safe underground while grain might be carried away, burned or trampled underfoot; and when people took to the hills with their cattle, potatoes they might grow, but hardly grain.

These, however, are incidental recommendations of the potato: essentially, it displaced the traditional foods because it provided a family's subsistence on a smaller area of land. Still, in the seventeenth century, the pressure on land was maintained by the dislocation of war; and later, in more tranquil times, by the growth of population: continuously, however, and most insistently, land was made scarce by the landlord's demands.

Irish property was rooted, much of it recently, in confiscation: sudden gains might be suddenly lost: principles of estate-management were sharpened, there-fore, by the owner's desire to get the most from his property while it remained his. The grantees, moreover, might be landlords already, attached to their English es-tates, administering them with feeling for their tenants as well as for their rents. The Irish, if they accepted the popular view, were a barbarous people, amongst whom it was foolhardy to live: certainly they were a people alien in language, loy-alty and religion. Little, therefore, induced a man with ties in England to settle on his Irish estate, to get to know his tenants and sympathize with their problems. More often, they were reduced simply to a source of rent, the landlord's refuge when creditors encroached on his English property or his thriftless living. But duty, as well as necessity, turned the screw. England, the mother-country, reckoned to profit by her colony: a landlord's leniency lightened his country's purse as well as his own. The Irish, moreover, were disaffected and lazy: they needed punish-ment and reform: a sharp rent was a blend of both, perhaps of more lasting ben-efit to the man who earned it than to the man who spent it.

The institutions of Irish landlordism were as predatory as the spirit. Land-agent, middleman and rack-renting:[4] many a head-landlord felt ill-served by this apparatus of exploitation — but rarely because it failed to impoverish his tenants. Few of them ever had the chance of getting a living in the Irish towns; emigration became a likely escape only in the nineteenth century: land, therefore, a man must have to feed his family — and for a foothold on land he offered an extrav-agant rent. Commonly, in the topsy-turvy Irish economy, the more onerous the rent, the less productive the farm, the landlord who exacted an elastic rent was no improver; and the tenant who paid it was neither inclined nor able to better his farming.

Spurred on, then, by the fear of eviction and the loss of his livelihood, the ten-ant struggled to increase his rent. But, with a stagnant technique of farming, to earn more rent meant earmarking a larger proportion of his land for rent crops — a smaller proportion, in consequence, for his family's subsistence. And the less

---

[4] The practice of charging excessive rent, nearly equal to the full value of the land.

land on which a family must grow its food, the more imperatively was the potato its staple — for on no other crop could it live more economically of land. Where landlord-tenant relationships were milder — as in Ulster — there might be supplements to the potato; where, incessantly, they were harsh, people lived, not simply on the most prolific crop, but on its most prolific varieties.

Now, if the elasticity of rent tended to make people live on the potato, it tended also to reduce them to the bare quantity that would keep them alive and working. But, in fact, until the two or three decades before the Famine, the potato was lavishly consumed: people retained more potato-land than their subsistence required. But we have not, I think, made too much of the landlord's exigence, too much of the expansiveness of rent-land. There were kind-hearted landlords; landlords restrained by leases, by the fear of violence, even by the realization that profits were related to a tenant's productivity as well as his promises. So bountiful, moreover, was the potato, that a couple of acres, even less, gave a family all it could use, and conveniently waste: a little more gave real abundance. Then there was much land, doubtfully capable of earning rent, but available for the people's subsistence: it might grow potatoes well enough, but so bulky a crop was hard to sell when most country families grew their own, and communications were poor. On the whole, too, potato harvests were good until towards the 1820s; and in the occasional bad year the pig, not his master, pulled in his belt.

Certainly until the 1820s the monotony of the Irishman's diet was usually offset by its abundance. There are scores of accounts from the late eighteenth and early nineteenth centuries of the quantity of potatoes people ate. A small farmer from co. Down told a royal commission in the 1830s that "a stone of potatoes is little enough for a man in a day, and he'd want something with it to work upon". . . . There is little doubt that, day in day out, except when the crop was poor, the adult Irishman ate some ten pounds of potatoes a day. If he ate nothing else and drank only water he was hardly disastrously undernourished: if, as commonly happened, he had a cupful of milk with each meal, to the biochemist, if not the gourmet, he was admirably nourished: he had some 4,000 calories a day, compared with the required 3,000; he had enough protein, calcium and iron; he had a sufficiency, or a superabundance, of the listed vitamins.

The Irish, then, burdened with predatory landlords, practised a primitive farming: food, clothing and shelter were about the extent of their material comfort; the potato was their food; they were clothed in rags; their hovels, not infrequently, they shared with their animals. But for all their wretchedness, they were admirably nourished — better, maybe, than the mass of the people of any other country during any recent century.

Now, for much of the time that they lived on the potato, the number of the Irish increased with astonishing vigour. The population of Ireland in 1780 was probably something over four million — much what it is today. But, sixty years later, on the eve of the Famine, the four million had doubled to eight million — and contributed nearly another two million to the population of Britain and North America. Probably in no other western country has so rapid a rate of natural increase been so long sustained. Was it fortuitous that an extraordinary dependence on the potato was accompanied by an extraordinary excess of births over deaths?

During the years of this coincidence, and drawing partly on Irish experience, Malthus[5] evolved a theory of population growth plausible enough to come rapidly into vogue: population, his contemporaries agreed, tends to increase more rapidly than the resources needed for its sustenance: unless births are checked, population is limited by premature death — the result of scarcity of food or some like calamity. Was it, then, simply the lifting of this traditional restraint that caused the population of Ireland to bound upwards towards the end of the eighteenth century; was it that a people, formerly ill-nourished, lived longer as they were plentifully fed on the potato?

We lack the statistics to answer this question with assurance. But the presumption is that the potato facilitated the growth of population less by reducing mortality than by increasing fertility — and helping then to forestall an off-setting increase in mortality. Acceptance of the potato tended, no doubt, to improve physique and lessen the incidence of deficiency disease. But, advancing piecemeal over more than a century, the potato in much of the country was all but fully accepted by the 1730s: it tended, that is, to reduce mortality too gradually and too early to be the direct cause of a sharp increase in population in the 1780s.

More probable, in the 1780s, than any reduction in mortality was an increase in fertility, the result of more-youthful marriage than had been customary. Today, the Irish marry later than any other people whose statistics are available. And latest of all to marry is the would-be farmer. He is expected to have "a hold of the land" before he thinks of marrying: a farm, that is, must be his or earmarked for him. Farms, however, are rarely divided; there is little reclamation: typically, in consequence, the only land a man can acquire is his father's, but fathers are rarely anxious to give up the reins. The transfer of the land is probably put off until the old man is in his seventies: his eldest son, by then, is probably in his mid-thirties — and 38 is the average age at which farmers' sons marry in the Republic.

Now it is plausible to argue that this kind of restraint to marriage was also felt during much of the eighteenth century — though less severely than today, for fathers, no doubt, died younger. The critical change towards the end of the century was that land became more readily available — and, therefore, youthful marriage more readily possible. By the 1780s and 1790s holdings were less commonly passed intact from father to son. It was possible, often imperative, for a father to mark off a piece of his land and make it over to a still-youthful son, and later, maybe, provide for a second, even a third, son. Essentially, this subdivision of holdings was a consequence of the extension of arable farming. Irish patriots had long pleaded for legislation to encourage corn-growing. But the Irish towns were a useful market for surplus British grain; and Irish supplies would have been re-

---

[5] Thomas Malthus (1766–1834), English economist, author of *An Essay on the Principle of Population*.

sented in Britain. There was, therefore, no effective legislation until the second half of the century. By then the growth of Britain's own population was turning her from an exporter to an importer of corn; by the 1780s constitutional changes allowed Irish patriots to try their hand at moulding the Irish economy. Foster's[6] corn law of 1784 imposed duties on the import of grain and offered bounties on its export; war, from 1793, further inflated corn prices — the more effectively after 1806 when, at last, Irish grain entered Britain duty-free. Between the 1780s and the early years of the new century oat prices more than doubled: on more and more estates the tilling tenant could pay most rent; he, therefore, was preferred by the landlord.

But more tilling tenancies meant smaller tenancies: the grassland a family could conveniently manage was embarrassingly large to cultivate by spade or plough; there was no class of people with the capital and the skill to manage large arable farms; tillage, moreover, needed the labour of the larger population subdivision induced.

By the closing decades of the eighteenth century, then, tenant farmers, anxious to provide for their sons, were encouraged by their landlords to divide their holdings. Their sons — and daughters — were scarcely aware of the inducements in other societies to postpone marriage: with an elastic rent, there was little reward for industry, little opportunity for thrift — almost no hope that by deferring marriage a family might be reared on a firmer foundation. Living conditions were wretched and hopeless: marriage could hardly make them worse; it might make them more tolerable.

When, therefore, land was within their grasp, young people seized the opportunity it offered of marrying younger than had been customary. Few of them knew of the possibility of restricting family size: almost none wanted to do so; it cost little to rear a child; even young children helped on the land; and, in a country without a poor law, a numerous family was some assurance against a destitute old age. The earlier a girl married, therefore, the more children was she likely to have; the sooner a new generation was added to the old.

Largely, then, the impetus to the rapid growth of population seems to have come from earlier marriage facilitated by subdivision, and followed by larger families. But where does the potato come in?

The incidence of sterility and still-birth varies, no doubt, with the nutrition of husbands and wives — and of their parents. Insofar, then, as the potato was improving nutrition — even before 1750 — it tended to increase fertility in the closing decades of the century. And, without the potato, subdivision could hardly have persisted for some three generations until, on the eve of the Famine, half of all holdings were of five or fewer acres. Much hilly land, mountain and bog was included: holdings so small and unrewarding could earn a rent, and support a family, only if it lived on the potato. Had the popular dietary been more varied, sub-

---

[6] John Foster (1740–1828), Chancellor of the Exchequer in Ireland.

division would have halted earlier; marriage, presumably, would have been delayed and fertility reduced. Already by the 1820s and 1830s, some farms were so
reduced in size that nothing could be pared from them for a son wishing to marry:
increasingly he was tempted to emigrate; but sometimes he settled in Ireland on
a scrap of waste, otherwise of little use, but able to grow potatoes.

The potato, then, tended to increase fertility; but its significance in population history is more for what it prevented than for what it did. Malthus was an accurate observer: population in his time pressed on resources: rising fertility tended
to make food scarce, and to be offset, therefore, by rising mortality. But Ireland,
for some sixty years, was exceptional: not only were additional children born, but
many of them survived and contributed to the astonishing rapidity of population
growth: crucial to their survival was the abundance and nutritional excellence of
the potato.

The effects of the potato mentioned so far — its tendency to keep mortality
down and, indirectly, to increase fertility — these tendencies depended on its
being steadily and abundantly available. But the perils of living on a single food
are more than usually acute when this food is the potato. Its yield, maybe, is
more erratic than that of oats or wheat; yet it keeps so badly that the surplus of
one year does nothing directly to make good the deficiency of the next; it is bulky,
too, difficult, if communications are poor, to move from areas of abundance to
areas of scarcity. It is planted late — lest it be damaged by frost: usually, therefore,
the season is advanced when its failure becomes apparent, too advanced for other
foods to be grown. Nor, in all probability, can its victims buy a substitute: growing their own potatoes, they have no money earmarked for food; reduced to the
most frugal of foods, they hardly have money at all; their society, too, will have
needed — and reared — only a rudimentary food trade. And even if there is public or charitable provision of grain, their troubles are not at an end: accustomed
to a crop prepared simply with a pot and a fire, they are ill-equipped with the mills
to grind corn; with the ovens and skills to bake it — even with the stomachs to
digest it.

The potato, then, is a capricious staple, liable to fail and hard to replace. Yet
not until after 1815 were the perils of Ireland's potato economy persistently
demonstrated. In 1740 — and again in 1807 — early and severe frost destroyed
much of the crop while it was still undug: 1800 and 1801 were lean years for Ireland as for much of the rest of Europe. By and large, however, from the middle
of the eighteenth century until after 1815, the Irishman had his fill of potatoes.

Why was the precariousness of life on the potato so long concealed? It is
hardly respectable to attribute more than incidental movements in economic development to shifts in the weather. Over three-quarters of a century, nevertheless,
few seasons disagreed with the potato; partly, too, it yielded well because year after
year, as more people depended on it, it was planted on land, not all of it poor, on
which it had never grown before. But it is easier to explain the frequency and
severity of failures after 1815 than their rarity before. Again, it seems, the weather
played a part: year after year, between 1820 and the Famine, the potato succumbed to cold, wet seasons; it may have succumbed also to diseases unknown

in Europe until steam navigation brought them across the Atlantic. Inherently, too, it probably became less resistant to disease as old varieties degenerated, and the new were chosen for their prolificness more than their vitality. And its yield became even less certain as it was grown on old land, starved of manure and exhausted by over-cropping; on new land, recently waste and ill-adapted to its needs — on so much land that once disease appeared, it quickly spread.

In the 1820s and 1830s the potato failed, partially or locally, at least as often as it yielded well. No longer, almost certainly, was rising fertility unaccompanied by rising mortality. But, it seems, there was little slackening in the rate of natural increase. The fickleness of the potato may have been countered by increasing the area on which it was planted: certainly the agrarian troubles and the unpaid rents of these years suggest an unwonted encroachment of subsistence-land on rent-land. It is probable too — for vaccination was spreading — that rising mortality from malnutrition was offset by falling mortality from smallpox. Marriage in these decades was postponed — as subdivision reached its limits, as the supply of food became less certain: but later marriage did not necessarily mean fewer births; the abnormal number of births in the previous twenty years was followed now by an abnormal number of potential parents.

Rapid natural increase, then, depended no longer on the bounty of the potato. But more and more its effects within Ireland were offset by mounting emigration, motivated, much of it, by the treachery of the potato. It was not until after 1845 that population began to decline: then, with three failures of the potato, two of them virtually complete, the population, in five years, was reduced by a fifth: half a million, perhaps more, died of starvation and associated diseases; a round million fled, like refugees.

The victims of so vast a catastrophe speculated, of course, on its cause. Was it brought by the fairies, the weather or atmospheric electricity; by the people's saintliness or sinfulness — by God's spreading the faith by spreading the Irish, or by his chastening a people who wasted the potato in its abundance, violated their pledge of temperance, emancipated the Catholics and subsidized Maynooth?[7] In the most pervasive of the popular explanations, the Famine was the work of the British government: "the Almighty . . . sent the potato blight, but the English created the Famine."

At the time this explanation had a rational and an emotional appeal. It is true enough that there was no escape from famine unless the government provided it; and there was the ring of salvation neither in allowing the export of Irish grain, nor in public works more obviously penal than benevolent. And a people, so beset by catastrophe, shied from the further agony of self-incrimination: if England, indeed, created the Famine, its victims had no call to dwell on their own defects; not even on their tolerance of the landlordism that made them idle and improvident.

---

[7] A Roman Catholic seminary in Ireland, the permanent endowment of which was controversial in the 1840s and 1850s.

Commonly, the historians of the Famine have reiterated the indictment of England. Their sympathies, very often, have been nationalist: nationalism in Ireland has been reared less on the rights of man than on historical wrongs, and the most grievous wrong was England's murder of a million. . . .

The scholarly studies of the Famine sponsored by the Dublin government and the Irish Committee of Historical Sciences enable us to re-assess England's guilt. . . . Mr. Thomas P. O'Neill allows us to believe no longer that the government, by staying the export of grain, could have staved off the famine: there was, he makes clear, an acute shortage of food, and it was relieved, not aggravated, by trade with Britain and the outside world.

Other measures of relief failed, not because the government so willed, not even because it was callous or negligent, but simply because the Famine was an intractable problem, an insoluble problem in the knowledge and opinion of the time. Once famine was imminent, epidemics of typhus and relapsing fever were all but certain: the doctors, backed however fully by the state, could do little to arrest their spread, or cure their victims. Famine — and therefore fever — could be averted only if the potato were saved, or if, by some administrative miracle, five million people were otherwise fed. The government, without delay, sought scientific advice on the potato; but the botanists knew nothing of the cause of the blight, nothing of how its spread might be arrested or its recurrence prevented. Nor were the economists and political theorists more effectual. The rotting of the potato was no excuse for corrupting their "scientific" poor law; and it was on their principles that Russell's[8] relief works foundered, their faith in unproductivity, central control and payment by results. Their insistence on free trade ruled out what relief there was in a ban on the export of Irish grain; and back of Russell's laggardly and niggardly import of food lay their refutation of state intervention, their certainty that it must aggravate more than alleviate.

A native government, it is true, might have deferred less to politics and economics more plausible in England than in Ireland. But no government could have contained the Famine: given the dominance of the potato, some such disaster was all but inevitable; given the growth of population, the more it was delayed, the more malevolent it must be. If, indeed, "England created the famine," it was not . . . in pursuit of a "deliberate policy of extermination": it was because, centuries earlier, she had geared the Irish economy to the elastic rent which ensured the diffusion of the potato and the unbridled growth of population.

No survivor of the Famine forgot the perils of life on the potato: fifty years later, the sight of a bowl of floury potatoes could bring tears to an old man's eyes. Yet in much of the country, as the blight receded, as seed became available, the potato was restored almost — but not altogether — to its former eminence. The yellow meal, eaten at first to save life, soon was enjoyed; and turnips and cabbage also became more familiar: none of these foods strained much more than the

---

[8] Lord John Russell (1792–1878), Whig prime minister from 1846 to 1852, an exponent of free market economics.

potato the peasant's resources, or his wife's cooking: all, therefore, encroached on the potato, or eked it out in the bad year, or before the new crop was dug. In north-eastern Ulster the potato was forsaken more rapidly — because, no doubt, it was never so firmly established. But elsewhere, its real relegation began, not in the 1840s, but in the 1870s and 1880s: "it was spuds, morning, noon and night," an old Donegal man recalled of his boyhood in the 1870s: a dozen years earlier, Clare families still lived on potatoes and sour milk; still in Cork and Limerick people reckoned on their ten pounds a day. And from the western seaboard, into the present century, the smaller holders "have nothing else to rely on: potatoes are their sole support."

Now for long, in the Médoc, it had been the custom to give grapes by the roadside an unappetizing appearance by spraying them with a mixture of copper sulphate and lime. But it was not until the 1880s that a passing botanist noticed that the sprayed plants were healthier than the rest, and, after some experiments, advocated Bordeaux mixture as a preventive of blight on the potato. In the following decade the Royal Dublin Society organized tests in Ireland, and, together with government agencies, landlords, teachers and doctors, it endeavoured to overcome the peasant's reluctance to spray. Spraying, some of course thought, was "going against nature": others, having started to spray, were lulled by a good season or two; or they lost faith because their mixture was adulterated or improperly prepared; or because, too poor or too unmechanical to use a knapsack, they had ineffectively shaken the mixture from a broom, or a handful of heather. By the time of the first war, the resistance was mostly overcome; spraying was all but universal. Before then the only safeguard against the blight was to plant a resistant variety; but the resistance even of the Champion had proved to be partial and diminishing. As long, then, as the hold of the potato persisted, famine recurred: several times in the second half of the nineteenth century scenes were enacted reminiscent, if not of the forties, at least of the twenties and thirties. But by the end of the century, the failure of the potato brought acute suffering only to the poorest families, most of them in the worst-congested districts: almost everywhere else the potato — with the milk that went with it — was yielding to stirabout (made increasingly of oats, instead of Indian corn); to bread, oaten and soon wheaten; to American bacon; to sugar, jam and tea — perhaps, where smuggling survived, to coffee in place of tea. The potato, of course, has never been ousted; but, in the words of its devoted historian, "it is eaten because it is liked, not because it is necessary."

There are two problems: why, after the Famine, did people revert so largely to a food they knew might fail again; and why, by the last quarter of the century, had they reduced it to one of several staples?

For all the agony that followed its failure, there was feeling still for the potato. People accustomed to stomachs distended three times a day by three or four pounds of potatoes, felt hungry and uncomfortable, though nourished enough on porridge or bread; or they complained of their difficulty in digesting grain stuffs. After the Famine, then, they welcomed the potato; and it was, very probably, a better food than any alternative widely available. And the people sensed also that, though the potato should fail again, they would hardly suffer as in the forties: the relieved (not only the relievers) learned by their mistakes; publicity and politics increasingly loosened the purse-strings: American relatives were a growing resource; and to join them became the conventional response to hardship at home.

The potato, before the Famine, meant more than nutriment; and people were drawn back to it by more than the need for food and bodily comfort. The open door and a meal for all-comers was a custom that sprang from the heart, but depended on the potato: hearts were hardened when the potato rotted — and any traveller might bring the fever. But when famine was past, it was good once more to disregard the cost of food — to return to the potato.

In reality, no doubt, as well as in the novels and travellers' tales, the Irishman was an indolent creature — not surprisingly if his family were large and his holding small; if industry, in his society, were robbed of its reward. For the lazy man there was no crop like the potato: it needed merely a few days' planting in the spring, possibly earthing up in the summer, and some more days' digging in the winter: with another week, cutting and carrying turf, a family might be fed and warmed for the year. By reverting to the potato, people with the taste for travel could take to the road soon after St. Patrick's Day, return temporarily to cut the turf, and settle down eventually to a leisurely winter with all the comfort they knew: the restless, ambitious man could spend his summer lifting the English harvest — even hewing stone in an American quarry; his family he might send out to beg, or leave at home to win the turf — and earn the rent if there were butter to be made.

But like its original diffusion, the re-establishment of the potato after the Famine probably owed more to the landlord's exigence than to the people's inclination. In the years of unpaid rents, and heavy taxes, the debts of already-embarrassed landlords piled up. In 1848, accordingly, the Encumbered Estates Act eased the transfer of Irish property — and patriots looked to it for the return, at last, of native, benevolent landlords. Much land changed hands under the act — a third of the whole country, it is said, in three years. The buyers, too, were mostly Irish; but Irish who were the patriots' despair. Few of their countrymen in 1849 had the money and the will to play the landlord and the assurance that they could make it a paying game. Much encumbered property was bought by petty shopkeepers and land agents, by gombeen men[9] and publicans, men, it might be, who had done well in the Famine, selling grain to a people unused to buying food, buying land from a people forced to abandon it. The central tradition of Irish property was safe in their keeping — perhaps, indeed, more rigorously applied, for their properties, by and large, were smaller than their predecessors'; more of them lived on the spot, and, stemming very often from the people they exploited, they were better informed of their hidden resources. There was probably no real relaxation of the pressure of rent-land on subsistence-land until the organized

---

[9] Moneylenders.

withholding of rent: for every peasant, then, who willingly returned to the potato after the Famine, others went back to it willy-nilly.

In the 1870s and 1880s, the land war was followed by the land legislation. In many respects it is this, not the more spectacular Famine that divides the nineteenth century: until then the social and economic life of the countryside was geared to an elastic rent; but the land acts first stabilized rent, then made it a dwindling real charge. With industry and its reward at last united, there was point in farming more productively. Costlier foods were now within the peasant's reach: no longer must he live on whatever supported him with the greatest economy of land. Sometimes, it is true, the tenant-at-will, blown up to be head of a landowning family, shied too far from his old improvidence: his family must eat potatoes so that he might buy more land, make a priest of his son, or dower his daughter beyond her station. But prudence so extreme was not typical: an owner-occupier had his status to think of: he looked with "modest shame" not just on the potato, but on home-baked bread: commonly, moreover, he had relatives "in emigration," brothers and sons who mocked at his potatoes and milk, who expected when they came home to find baker's bread and jam and tea.

VICTORIAN ENGLAND:
THE HORSE-DRAWN SOCIETY
F. M. L. Thompson

F. M. L. Thompson, emeritus professor of history at the University of London, contrasts the myth of the "railway society" with the growth of the horse population in nineteenth-century England. He uses contemporary treatises, government records (such as censuses, tax returns, and parliamentary investigations), and reports of contemporary social observers to study the social and economic functions of the horse in industrial society.

What was the specific role of the horse and carriage in Victorian England? Expensive and inefficient as commercial means of transportation, horses were exceptional pollutants whose droppings made urban life nasty. We hear much today about the pernicious effects of automobiles on the urban landscape, but Thompson's analysis of horses' noxious contributions to the atmospheric stench, street muck, and noise level of the last century makes our cities appear to be centers of pristine tranquillity by comparison.

Even modern complaints about traffic congestion must be muted when contemplating the Victorian street, prey to the chaotic mixture of horses and horse-drawn vehicles. How did city governments attempt to cope with the numerous and unpleasant problems that horses caused?

Another erroneous assumption Thompson lays to rest (in addition to the one that modern cities are dirtier than those of the past) is that railroads made horse-drawn transport obsolete. Why did railways in fact require horses, and how did the railroads stimulate transportation by horse-drawn vehicles?

Along with horses, carriages constituted a prominent feature of the Victorian city. What social functions did carriages serve, and how did carriages affect urban life and space?

Finally, what conditions led to the demise of horse-drawn transport? We have moved from the omnipresence of horses to that of cars. Thompson does not miss the bygone world of horses, yet in some ways cities may have been better off with horses than they now are with automobiles.

F. M. L. Thompson, "Victorian England: The Horse-Drawn Society" (lecture given at Bedford College, University of London, October 22, 1970).

Horses are hard work. Their food is bulky, heavy, and they demand enormous quantities of it. It all has to be manhandled. . . . Two and a half tons for one horse for one winter. In this they differ sharply from the motor car, whose food comes expensively but effortlessly out of a pipe. I would assert, but not offer to demonstrate, that stoking a horse is almost as hard and almost as continuous a labour as stoking a locomotive. Horses also work hard. So hard for so long, historically, that of course horsepower naturally became the measure of the strength of the steam engines and internal combustion engines which eventually replaced them. Animal horsepower was most versatile in its applications. Anything a petrol[1] or diesel engine can do a horse can do, worse. . . . At one time anything on wheels had a horse in front of it, and anything which was dragged through the soil was dragged by a horse; the horse was, indeed, made to turn its feet to almost anything, and when harnessed to a contraption rather like a giant capstan it supplied, through the horse-gin, cumbersome but reasonably reliable rotary power for driving machinery as diverse as spinning jennies, portable threshing machines, pumps, flour mills, and colliery[2] hoists. Though there was something to be said for this form of industrial power, since it was neither so fickle as wind nor so localised and unsteady as water, I do not propose to say it, since it had to all intents and purposes been technologically superceded by cheaper and more efficient stationary engines — whether water- or steam-powered — before the Victorian period. I am concerned, rather, with the locomotive power of horses. Why should I be concerned?

It is a question which can be approached on many levels. One at least, . . . the most fundamental, . . . is the level which leads straight to the nature and purpose of history. For, history being the study of the past, past horses are as fit a subject for that study as past politics, past ideas, or past buildings, though it may not have been widely recognised hitherto that they are of similar moment. That being the case, there is no difference in principle between the answer to the question: Why study Victorian horses? and the answers to the question: Why study history at all? which might be preferred by any historian who turned his interest to anything in particular which has exercised significant influence on human society in the past. . . .

. . . Horses and carriages were so much a part of ordinary life until the death of Queen Victoria[3]—and indeed until 1914 — that as with other everyday objects they tended to be taken for granted, exciting little contemporary comment apart from attention to the technical side of their management and construction — much as today there is an abundant supply of manuals on the driving, maintenance, and production of motor vehicles, so the Victorian literature made ample provision for those whose business it was to look after horses or to build carriages.

---

[1] Gasoline.

[2] Coal mine.

[3] Queen Victoria reigned from 1837 to 1901.

The disappearance of horses, from the streets in the 1920s and from the farms in the 1940s, is still so comparatively recent that it has only lately begun to strike some historians that there is something interesting to be said about the period of their ascendancy. . . .

It is the role of the horse and carriage in Victorian society and in the Victorian economy which lends the subject some importance, an importance which has not so much been denied by other historians, as somewhat overlooked. It has been overlooked for the very good reason that the historian's eye tends to be caught by what is dramatic, and what is dramatic is usually what is new. If we think of the Victorian age in transport terms at all, we think of railways and steamships; if we think of its social structure, we think of a developing class system, based perhaps on differences of wealth, of source of income, of religion, of education, of place of residence, or on some blend of all of these; if we think of its economy, we think of steam, iron, steel and electricity, the mechanisation of the processes of production and the application of power; if we think of the consequences of all this, we think of massive urbanisation, slums, and urban poverty, and possibly also of large Victorian mansions now converted into flats, with the large households of domestic servants which used to inhabit them. What I wish to suggest is that for all its bustle, smoke, and modernity, this was still at heart a horse-drawn society, and to argue that the degree of its dependence on the horse set some of the more important limits to its social and economic development. The horse is often regarded as the most noble of animals; and when serving as the vehicle of pleasure, sport, and entertainment it may well be so. It is integral to the argument, however, that as a practical and commercial means of locomotion the horse is expensive and inefficient. The corollary is that if some dreadful fate, such as the non-invention of the railway, had thrust the horse even more into the Victorian limelight than it actually was, the result would have been an extremely impoverished society. . . .

The pervasiveness of the role of the motor car today gives us a clue to the possible role of its predecessor, the horse and carriage. Not only is car production at the very centre of the economy — which carriage-making never was — but . . . it is farmed out among a number of component manufacturers, stoppage in any one bringing the assembly plants to a halt. Car makers anxiously scrutinise the trends in their sales, trying to forecast their future market as the initial demand due to the expansion of car ownership threatens to reach its limits and replacement demand takes over as the major component, only to have their gloomiest predictions upset first by the appearance of the two-car and then of the three-car family. Builders and estate agents find first that houses without garages, and then that houses in select districts without double garages, are unsaleable, and building societies[4] decline mortgages on the unfashionable properties; but at a later stage the city streets become so blocked with traffic that a car in town is a nuisance

---

[4] Roughly equivalent to savings and loan associations in the United States.

and town houses without garages are once more a highly-prized article, the owners being affluent enough to keep the car out at their country place. Meanwhile the cars themselves, having passed through a phase in which multitudes of makes and shapes flowered in luxuriant abandon, have settled down to a handful of basic sizes each suited to particular functions and definite markets. The affairs of buying and selling cars, and driving them, have given rise to a whole branch of the law, with special motoring offences, special enforcement officers, and very special social attitudes towards offending motorists, who are sharply differentiated from other kinds of law-breakers. Above all perhaps we nowadays cannot avoid entertaining views about the social implications of cars — as status symbols, sex symbols, emulation objects, group definers, and community creators and destroyers — and about their social effects — as producers of congestion, noise, and pollution, potential destroyers alike of our cities and of the peace and solitude of our countryside, able contestants for the place of chief enemy of the environment, but still indispensable possessions for all those who possess them.

. . . If then we confine attention to the topical problem of pollution, the horse struck his blow at the quality of urban life long before the waste products of modern technology began to cause trouble. Contemporary experts of an experimental turn of mind differed somewhat in their results, but agreed in their measurements on a range of 6 to 7 1/2 tons as the amount of droppings which one horse on normal feeding and workload produced in a year. Individually modest, cumulatively the amount could be rather more than simply a messy embarrassment. In their proper place, and mixed with about equal quantities of straw litter, the droppings of course formed the best kind of farmyard manure; and with an annual output of 12 tons of finished manure the average farm-horse could manure all the land which was used to feed it about once in four years, a neat example of the re-cycling process which is now the fashionable answer to the problem of awkward effluents. The trouble was that many horses lived far away from farms. The best estimate I can make is that already by the 1830s English towns had to cope with something like 3 million tons of droppings every year, and that by 1900 they had more like 10 million tons on their hands. It is true that if this could be recovered it was valuable agriculturally, particularly for the market gardens and intensive hay farms which clustered round the larger towns. But since the town droppings were worth barely five shillings[5] a ton to the farmer they could only stand transport over a couple of miles or so by road and ten times as far by barge, if there happened to be a canal handy. The result was that a high proportion never was recovered, and many scraps of waste land in the poorer quarters of towns were turned into vast dung heaps, considerably aggravating the squalor, stench, and unhealthiness of such parts of the urban environment. It was in any case exceedingly difficult to keep the streets clean in the press of daytime traffic, and pick-up operations had to be left largely to night squads who could shovel

---

[5] A former unit of British currency; one-twentieth of a pound.

away without causing traffic jams. In this situation the crucial role of the crossing-sweeper in keeping town life tolerable can be readily appreciated. And while there is no question that the streets did improve considerably in appearance during the Victorian period, especially with the introduction of hard, smooth surfaces of tarred wood blocks or of asphalt, and with the construction of kerbside gullies and drains, which reached the main streets in the last quarter of the nineteenth century, there can equally be no question that the motor vehicle has raised the quality of urban life by driving the smell and the squelch off the streets.

Consideration of the waste products of society, and their disposal, has never been a subject for the fastidious; and you will remember that the Victorians of both sexes, if they could possibly afford it, never ventured out into the streets unless wearing ankle-length outer garments or other enveloping protective clothing, which had very necessary anti-splash functions. To suppose, as some have done, that such fashions were dictated purely by modesty, or that their primary or sole purpose was to muffle sexual excitement, is to forget that no one could set foot in a Victorian street without encountering dozens and dozens of horses. Henry Mayhew,[6] in the course of his fascinating investigation of the conditions of *London Labour and the London Poor* in 1851, attempted a computation of the annual droppings of horses — and other livestock on their way to markets — in the London streets. . . . As it happens Mayhew's estimate is not very useful, since it is concerned only with the refuse problem facing the public authorities in the City and Westminster, and for this purpose he assumed that the average City horse only spent 6 hours of each day out and about on the streets and the remaining three-quarters of its time in off-street stabling where its wastes became a purely private problem. Hence the difference between his figure of 52,000 tons a year and the Board of Health's estimate of 200,000 tons for the same date and same area. . . .

Next to smell and dirt, noise is the most resented intruder in our time. It cannot be pretended that any number of horses could out-neigh a jet engine in any conceivable equine chorus. But for mere street noise hooves and iron-rimmed wheels clattering on cobbles, stone setts, or granite chippings did not do at all badly. Residents on main thoroughfares certainly complained about the incessant rattle and rumble of horse-drawn traffic and said that the noise drowned their dinner-time conversation. And it was to deaden horse-drawn noise that the streets were habitually covered with layers of straw in front of hospitals, and of private houses whenever anyone was ill in bed. No one had thought of decibles or of measuring them before horse-drawn traffic vanished, so it is impossible to make any statement about the comparative noise levels of town streets in 1900 and 1970; but the possibility that the motor car made our streets quieter as well as cleaner should not be ignored. As to congestion, it was horse traffic which seemed to be threatening to bring our cities to a standstill in the closing years of Victoria's reign,

---

[6] Author and magazine editor (1812–1887), best known for his pioneering social research on London's working classes of the 1850s.

and which caused a major part of the problem investigated by the Royal Commission on London Traffic which reported in 1906. . . . [I]t has sometimes seemed laughable to suppose that London could ever have imagined it had a traffic problem at that time: there were barely 10,000 motor vehicles in the entire country, compared with over 10 million today. Quite true; but in the peak year of horse-drawn traffic, 1902, there were close on half a million private carriages on the roads, 133,000 public passenger vehicles and cabs, and a fleet of commercial vans, wagons, carts and drays which was completely uncounted but which must have amounted to not far short of another half million. What proportion of all these were driving about London is not known, but it was enough to overload the road system; the evidence for this was plain enough by 1906, in terms of a 25 per cent fall in the average speed of the traffic in the previous 30 years owing to the growing congestion, and in terms of an equally sharp decline in the normal working life of bus horses due to the mounting strain on them of a crescendo of stopping and starting.

The reasons why what appear to us rather puny numbers of vehicles created very genuine and nearly desperate traffic chaos are not too far to seek. In the first place, the behaviour of horse traffic is unpredictable, its control of direction erratic, and its road discipline poor, in comparison with motors; hence any given number of horse-drawn vehicles occupied a good deal more road space than the same number of motor vehicles simply because of the extra elbow room required. But of far greater importance was the highly favourable ratio between useful space and overall length of horse-drawn vehicles. It was normal for the tractive power source to be at least as long as the vehicle being drawn, and it was frequently longer. Any given horse-drawn payload was therefore likely to occupy two or three times the road space of its motorised successor, on this score alone. This issue of the overall length of vehicles and horse teams was, indeed, seen as crucial to the traffic problem of the early 1900s and its solution. One witness to the London enquiry, a traction engine enthusiast, pointed out that one steam roadster with a train of trailers could do in 72 feet the work of 18 horses and carts stretched out over 360 feet of road, which at once promised to cut congestion to one-fifth of its current proportions. Another saw salvation in electric trams, which would remove traffic jams by cutting the length of tramcar and horses in half. In the event, of course, the jams were removed by motorisation. Or rather they were removed for half a century. It is hardly my province to suggest the form of technological miniaturisation which might push back our own problems for another half century.

All this amounts to saying, in short, that horse-drawn transport had its drawbacks and limitations. But until a substitute became available — and the demonstration that motors were something more useful and reliable than mere playthings of the eccentric rich dates almost precisely from the year of Victoria's death — horse-drawn transport was quite indispensable. The mistake is sometimes made of supposing that the railways dealt it a mortal blow. This is because railway competition did indeed kill off long-distance road transport very rapidly, and by 1850 the mail-coaches and stage-coaches, with all the elaborate organisation of coaching inns and post-horse establishments which had supported them, had all but vanished. . . .

. . . Without carriages and carts the railways would have been like stranded whales, giants unable to use their strength, for these were the only means of getting people and goods right to the doors, of houses, warehouses, markets, and factories, where they wanted to be. All the railway companies kept their own establishments of horses and assorted wagons and vans for goods collection and delivery, and it is in railway records that one may find the best series of prices of van-horses and horse-fodder covering the whole Victorian age. In addition to the company fleets there was plenty of scope for independent operators in these feeder services. A firm like Pickfords, which had grown up as canal carriers of inter-city through traffic, soon adapted itself to the new railway situation and flourished as never before, as a distributor from railheads; the 4,000 horses which this firm had maintained in the 1820s to run its canal fly-boats between London and Birmingham were before long insufficient to cope with the new local town traffic generated by the London and Birmingham Railway. No wonder that a big railway terminus came to require about as much space for stabling as it did for locomotive sheds. As one elderly commission stablekeeper remarked in the 1870s, when his annual turnover had grown to 1,200 horses, "We thought when the railways first came in that we should have nothing to do, but it has not turned out so . . . for every new railway [that is built] you want fresh horses . . . because there is the work to be done to and fro." To and fro may be very commonplace, but there was a lot of it. The railway age was in fact the greatest age of the horse, albeit in terms of its total contribution to the economy rather than in terms of any heroic qualities in its unaided achievements. The threat of redundancy because of technological change, in other words, turned out to be as unreal for horses as it has so often been for men, and given adaptation to new or modified tasks the new technology did not diminish, but substantially increased, the demand for horse-labour. Taking all the varied forms of horse-drawn and horseback activity together, British society required about one horse for every 10 people — men, women and children — in order to keep going in the late Victorian period. The USA, with vastly greater spaces and distances, needed about one horse to every four inhabitants at that time. As in parallel situations, the increased demand brought higher rewards for horse-labour; or to put it more normally, raised its cost. The price of van-horses and cart-horses went up by 25 to 30 per cent between 1850 and 1873; and though it subsequently fell, in the last quarter of the century, it did not fall by as much as the general price level.

Railway travel also stimulated the transport of passengers by road, most obviously in cabs to catch trains and in inter-station horse buses. In London, for instance, the number of cabs increased virtually tenfold between 1830 and 1900, while the fleet buses grew from 1,000 in 1850 to 4,000, rates of growth which greatly exceeded the simple increase of population so that a provision of one cab to 1,000 head of people at the start of Victoria's reign had improved to one cab to every 350 people at its end. Less obvious was the effect of railways in stimulating horseback riding, but Trollope[7] fans will remember how, in *The Way We Live Now,* it was the ease and speed of railway travel which made it obligatory for young men about town to keep a string of hunters in the country, which they would pop down to use for a day's mid-week hunting without seriously interrupting their course of dissipation in the London clubs. At this point, however, the impact of railways simply acted alongside the general influences of economic growth and increasing affluence, and it would be absurd to attempt to disentangle it from them. The cabs, the horse buses, and the horse trams which developed from the late 1860s, were after all very largely employed in carrying traffic which both originated and terminated within their city catchment areas, and which never at any point touched a train; the trams in particular were almost exclusively devoted to serving this urban-generated traffic, and never had more than a very minor role as railway auxiliaries. As to the increase in hunting, it was an admiral who offered the most profound analysis when he was asked to explain the great increase in the turnover of the London horse sales in the fifty years before 1873: "I think it is the money, the enormous wealth of London," he said; "so many people keep hunters now, who never dreamt of keeping them before. I know that at Melton there are 500 people in a field, where formerly there would not be 100, and many of them have two or three horses each in the field." In answer to the further question "whether in former days would not those gentlemen have hunted in their own countries in preference to going to Melton?" he replied "My idea is that it is owing to their means; that their riches have increased, and that the love of hunting has increased in proportion to their means of being able to indulge their fancy." Hunting in fact increased three- or four-fold in the period, in terms of numbers of separate hunts and packs of hounds; what demands this made on horseflesh we do not know, but by 1900 it was thought that some 200,000 horses were kept exclusively for hunting, at an annual cost in upkeep of £8 million, to which should be added a couple of million for remounts. It may help put the annual expenditure on hunting into perspective to point out that it was about half as large as the total expenditure on tobacco by all the smokers in the United Kingdom.

The hunters were a form of consumer durable. Rather more durable, indeed, than most cars or television sets today, but somewhat less durable than the private carriages which performed for the Victorian age many of the functions which are currently associated with consumer durables, in particular the functions of conferring prestige and defining status. Everyone has heard of the "carriage trade" and "carriage folk" as concepts which defined the standing of desirable residential suburbs, epitomised the social aspirations of people on the climb, outlined the markets aimed at by the producers, sellers, and advertisers of quality goods, and summed up one of the critical lines of class division. Surprisingly few people have attempted to define what the carriage trade was, to estimate its extent, or to

---

[7] Anthony Trollope (1815–1882), English novelist.

examine its development. Luckily the taxman was as interested in private carriages as he now is in private cars, and his attentions have left behind a trail which indicates the broad dimensions of carriage-ownership and the directions of change. As with all tax returns, the figures must be handled with caution: they record licenses issued, which may or may not be the same thing as carriages on the road. Evasion of carriage duty was probably not a serious problem, since possession was not easy to conceal. But the Revenue classification of carriages, and changes in the categories, make interpretation of the returns a complicated and specialised task. The old horsepower rating car licenses were simplicity itself beside the classes of carriages: 4-wheel carriages drawn by 2 or more horses of over 13 hands, 4-wheel carriages drawn by 2 or more ponies under 13 hands, or by oxen, 4-wheel carriages drawn by 1 horse over 13 hands, 2-wheel carriages drawn by 2 horses, 2-wheel carriages drawn by 1 horse; these are but a few of the taxation classes which were used to apply differential rates of duty with refined precision. The more fashionable, prudent, or plain accident-prone among carriage owners used sometimes to keep spare bodies in their coach-houses, which could be mounted on the chassis in case of change of mood or of outright disaster: these additional bodies, also, had their special niche in the taxation manual.

. . . In the early, pre-railway, decades of the nineteenth century carriage-ownership increased quite fast, but possession of this coveted form of personal transport was still largely confined to the "upper ten thousand" who comprised the ruling class — the aristocracy, gentry, and very wealthy commercial men. There were 15,000 privately-owned large carriages in 1810 and about 30,000 in 1840; the smaller 2-wheeled runabouts, over 40,000 of them by 1840, were partly owned by the same people, and partly formed the necessary stock in trade of businessmen, doctors, and solicitors.[8] The wealthy frequently had several carriages, for different functions, different types of weather, or to be kept in different parts of the country; they were in fact subject to progressive taxation with a scale of duties running from £12 per carriage for a person keeping only one up to £18.3. per carriage for a person keeping nine or more. In this period something like 20 per cent of the large carriages seem to have been owned by two-carriage families. After 1840, however, the early railway age witnessed a remarkable social deepening of the carriage trade. By about 1870 the number of large carriages had increased four-fold, to some 120,000, owned by some 100,000 individuals; this proved to be saturation point, the numbers remaining fairly static until decline set in after 1902. The light 2-wheelers proliferated even more rapidly, growing more than six times between 1840 and 1870; these were the vehicles of the middle classes *par excellence,* and were very largely in the hands of one-carriage families. In contrast to the large carriages these light ones continued to grow in number after 1870, but at a very much slower rate so that the 250,000 of 1870 had only become 320,000 by 1902.

---

[8] British lawyers who prepare briefs but who do not present cases in court.

Figures of this order establish that it was in the Victorian age that carriage-ownership spread right through the middle class. The upper class left its mark on its carriages in the shape of the coats of arms with which "the quality" emblazoned their doors; these, too, did not escape the tax net, and the number of armorial bearings painted on carriages remained throughout very stable in the range of 15,000 to 19,000, so that all the rest of the carriages, ultimately over 400,000 of them, may be presumed to have been solidly bourgeois. It is perhaps more significant that carriage-ownership, having grown from 4 per 1,000 inhabitants in 1840 to 14 per 1,000 in 1870, thereafter subsided gently to a level of 12 per 1,000 in 1902. Of course all these proportions are chickenfeed beside present day levels of car ownership, which are running at the order of 206 per 1,000 inhabitants in this country; though it should be noted that it was not until 1926 that car ownership surpassed the 1870 peak rate. The very sharp check to the growth of the carriage trade after 1870, however, has a number of interesting implications, because it is not at all what we might have expected to accompany the increasing affluence, the rising per capita real incomes, and the growing appetite for luxury, of the late Victorian period. The check was due, I believe, not at all to any lack of potential demand for personal transport, but to physical constraints on the supply side, in short to problems of horsefeed and carriage space.

A private carriage is a labour-intensive object, requiring a coachman and a groom for its management. It is possible that the available slack in the labour force was all taken up in the years before 1870, and that in the late Victorian economy the labour force, with all the other competing demands upon it, simply could not expand fast enough to sustain the earlier rate of carriage growth. At any rate the number of domestic coachmen and grooms barely managed to increase at all between 1881 and 1901. Space to keep a carriage was probably a more important constraint. A horse and carriage simply could not be parked in the street like a car. Ancient City regulations, dating from the late seventeenth century, were very firm about off-street stabling, and provided penalties for drivers who so much as fed their horses in the streets "except with oats out of a bag, or with so much hay as he shall hold in his hands"; while impounding by police was avoided by the economical custom of London that "if a horse stands at an inn till he eats out his value, the innkeeper may take him as his own, upon reasonable appraisement of four of his neighbours." Possession of a horse and carriage implied possession of a stable and coach-house, either within the private grounds of the larger mansions, or in a separate mews[9] block provided for a group of houses. My contention is that a number of influences converged about 1870 to reduce very sharply the rate of mews provision. One was the competition for urban land, which yielded higher returns if covered with houses; another was the realisation that mews quarters introduced unwelcome lower class elements into otherwise respectable and refined residential districts; a third, connected with this, was a certain middle-class feel-

---

[9] An alley behind a residential street containing stabling for horses.

ing that outdoor servants living at a distance were not amenable to the discipline and moral supervision proper for domestics; and a fourth was the appreciation that the growing scale of cities had thrown up tolerably adequate public services in buses and cabs, so that suburban carriage-owning was no longer worth so much candle. It was for reasons like these that one comes across cases of radical revisions in speculative builders' plans in the 1860s and 1870s, schemes for building estates with mews quarters being abandoned as they went along in favour of pure housing estates. . . .

While sections of the middle class adapted their style of living to the approach of carriage saturation point, and peopled the carriageless suburbs of late Victorian England, the upper classes also were not unaffected by the physical difficulties of the carriage world. The demand for horses threatened to outrun the supply, and one large dealer announced: "If you told me you would give me £400 for a pair of carriage horses that you dare put your wife behind, a pair of nice good horses worth £200, and gave me a fortnight to get them, I would not guarantee to buy them." Scarcity of good horses apart, many gentlemen found that it was ceasing to be worth while to run their own carriages in London, the traffic was getting so intolerable and the recruitment of staff so difficult; instead they hired carriages for the season from one of the great jobbing masters — the Hertz rent-a-car people of their time — who flourished with their thousand-horse stables in late Victorian London.

The horse-drawn society did not in the event grind to a halt. But its progress slowed down, and it slowed down because in the final analysis there loomed behind these physical limitations the horse himself and the question of his feed. . . . [E]very horse . . . got through the produce of four to five acres of farmland every year. It is perhaps doubtful whether enough land existed anywhere in the world to support very many more horses than did in fact exist.

. . . Counting horses was not a habit with the British, their curiosity being satisfied when they had totted up the farm-horses, a mere fragment of the total population, and even that was tardily done. To conduct a horse census was the mark of a military nation, anxious about its potential horse supply in case of war. Hence one of the earliest acts of Italy on the morrow of her unification,[10] eager as in so many other spheres to cut a correct figure as a fledgling great power, was to hold a solemn census of equine population and to pass a law of horse conscription providing an apparatus of draft tickets and mobilisation centres for the nether part of the cavalry: running true to form Italian style, the first was wildly inaccurate and the second hopelessly elaborate. Peace-loving, or naval, Britain did without such bureaucratic trimmings; though the figure-conscious Americans counted horses methodically, along with almost everything else susceptible of enumeration.

The upshot is that in the year of peak horse populations, 1902, there were something like 3 1/2 million in Britain, and about 30 million in the USA. Scattered

---

[10] That is, in 1860.

over the world, some 15 million acres were set aside for the sustenance of the British herd; for by this date only part of the hard stuff in the horsefeed — the oats and corn — was grown at home, and much was imported. In America the farm-horses by themselves ate their way through the produce of 88 million acres each year, or one quarter of the entire crop area of the nation; when the consumption of American city horses and other non-farm horses is added, horse-feed is seen to have pre-empted more like a third of the crop area, and even then there were export crops destined for overseas horses on top of this. All this, it should be re-membered, refers to a world served by highly developed railway systems in which coal had been substituted for oats as the fuel of the railway sector. It provides grounds for supposing that any appreciably greater numbers of horses would have been quite literally insupportable.

Hence the somewhat stunted growth of the late Victorian carriage trade to which I have referred may owe much to the impossibility of expanding the sup-ply of horsefeed at any appreciably greater rate than was in fact achieved; or more strictly, to the impossibility of devoting a greater proportion of cultivated lands to horsefeed without doing great injury to other demands for agricultural produce, principally those of humans. Behind this modest conclusion there lies a rather startling prospect for those who have sought to measure the impact of railways by asking themselves what things would have been like if there had been no railways. Perhaps so many extra horses would have been required that everyone else would have starved. . . .

THE CHALLENGE OF CHOLERA
IN HAMBURG
Richard J. Evans

Cholera first visited the German port city of Hamburg in 1832 and reappeared at various times throughout the nineteenth century. Cholera was not the most deadly disease ravaging nineteenth-century Europe (tuberculosis, smallpox, typhoid, and measles killed more people), but it was perhaps the most vile. A seemingly healthy person who contracted the cholera bacillus succumbed to diarrhea, fever, and vomiting. The body shriveled, the skin discolored, the extremities turned blue with cold, and the victim died a miserable death, albeit a quick one. Unlike other diseases, cholera was socially unacceptable. Why was this the case?

Social historian Richard J. Evans is interested in industrialization's impact on social and political inequality. Using newspapers, letters, government documents, and medical publications, Evans describes the terror that cholera epidemics inspired, especially in bourgeois society. Because the bacillus had to be ingested, it spread through contaminated water, food, and clothes. Port workers and slum residents most easily contracted the disease. Thus cholera affected the poor disproportionately.

How did the medical profession and Hamburg's leaders deal with this new disease? What explanations did physicians offer for the spread of cholera, and how did they advise the state and medical community to contain the epidemic? How did their opinions reflect bourgeois disgust with the poor inhabitants of Hamburg? Note why scientist Max von Pettenkofer's theory of cholera and a voluntaristic, individualistic approach to health and hygiene proved so attractive to the bourgeois and commercial elite that controlled the city government.

Nineteenth-century Europeans debated the extent to which states should intervene to regulate epidemics. This debate was part of a wider discussion of governments' role in society. In Hamburg, how did the association of cholera with individual morality tie in to the discussion about the city's proper role in combating the disease?

Richard J. Evans, *Death in Hamburg: Society and Politics in the Cholera Years, 1830–1910* (New York: Oxford University Press, 1987), 226–252, 254–256.

In the early 1830s European society was suddenly confronted by the appearance of an entirely new and very serious disease: Asiatic cholera. It came to Europe as a consequence of European mercantile and industrial enterprise, and once it had arrived, it fastened on to the industrial society that was then in the making and exploited and exaggerated many of its most prominent aspects, from urbanization and overcrowding to environmental pollution and social inequality. The disease had long been endemic on the Indian subcontinent. But the expansion of the British Empire, with its frequent and large-scale movements of goods and people, and the rapid growth in trade between India and Europe that accompanied the industrial revolution in the United Kingdom, combined in the early nineteenth century to export the disease to the rest of the world. By 1819 the major outbreak that had begun in Bengal two years before had reached Mauritius; by 1824 it covered the whole of South-East Asia. More ominously still, it had been carried by traders across Afghanistan before being halted by a military cordon sanitaire in Astrakhan in 1823. It was indeed by this route that it eventually reached the West. After a brief respite in the mid-1820s, it returned to Persia and crossed the Caspian once more, making its way north to Orenburg, at the south-western edge of the Urals, in August 1829. From this new centre it was spread by merchants travelling to and from the great annual fair in Nijhni-Novgorod, as well as making its way independently up the Volga past Astrakhan, where this time the military cordon sanitaire failed to work. In September 1830 it reached Moscow. And in 1831 a major Russian military campaign against a rebellion in Poland spread it rapidly further west. By July it had reached the port of Riga, on the Baltic.

Reports of the horrifying and deadly effects of the new disease soon began to reach Western Europe. It began to affect the victim through a vague feeling of not being well, including a slight deafness. This was followed fairly quickly by violent spasms of vomiting and diarrhoea, vast and prolonged in their extent, in which the evacuations were usually described as being like "rice-water." In this stage up to 25% of the victim's body fluids could be lost. This led, not surprisingly, to a state of collapse in which, in effect, the blood coagulated and ceased to circulate properly. The skin became blue and "corrugated," the eyes sunken and dull, the hands and feet as cold as ice. Painful muscular cramps convulsed and contorted the body. The victims appeared indifferent to their surroundings, though consciousness was not necessarily lost altogether. At this stage death would ensue in about half the cases from cardiac or renal[1] failure, brought on by acute dehydration and loss of vital chemical and electrolytes, or the victim would recover more or less rapidly. The whole progress of the symptoms from start to finish could take as little as 5 to 12 hours, more usually about 3 or 4 days. Modern medical science would add that the incubation period appears to last for a minimum of 24 hours and up to a maximum of 5 days, and though the carrier state may last longer, it too is usually of similar duration (roughly 24 hours to 8 days).

---

[1] Of the kidney.

The most important causative agent in the disease is now agreed to be a microscopic bacillus known as *Vibrio cholerae*. It thrives in warm and humid conditions, above all in river water (up to 20 days). It multiplies very rapidly when the water is warm, though it can survive in colder temperatures. Although the bacillus is transmitted most easily in water, it can also survive on foodstuffs, especially on fruit and vegetables which have been washed in infected water. It can live in butter for up to a month. Milk also provides a hospitable environment. These facts are important because the disease can only strike if the bacillus enters the human digestive tract. In effect, it can only be caught by putting an infected foodstuff or other substance into the mouth. It is transmitted easily enough by touching the mouth with infected hands. This opens up a further range of possibilities. The bacillus survives for up to 15 days on faeces and a week in ordinary earth dust. Infected clothes and linen, especially the bed-linen of victims, are important sources of transmission, should they be touched by others who then later unsuspectingly put hand to mouth. Person-to-person transmission usually occurs indirectly through infection of food or clothing or bathroom and toilet facilities. The bacillus can also be transmitted by flies as far as their limited range takes them. The best way to combat the bacillus is through scrupulous personal hygiene. Frequent washing of the hands, especially after contact with infected persons and things (e.g. communal lavatories), is vital. During an epidemic, bacilli in the water-supply, in milk, or on foodstuffs can be killed by heat (boiling or baking). The bacillus cannot withstand acid. This includes some gastric juices and most disinfectants. It only lasts for a few minutes in wine or spirits, a few hours in beer. It can be prevented from entering the water-supply by the process of sand filtration. This introduces hostile bacteria into the water and the cholera bacilli are quickly exterminated. It follows from all this that cholera epidemics tend to break out in warm and humid weather. They are often spread by infected water-supplies, especially if allied to inefficient sewage systems. Personal contacts also play a role. Dirty and overcrowded living conditions and shared toilet facilities are especially dangerous. On a wider geographical scale, the disease is spread by victims and carriers as they move about the country. River-water is sometimes infected and spreads the disease as it flows downstream. All these factors marked out an insanitary port city such as Hamburg as a major potential centre if the disease should continue to spread.

For nineteenth-century sensibilities, cholera was a disease truly terrifying in its effects. Society had in many ways come to terms with infant deaths and with long-term, permanently present killers such as consumption. A whole set of attitudes had evolved to help people confront the reality of such everyday deaths. This was "the Age of the Beautiful Death," . . . when literature was full of edifying death-bed scenes, in which death crept up on people slowly, transformed their physical suffering into an ethereal beauty, and lent them, in its slow but inexorable progress, a moral purity unattainable in everyday life. Death's permanent presence in the family made its emotional costs easier to bear. In most cases where death was exceptionally sudden and violent, as on the battlefield, it was usually possible to come to terms with it through the ideology of heroism, chivalry, or self-sacrifice. Even an ignominious death, by suicide or on the gallows, had its appointed rituals — the suicide note, often with its claim to a noble motive, the last meal of the condemned, the speech from the scaffold.

Death from cholera was, almost by definition, anything but beautiful. It was a new disease, which people found hard to fit into the patterns of coping with death evolved across the preceding centuries. Moreover, the occurrence of cholera epidemics was sufficiently rare for people to be able to suppress their consciousness of its visitations. The threat which it posed was not permanent, and therefore not psychologically manageable. Its impact was unpredictable, its causes unknown or disputed. It affected every group of the population. Thus when a cholera epidemic did occur, it stamped itself on the public consciousness with all the force of a natural disaster. Tuberculosis, though a great killer, was usually a slow disease. It spread through the city's population at a pace so leisurely that no one could notice whether it was increasing or decreasing in incidence. Cholera raged through the population with terrifying speed. People could be walking about normally, with no symptoms one day, and yet be dead the next morning. The mere onset of the symptoms could sometimes be enough to kill. People were appalled by the terrifying and unpredictable suddenness with which the disease struck. A businessman could leave his house in good order in the morning and return from work in the evening to find a note on the door saying his wife and family had been taken to hospital after being stricken down during the day. A woman could begin her supper in good health but not live to eat the pudding. Such stories, and the fact of their wide circulation during epidemics, attested to the fact that the suddenness with which cholera attacked people was one of its most frightening aspects.

In addition, the symptoms of cholera were peculiarly horrifying to nineteenth-century bourgeois sensibility. Consumptives exhibited few symptoms that caused embarrassment or discomfort in the onlooker, and then only from time to time. On the whole, they merely became pale and interesting. Even typhoid, despite some unpleasant symptoms, was considered socially acceptable and claimed a number of prominent victims. It presented symptoms of fever that took some weeks to progress and could be understood in terms of a drama of life and death, so that spectators were frequently present at the bedside to watch the whole performance and converse with the patient in his or her moments of lucidity. Not so cholera. The blue, "corrugated" appearance of the skin and the dull, sunken eyes of sufferers transformed their bodies from those of recognizable people, friends, family, relatives, into the living dead within a matter of hours. Worse still, the massive loss of body fluids, the constant vomiting and defecating of vast quantities of liquid excreta, were horrifying and deeply disgusting in an age which, more than any other, sought to conceal bodily functions from itself. Bourgeois society . . . took increasing pains, as the century wore on, to make private the grosser physical acts of daily living and to pretend that they did not exist. Cholera broke through the precarious barriers erected against physicality in the name of civilization. The mere sight of its symptoms was distressing; the thought that one might oneself suddenly be seized with an uncontrollable, massive attack of diarrhoea in a tram,[2] in a restaurant, or on the street, in the presence of scores or hundreds of respectable people, must have been almost as terrifying as the thought of death itself. It is telling that while quiet diseases such as cancer and tuberculosis were widely used as literary metaphors, cholera's appearance in the literature of the nineteenth century is rare. . . .

Such was the nature of the disease that broke out in Hamburg on 5 October 1831, when a sixty-seven year-old former sailor called Peter Petersen, who mainly lived from begging, fell ill with "violent vomiting and diarrhoea." Police surgeon Hauptfleisch found him on 6 October suffering from severe cramps, "the extremities ice-cold, hands and feet blue, and eyes sunken." At 6 P.M. on 6 October 1831, Petersen died. At this point the authorities learned of another case that had occurred on 2 October on board a barge that had travelled down the Elbe from Wittenberge. It is most likely that the disease had entered the city by this route, through infection of the river-water upstream from Hamburg, where the barge lay in quarantine in the port of Geesthacht. Probably Petersen had for some reason come into contact with the river water; or it had infected the sour milk which he often drank. Several of the 41 inhabitants of his cellar lodgings, who "consisted in their entirety of vagabonds and beggars" as a history of the epidemic written later in the same year subsequently noted, also fell ill with the same symptoms. So too did some of Petersen's companions in the begging trade. Soon cases were being reported all over the city. Already on 11 October 14 new cases were reported; on 16 October there were 44, and on the 18th day the epidemic reached its height, with 51 new cases. Thereafter it declined rapidly. Hamburg breathed again. The epidemic had, all things considered, been a good deal less severe than many people had feared.

. . . But it had not yet disappeared from Hamburg. The epidemic was officially regarded as having ended in January, and the various precautionary measures ordered by the authorities were relaxed. No cases occurred in February or March. Already on 1 April, however, a new case was reported, and eight further cases, with five deaths in all, were confirmed before the Senate, on 27 April 1832, finally concluded that cholera had broken out once more. The disease spread throughout May and June, reaching a first peak on 16 June, when 92 cases were reported within the space of a few hours. In July it declined, so that towards the end of the month there were only half a dozen or so new cases reported each day. But in August it grew in intensity once more, with 30 new cases reported on the 26th. Throughout September and October it showed no signs of departing, with anything between 5 and 15 new cases occurring each day. In November it finally began to abate. The last case was reported on 17 December. All in all, 3,349 people in Hamburg fell victim to the disease in the epidemic of April–December 1832. 1,652 of them died. In the end, therefore, Hamburg was quite seriously affected by the epidemic of 1831–2.

---

[2] Streetcar.

How the medical profession and the authorities dealt with the new disease depended on what they thought caused it. Here opinions were divided. The obvious model to which cholera seemed to conform was the plague. . . . Two Berlin medical men, writing in 1831, argued that it was "solely and exclusively caused and transmitted by an infectious material" which was spread in people's breath, in their clothing, in their excretions, and in the things they touched. They drew optimistic conclusions from their theory. If cholera was caused by a miasma,[3] they declared, there would be no means by which the individual citizen could protect himself. A contagionist theory[4] placed the means of prevention in everyone's hands. . . .

The doctrine of contagion was a very old one. It went back at least as far as the plague writings of the sixteenth century, which postulated transmission by touch, by infected clothing or goods, and (exceptionally) inhalation of an infected atmosphere. By the 1830s, however, many medical scientists seriously doubted the adequacy of the contagionist model. A second type of theory stressed instead the importance of local miasmas, in which the air was polluted by factors peculiar to certain localities under specific conditions. This too was an old theory, with parallels in medieval plague medicine. . . . Even before the disease arrived in Hamburg the local medical profession was split over the issue. On 21 June 1831 the Doctors' Club decided to meet once a week to study and discuss the reports of cholera coming in from further east and prepare for its possible arrival. Letters from doctors in Königsberg, St. Petersburg, Warsaw, and other cities where the disease had broken out were read aloud and debated. Here the first battles took place between the "contagionists" and "miasmatists." . . .

What particularly impressed the anticontagionists was the universal failure of quarantine. Time and again this was the major reason given for concluding that the disease was not contagious. . . . So certain were some writers of the noncontagious character of the disease that they predicted in advance of its arrival that cholera would never reach Hamburg. Dr. H. W. Buek, the City Medical Officer (*Stadtphysikus*), . . . gave it as his firm opinion in December 1830 "that this oriental form of disease should appear in the heart of Germany . . . seems to me . . . to be very unlikely, indeed almost unthinkable." Yet appear it did; and soon the idea of contagion was in disrepute because quarantine had failed to work. Doctors began to be converted to the idea that cholera was produced by a miasma. F. Siemerling, writing in 1831, called it *malaria animata* or "animated swamp-air" released by rotting plants in marshy land. . . .

If cholera was caused by a local miasma, then how was the disease transmitted from place to place? One writer, Karl Preu, noting that it appeared to travel along waterways, hypothesized that the miasma was carried along by "the strong airstreams that prevail along such great rivers." From there it sank into the ground

---

[3] Bad-smelling vapor thought to transmit disease.

[4] The belief that diseases are transmitted from one person to another.

on the river banks. He denied that the miasma was produced by any particular type of weather. Dr. C. F. Nagel, writing in Altona, went further in the direction of a "contingent contagionism." He argued that the disease was in part the consequence of conditions in the ground the nature of which was not yet properly understood; it also seemed to be carried by "infection by people, perhaps also by goods and effects." However, though he practised in state-interventionist Altona rather than free-trade Hamburg, Nagel did not go so far as to argue for quarantine and isolation as preventive measures. He preferred instead to place his main emphasis on personal behaviour. "Nothing encourages the outbreak of this disease more than excessive, persistent fear of the same." If people kept calm and avoided a "disorderly . . . way of life," they would be safe. In particular dirt, damp, and neglected living conditions, and above all, the "abuse of alcoholic beverages" encouraged infection. "Old drunkards" were particularly vulnerable. Thus Nagel inserted his theory within a powerful current of opinion which ascribed disease to the moral weakness of the victims.

The tendency to ascribe infection to moral failings or psychological disturbance in the victim was very widespread. "Just don't be afraid!" people were advised, "be moderate and sober!" Fear, wrote Wilhelm Cohnstein of Glogau, in a pamphlet circulating in Hamburg before the outbreak of cholera, had a "paralysing influence on the nervous system." . . .

In general, therefore, three basic explanations of cholera seem to have been circulating in Hamburg in the early 1830s: the contagionist, the miasmatist, and the moral or psychological. . . .

However, the experience of the first epidemic was enough to persuade most medical men in Hamburg — as in other parts of Europe — that whatever else cholera was, it was not a contagious disease in the accepted meaning of the word. As Zimmermann[5] remarked in 1832, "a conviction that cholera is not contagious has become so fixed here, as everywhere, among the medical and lay public, that it would be difficult to bring them over to any other point of view." It was particularly important that the Chief Medical Officer of the city, *Stadtphysikus* Dr. Heinrich Wilhelm Buek (1796–1879), was from the outset a convinced anticontagionist; his influence was doubtless a contributing factor to the spread of anticontagionist views in the Hamburg medical profession after 1831. In his official report on the next major cholera epidemic to hit the city, in 1848, Buek repeated "that an *import,* a transmission from one victim to another, an assumption that is still to be found here and there, has *not* happened here." This was proved, he considered, by the fact that the first cases to occur broke out in different parts of the city and were thus not connected. Yet "the manner in which cholera is *spread,*" he was forced to confess, "is still a riddle, nor has the present epidemic given us any clues to it." Indeed, so insoluble did the problem seem that the Doctors' Club did not think it worth discussing at all in 1848–9. The medical pro-

---

[5] K. G. Zimmermann, physician and chronicler of the Hamburg cholera epidemic of the 1830s.

fession remained anticontagionist in its majority. . . . But its unity was essentially negative: the doctors could agree on what cholera was not, but they were completely at a loss when it came to explaining what it actually was.

By 1860, however, all this had changed. A new theory of cholera had been developed which seemed to offer the answer to all these problems. Its author was the Bavarian scientist Max von Pettenkofer. . . .

. . . In his own day, and indeed in his own mind, Pettenkofer was the best-known and most implacable of the contagionists' opponents. His ideas evolved and changed in various respects over the years, but the central elements in his mature theory remained constant, and it is important to look at them briefly since their consequences proved to be practical as well as theoretical.

Pettenkofer's theories of cholera took their starting-point in the ideas of his mentor Justus Liebig.[6] These stressed, among other things, the importance of the fermentation of decomposing matter as an influence on the receptivity of a given area to epidemic diseases. Pettenkofer began to apply these ideas in his account of the 1854 epidemic in Munich, published the following year. While accepting the existence of an infectious element which enabled cholera to be transported from one place to another, he denied that the disease was spread "by contagion in the narrow sense of the word." Nor, he asserted, could it possibly be carried by drinking-water. Indeed, he wrote that "in my report in Munich, I have disposed, once and for all, of causation by drinking-water." Nor, finally, was the disease carried in infected clothes or goods. It was most probably transmitted from place to place by human beings, even those who had not suffered the symptoms of cholera. But they could have no effect unless they infected the soil with their excreta. Influenced by Liebig's work on fermentation, Pettenkofer developed over the decade 1855–65 an elaborate theory of the conditions under which a cholera miasma could arise. It depended, he argued, on a series of changes in the level of the water-table or "ground-water." The water-table would suddenly rise, and the moisture content of the soil increase. These events were followed by a dry period in which the water-table dropped and the moisture content of the soil fell. Thus a layer of soil would be left above the water-table; cholera would "germinate" in this soil, provided of course that the soil had been infected with the cholera germ. A miasma would then be created, in which the disease was transmitted through air polluted by the germination process. Thus people living on high ground, or even on the upper storeys of apartment blocks, could enjoy a relative immunity, while those living on low-lying or marshy land, in cellars, or in cramped and confined conditions, where the circulation of air was restricted, were most at risk.

Pettenkofer thus became the self-appointed champion of the "localist" school, which emphasized meteorological influences operating through changes in the water-table. Though he accepted a contagious element in cholera, he did not con-

---

[6] German chemist (1803–1873).

sider it very important, and the bulk of his writings on the subject was devoted either to proving that the disease could not be transmitted by drinking-water, or to elaborating and further refining his own "ground-water" theory and providing a statistical basis for its major assertions. On these fundamental points he did not change his mind over the decades. Pettenkofer's theory achieved widespread currency, helped by his enormous influence in the field of hygiene, a discipline of which indeed he has some claim to be regarded as the founding father. . . .

In the 1860s and 1870s, therefore, there can be little doubt that Pettenkofer's "ground-water theory," and his dismissal of the notion that cholera was a water-borne disease, dominated official and medical approaches to the cholera problem in Germany. His ideas were never undisputed, and many doctors continued to emphasize moral and other factors in the aetiology[7] of cholera. But Pettenkofer's influence is unmistakable not only in a large body of medical writings on cholera by many different commentators, but also in official policy as well. How can it be explained? Certainly it would not have been possible without his indefatigable energy and the ceaseless flow of publications on cholera that streamed from his pen. Equally certainly, it owed a lot to his enormous reputation in the field of social hygiene, with which the problem of cholera had long been recognized as having an intimate though hotly disputed connection. But there were more general reasons for Pettenkofer's influence. Pettenkofer was a pioneer of preventive medicine. He advocated a broad approach and believed strongly in public education as a means of improving public health. Against some opposition from his own university, he was a determined popularizer of his own views, both on paper and by word of mouth. He was an advocate of temperance, of cleanliness, of regular bathing, of a "rational diet," of warm clothing, and above all of fresh air. Indeed, if anyone deserved to be called a "fresh-air fanatic" it was Max von Pettenkofer. He opposed drinking not least because it took place in "the horrible atmosphere" of smoke-filled, overcrowded taverns. He maintained that "our children's health suffers when they are exposed for a number of hours to the atmosphere of ill-ventilated schoolrooms." He poured well-deserved scorn on the Germans' traditional horror of draughts. He admired the English habit of maintaining an open fire in every parlour because, as he perceptively remarked, "the English fireplace is a very poor heating device but good for ventilation." All these improvements could be achieved, he thought, by means of public education and propaganda. Legislation was not only largely unnecessary, it was also impracticable.

Pettenkofer was, to be sure, an advocate of state regulation and reform where he considered it absolutely necessary in order to reduce the possibility of creating an unhealthy miasma through contamination of the soil. He insisted on the provision of adequate sewage and waste disposal. He believed that every dwelling, even a garret apartment, should be supplied with water from a central source, because this meant people were more likely to wash frequently than if they had to

---

[7] The causes of a specific disease.

fetch the water from a distance. The water, therefore, had to be clean, for if foul water was repeatedly used for washing it could turn the surfaces which it affected into breeding-places for disease. It was largely due to Pettenkofer's insistence that a slaughterhouse was constructed in Munich in 1878, that the city acquired a new water-supply from the mountains, and that a new sewage system was installed, channelling the waste into the river downstream from the city and so preventing it from getting into the soil, where he thought it did so much harm. Pettenkofer warned against regarding sewage disposal and the provision of a fresh water-supply as all that were necessary to the improvement of public health, however. He asserted that a nutritious diet and fresh air were far more important. Moreover, he does not seem to have thought it necessary to provide a filtration system for the water-supply. It was enough for the water-supply to avoid direct contamination by contact with ground-water in the soil. Thus spring-water carried from the mountains was superior to water drawn from wells in the city. The water with which he arranged for Munich to be supplied certainly was not filtrated, and indeed, shortly after the water began flowing a massive typhoid epidemic hit the city, spread by the new supply system. Pettenkofer continued to believe none the less that epidemic diseases could not spread in water. He did advocate reducing overcrowding in houses "partly by education and partly by regulations," but again he insisted that "we do not solve the problem by providing the poor with the most necessary food, housing and clothing unless we at the same time educate them in painstaking cleanliness."

. . . Pettenkofer sought to prove that prevention would result in a massive saving in hospital costs by reducing disease. It thus offered municipal authorities a substantial return on their initial investment. He called hygiene "health economics." Such preventive measures as proper sewage disposal and the provision of drinking-water were analogous to the minimal state intervention necessary to guarantee the smooth running of the economy, rather like the standardization of weights and measures or — in Hamburg — the construction of the harbour. Once they had been provided, the real responsibility for health and well-being lay with the individual.

In keeping with this voluntaristic approach to health, Pettenkofer was opposed to the massive state intervention favoured by the contagionists. Prevention, he believed, was all: once an epidemic had actually broken out, the state could do nothing to check its progress. In a major series of articles published in 1886–7, Pettenkofer declared that quarantine measures were useless against cholera. They would always be ineffective, he said. They were irrelevant to the decisive factor, which was the condition of the soil. The isolation of cholera cases after the outbreak of an epidemic, he wrote, "is equally useless; and so is the special cholera hospital." Moreover, he added, "it is obvious that I consider the disinfection of the excreta of cholera patients to be as ineffective as the isolation of cholera patients." This was because "cholera patients produced no effective infectious material." Flight was a reasonable precaution since it removed people from the miasmatic local influences. The closing of markets, fairs, and other gatherings would achieve nothing, unless they were held in a locality where the soil factor was powerful. Finally, he continued to deny categorically that cholera was transmitted by drinking-water, so all measures during an epidemic to provide people with alternative supplies of pure or boiled water were futile.

The parallels between Pettenkofer's theory of cholera and liberal theories of the state[8] are obvious. Pettenkofer attracted the adherence of medical opinion by offering a synthesis of many previous accounts and linking it to the established scientific principle of fermentation. But his ideas also had a broader appeal. His emphasis on sanitation, cleanliness, fresh air, and a rational diet were more than welcome to the German middle classes at a time when the urban environment was rapidly deteriorating, and when bourgeois consciousness of the presence of dirt and excrement, noxious vapours, and polluted or adulterated food was growing stronger. The stress he laid on temperance and regularity accorded strongly with bourgeois values, as did the belief he expressed that hygienic improvement depended above all on the individual. But the seductiveness of Pettenkofer's theories went even further than this. As we shall now see, they found a ready response not only because of the values which they expressed and the promise of environmental improvement which they held out, but also because of the direct appeal they directed to bourgeois self-interest.

When cholera first appeared on the European scene, governments everywhere went to great lengths to try and halt its progress. In Russia, military cordons were thrown around infected areas; in the Habsburg Empire, stringent quarantine measures were introduced. These activities were almost invariably ineffective. Not only did they fail to stop the cholera, they also provoked widespread popular unrest. The government and military presence in the stricken areas, the isolation of hospitalized victims, and the sudden appearance of large numbers of doctors, including many from other areas and countries who had come to observe the disease, convinced many Russian peasants that the government was trying to kill them off. Several physicians and officials were massacred amid widespread rioting. In the Habsburg Empire castles were sacked and quarantine aid officers and doctors were slaughtered. When the disease reached Prussia, official efforts to control it met with a similar response. Popular resentment against official interference in the livelihood of journeymen, peasants, traders, and many others found symbolic expression in the belief that the disease was the product of poisoning by physicians engaged in a secret campaign to reduce the excess population. . . .

Public order was very much at the front of the mind of authority as the cholera epidemic spread across Eastern and Central Europe in 1831. Even Hamburg did not escape; in September 1830 popular unrest in the city expressed itself in prolonged though minor anti-Semitic disturbances. Nevertheless, in common with the authorities elsewhere in Europe, the government of the city-state

---

[8] The belief that the state should improve the population by inculcating middle-class values.

proceeded in the summer of 1831 to impose restrictions on the movement of people and goods in an attempt to stop the approach of the cholera epidemic. Incoming ships and river barges were subjected to medical quarantine from the summer of 1831 until the beginning of 1832. From 8 October the Senate refused to issue clean bills of health to ships leaving the port. For the duration of the 1831 epidemic, Hamburg was under medical quarantine with severe restrictions on trade.

The Hamburg Senate was no less energetic in the measures which it took to combat the disease once it actually arrived. In July 1831, indeed, well before the outbreak of the disease, it issued an elaborate set of ordinances, to come into force immediately the epidemic broke out, as it eventually did in October. A General Health Commission was established, with special local commissions for the various districts of the city. All cases were to be reported to these commissions as soon as they broke out. "Houses in which there are people stricken with cholera will be signified with a poster, on which the word 'cholera' is written, so that everyone knows that they are infected." Such houses were to be isolated and disinfected. A special commission was established, to supervise disinfection work. This included chlorine fumigation in the streets, to clean the air. The cheap lodging-house where the disease had broken out was evacuated and fumigated some five days after the first case was reported, and other affected houses were similarly treated. . . . All these measures, of course, were predicated on the assumption that cholera was an infectious disease.

But they met with increasing criticism as time went on. In the first place, they were clearly unable to prevent the arrival of the disease or its spread through the city and beyond. Secondly, in Hamburg as elsewhere, they were seen as posing a threat to public order. Like other German cities, Hamburg was walled in the 1830s, but its expansion with the growth of trade had already led to the creation of a substantial built-up area of urban settlement outside the walls, in St. Pauli and St. Georg. The inhabitants of these areas resented their exclusion from the governing institutions of the city and had been petitioning for equal rights for some time, with little success. When the General Health Commission was founded in July, the Chief of the St. Georg Battalion of the Citizens' Militia demanded a seat on it, and was dubbed a "trouble-maker" for his pains. The incident led to a series of demonstrations in which the inhabitants of the suburb attempted forcibly to prevent the nightly closure of the city gate, the symbol of their exclusion from equal participation in the city's affairs. Eventually the problem was solved, but it was now felt in the Senate that any further organizational measures against the epidemic might easily offend popular sensibilities in a similar way. Finally, the measures taken in 1831 were very expensive. They involved, for example, the employment of some 700 workers to carry out the hospitalization, quarantine, and fumigation measures ordered by the Senate, as well as the construction of the special hospitals and isolation wards where the sick were housed.

Medical and bourgeois opinion all over Europe was now mobilizing against quarantine and the other interventionist policies adopted in the face of the first cholera epidemic. Quarantine, maintained a pamphlet published in Danzig in

1831, was not only useless but dangerous. It exhausted state finances, disrupted trade, and so increased poverty. It caused terror and panic flight in the population and prevented the support of the afflicted and isolated families by welfare agencies. . . . There was thus ample support for the decision of the Hamburg authorities to drop early in 1832 all the precautions they had taken against cholera the previous year. These precautions had contributed, it was believed, to "fear and terror" among "the gentlemen who frequent our Exchange," and the sealing-off of the borders by the Prussian and Danish authorities had done untold damage to trade.

The Senate was fortified in its decision by the general swing of medical opinion against contagionism, and by the fact that the epidemic had in the end proved a good deal less severe than originally feared. The quarantine measures were thus not renewed; and the state sanitary stations (*Sanitätswachen*) set up to deal with the disease were disbanded. When cholera broke out with increased virulence later in the year, the burden of combating the disease was placed entirely on the medical profession. The Doctors' Club set up a sanitary station in its rooms, staffed by two physicians at a time, working shifts, during the day. There were no medical services available after 10 P.M. To the Doctors' Club also fell the task of compiling lists of the sick and the dead. It was the medical profession, not the state, that arranged for hospitalization of victims and supplied ambulancemen and nursing staff, though expenses could be claimed for these measures, in arrears, from the authorities. There were no quarantine measures and no isolation wards: cholera patients were simply put alongside the normal hospital inmates. No official announcements were made of new cases, or even of the presence of an epidemic. It was hardly surprising, therefore, that while the 1831 epidemic cost the authorities fully half a million Marks Courant,[9] that of the following year cost them only twenty thousand, even though it was considerably more severe.

The widespread concern with cholera as a problem of individual morality found its way into the handbooks of medical advice on how to prevent the disease. Disease appeared here as the consequence not so much of immorality as of emotional disorder or excitement — the very factor which was also seen as at the root of the riot and rebellion with which cholera was so often associated. Virtually all the early literature, including the official leaflet issued in 1831, prescribed personal cleanliness and much of it also offered dietary advice, including the avoidance of "acidulous, watery foods and those which cool down the stomach and abdomen." Miasmatists stressed the need for fresh air, while the widespread belief that cholera was an extreme form of "the common cold" led many to urge the importance of keeping warm. Most widespread and insistent of all was the advice to avoid physical or emotional excess. Many doctors in 1831 considered that fear of the disease was a sure invitation for it to strike. Correspondingly they urged people to lead a sober and moderate life and to avoid any kind of upset. People were told to avoid "passions," to trust in God, and to maintain an "orderly

---

[9] Standard Marks, the basic monetary unit.

way of life." The classic formula was provided by the Prussian physician Wilhelm Cohnstein, who declared that a calm and positive frame of mind was best maintained by "unconditional trust I: in Divine Providence and II: in the orders of the authorities." . . .

The association of cholera with individual immorality was thus expressed in the very theories which medical men developed to account for it. It was felt that emotional excess could lead to increased receptivity to infection. But there was another reason for the widespread association of cholera with lack of self-restraint. Not only did it lead to public disorder in itself, but the threat which it posed was magnified by the fact that it generally appeared at moments of tension in European society, because social and international conflict both led to large-scale troop movements which tremendously accelerated the pace and scale of epidemic infection. In 1830 these troop movements were taking place everywhere in Europe, from Poland, where the Russian army was engaged in putting down a major nationalist uprising, through to the West where military engagements were taking place in many countries in connection with the successful or unsuccessful revolutions of that year. During the revolutionary upheavals of 1848–9 there were even more extensive troop movements, with the Russian army in Vienna and the Prussians marching as far west as Baden, in the deep south-west of Germany. Similarly, Bismarck's[10] wars of 1866 against Austria, and of 1870–1 against France, both brought cholera to Hamburg and spread it to other areas as well. Because the disease was notoriously liable to appear at moments of acute political tension, it is hardly surprising that the first reaction of the authorities was to appeal for calm.

Such an appeal, understandably enough, was issued with greater force than ever in the revolutionary year of 1848. On that occasion, Dr. Friedrich Simon, a Hamburg medical practitioner, urged that inns and bars be closed early for the duration of the epidemic and urged his readers to lead "a moderate, sober, and regular life-style" and "to avoid any excesses." Not only did this mean the avoidance of alcohol. It also meant, Simon explained, that

> altogether a state of mind that is as evenly balanced as possible is an essential and important means of protection. . . . Tiring intellectual exertions, especially deep into the night, have a disadvantageous effect; but strong and long-lasting spiritual excitements of other kinds, powerful passions and changes of mood, even exaggerated joy and sprightliness, are just as much to be avoided.

In 1848 there was no doubt that for the Hamburg Senate the preservation of public order was the first priority. In July, the medical representatives on the Health Committee held a meeting to discuss measures to be taken in view of the fact that after an interval of sixteen years, cholera was once more approaching the city from the east:

---

[10] Otto von Bismarck (1815–1898), Prussian statesman who unified Germany.

The first thing that we feel impelled to express, before anything else, is the wish that the public be alarmed and disturbed as little as possible. Therefore we would like to see the avoidance of all sensation during the preparations and right up to the actual outbreak of the epidemic. We do not want the release of public notices calling attention to this so widely feared disease, nor, later, when the epidemic has really broken out, do we want measures to be taken which allow the disease to appear as particularly dangerous or extraordinary.

Such measures, in their opinion, would only cause panic and make things worse. The previous epidemic had, they argued, showed beyond doubt that cholera was not a contagious disease. So it was decided on these grounds not to establish a quarantine, not to isolate the sick, nor to make any special arrangements for burying the victims. Such measures, the doctors warned, "are no help at all, but rather cause endless damage by getting people excited." The most that was necessary was the printing of a pamphlet advising people what to do in the event of an epidemic, together with arrangements to feed the poor, control the quality of food in the markets, ensure the cleanliness and airiness of doss-houses,[11] and hospitalize the victims should there be any. . . .

The unusually strong concern with public order, reflecting the fact that the political conflicts and disturbances of the revolutionary year reached their height in the first week in September, just as the cholera broke out, led once more to a policy of inaction on the part of the Hamburg authorities. Clearly they were anxious not to give further cause for lower-class discontent, which had already led to barricades and demonstrations in August. As in 1832, therefore, virtually nothing was done to cope with the epidemic. . . .

The epidemics of 1832 and 1848 thus established a firm tradition in Hamburg, according to which the state did virtually nothing to prevent or combat the disease, and took no steps to confirm or announce its presence in the city. The burden of coping with cholera fell instead on the medical profession and voluntary organizations such as the Doctors' Club. Here too, as we have seen, anticontagionism reigned supreme. The Chief Medical Officer, Dr. Buek, had been an anticontagionist even before the arrival of cholera in 1831; he remained one in the epidemic of 1848. There were further minor epidemics in the 1850s . . . and more serious ones in 1859 and 1866. . . . But the tradition of inactivity was only strengthened by the appointment of Buek's successor as Chief Medical Officer, Dr. Johann Caspar Theodor Kraus, a "convinced supporter of Pettenkofer's views." . . .

One of the most striking features of the history of medical administration in nineteenth-century Hamburg was the continuity of senior personnel. Dr. Buek was closely involved in dealing with all the epidemics from 1831 to 1873; Dr. Kraus, whose first experience of cholera came in 1873, was still in office in 1892.

---

[11] Cheap, overnight shelters for homeless men.

. . . [N]othing happened between 1873 and 1892, not even Koch's discoveries,[12] to make Kraus change his mind on the subject of cholera. In 1892, as in 1873, Kraus and the medical authorities were still operating to an "absolutely definite plan" which obliged them to deny the existence of Asiatic cholera in Hamburg until after the disease had reached epidemic proportions. This policy could be justified to some extent by the anticontagionist views which Kraus espoused, but there could be little doubt that it had its origins in the fear of the quarantine measures that would immediately loom over the city if an official declaration of a cholera epidemic was made. . . .

The influence of Pettenkofer since the 1850s had diverted the attention of the medical profession to the soil factor. In many cases, it was agreed in 1874 that "one is inclined to regard possible harmful substances in the soil as a direct cause." But Pettenkofer and his supporters never thought it was possible to eliminate these "harmful substances" altogether. Improved sewage disposal would certainly help, they thought; and indeed great improvements had taken place in this area since mid-century. The faith they placed in a centralized water-supply, uncontaminated, as drinking-wells often were, by infected "ground-water," was not matched by any corresponding belief in the importance of filtration. In most respects, the influence of Pettenkofer in Hamburg simply confirmed the existing way of doing things. In 1873, as in all previous cholera epidemics since the defeat of contagionism in 1831, the medical profession and the Senate did their utmost to avoid official confirmation of the disease's presence in the city, and once they were forced to concede this point, made no attempt to impose quarantine, to isolate the victims, or to mount a campaign of disinfection. By 1871 at least the Senate was agreeable to undertaking a limited amount of state action, lending the police to collect the sick and the dead, and providing funds to stop the contamination of the ground-water. But the avoidance of financial costs and the maintenance of public order remained the highest priorities. Those who disapproved of this policy of state inaction remained a tiny minority.

---

[12] Robert Koch (1843–1910), German physician who received the Nobel Prize in 1905 for his work in bacteriology.

MAKING CONNECTIONS:
DISEASE AND DEATH

1. In Part One, John McManners, in "Death's Arbitrary Empire," chronicles the poor living conditions, diet, and health of the mass of the French population in the eighteenth century and notes the most frequent causes of death. Compare the selection by McManners to the one you have just read by Evans. What significant differences existed in the ways of living and dying in the eighteenth versus the nineteenth century? How do you account for these differences? Which diseases or types of death offended eighteenth-century sensibilities as cholera offended nineteenth-century cultural mores?

2. Evans explains that cholera, unlike other diseases, was socially unacceptable because of its suddenness, unpleasantness, and links to the lower classes. Other ways of dying appeared possibly heroic, or at least dignified, to the nineteenth-century elite — aristocrats, industrialists, and merchants — who could respect death on the battlefield or a passing away from a slow, lingering disease. How did cholera upset the traditional patterns of coping with death?

3. Do you think the elite's collective opinion of the "little people" differed in the eighteenth and nineteenth centuries? What connections do you see between lower-class discontent and the Hamburg government's handling of cholera epidemics?

4. McManners underscores the economic insecurity that lay behind "death's arbitrary empire." Did the economic prosperity that international trade brought to Hamburg make death's empire any less arbitrary in the nineteenth century? Explain.

IS GOD FRENCH?
Eugen Weber

Many European historians have expanded the study of religion by adding social history to the more traditional studies of theology and church politics. Examining parish registers, wills, sermons, visitation reports by clergy, diaries, letters, and tracts and pamphlets written for the populace, historians have attempted to describe both daily religious behavior and the thoughts of the masses. Eugen Weber, a historian who has written numerous books on nineteenth- and twentieth-century France, here elucidates the meaning of religion to nineteenth-century French people.

France in the second half of the nineteenth century appeared to be a solidly Roman Catholic nation. In the census that Weber cites, over 98 percent of the French affirmed themselves as Catholic, and there were certainly enough priests to minister to the spiritual needs of the populace. Yet today the major religion of the French is indifference. What developments (from the French Revolution on) does Weber discuss that reveal a decline of religiousness?

Some people may have rejected supernatural religion altogether, or they might just have lost faith in the institutional Church. After all, it is not uncommon for sincerely religious people to stay away from churches. Scholars, in fact, often debate the extent to which Church attendance measures religious belief.

Note the varied roles the Church played in the lives of the nineteenth-century French. Weber describes a panoply of popular religious beliefs, including attitudes toward saints and miracles. Ever since the Middle Ages, there has been perennial tension between the institutional view of religion and the popular attitude toward religious practice. How did the Church feel about parishioners' veneration of saints and craving for the miraculous? What functions did miracles serve? How did the flock view priests' functions? Could a priest be considered a magician? What Church rules and prohibitions did the French come to disregard? The popularity of Lourdes, a pilgrimage site in southern France

Eugen Weber, "Is God French?" adapted by Eugen Weber from "Dieu Est-Il Français?" in *Peasants into Frenchmen: The Modernization of Rural France, 1870–1914* (Stanford: Stanford University Press, 1976), 339–356.

where a girl had eighteen visions of the Virgin Mary in 1858, is a marvelous example of the strength of popular devotion and the Church's desire to control its flock's religious expressions.

Religion did not simply mean belief and practice; there was a commercial side to religion that Weber does not neglect. Thus a pilgrimage signified more than a possible cure for a crippling disease or improved chances for salvation. There was money to be made from pilgrims, and, for their part, the pilgrims could play tourist and enjoy an escape from their daily routines.

Weber concludes this selection with a story that illustrates "the requiem of nineteenth-century religion." Perhaps Weber is a bit premature, for the 1890s unleashed a torrent of religious feeling in the form of virulent anti-Semitism that colored the notorious Dreyfus affair. There is no doubt, however, that by the end of the century the traditional faith of the peasantry had changed in dramatic ways and the Church had lost its hold on the hearts and minds of many French people.

In the mid-1870's 35,387,703 of the 36,000,000 people in France were listed in the official census as Catholics. The rest declared themselves Protestants (something under 600,000), Jews (50,000), or freethinkers (80,000). The secular clergy of the Catholic church alone included 55,369 priests, one for every 639 inhabitants. Roman Catholicism remained, as it had been in 1801, "the religion of the majority of Frenchmen."

Whatever else this meant, it meant that the Church was an integral part of life. It presided over all the major occasions in a person's life — birth, marriage, death — and over the welfare of the community and the conduct of its members. It helped the crops increase and the cattle prosper. It healed, taught, and preserved from harm. . . .

Religion provided spells and incantations, often written down and passed on preciously like amulets. These, like its ceremonies, were efficacious and protective. The peasant . . . was proud to recite his prayers. "He has prayers for thunder, for sickness, for going to bed at night. They are good, very good, these prayers, says he, though he doesn't understand them very well, since they are in French," or in Latin. The ritual lent solemnity to private and public occasions, as the term solemnization applied to ceremonies like marriage attests. This was particularly important in rites of passage. The first communion, the first time one received the Eucharist, was crucial — a "great matter for country children; many cannot find a job before they have done it." Marking admission into the world of workers and of earners — almost an adult world — the first communion and the preparation for it, the catechism, provided the basic initiation into the moral mysteries of life. "The children did not know how to read, so the priest was teaching them the catechism by heart [which was] full of extraordinary words and which they laughed at," recorded Charles Péguy.[1] They must have had a sense that obscure powers were properly invoked with obscure incantations. . . .

Was Christ's personal message communicated in many a village church? We cannot tell. Those sermons that one finds concern themselves with the proprieties and transgressions of everyday behavior. Policemen were less concerned with immanent justice than with infringements of petty human laws; and village priests seem to have taken a similar view. This was their civilizing function. Along with this, it was their duty to see that their flock observed all of the formal and routine religious rites. It is by the practice of such rites that adherence to religion is generally measured. When there is little participation, even on high holidays, or when it declines, religion is said to decay. Yet what did church attendance mean to churchgoers?

"Sunday, the peasants go to church . . . some moved by religious feeling, most by habit or by fear of what people say." One went to church because it was the thing to do on Sunday, because it was one of the few social occasions of the week, because it was an opportunity for talking business or meeting friends, acquaintances, relatives. It was — especially for the women, once men had grasped at the opportunities that fairs held out — the sole occasion to escape the isolation in which many lived, the major recreation or diversion in a restricted life. Observance, business, and pleasure were combined. One went to mass wearing one's Sunday best. . . . Public announcements were made by the village crier as the congregation left the service, public sales were often timed to fall after it, one could slip off later to call on the notary or the doctor, or drop in to the tavern, circle, or café. Even if a majority did not attend the service but went about their work as on any other day, "a multitude of peasants gathered in front of the church, discussed politics, made deals, filled the taverns."

In a world where entertainment was scarce, church provided a certain festive diversion. Those attending might well "love the high mass, the rich ornaments, seeing a great many statues of saints in their churches." Writing about his grandmother, Charles Péguy presented church attendance as a treat for the lonely child raised in a woodcutter's hut in Bourbonnais in the early 1800's: "When she was good, she was allowed to go on Sunday to mass in the village — she wore her sabots[2] because one doesn't go to church barefoot, and she was happy because that's where everybody met, where they exchanged news, where one heard about deaths, marriages, births, where gossip flowed about what was going on, where servants were hired."

. . . But the belief and behavior of the peasants never ceased to oscillate between observance and transgression. Until the Revolution church attendance was compulsory, and religious sanctions that could cause serious social embarrassment menaced those who skipped their Easter duties.[3] The elimination of constraints

---

[1] Essayist and poet (1873–1914), from a working-class background.

[2] Wooden clogs.

[3] That is, to attend Mass and to receive Communion.

broke this decreed unanimity. Those who had been quietly uncommitted (as in Aunis-Saintonge, where the forced conversion of Protestants had made lukewarm Catholics) were free to fall away. Political divisions and internal schism during the 1790's confused many more, and deprived parishes of pastors or cut sections of a community off from the only priest. For a decade or more, at least until the Concordat of 1801,[4] a good number of young people grew up without catechism, whole communities did not attend church, and others ceased to celebrate traditional festivals. The Décadi[5] created the habit of working on Sunday. The absence of priests left marriages to civil authorities and led to prolonged delays before baptism, if the ceremony was performed at all.

Some communities came to rely on the services of laymen, who took over the functions of absent priests, performing baptisms, marriages, and burials. . . . Ad hoc arrangements of this sort could prove enduring. . . .

Canon Fernand Boulard doubts that the Revolution really affected rural religious practice very profoundly, or that much changed in this realm until the last decade or two of the nineteenth century. He may be right. But there were discordances where there had been at least outward unity. Men who had acquired Church property and would not submit, men who had married in a civil marriage and would not seek absolution for their sin, became centers of local opposition. Not many cases of this kind of sturdy opposition developed in communities that remained cohesive, but it flourished in areas where, as in Burgundy, the memory of clerical harshness and exploitation survived, along with the fear of a reconstitution of their great domains. In Mâconnais . . . the devil appears as the hero in some local legends and triumphs over Christ, disgraced by the men who served him. The peasants had burned churches there in the Middle Ages and did so again in 1789, or stayed away thereafter. But even where the road had not been so prepared, hard times frayed clerical authority. Priests were forced to ask for help from their parishioners. Rival clergymen accused each other of the worst transgressions, diminishing still further the influence of the cloth. "People begin to separate religion from its ministers," asserted the *Statistique*[6] of Lot in 1831. But religion *was* its ministers, just as the state was bailiffs and gendarmes. And when, after 1830, liberal local mayors opposed the influence of priests loyal to the old order, they sought to sap their authority by encouraging the drift of men away from the sacraments.

We see that in the churches, as in the schools, non-attendance is a way of measuring ineffectiveness. The growing numbers of migrant workers going to the cities added to this trend. Urban workers worked Sundays and holidays, or did so very often. The more earnest the man, the more he worked. The less re-

---

[4] Agreement between the pope and the French government reestablishing religious peace and recognizing Catholicism as the religion of the majority of the French.

[5] The ten-day week created during the French Revolution to replace the seven-day week.

[6] *Statistics,* a publication.

sponsible were the more likely to get drunk during their free time. The Church did not see them either way. Like the Revolution, acquaintance with the city did not destroy religious sentiment. It simply made nonconformity possible or created another kind of conformity. Men who attended church at home because their peers did ceased to attend church where such attendance was exceptional. The city merely provided an opportunity for the collapse of practices "shallowly rooted in the personality." Returning migrants may well have lost whatever impulse to religious conformity they had left with. They did not necessarily bandy this about so long as the priest retained his influence in the community. But they were ready to welcome emancipation when it came.

At any rate, all observers seem to have sensed the shallowness of faith behind the slackness of observance. In Beauce respectable farmers, "preoccupied by the care to augment their fortune, work to this end even on Sunday during the services, so that the churches are deserted." Not that they lacked respect for religion, "but they consider that the time they would spend in church would be lost for their work and their fortune." Not challenge, but indifference and hardheadedness. . . . "The absence of religious sentiment [in the countryside, especially] is such that there are communes where scarcely one marriage in six is blessed in church." . . .

Whether unconverted or disaffected, people lost their respect for Church rules and Church prohibitions. The proportion of civil marriages grew, the delays between birth and baptism became longer. Once set at 24 hours of birth, the outside limit for baptism was extended to three days in 1830, to eight days in 1887, to "the soonest possible time" in the twentieth century. In one Sologne parish the average delay between birth and baptism, which was 2.73 days in 1854, had stretched to 15.12 days by 1901; in 1950 it ran well over three months. Less fear for the newborn's life, fewer epidemics, greater closeness between husband and wife, who was increasingly expected to play a part in the ceremony, but also indifference to what the sacrament of baptism meant and to the authority of the priest. . . . One could do without the priest if one wanted to get married when he could not, or would not, perform the ceremony.

From the Church's point of view, every innovation only made things worse. The bicycle was blamed for enabling young people to avoid mass. Tourists, visitors, and returning emigrants felt increasingly free to speak of their indifference to religious practice or even their scorn of it. Military service side by side with "pagan" urban workers made some peasants ashamed of a show of piety as a mark of their bumpkin backwardness. Finally, with war in 1914 there came a culmination of the pressures toward detachment. . . .

Religion was an urban import, like education, and, just like education, it reflected the scholarship of the Counter-Reformation and the Enlightenment — the two at one, at least, in being alien to the countryside. Tridentine[7] and post-

---

[7] From the Council of Trent (1545–1563), which clarified doctrines and reformed the Roman Catholic Church.

Tridentine missionaries, where they could, replaced familiar native rites and practices with new ones that were strange. These had no time to settle into tradition before the Revolution and the cascade of changes following it. Religious custom remained superficial, even though convention and the need for ritual kept it in being. In this respect, reputedly devout areas appear little better than incredulous ones. For the outwardly pious Solognot, religion was "an artificial system that he bore without understanding, lacking in efficacy and well above his preoccupations." . . .

Such comments may explain the frequent conjunction between indifference and some form of practice, as in Bourbonnais where peasants "have recourse to religion in all great circumstances, but following ancestral traditions rather than any real faith." Religion had didactic uses: "It fills the young with fear," and that was good and necessary, "but when we're dead we're dead," and that was common sense. Even those peasants who eschewed religious practice wanted a resident priest, for one thing, because he would teach the children to respect their parents and authority, but above all "for rites needed in social life and to ensure good crops, for festivals often connected with a healing saint." In short, the ritual and the ceremonies that were the very core of popular religion were fundamentally utilitarian. Accordingly, we might expect such pragmatic formalism to decline when its utility no longer seemed apparent, or when rival authorities and formalities beckoned.

This of course is advanced as merest supposition. I know no way of telling the spiritual hold that the Church had on people. At the visible level, however, its influence was based on practical services and subject to its ability to keep these up: consecration (in an officially acceptable sense), healing, protection, making wishes come true, and not least providing a center for traditional practices. In all these things, official religion drew generously on the popular cult of saints, of healing agencies and other useful "superstitions." Superstitions have sometimes been described as religions that did not succeed. Perhaps, in our case at least, it is they that should be called successful, since so much official religion depended on them and survived largely by indulging practices endorsed by popular belief. The people of Balesta in Comminges, noted the village teacher in 1886, "are the more religious, the more superstitious they are." . . .

We know about the widespread usage of the cross — about how the plowman signed himself before he drew the first furrow, and again before he sowed the first handful of grain; about how he would not cut a slice out of a loaf without first tracing a cross on it. But how far did this, or prayers, or kneeling in the fields when the Angelus[8] tolled, go beyond the propitiation of powers that were feared but little understood? . . .

Much that was expected of the priest indeed fell in the category of magic — white, of course, as when the priest said masses to cure animals that were under

---

[8] A Roman Catholic prayer said three times daily upon the tolling of the Angelus bell.

a spell, or when, during the traditional processions that wound their way through communal territory on Rogation Sunday,[9] he threw stones plastered with a small wax cross (priest's dung in Franche-Comté) into the fields to keep the storms and hail away. We have already seen the power over natural phenomena attributed to priests, and the logical belief that some men of the cloth wielded more powers than others. . . . It seems quite natural that when, in the early 1890's, the bishop of Mende visited the village of Saint-Enimie (Lozère), his flock should find that his blessing of their valley made the almond harvest more abundant. . . . In Meuse several priests were held to sit on clouds, thus helping to disperse them; and the Abbé Chévin, of Bar-le-Duc, who died in 1900, was accused of having made a violent storm break over his own parish.

For those who connected Catholicism and sorcery, plainly, priests could be sinister figures, holding the powers of black magic as well. As a result of natural associations, the Limousins of the twentieth century still dreaded that "priests would usher death" into the homes they visited. The fear that stalked all the inhabitants of the countryside found in the church service not only appeasement but fuel. When sermons did not deal with public discipline, they frequently stoked the fires of brimstone and hell. That was the only way "to move such an almost savage populace," remarked a Breton. "A voice like thunder, dire threats, fists belaboring the pulpit, sweat running down his cheeks, the eloquent pastor fills his hearers with delicious terror."

Benoît Malon (another hostile witness) has denounced the obsessive effects this sort of thing could have on people, especially children, haunted throughout life by the dread of hell-fire, torments, retribution, and circumambient fiends. But priestly menaces were bound to be intimidating to the most sober when menace was the staff of everyday life. Living was marginal, disaster inexplicable and uncontrollable. . . . Where harm and ill-fortune were swiftly come by, nothing was easier than to claim that they were punishments of heaven. Long centuries of trying to mollify and coax the powerful conjured up a religion where fear almost excluded love, a faith bent to flatter and do honor to the heavenly lords in order to obtain their protection or avoid their ire. Power and irascibility were what impressed. The peasants would not work their cattle on the feasts of the nastiest saints, the ones most likely to resent and revenge any irreverence. . . .

God was far away. The saints were near. Both were anthropomorphic. Saints were intercessors. One did not address God directly, but prayed to saints to request his favors, rewarded them if the crop was good or the weather fair, even chastised them, as at Haudimont (Meuse), where Saint Urban, accused of permitting the vines to freeze on May 25, his own feastday, was dragged in effigy through the nettles around his church. The greatest saint of all, of course, was the Virgin, an unparalleled source of delivery from harm. The *gwerz* (ballad) made up when a new pilgrimage to her was launched in 1894 at Plounéour-Menez recited

---

[9] The Sunday before Ascension Day, which marked the supposed bodily ascent of Jesus to heaven.

only recent and concrete miracles: saving men from falling, drowning, prison, and so on. These were the functions of a saint.

But the chief function of saints on earth was healing, and every malady was the province of a particular saint. The attribution could vary from region to region, with some local patron saint taking over duties another saint performed elsewhere; but it was a creation of popular design. The conjunction between saint and illness was determined by associations, some naively evident, others lost in the mists of time. Thus Saint Eutropius healed dropsy . . . ; Saint Cloud healed boils . . . ; Saint Diétrine dealt with herpes and scurf . . . ; Saint Aignan coped with ringworm and scurvy. . . . Berry had its own array of saints destined by alliteration or obscure fiat to heal. For the deaf there was Saint Ouen; for the gouty, Saint Genou; for crabbed and peevish women, Saint Acaire. . . . In Finistère Our Lady of Benodet healed aches, depressions, madness, or simplemindedness — disorders associated with the head. Benodet literally means head of Odet, that is, the mouth of the Odet river. . . .

Probably the most notorious saint born of popular whimsy and need was Saint Grelichon or Greluchon (from *grelicher,* which means to scratch or tickle). Saint Greluchon had started life as the funeral statue of a local lord of Bourbon-l'Archambault, Guillaume de Naillac, but we rediscover the figure in a recessed nook of that city's streets. Childless women came from afar to scratch a little dust from the statue's genital area and drink it in a glass of white wine. By 1880, when Sir Guillaume's lower parts had been scratched down to nullity, the dust was obtained from under the statue's chin. Finally, the statue — which had become a bust — was transferred to the museum for safekeeping.

. . . [M]iracle-working agents enlisted strong popular loyalties. So did the traditions that called for rites to be performed in scrupulous detail, or otherwise fail in their intent. At Maizey (Meuse) the relics of Saint Nicholas were carried in procession through the streets in May, and the following Sunday's services then had to be celebrated in a country chapel about a mile away. In 1889 the priest tried to avoid the chore and to say mass in his own church. This disturbed his flock, and most of the men in his congregation, dressed in their holiday clothes, marched to the designated chapel so that the rite would be carried out properly. On the other hand, it appears that the change of a patron saint was often treated with equanimity, as was a substitution of the supposedly sacred image itself. At Villeneuve-de-Berg (Ardèche) the blacksmiths had no statue of their patron, Saint Eloi, to parade on his feastday. They solved the problem routinely by borrowing Saint Vincent from the vintners' corporation, removing the statue's pruning knife, and replacing it with a little hammer. Similarly, in the Alps, at the feast of Saint Besse the saint's devotees brought medals "of him" bearing the legend "St.-Pancrace." When the discrepancy was pointed out to them, it bothered them not at all. The fact was, they said, the likeness was close, and the effects were the same. To the traditional mind the patron saint was secondary to the rite, and to the site as well.

We can see this in the cult of "good" [i.e. healing] fountains, a cult that was generally abetted by the clergy on the theory that the saints who protected the fountains would be given a share of the credit for their restorative powers. Yet popular customs connected with healing fountains were, as a student says, "often purely secular," and certain spas kept their appeal with or without the Church's blessing. . . . On Batz island, off the Breton coast, the old chapel dedicated to Saint Pol (de Léon) was shifted to the patronage of Saint Anne when, at the end of the nineteenth century, she was officially declared the patron saint of the peninsula. The pilgrimage continued as before. It was the place that mattered! . . .

Alphonse Dupront has written that all pilgrimages are made to a source of healing. But we should add that the pilgrims as often seek protection and favors, too. In Bresse one went to pray to Saint Anthony that one's pigs should "gain" during the year. In Bourbonnais shepherdesses attended the annual pilgrimage to Saint Agatha's shrine at Saint-Désiré "in the first place to divert themselves and to secure a blessed hazel switch" with which to control their herds and be free of the fear of wolves.

Conditions obviously varied depending on the stand of the local priest; but priestly decisions were interpreted without illusions. At Carnac (Morbihan) the pilgrimage to the shrine of Saint Cornelius (Cornély), patron of horned beasts, was very profitable. Oxen and calves were offered to him; they were made to kneel in adoration of his statue, which stood above the portal of the church, then blessed by the priest and auctioned off under the saint's banner. Then, in 1906, the priests refused to bless the gathered beasts. "They haven't been paid enough," explained a hawker selling his toys at the local fair. . . . [P]riests too galled or too rigorous to keep up traditional devotions were in minority. As a general rule, they accepted current beliefs in healing fountains, stones, and megaliths. For one thing, as all observers hastened to point out, the gifts offered to their patron saints contributed to clerical revenues. Saint Anthony was offered pigs' feet, Saint Eloi horses' tails, and Saint Herbot cows' tails. More important, many saints were offered the beasts themselves, calves, lambs, chicken, and other gifts in kind. These would be sold by the verger after the ceremony, and the revenue could rise to as much as 1,500 or 2,000 francs — riches for men whose yearly income was only half as much.

For some priests the launching of a new pilgrimage spot meant big business, like the shrine in Picardy, complete with publicity, signposts, hostels, and eateries, which had to be suppressed in 1882 by the bishop of Beauvais. Others were satisfied with a modest but regular income gained from the sale of some small item, like the *saint vinage*[10] at Miremont in Combrailles, a mixture of 10 liters of water and one liter of wine that was blessed by the priest and sold by the sexton at very moderate prices, and that was said to cure all cattle ills. . . .

That priests and their parishes profited from such religious undertakings does not make the undertakings any the less valid or the participants any the less sincere. Utility underlies most human enterprise, and in no way demeans it. The

---

[10] Consecrated wine.

mother who trudged off carrying her child that it might be strengthened or healed was an admirable figure. The priest who sought funds to glorify the source from which such healing sprang — and perhaps its guardian as well — was human and perhaps even saintly.

But to return to pilgrimages: these were perhaps important above all as a form of access to the extraordinary. . . . The pilgrimage offered an excuse to leave the village, and with it, for a time at least, an inescapable fate. Pilgrimages were festive occasions involving food and drink, shopping and dancing. The most ancient pilgrimages coincided with great fairs; markets and sanctuaries went together. . . . Bakers and butchers, clothiers and peddlers, set up their stalls; people treated themselves to sweetmeats, wine, or lemonade, and purchased images, traditional cakes, and other ritual ex-votos[11] to deposit in the sanctuary or tie to the branch of a nearby tree. The healing statue of Saint Stephen at Lussac-les-Eglises (Haute-Vienne) was invoked, like a good many others, by binding a ribbon on the statue's arm. The ribbons were bought from cloth merchants or from the stalls local women set up in the village streets. So were the wax limbs carried in the procession of Saint Amateur at Lamballe (Côtes-du-Nord); the "saffron-flavored cakes shaped like hens," sold to the devotees of Saint Symphorien at Vernègues (Bouches-du-Rhône); the yellow wax breasts offered by women to Saint Anthony's fountain near Brive (Corrèze); and the amulets or priapic[12] figures, in cake or wax, sold from Normandy to Var at least since the seventeenth century. No wonder the peasants felt that priests were necessary because they made business go! And it is easy to dwell on the commercial aspects of religion. The point is that there was commerce because there were people, and people congregated because this was the only sort of festivity they knew.

"It's more a pleasure trip than a pious action," caviled an eastern teacher in 1888. What was wrong with its being both? At this unexalted level, the pilgrimage and traveling were one and the same thing. . . . Relations and friends met at pilgrimage places regularly every year, and such predictable gatherings were convenient in times when communications were rare and difficult. They also afforded welcome breaks, especially to women. The pilgrimage was chiefly a feminine activity — perhaps because it was the woman's only socially sanctioned means of escape from home and its daily routine. Men had opportunities to visit fairs or to travel to farther places. Their lives were far more varied than those of womenfolk. These found their opportunity in pilgrimages, which they often undertook alone over great distances. . . .

But let us hazard further. Even quite humble trips, for secular or devotional ends, took a person out of his element and opened up unfamiliar spheres. The extraordinary began much closer to home then than it would do today, and a trip of any kind was an understandable aspiration for those whose ordinary lives offered so little change.

---

[11] Offerings made in pursuance of a vow, in gratitude, for example, for recovery from sickness.
[12] Phallic.

What could be more extraordinary than the miraculous? Perhaps this was what humble people welcomed in the news of the great miracles of the time. Miracles promise deliverance from the routine unfolding of predictable destinies; and they create a sense of expectancy and excitement the more potent for being the more vague. Millenarianism, which embodies all this in its most extreme form, is commonly attributed to bafflement — a sense of privation and restraint with no conceivable relief in sight. The promise carried by evidence of supernatural forces heals bafflement and frustration, and reinforces hope. It also holds out an opportunity to escape from the commonplace into the realm of the prodigious, to wonder over marvels and possibilities beyond familiar ken. . . .

Whatever the explanation, the rural world was eager for miracles. . . . Most of the time rumors of local miracles did not go beyond a limited radius. In 1840 the Holy Virgin seems to have manifested herself in several places in Vendée. But this was treated as local superstition. In the early 1860's the Ursuline nuns of Charroux in Poitou discovered what they claimed to be the Sacred Prepuce, removed from the Infant Jesus at the circumcision and, in the words of Monsignor Pie, bishop of Poitiers, "the only part of Christ's body left behind when he ascended into heaven." The name Charroux was associated with *chair rouge* (the red meat of the cut-off prepuce!), and an elaborate festival in 1862 brought the fortunate convent into the public eye. . . .

At about the same time, in the fall of 1862, the sixteen-year-old daughter of a rural postman of Saint-Marcel-d'Ardèche began to preach, predict the future and promise miracles. The people came en masse from all surrounding communes until, in a few days, the furor died down.

In other cases the feverish excitement did not pass so quickly. When, in September 1846, two shepherd children guarding their herds on the deserted mountainside of La Salette saw an unnatural light and a tearful lady announcing the wrath of Christ in their own patois,[13] curious pilgrims hastened there at once. The veracity of the children was contested, especially by the Church authorities, but the enthusiasm was too great to stifle. The evidence makes clear that miracles were validated and imposed by popular opinion, which the authorities — civil and clerical — accepted only unwillingly and under pressure. In a notorious trial of 1857, concerned with the reality of the miracle of La Salette, the lawyers continually referred to the supernatural needs of the lower classes (explained presumably by their ignorance). It was wholly understandable, they said, that the common people should believe in such things, but they expressed some surprise at finding members of the upper classes sharing these views.

This same division and the same pressure of popular need appear in the earliest stages of the first and perhaps the greatest modern pilgrimage site — Lourdes. In February 1858, eleven-year-old Bernadette Soubirous encountered a "Beautiful Lady" beside a stream. The local nuns, priests, and civil authorities, afraid of

---

[13] Local dialect.

complications, refused to believe Bernadette's story. The local gendarme sought to tell "the people . . . that it is not in the nineteenth century that one lets oneself be carried away by such a belief." Yet belief was stronger than skepticism. It spread like wildfire. Within a few days large crowds, mostly women and children, began to gather at the grotto of Masabielle. By the beginning of March they numbered 20,000 (the population of Lourdes was less than a quarter of that). "Disorder caused in the name of God is none the less intolerable disorder," warned the gendarme. All his superiors clearly thought the same. The records are full of it: "disorder," "regrettable agitation," "preserve order," "undeceive the population," "regrettable facts." But the population did not want to be undeceived. For it, disorder was hope and holiday. "The population . . . wants to believe. When there are no miracles, it invents them; it insists on baring heads, kneeling, etc."

There were few priests, sometimes no priests, in the assembled crowds. The clergy, as the imperial prosecutor reported, "maintained an excessive reserve." But the ritual pilgrimages developed without their intervention and despite that of the civil authorities. It was several years before the bishop of Tarbes confirmed the miracles in 1862, proclaiming the authenticity of the Virgin's appearance and the healing virtues of the grotto's spring. But clearly the voice of the people preceded the voice of God. In 1867 a railway line became available. By 1871 the pilgrimage had become international, and in 1876 the great basilica was consecrated before 100,000 pilgrims — a new tide in the affairs of men, flowing in the wake of the railroads. . . .

What does all this tell us about religion? Conclusions do not come easily. That it was local and specific. That a peasant who did not believe in the Church, its foolishness or its saints, to quote a country priest, could share in local reverence and worship Saint Eutropius. That men who would not go to mass would undertake long pilgrimages to be healed or to have their beasts healed. And that, in one way or another, religious practices were interwoven with every part of life, but hardly in a manner that one would call specifically Christian. Leaving aside the entertainment that these practices offered, divinity was associated with vast unknown areas. God and saints — like fairies — possessed knowledge that was forbidden to men. They had to be propitiated and persuaded to perform tasks that men accomplish only imperfectly (like healing) or not at all (like controlling the weather). The more men came to master such tasks, plumb the unknown, shake the tree of knowledge, the less they needed intercessors.

The sales of the *saint vinage* at Miremont declined, to the despair of the sexton. In Sologne good Saint Viâtre, who had done so much to heal the local fevers (malaria), was badly hurt by the spreading use of quinine and by the drainage and sanitation projects beginning to show results in the 1880's. At Hévillers (Meuse) the priest read the Lord's Passion every day from May to September "to bring heaven's blessing on the goods of the earth"; then, before Christmas, the church treasurer went from door to door to collect grain in payment for this service. In the 1850's the treasurer got 800 lbs. and more. By 1888 . . . he garnered only 330. Things were worse still in Périgord, where the popularity of Saint John the Baptist, whose accompanying lamb had made him the patron of the local sheepruns, declined with the century. . . .

. . . The observance of Rogation week declined — even in Brittany. The turn of the century saw fewer processions across the village fields with cross, banners, and bells to drive off evil spirits and to bless the crops. In the Limousin, where in 1876 many peasants still reckoned their age according to ostensions — great septennial processions with scores of villages in their entirety parading behind relics, drums, and banners — the emotional content gradually seeped away, and the penitents in their colorful costumes disappeared; and new religious groups that borrowed nothing from the old traditions meant little to the popular public. . . .

Local pilgrimages of the popular sort leveled off or declined. Some were domesticated into the Marian cult.[14] Others were suppressed because they gave rise to scandalous practices, as when Morvan women seeking a cure for barrenness too often found it in adjacent woods; or because they always brought disorders, like the wrestlers' *pardon* of Saint Cadou at Gouesnac'h (Finistère) that never failed to end in fights and brawls. The mercantile activities that had grown around traditional devotions killed them, like trees stifled by ivy. Easter Sunday processions had to be given up in some places because the streets and squares were too crowded with stalls and carrousels. Tourists and sightseers helped to keep observances alive as pure pageantry, but finally, "when everyone wants to watch the procession, there is no one left to take part in it." Between the wars, automobiles denied the roads to those pilgrimages traditionally made on horseback, and the enclosure of fields discouraged them. In 1939 the *Courier du Finistère*[15] noted that the traditional procession stopped at the wires barring access to the ancient chapel of Saint-Roch at Landeleau. "What is the use in destroying the grass of a field to enter a building in ruins and without a roof?" No such reasoning could have been accepted half a century earlier.

Yet phosphates, chemical fertilizers, and schooling had spelled the beginning of the end. In 1893, a drought year in Bourbonnais when many men were having masses said for their emaciated cattle (which died anyway), the priest reproached Henry Norre, a self-taught man who farmed not far from Cérilly, for not attending church. "I haven't got the time," he answered. "And really, I haven't got much confidence in your remedies for the beasts. My remedies are better; you can check." Daniel Halévy[16] quotes another story about Norre. This time the farmer returned from the railway station with a cartful of fertilizer and met the priest. "What are you carting there?" "Chemicals." "But that is very bad; they burn the soil!" "Monsieur le curé,"[17] said Norre, "I've tried everything. I've had masses said and got no profit from them. I've bought chemicals and they worked. I'll stick to the better merchandise." It was the requiem of nineteenth-century religion.

---

[14] Cult stressing veneration of the Virgin Mary.

[15] A newspaper.

[16] French historian (1872–1962).

[17] Chief parish priest.

THE PERFUMES OF INTIMACY
Alain Corbin

Recently, historians have begun to study topics previously unexplored, such as the body, cleanliness, and odor. We have learned that these subjects have a rich background, that conceptions of the body and particular body parts, of hygiene and cleanliness, and of odor are culturally derived and change over time and from one society to another. A historian at the Sorbonne, Alain Corbin has studied several subjects that traditional historians have generally overlooked, such as the social history of odors.

Relying on hygiene manuals and medical books and treatises, Corbin argues that the French bourgeoisie in the late-eighteenth and nineteenth centuries began to pay more attention to smells and fragrances, and hence to sanitation. The bourgeoisie became less tolerant than previously of the stench that permeated cities and especially of the smells they associated with the poor. The bourgeoisie wanted to deodorize cities and favored floral scents over heavy and musky scented perfumes. This new sensibility also affected concerns about the disposal of sewage, the need for urban space, and personal cleanliness.

What does Corbin mean when he refers to "the new alliance between woman and flower"? How did the French interpret cleanliness, and how was bodily hygiene encouraged? What obstacles inhibited the development of hygiene and the elimination of putrid odors? Note the means the French used to achieve olfactory satisfaction: lotions, frequent partial baths, the removal of human waste from cities, new hair hygiene, and the deodorization of breath. How did the new perceptions of elegance and delicacy affect the use of perfumes and cosmetics? To what extent did the new olfactory perceptions and new attitudes of cleanliness serve to further separate the bourgeoisie from the poor?

Though history textbooks frequently mention the development of urban sewer systems, they rarely pay attention to humans' changing perceptions of smell and the implications these attitudes have for standards of health, living conditions, and class prejudices, not to mention the links between scent and sex-

---

Alain Corbin, *The Foul and the Fragrant: Odor and the French Social Imagination* (Cambridge: Harvard University Press, 1986), 176–188, 193–194, 199.

uality. Corbin, however, argues that the history of smell, including his account of floral perfumes, is important to understanding nineteenth-century society.

The new control of odors that accompanied the increased privacy inside bourgeois[1] dwellings permitted a skillful change in the way women presented themselves. A subtle calculation of bodily messages led to both a reduction in the strength of olfactory signals and an increase in the value assigned them. Because, in the name of decency, women's bodies were now less on show, the importance of the sense of smell increased astonishingly. "The woman's atmosphere" became the mysterious element in her sex appeal. However, exaltation of the young girl's virginity and new perceptions of the wife, her role and her virtues, continued to forbid any open advances. To arouse desire without betraying modesty was the basic rule of the game of love. Olfaction played a crucial role in the refinement of the game, and it turned primarily on the new alliance between woman and flower.

New medical arguments were invoked to justify practices aimed at eliminating putrid filth so as to diminish the risks of infection. Since the time when Lavoisier[2] and Séguin[3] had precisely measured the products of cutaneous perspiration, there had been increased concern that perspiration not be impeded. Broussais's[4] physiological approach to medicine called for greater attention to the hygiene of the secretory organs, which ensured that the body was freed from impurities. Medical theory indicated the "geography" of the body that governed the ritual of the toilette. The key was to supervise cleanliness of hands, feet, armpits, groin, and genital organs. The importance that Broussais accorded to the concept of irritation strengthened the ban on oxymetallic cosmetics. Sensualism, which still had considerable influence though it was now questioned, enjoined sensitivity and lightness of touch by means of a scrupulous toilette.

The canons of bodily aesthetics urged the most scrupulous hygiene. Cosmetics were governed by the aristocratic ideal of pearly skin, through which the blue blood could be seen pulsing. For nearly a century the supreme reference points remained the brilliant whiteness of the lily and of the Pompadour's[5] complexion; the aesthetic code decreed that all visible parts of the body be washed — as it also prescribed a sedentary life, the cool shade of trees, and the protection of gloves for "soft, white, firm, plump hands."

Removing the dirt from the poor was equivalent to increasing their wisdom; convincing the bourgeois of the need to wash was to prepare him to exercise the

---

[1] Middle-class.

[2] Antoine Laurent Lavoisier (1743–1794), chemist and royal administrator.

[3] Armand Séguin (1767–1835), chemist, physiologist, and scientific writer.

[4] François Broussais (1772–1838), physician and medical educator.

[5] Mistress of King Louis XV (1721–1764).

virtues of his class. Cleanliness was the tenth of Franklin's[6] thirteen principles of wisdom, coming just before moral balance and chastity. "Hygiene, which maintains health, which nurtures the mind with habits of order, purity, and moderation, is for that reason alone the soul of beauty; because this precious advantage depends more than anything else on the freshness of a healthy body, the influence of a pure soul." Vidalin[7] put his finger on the unexpected link between economy and cleanliness. Cleanliness, in its widest sense, reduced waste of food and clothing and facilitated the identification, control, and even possibly the salvage of waste; it became another method of fighting loss. From this point of view, the best preventive measures consisted in learning not to get dirty, to avoid contact with the putrid, and to get rid of all excreta on the skin. . . .

Nevertheless the progress of bodily hygiene encountered numerous setbacks; the most important was the slowness with which houses were equipped, authorized by doctors' persistent distrust of immoderate use of water, as is evidenced by the long list of prohibitions and precautions that larded public health discourse. Menstrual frequency still ruled the cycle of bathing. Few experts advised taking more than one bath a month. . . .

Plunging into water involved a calculated risk. It was important that the duration, frequency, and temperature of baths be adapted to sex, age, temperament, state of health, and season. Baths were thought to exert a profound effect on the whole organism, because they were not an everyday event. Mental specialists and sometimes even moralists pinned their hopes on them; gynecologists feared them. Delacoux[8] noted that the courtesan[9] owed her infertility to her excessive preoccupation with toilette. According to him, numerous women had been deprived of the joys of motherhood by this "indiscreet attention." Even more serious, baths endangered beauty; women who overused them "were generally pale and their fullness of figure owed more to fleshiness than to the bloom of the skin." Young girls who bathed too much risked debility. . . .

Until the triumph of the shower, which shortened the time spent in bathing and rendered self-satisfaction harmless, baths aroused suspicion. The ban on nudity acted against the spread of baths. Drying the genitals posed a problem. "Close your eyes," Madame Celnart[10] ordered her readers, "until you have completed the operation." Water could become an indiscreet mirror. Dr. Marie de Saint-Ursin[11] described the young girl's confusion in the bath: "Inexperience descends, blushing, into the crystal of the waves, meets the image of its new treasures there, and blushes even more." In affected phrases, the author confirmed the synchronism

---

[6] Benjamin Franklin (1706–1790), American statesman and ambassador to France.

[7] Félix Vidalin, author of the *Treatise of Domestic Hygiene* (1825).

[8] A. Delacoux, author of *Women's Hygiene* (1829).

[9] Mistress of rich and powerful men.

[10] Elisabeth Celnart, writer on etiquette and women's beauty, ca. 1820s.

[11] Physician and writer on health (1763–1818).

established between female puberty and initiation into the practices of bodily hygiene. "Bathe, if you are ordered," concluded the comtesse de Bradi;[12] "otherwise take only one bath a month at the most. There is an indefinable element of idleness and flaccidity that ill becomes a girl in the taste for settling down on the bottom of a bathtub in this way."

These attitudes account for the obvious disparity that grew up between the volume of discourse and the scantiness of practice. Bathing still required therapeutic justification. It is therefore not surprising that the ritual was complicated. Transporting the water and filling and emptying the tub, bucket, or metal bath entered, like laundry or seasonal housework, into the timetable of major domestic rites.

Accordingly, the major innovation was an increase in partial baths, as shown by the spread, still limited it is true, of footbaths, handbaths, hipbaths, and halfbaths. The concern to avoid getting dirty, the new frequency of ablutions, and the stress on the specific requirements of washing shaped the bourgeoisie's apprenticeship in hygienic practices. The physiology of excretion, which appeared even more important in the light of Broussais's theories, governed the fragmented ritual of the toilette in the same way that it obsessed both the actual practices and utopian fantasies of municipal policy. The same rationale underlay both the insistent hygiene advocated for the bourgeois body and the ceaseless evacuation of urban waste that was the sanitary reformers' aim: the abolition of the threat from excrement, no longer so much determined by the risk of infection as by the risk of congestion.

A proliferation of lotions accompanied the increase in ablutions. This was the result not only of a process of substitution encouraged by the disrepute of perfumes, but also of the alliance between lotions and friction, highly recommended for its energizing properties. The other activities of the toilette ritual can be quickly listed. The fashion for plastering pomade on hair had disappeared. Hair hygiene consisted of periodic untangling with a fine comb, brushing, and plaiting before bed. The Salernitan[13] prohibition remained: the head was not washed. Madame Celnart recommended rubbing hair with a dry cloth to remove dust; at the most, and then with caution, the fashionable lady could use a soapy lotion applied with a sponge. The practice of shampooing developed only during the Third Republic[14] — fortunately, because until then the strong scents of her hair remained one of woman's strongest trumps; she had, after all, been forbidden to use too much perfume.

Mouth hygiene was becoming more specific; Londe[15] advised daily brushing of all the teeth to deodorize breath, and not, as was most often the practice, only the front ones. Madame Celnart prescribed the use of aromatized powders.

---

[12] Early nineteenth-century poet and author.

[13] Referring to the medical school at Salerno.

[14] Democratic government of France, 1870–1940.

[15] Charles Londe, physician and writer on the benefits of exercise during the 1820s.

Fresh bodily odor depended even more on the quality and cleanliness of underwear than on scrupulous hygienic practices. Development in this area too moved at an accelerated pace. Sanitary reformers endeavored to institute weekly changing of underwear. The new timetable for changing clothes and the new appreciation of the pleasant odor of clean linen were incentives to perfume washtubs, chests, and drawers. These practices spread long before those of bodily hygiene proper.

In fact the new behavior patterns were accepted only slowly even by the bourgeoisie, as the rareness of bathrooms attests. The bidet[16] was popularized only at the very end of the century. The use of the tub, imported from England, long remained a sign of snobbishness. In 1900 a Parisian bourgeoise of good social standing was still quite happy with periodic footbaths. Inventories suggest that contemporary doctors may have possessed a fair number of halfbaths, but this was because they formed an avant-garde responsible for encouraging hygiene.

For the time being there could be no question of obliging the masses to follow a ritual that the elite was still neglecting. Consequently, they remained condemned to steep in their oily, stinking filth, unless they braved the putrid and immoral promiscuity of public baths. . . .

Nevertheless, several segments of the population were already confronted with the norms formulated for the bourgeoisie. Prisons rather than boarding schools were serving as the laboratories for personal hygiene. As early as 1820, Villermé[17] ordered that convicts comb their hair before washing their faces every morning, and that they wash their hands several times a day and their feet every week. He advocated a weekly review of cleanliness; he wanted new arrivals to be bathed and the administration to insist on short hair. Sanitary reformers asked no more of school children a century later.

Wet nurses for the bourgeois newborn were compelled to follow norms that were probably stricter than those prevailing in the nurseling's family. Doctors advised that they be bathed once a month and forced to wash their mouths, breasts, and genitals every day. It is hard to assess the influence these women exerted when they returned to the village. . . .

Under the July Monarchy,[18] the elegant gentleman had stopped using perfume — unless he played the dandy or practiced "antiphysical" love. At the most, his person emitted a vague smell of tobacco, which he had to try to keep from the ladies. For him, the time for ostentation was past, as historians of fashion and costume have clearly demonstrated. The new code of male elegance was subtle; there was no longer a place for nuances of smell. It was precisely the absence of strong odor, evidence of careful hygiene, that was regarded as the decisive criterion of good taste. The symbolic, barely perceptible, odor of cleanliness that emanated from linen characterized the deodorized bourgeois.

---

[16] A low oval basin used for washing the genitals.

[17] Louis-René Villermé (1782–1863), physician and writer on social issues.

[18] Government of King Louis-Philippe, lasting from 1830 to 1848.

The wife, on the other hand, had become the man's standard-bearer and "the ceremonial consumer of goods which he produces." She was invested with the function of representing the position and wealth of father or husband. Silken draperies, bright colors, ostentatious luxury were henceforth her preserve; they testified to extravagance that placed her above all suspicion of work.

In terms of scents, the code of elegance became more refined. Up to the end of the century, the range of permitted scents remained very small; despite short-term oscillations in fashion, good society respected the aesthetics established at the court of Marie Antoinette.[19] Particularly during the July Monarchy, the hygiene advocated by doctors in matters of smell was an invitation to keep faith with the values of delicacy, to be content with the sweet perfumes of nature, and to eschew the heavy animal scents of musk, ambergris, and civet.

A new use of cosmetics accompanied this quest for delicacy. It caused beauty to be identified with "elegant cleanliness." Paint (red and white) and powders were abandoned and pomades used in moderation. Tourtelle[20] gave a perfect summary of the new requirements of fashion and hygiene: "True cosmetics are aqueous lotions for cleanliness, and unguents, which can be used to cleanse and soften the skin, like emulsive substances, fresh oil, whale soap, butter, cocoa butter, soap, almond paste," and, most of all, he added, "no metallic oxide." What was important was to tear off mask and plaster, air the skin, open the pores, and thus allow the woman's atmosphere to be diffused.

All observers provided evidence of the decline in perfumes; the professional perfumers deplored the trend. . . . Bath perfumery had practically disappeared. . . . Once powder had been abandoned, the practice of perfuming hair was the subject of protracted debate; it seems that only the most coquettish dared be bold in this respect.

Good taste forbade the young girl to use perfume; this indiscreet solicitation might reveal her ambitions for marriage too crudely. It might also compromise one of her main trumps. There was absolutely no need to mask, however lightly, the effluvia that emanated from the slender body, the nature of its odor as yet unspoiled by male sperm: "the tender odor of marjoram that the virgin exhales is sweeter, more intoxicating than all the perfumes of Arabia."

In no circumstances should real perfume be applied to the skin. Only aromatic toilet waters — distilled rose, plantain, bean, or strawberry waters — and eaux de cologne were permissible. Keeping perfume at a distance from the body was more important than ever. This increased severity was accompanied by a reduction in the range and volume of objects carrying perfume. Whereas it might be in good taste to impregnate linen with delicate scents from cupboards, it was no longer so to perfume the towels used for the toilette. Sweet odor was concentrated on handkerchiefs and one or two accessories: fans, the lace surrounding the

---

[19] Wife of King Louis XVI (1755–1793).

[20] Etienne Tourtelle (1782–1863), physician and writer on hygiene.

tiny bouquet carried to the ball, and, for the most sensual, gloves, mittens, and slippers. . . .

   This complex plan dictated and justified the abandonment of animal perfumes and the rise of the fashion for floral odors; the latter, without competing with the odors of the flesh, echoed the traditionally mysterious collusion between woman and flower. "It is on the perfumes of nature at the first rays of the sun that the sense of smell must be exercised," decreed Londe in 1838. The comtesse de Bradi added, in a conciliatory vein: "I have forbidden you prepared perfumes; but those spread by natural flowers seem to me very permissible, when they are in no way disturbing." The proportions as much as the nature of the products set the seal on elegance. The list of acceptable perfumes and toilet waters remained essentially unchanged until the middle of the Second Empire.[21] When perfumers set to work around 1860 to refine their products, their basic range of preparations for handkerchiefs remained very small. According to Rimmel, it comprised six elementary odors: rose, jasmine, orange blossom, acacia, violet, and tuberose. The perfumer invented bouquets by combining these six odoriferous bases. To produce pomades, he could also use jonquil, narcissus, mignonette, lilac, hawthorn, and syringa. The Parisian masters, Debay[22] stated in 1861, "have banished strong and intoxicating odors that are harmful to the nerves . . . and offer only innocent perfumes."

   Contemporaries justified this timid attitude to smells. Doctors endlessly repeated the old arguments refined at the end of the eighteenth century to discredit animal perfumes, thereafter regarded as putrid substances. They congratulated themselves on their virtual disappearance. The acknowledged need for a good hygiene of respiration created even greater mistrust. There was an increased fear of the ravages made by animal perfumes on the psyche of those who wore them; it accompanied the development in psychiatry. . . .

   The ambiguous theme of the immorality of penetrating, stifling scents is implicit in medical discourse at those points where it explicitly warns its female readers. Early in Pasteur's revolution[23] the diatribe took on new violence. The charm of perfumes, the search for "base sensations," symptoms of a "soft, lax" education, increased nervous irritability, led to "feminism," and encouraged debauchery. . . .

   But the survival of the fashion for natural perfumes and the persistent ostracism of those who wore provocative animal perfume clearly had a much larger significance. These refined behavior patterns in relation to smells are a source of information on social psychology. I would like to indicate a few, still dimly lit, paths, without suggesting that any one of them is more important than any other.

   "The bourgeois does not employ his wealth to make a show" . . . ; he needed it in order to exist. This view would be enough to explain the hostility displayed

---

[21] French government of Napoleon III, 1852–1870.

[22] A. Debay, author of *Perfumes and Flowers* (1846).

[23] Louis Pasteur (1822–1895) established the connection between bacteria and disease.

toward perfume: it was a symbol of waste; its dispersion was evidence of intolerable loss. But this argument does not seem to fit the nineteenth-century bourgeois. He was no longer solely that man of duty, the moralist, opposed to enjoyment and even all sensuality. . . . Obsessed by the desire to legitimate his position, the bourgeois now envied and tried to emulate aristocratic nonchalance. As the years went by, he ceased to give the impression of being socially inhibited. Where ostentation was concerned, it could even be said that he went too far; the fashions of the Chaussée d'Antin[24] rapidly outstripped in magnificence the discreet charm of the boulevard Saint-Germain.[25] Until well into the July Monarchy, it was among the elite that the criteria of good manners were determined. . . . From the Restoration[26] on, the hierarchies became more refined, the symbols more complicated; unforeseen divisions became apparent. While the new practices of cleanliness distinguished rich from poor, criteria imperceptible to outsiders fragmented the world of wealth. The cultivated delicacy of the messages of smells undoubtedly formed part of the complex tactics of this set of distinctions. . . .

The arbiters of nineteenth-century morality placed modesty above all other feminine virtues, and the prohibition on cosmetics, as well as on indiscreet perfume, was part of a complex system of visual, moral, and aesthetic perceptions. "Unaffected cleanliness, the natural elegance and graces of body and mind, *sprightliness* and modesty are the most powerful cosmetics." The thick vapors of impregnated flesh, heavy scents, and musky powders were for the courtesan's boudoir or even the brothel salon. The obverse model furnished by the venal woman facilitated the definition of true elegance.

The increasingly prevalent symbolism of the natural, sweetly perfumed woman-flower disclosed a firm wish to control emotions. Delicate scents set the seal on the image of a diaphanous body that, it was hoped, simply reflected the soul. . . .

Modesty seems to have become an erotic science. The allusive coldness, the delicate invitation, the admission of imperceptible anxieties, the blushes, the constant reference to the thoughtlessness of the misconduct about which it was fitting to know nothing — all appear to have been skillful sexual tactics that integrated the subtlety of the messages of smell. Were not the natural effluvia from the virgin's body and her airy toilette perceived as the most erotic traps? . . . A new role devolved on olfaction within the framework of these global tactics. The perfumed invitation was more delicate, less obvious, and less coarse, perhaps more disturbing, than the charms of nudity; it was more in tune with the ambiguous wish to seduce. It had the additional advantage of preserving the appearance of innocence. The message of love that emanated from the sweetly perfumed body

---

[24] A street in Paris.

[25] A fashionable Parisian boulevard.

[26] Ultra-conservative government of the restored Bourbon monarchy, 1815–1830.

could no more implicate modesty than could the involuntary curves, hidden but revealed, even accentuated, by the fabric of the bodice. . . .

For the time being, doctors unanimously refused to acknowledge the erotic role played by the odor of sexual secretions in man. This odor whetted the generative instinct in animals, stated Rostan,[27] but "the same is not true of human species." Among humans, explained Londe, the erotic function devolved on the sense of touch; caresses alone were exciting. In animals, wrote Hippolyte Cloquet,[28] the sense of smell was the sense of violent appetites; in man, of sweet sensations. . . .

Placed in the center of the domestic scene, woman became its stage director; within the bounds of what her modesty permitted, she skillfully calculated the erotic possibilities provided by the framework of her life, transforming it into a veritable forest of symbols. These images are more clearly apparent in the interiors of homes than anywhere else. . . .

Perfume-pans were still an essential part of the fashionable young girl's equipment. Fragrant pastilles[29] had not disappeared, but they tended to be reserved for sickrooms. The new fashion was for the perfumed candle, its innocence guaranteed by the fact that it was useful. The main thing now was to conceal the plan to seduce behind a utilitarian pretext. Perfuming linen was nothing more than a hygienic practice. Stationery emitted delicate scents; there was nothing to stop one thinking that they came from natural perfumes emanating from the writer. . . .

Proximity to flowers, like proximity to birds, was innocent. "It is a taste natural to woman," the comtesse de Bradi confirmed; even prostitutes retained it when they fell from grace. According to the Romantics, . . . the angelic, secret young girl, sensitive to the calls of the infinite, like the country flower opened a perfumed way to the other world of poetry. This proximity, this discreet harmony created the symbolic metamorphosis, kept alive the confusion. . . .

Flowers also proliferated inside the home; they were no longer restricted to the woman's toilette. They decorated "floor boxes," "window boxes," and "massive vases of greenery." There bloomed the roses, jasmine, lily of the valley, reseda, and violets that the arbiters of elegance recommended. Exotic plants were judged too disturbing; it was not yet good form in France to transform the house into a museum of vegetation.

During the Second Empire, fashion decreed that women decorate their clothes with flowers. "Natural flowers are used to decorate bodices; they are put on sleeves, often on skirts, not only in slashes and flounces, but in two or three rows in front." Roses, wallflowers, lilies of the valley, jasmine, and forget-me-nots were artistically arranged in the hair and framed the faces of young, fashionably

---

[27] Camille Rostan (1774–1833), professor of botany at the Parisian horticultural garden.

[28] Anatomist and medical writer (1787–1840).

[29] Aromatic pastes, burned as a disinfectant or deodorant.

dressed ladies. On the other hand, the code of good manners forbade the mature lady to use natural flowers. Harmony existed only between the young girl and flora. Those who had forfeited these youthful scents still had artificial flowers, but again, to be used with discretion. . . .

Flowerpots and bouquets spread to the masses, "down to the little working-girl who likes decorating her attic," noted Debay. . . . The image of the beflowered little dressmaker was cheering. Scented with natural perfumes, the garret was the symbolic antithesis of the stinking hovel or licentious factory. The presence of flowers was evidence of a workplace that was consistent with the cheerful, clean, and hard-working young girl. Even indoors, the innocence of flowers bore witness to virtue. Lit up and framed by curtains, the bouquet could, of course, be transformed into an inviting signal; clandestine prostitutes also knew the language of flowers. . . .

Over the decades, the aesthetics of the sense of smell became commonplace; the moderate price of perfumed soaps, the industrial manufacture of eau de cologne, the expansion of the network of drapers who distributed the products of perfumery enlarged the range of the clientele. Flasks began to adorn the shelves of doctors and minor provincial notables. Even before toilet soap came into general use, the downward social mobility of eau de cologne was evidence that the poor man too had joined the battle against the putrid odor of his secretions.

POPULAR JUSTICE, COMMUNITY, AND CULTURE AMONG THE RUSSIAN PEASANTRY, 1870–1900

Stephen P. Frank

We in the West tend to have a negative view of vigilante justice, but what the rule of law is or is not depends on a particular culture. Laws are culturally relative and differ according to people's socioeconomic status. Nineteenth-century Russian villagers frequently meted out justice according to their own community mores and values, apprehending and punishing those who had broken the law or transgressed village norms. Known as *samosud* (self-adjudication, as Stephen P. Frank defines it), this collective activity was organized, even ritualized in some instances, and certainly legitimate in the eyes of the peasants, though not according to government and judicial authorities. Frank, who teaches history at Boston University, analyzes three types of popular justice: *charivaris* (raucous demonstrations intended to shame people who transgress community customs), the harsh punishment of serious theft, and violence against witches. Frank bases his research on newspaper accounts, legal journals, government commission reports, and materials gathered by an amateur ethnographer.

What sorts of behavior led to a *charivari*? Frank explains how the Russian *charivari* differed from its counterparts in England and France. How did villagers express their moral authority in *charivaris* and in punishments for property crimes? Did harsh violence and penalties work successfully to reinforce collective rules of behavior? Notice that villagers distinguished between insiders and outsiders when punishing victims. Why were horse thieves punished more brutally than those guilty of other crimes? Why did peasants not rely on courts to punish those who violated the law and community customs?

Agrafena Ignatieva was known as a sorceress and a fortuneteller in the village of Vrachev (Tikhvinskii district, Novgorod province). An impoverished widow

Stephen P. Frank, "Popular Justice, Community, and Culture among the Russian Peasantry, 1870–1900," in *The World of the Russian Peasant: Post-Emancipation Culture and Society,* ed. Ben Eklof and Stephen Frank (Boston: Unwin Hyman, 1990), 133–150.

with no means of livelihood, she was forced to beg for her daily subsistence. Unfortunately for "Grushka," as the peasants called her, an outbreak of "falling sickness" in the locality where she lived brought suspicion on her. Most people knew that such an illness resulted from a spell, or *porcha,* and Ignatieva appeared to be the most likely culprit. Early in January 1879 Grushka had asked her fellow-villager Kuzmina for some cottage cheese but was refused; shortly thereafter Kuzmina's daughter fell sick and began crying out that Grushka was the cause. With this episode still fresh in everyone's mind, the illness reached Katerina Ivanova, whose sister had died from the same affliction, also "hexed" by Grushka. Ivanova attributed her sickness to the fact that she had once forbidden her son to chop firewood for the sorceress; Grushka was obviously seeking revenge. Ivanova's husband even lodged a complaint against Ignatieva with the local constable *(uriadnik),* but few villagers expected that she would be punished.

Because of the number of misfortunes attributed to her, the peasants of Vrachev decided to burn Grushka. They made their decision during a meeting of the village assembly, which had gathered to divide the property of four peasant brothers. After settling this case, the villagers reached an agreement among themselves, took some nails, and set off to "seal" Grushka, as they put it. On reaching Agrafena Ignatieva's hut, they found the entrance shed locked and broke down the door. Four peasants entered the storeroom in search of charms and potions while six others went into the house itself. After parleying for some time with the woman, they proceeded to "seal" the house. First a pole was set into the entranceway and nailed in place. Next they nailed a plank against the larger window and sealed off two small windows with logs, so that all exits were completely blocked. At about five P.M. they set fire to a bundle of straw and rope in the entrance shed, and the hut burned to the ground while nearly 200 people from Vrachev and a neighboring village looked on. Though certain they had done the right thing to protect their village, the peasants nevertheless sent the local constable 22 rubles so he would forget the case, but he declined their offer. Those most guilty in the burning of Grushka — sixteen persons — were brought before the circuit court, where three confessed their guilt and were sentenced to church penitence, while the others went free.

Community or "mob" violence of this sort frequently found its way into the pages of Russia's urban and provincial press. It was by no means limited to persons accused of sorcery; thieves were commonly subjected to community reprisal, as were those who transgressed certain village norms of conduct. Nor was the phenomenon peculiar to backward, isolated regions. . . . [S]*amosud* (literally, self-adjudication), as educated Russians called it, was primarily an activity of rural villagers and occurred most often in areas where the effects of capitalist development had been least felt, for there the presence of police and other agents of state coercion was weak and traditional peasant institutions retained greater strength. It existed in nearly all provinces of the empire and remained widespread throughout the nineteenth century and after, accounting for as much as 1 percent of all rural crimes tried before the circuit courts.

Samosud in the Russian countryside was a far more complex phenomenon than contemporaries believed it to be. Most of Russia's educated elite saw *samosud* as little more than mob violence or lynch law, and the greatest attention was paid to just these types of extralegal reprisal. The best dictionary of the period, however, took a broader view, defining *samosud* not only as willful punishment but also as arbitrariness and "adjudication of one's own affairs." In fact, many instances of *samosud* did not involve violence but bore close resemblance to the *charivaris,* "rough music," and shivarees of Western Europe and North America. Although peasants rarely offered definitions to investigators who questioned them about their juridical beliefs and practices, they did include such nonviolent acts in their conception of *samosud.* In addition, although they did not categorize the types of *samosud* practiced in the village, close examination of the acts themselves reveals that peasants distinguished sharply between punishments inflicted on community members and those used against outsiders. With fellow villagers *samosud* took on a highly ritualized character; violent forms were reserved almost exclusively for outsiders whose crimes posed a threat to the community.

This distinction between punishing members of the community and outsiders is perhaps the most useful framework for analyzing the nature and function of *samosud* in rural Russia and for understanding such acts from the perspective of the villager rather than of the urban elite. For this reason I will consider three frequent forms of popular justice, all of which were termed *samosud* by the participants: ritualized disciplinary action such as *charivari,* in which villagers inflicted shame and public disgrace on the guilty party, usually without resorting to violence; punishment of theft, particularly the theft of horses; and, briefly, violence directed against those suspected of witchcraft. . . .

. . . Invoking the commune's moral authority was one of the most notable features of *samosud.* Peasants usually brought a case before the village assembly before inflicting punishment, especially if the offender was a community member, and the assembly frequently sentenced the guilty party to some form of *samosud.* In this way the assembly sanctioned what outsiders would deem an illegal action and lessened the chance that a criminal would complain to the authorities or seek revenge, considering that to do so challenged a decision of the assembly as well as the authority of the community itself.

Other distinguishing features of *samosud* included community participation in the punishment, a real or perceived threat to local norms or to the community's well-being, and an attempt to prevent repetition of a crime through ritualized public humiliation of the offender or, in more serious cases, by ridding the community of a criminal altogether. Because the presence of these characteristics in a given act of *samosud* depended on the nature of the crime and the offender's status as villager or outsider, they helped both to differentiate the various forms of *samosud* and to join them together in a common meaning, as we shall now see.

At its simplest level, *samosud* might be inflicted for a multitude of petty infractions such as *potrava* (damage caused to another's crops by one's livestock); it was also used to discipline minors if the case warranted serious attention. One of the most widespread types of *samosud* in rural Russia, however, was called "leading of the thief" (*vozhdenie vora,* or simply *vozhdenie*) — a punishment that had the ritualistic character of *charivari* and, unlike other acts of *samosud,* was visited only upon members of the community. Known by various names throughout Europe and North America, *charivaris* were a traditional means of public criticism or punishment in which the entire community could participate and a disciplinary technique by which family or community members were forced to follow collective rules. A strong, formal similarity existed between *charivaris* in Russia, where the practice endured as late as the 1920s, and in countries such as England, France, and Germany.

The typical Russian *charivari* consisted of parading an offender through the street either on foot or in a cart, in some cases wearing a horse collar, while villagers followed along playing *paramusique*[1] by beating upon oven doors (evidently the most favored instrument), pots and pans, washtubs, and other domestic or agricultural implements, sometimes carrying signs, mocking the victim, and singing songs. Women were often stripped naked or had their skirts raised before being led around the village; men might first be stripped, then tarred and feathered. Apart from minor differences of detail, the similarities here with European examples are striking.

. . . It is, in fact, with the function of the rituals and the victims themselves that Russian *charivaris* differed from those in other countries. The *charivari* in England and France most often expressed disapproval of marital mismatches or conjugal relations considered to be deviant, such as marriages between people of great age difference, socially ill-matched marriages, or a recently widowed villager marrying a single, younger person. Sexual offenders were also common victims of *charivaris,* as were cuckolded husbands, unwed mothers, persons (usually women) who committed adultery, wife-beaters, and household members deviating from accepted sex roles — for example, men who performed women's work or whose wives beat them.

In postreform Russia[2] we do find cases of *charivaris* involving adulteresses (and occasionally adulterers too), unwed mothers, and "immoral" women, but they account for only a small proportion of collective community actions that can be termed *vozhdeniia.* Nor did I find reports of cuckolded husbands or husbands beaten by their wives being subjected to rough music. The apparent scarcity of such cases in Great Russia[3] suggests that other matters occupied a higher priority when it came to the collective enforcement of local norms. Chief among these was petty theft.

Russian peasants treated many kinds of theft and pilfering quite leniently. Both unofficial and township courts used reconciliation far more than punishment in cases of petty theft. In the Volga region, for example, a peasant who perpetrated such a crime was not always viewed as someone capable of real harm to the community — a perspective clearly expressed in the popular saying, "The thief is not a thief, but a half-thief." Yet despite their apparent leniency, villagers did not simply dismiss the crime; in many instances *charivari* was a typical punishment, and

---

[1] Rough, raucous music.

[2] In Russian history, after the reforms enacted in the 1860s.

[3] The central and northeastern areas of Russia; home of the Russian-speaking people.

its magnitude was determined above all by the seriousness of the crime, and especially by the value of the stolen item. During *charivaris* involving petty theft, offenders would be marched through the village with the stolen object hung on them. In the village of Zabolonia, Smolensk province, for example, one peasant was caught stealing another's goose. Hanging the goose from his neck, villagers led the thief three times around the hamlet, pounding all the while upon oven doors. After this procession the thief begged forgiveness, bought drinks for everyone, and there the affair ended. In another case a woman from the village of Kozinkii, Orel province, stole a sheep from her neighbor and butchered it. She was discovered and brought before the village assembly, which sentenced her to a *charivari*. Village women gathered together with sickles, oven doors, and other "instruments," hung the sheep's head around her neck, and amid songs and banging, led the woman three times through the town before letting her go. . . .

The additional humiliation of being stripped for a *charivari* was reserved mainly for women. In one village of Novgorod province, Cherepovets district, a woman named Drosida Anisimova was caught picking berries before the time agreed on by the village assembly. A village policeman brought her before the assembly, where they stripped her naked, hung on her neck the basket of berries she had gathered, "and the entire commune led her through the village streets with shouts, laughter, songs, and dancing to the noise of washtubs, frying pans, bells and so on. The punishment had such a strong effect on her that she was ill for several days, but the thought of complaining against her offenders never entered her mind" (or so the report claimed). Likewise, Katerina Evdokimova, a peasant from the village of Ermakov, Iaroslavl province, was accused in 1874 of stealing linen. The assembly found her guilty and decided to undress her, wrap her in the stolen linen, and lead her through the streets. Evdokimova, however, pleaded not to be completely disrobed, so the assembly accommodated her by uncovering her only to the waist, then wrapping her in linen and leading her in public with her hands tied to a stake as everyone rang bells and beat upon oven doors.

Charivaris could also result from a refusal to obey the assembly's decision in a criminal case. In Orel province a peasant named Mikhail was found guilty of stealing a sheep and ordered to buy the village elder and his friends a half-bucket of vodka. This they quickly drank and demanded another, promising to forgive Mikhail afterward. But while consuming the second bucket the peasants continued berating Mikhail for his crime, and becoming concerned for his safety, he fled to his home. When they finished their vodka and noticed Mikhail's absence, the irate villagers went to the thief's house led by the elder. Demanding more vodka, they became even angrier when he called them drunks and robbers. For this new insult they took a wheel from his wagon and sold it for vodka, after which they seized Mikhail, tied a large sack of oats onto his back, and led him around the village accompanied by other peasants who beat upon oven doors while laughing and insulting the victim. When the *charivari* ended, Mikhail was forced to pawn clothing at the local tavern in order to buy the men still more vodka. With this they finally agreed to forgive him, but sternly warned that things would go much worse if he ever stole again.

Mikhail got off lightly, having not been beaten. Refusal to obey the will of the assembly could lead to more severe retribution involving violence and even expulsion from the community. To her misfortune, a peasant from the village of Meshkova, Orel province, learned this the hard way. Anna Akulicheva had been found guilty of stealing canvas, and the assembly decided to subject her to a *charivari* and then sell her own fabric for vodka. First the villagers knocked off her kerchief (a grave insult among Russian peasants) and dirtied her holiday shirt. Next they tied her sack-cloth on her back, bound her hands behind her, hitched her up, and led the woman through the village. Two peasants walked ahead beating with sticks upon oven doors while Anna followed in harness with the reins held by two others. The entire village turned out to watch and laugh, and children threw clods of dirt at her. Finally they brought her home and untied her, taking only the cloth they had placed on her back to purchase vodka. At this point, however, Anna attacked her tormenters with a chain seized in the shed and then fled the village to avoid further punishment.

On the suggestion of peasants from a neighboring village, Anna lodged a complaint with the local land captain.[4] He summoned the elder from Meshkova, who confessed in detail and was forbidden to do such a thing again. Furthermore, the land captain sentenced him to two days' arrest. When he returned home, the elder immediately summoned the assembly and told them what Anna had done. The members wasted little time in responding to this latest offense. They ruled that Anna should be whipped in public by her husband, Sergei, and that some of her clothes would then be taken to sell for vodka, after which she would undergo all sorts of public ridicule. The woman was brought before the assembly but resisted her husband's efforts to force her to lie down for the beating. Finally, other peasants threw her to the ground and held her there while Sergei administered thirty blows with a knout.[5] Following this severe punishment, he went to fetch his wife's clothes, but Anna had already taken all of her things to her family in Balasheva. As a result, Anna was ostracized. She fought with her husband daily. Worse, the community held her in contempt and mocked her, and village children pelted her on the street with clods of earth to shouts of "hurrah." At last she decided to leave Meshkova. With her husband's approval she received a passport and set off, first to the city of Orel and then to Odessa.

In all of these examples the obvious function of *charivaris* was to shame thieves so that they would not steal from fellow villagers again. With its wealth of symbolism and ritual, public humiliation of a wrongdoer brought both crime and criminal before the offended community for judgment, and it was the community that oversaw conformity to established rules, thereby asserting the primacy of its authority. At the level of symbolic discourse, the *charivari* held out a threat of greater sanction, for it acted as a ritualized, though temporary, expulsion

---

[4] Supervisor of peasant workers.

[5] Whip with a lash of leather thongs twisted with wire.

of an offender from the community and reminded all villagers — not only the thief — that expulsion could be permanent if someone repeated his or her crime or perpetrated a more serious infraction. Petty thieves were allowed to return to the collective fold only after publicly acknowledging their guilt and begging the community's forgiveness. Hence the equally symbolic payment in vodka which villagers demanded at the conclusion of a *charivari*. In "treating" the community to drinks, a thief won forgiveness and, more important, readmittance.

Beyond their immediate purpose of discipline, then, *charivaris* were a constituent element of village culture and an important means of social regulation. They played a significant role in governing behavior, regulating daily life, and ordering conduct "in a highly visible and comprehensive way." In this respect the *charivari* was only one of the tools in a village culture's arsenal of regulatory customs and rituals. *Charivaris* also helped to preserve local solidarity by preventing the taking of sides in a dispute and a subsequent development of open feuding, which would otherwise disrupt activities and social relations crucial to the peasant economy. The punishment thus acted to soothe ill feelings and hostilities by involving an entire village, often with the elder's authorization and active participation.

In the majority of recorded cases peasants first brought a thief before the local assembly for sentencing, though eight to ten assembly members together with an elder or a township headman were deemed sufficient to reach a decision. It is here, in fact, with the villagers' use of their assembly as a judicial organ, that we find the basis of the commune's exclusive right in the moral control of its members. . . . The assembly's decision legitimated a *charivari* in the eyes of all villagers and made revenge on the victim's part unlikely, because to seek retribution against the participants was tantamount to challenging the authority of the commune itself. The escalation of punishment during a *vozhdenie* resulted from just such a challenge. Similarly, escalation occurred when a demand for "payment" in vodka went unmet and the offender thereby refused to reach reconciliation with the community.

Charivaris directed against persons other than thieves do not fit so neatly into the conclusions drawn thus far. Many forms of *charivari* worked in a manner similar to the French *charivari* so often held up as a model for comparison — to maintain community norms of morality and to exert community control over sexual behavior and conjugal relations. To give one example, Evgenii Iakushkin[6] reported in 1875 that if a bride in Olonets province had not preserved her virginity until marriage, villagers would stick a peg over her door, hang a horse collar on it, and lead both her and her mother under it. Adulteresses, too, might be subjected to *charivaris*. Such events included all the common elements of *charivari*: leading offenders through the village, public derision, humiliation, and paramusic. Yet in some cases of adultery, the element of violence was used even when

---

[6] Ethnographer and jurist (1826–1905) who studied customary law among the peasantry.

a victim offered no resistance; the process of escalation did not function because violence seems to have been inherent to this type of *charivari*. Thus a woman named Oksana Vereshchikha was suspected by peasants in her village of Poznanka (Volynia province) of carrying on an illicit affair with the township clerk. For this they stripped her naked, placed her in irons, and tied her to a post, where she stayed all night. In the morning the villagers returned and ordered her to buy them a pail of vodka, even though they had already pawned her kerchief and sheepskin jacket for one pail on the previous day. Because she had no money, a *charivari* was organized with "musicians" marching in front, followed by Vereshchikha, the elder, and the villagers. This was a particularly creative procession in which a garland of straw and burdocks[7] was placed on the victim's head, and she was forced to dance before the crowd. They led her seven times along the street, beating her with fists and flogging her with the birch, all the while passing vodka around. At last they took her home, beat her again, and let her go.

Charivaris of adulteresses or of housewives who somehow had failed in their domestic duties reveal the ability of communities "to compel individual family members to follow collective rules," as well as the public control to which "the deviant relations of husband and wife are subject." As with cases of theft, collective responsibility and supervision constituted the basis of *charivaris*. Yet in the Russian village, communal authority was less concerned with punishing adultery than with punishing theft; adultery involved a different set of property and power relations that rested on the generally accepted position of male domination and the husband's customary authority to punish his wife with almost complete impunity. Neighbors rarely intervened to quell domestic violence between husband and wife. Thus few *charivaris* were directed against adulteresses by Great Russian peasants because villagers usually left it to a husband to mete out appropriate punishment. The expectation of corporal punishment, in turn, may account for the use of violence in those instances when villagers did subject an adulterous woman to *charivari*, for here the community symbolically took on the role of offended spouse and punished as custom dictated. Though signs of change can be found in some areas, the persistence of such punishments helps to explain the relative scarcity of incidents in which adulteresses were victims of *charivaris*. Marital violence was especially likely to occur when a wife had committed adultery or left her husband; both deeds could disrupt the household economy and bring a loss of honor to the husband.

Evidence from township courts shows that women tried to escape domestic violence or to seek justice through formal litigation. Yet peasant judges ruled in a woman's favor primarily when they found no justification for a beating, or when they deemed that the punishment had been overly cruel. In cases of adultery or "abandonment," however, litigation had little chance of success; the husband was within his rights to punish his wife as he saw fit. . . .

---

[7] Cockleburrs.

Russian *charivaris,* then, differed in important respects from those in many countries of Western Europe. Great Russian peasants used rituals of public shaming far more to punish theft than sexual and conjugal misconduct, perhaps because of the increased significance of property relations in the postemancipation period[8] and an attendant weakening of the primacy of kinship. When villagers did punish sexual misconduct, their attention focused primarily, apart from unmarried girls, on adulteresses whose husbands were absent or, in the community's view, required assistance in controlling their wives. Finally, the Russian *charivari* sought to bring offenders back into the community rather than drive them out altogether, using the symbolic threat of expulsion together with the forced purchase of vodka (i.e., symbolic reconciliation) as its main instruments for reestablishing normal intravillage relations. This fact helps to distinguish the *charivari* from other types of *samosud,* in which ritual was largely absent, violence was prominent, and expulsion constituted the overriding objective. It is to these manifestations of *samosud* that we now turn.

A second form of summary justice that clarifies the peasants' distinction between *charivari* and *samosud* brings us back to property crime, though this time to crime of a serious rather than a petty nature. Such acts were especially likely to meet with harsh penalties if the criminal was an outsider or had repeatedly committed theft in a given locality. Popular retribution involved beatings, myriad gruesome and often lethal tortures, and outright murder. These acts were almost always carried out by a crowd but lacked the organized, ritual character of *charivari.* Although an elder might direct the violence, meetings of the village assembly were not necessary before punishing a criminal.

Peasant reprisals could be merciless, especially if their aim was to rid the community of the criminal once and for all. In one part of the Mid-Volga region, for instance, a gang of six peasants had long caused trouble among their fellow villagers by stealing property and money, but attempts by the local population to catch the thieves met with no success. When the gang turned to highway robbery, villagers grew particularly enraged and selected three men to kill them, which they finally did. One thief in Kazan province was beaten savagely and then, before a large crowd on a riverbank, he was killed by the village elder and buried in the sand. Elsewhere a peasant named Vasilii Andronov had been exiled to Siberia by communal decree from his village of Grigorev, Samara province. In 1872 Andronov escaped and returned to Grigorev seeking revenge. Once there he committed theft and arson and threatened murder. On December 3 the peasants summoned their assembly and decided to end the matter by doing away with him. "At dusk the entire assembly, led by the village elder, surrounded the house where Andronov was hiding. He was caught and killed."

Here we have cases of straightforward, premeditated, collective murder by a community. Yet summary justice also included ingenious tortures, all described

---

[8] In Russian history, after the emancipation of the serfs in 1861.

in great detail by the urban press, popular writers, and scholars. In Vetluzhskii district of Kostroma province, according to one report, "this is what they do with thieves: they drive the handle of a whip into his rectum and shake up everything there. After this the peasant weakens and dies." Variations of this punishment could be found in other areas as well, where a jagged stick might be used so that it could not be removed. Some thieves and arsonists had nails driven into their heads or wooden pins behind the fingernails; others were stripped naked in winter and drenched with cold water until they died.

Horse thieves inspired the greatest fear and hatred in the Russian countryside. They usually operated in gangs, sometimes composed of several hundred members who formed networks or "societies," dividing a territory among themselves to carry out their trade. With organizations stretching into several provinces and controlling many officers of the rural police force, horse thieves worked with little fear of capture, wielding great power among the populace. Villagers knew that revenge was likely to follow if they reported the thieves' activities in their locality. Yet for peasants a horse represented the most valuable piece of property, without which farming would be impossible, as countless sayings attest: "Without a horse you're not a ploughman"; "Without a horse you're another's worker"; or "A peasant without a horse is like a house without a ceiling." Thus villagers encountering horse thieves confronted a situation in which they were prey to a parasitic gang that stole their major means of subsistence, and all too often the peasants could take no measures to prevent this loss.

When a horse thief did fall into their hands, peasants let loose an elemental fury with often deadly results. Ivan Stepanov, for example, was a well-known thief in one of Russia's central provinces. As a fellow villager later told the court investigator, hardly a person in the village had not suffered some loss from Ivan's trade. He had been publicly whipped on numerous occasions, and the last time he was caught the village assembly warned him that if he stole again, he would be exiled to Siberia. Many peasants shouted in protest that it was not worth it to spend community funds to send him away; it would be far easier just to kill him. After this Stepanov disappeared for eight months; rumors circulated that he had taken up work as a horse thief in another locality and had even sneaked into town several times to bring his wife some money. Following one of these nocturnal visits, Stepanov was leaving the village early in the morning when he spied a foal in Dmitrii Petrov's meadow, jumped onto the horse, and rode it into the nearby forest. Unfortunately for him, Stepanov was caught by a group of peasants who grabbed him and brought him back to the village, where a search had already begun for the foal. On learning of the thief's capture, a crowd gathered and started beating Stepanov. "They beat him for a long time, and Dmitrii Petrov beat him most of all. When Stepanov already lay motionless, Dmitrii cruelly kicked him in the back and sides. Seeing that he was dead, the assembly came together to discuss the matter. Petrov, a well-to-do farmer, begged them not to ruin him by turning him in, promising to help Stepanov's widow for the rest of his life. Because the murdered man was hated by all as a thief, whereas Petrov was a young man and a good worker, the assembly took pity on him. They asked the widow, who agreed to the deal, and the assembly voted unanimously to conceal the murder from officials."

Peasants reserved their worst punishments for horse thieves, who, if caught, were castrated or beaten in the groin until they died, had stakes driven into the throat or chest, were branded with hot irons, and had their eyes put out. Two punishments appear to have been particularly widespread. In one peasants first nailed a pully high onto a gatepost. Then the thief, with his hands and feet tied together, was raised into the air by a rope running through the pully. When he hung at a sufficient height, they released the rope. "He falls to the ground, striking the lower part of his back in a terrible way. This is repeated many times in succession, and each time the snap of the poor devil's vertebrae can be heard." The punishment might continue long after he had died. Another torture consisted of stripping a thief and wrapping his torso with a wet sack. A plank was then placed on his stomach and peasants beat on it with whatever they could find — hammers, logs, or stones — "gradually destroying the unfortunate's insides." The utility of such a punishment was that it left no external signs, so whoever found the abandoned body would suspect no crime. With the introduction of coroners as part of the court investigator's office in the late nineteenth century, however, the practice became far less foolproof. . . .

Given the availability of courts for punishing these crimes, why did peasants continue to employ *samosud* knowing that, if discovered, they too could be punished? One reason was their conviction that the official courts did not punish severely enough. Even in those instances when villagers turned a criminal over to the authorities, they first inflicted their own penalty. Horse thieves and arsonists might be sentenced to several years of incarceration or exile, but eventually they regained their freedom and often took up their old trade. None knew this better than villagers who had to deal with the criminals again, especially if they returned seeking revenge, and a few years in prison did not seem a just punishment. Furthermore, peasants could never be certain the thief would be punished. The overburdened, understaffed, and inefficient rural police, even if honest, were no match for professional thieves working in large groups and living secretly in prosperous, well-protected settlements. Peasants also mistrusted the official courts and attempts by outsiders to meddle in local affairs, feeling that they best knew how to treat criminals who threatened their community. They showed particular reluctance to turn a fellow villager over to an alien authority, for as one saying went, "He's *our* criminal and it's up to us to punish him."

Russian peasants also had ways of dealing with persons whose magical powers endangered the health and welfare of community members, crops, and livestock (recall Agrafena Ignatieva!). Belief in sorcery and maleficent spells remained an active element of peasant culture throughout the period, and villagers frequently utilized practitioners of magical or healing arts for many purposes. But when some disaster such as plague, epidemic, or crop failure befell the community, blame might be placed on the very people whose powers previously had appeared beneficial. Somehow, it was believed, they had been offended and were seeking revenge on the entire village or certain of its members. It proved difficult to accuse these people in court, for official law no longer recognized witchcraft as a criminal offense and often punished the complainants themselves while the sorcerer went free. As with horse theft, then, villagers confronted with maleficent spells felt that they were unprotected by state law and had to take matters into their own hands. When the "culprit" was identified, peasants meted out punishment of similar brutality to that suffered by horse thieves, and their justice often resulted in the murder of the accused.

The link between peasant culture and *samosud* appears most dramatically in instances of popular reprisal against suspected practitioners of magic. *Samosud* of sorcerers and witches could not be written off as an aberration as long as epidemics and other natural phenomena were explained within a framework of supernatural causation, and the ease with which devious charlatans and criminals exploited peasant beliefs merely confirms that such a mode of explanation continued to operate in the countryside throughout the late nineteenth century. Cases I have examined conform to the general, Western pattern of witchcraft accusations in which the main victims were impoverished elderly persons, itinerants, and the socially isolated. Despite peasants' traditional generosity toward wanderers and beggars, when such a person depended on others in the community for daily subsistence, she or he might come to be seen as a burden and, under the proper circumstances (such as an outbreak of disease), could easily become the target of hostility. Other cases might arise from a grudge held by one villager against the "witch." Having little or no say in community affairs because of their economic (and, hence, social) position, these people were particularly vulnerable to any accusation — a fact well known to neighbors and other villagers, who may have used it to their advantage.

None of this is to say that accusations of witchcraft were only pretexts for settling preexisting conflicts in the village. Persons who accused a "witch" may have known the charge was false. Still, despite such incidents, most peasants who leveled witchcraft accusations, and those who punished the accused, were directed by their belief in the supernatural. Evidence of the widespread persistence of such belief is far too convincing for us to conclude otherwise.

It is all too easy to attribute the brutality of such punishments to the peasants' lack of "culture" or "legal consciousness" and to overlook the interaction of peasant and elite cultures that was involved. Earlier criminal codes provided for severe punishment, mutilation, or execution of horse thieves (as well as other criminals), and these punishments were carried out in public settings. Even more important was the often brutal punishment of serfs on gentry estates, which certainly contributed to the peasants' concepts and practice of justice in the village (though this influence must have worked in both directions). Official codes such as that of 1839 made corporal punishment one of the few penalties that peasant courts could impose in practice. If not directly modeled on official and gentry treatment of offenders, the punishments employed by peasants had developed as a complex mixture of official and popular forms of retribution.

In the three areas discussed in this article *samosud* was a response to threats against the community or challenges to village norms and authority. It was not "lawless violence," as outsiders claimed, but action aimed at suppressing particular forms of behavior and criminal activity that could disrupt social relations or seriously harm the village economy. With little protection against danger other than that offered by their own local rules and institutions, peasants responded with the weapons available to them: *charivaris,* public beatings, ostracism, and murder.

These weapons, however, differed in both form and purpose. Directed against village members, the *charivari* employed an array of symbols and rituals designed to reconcile criminal and community and to restore peaceful relations among villagers. Only if reconciliation was rejected did peasants resort to harsher measures, for in such cases the offender became an outsider by spurning the community itself. Violent *samosud,* in contrast, focused on outsiders — defined either as nonmembers of the community or those who, through the harm caused by their crime or because of their social isolation, removed themselves from the community, thus the absence of ritual "processions" with their symbolic expulsion and reconciliation. Outsiders, by definition, could not be brought into the community except through bonds of marriage or kinship, and when they threatened the well-being of the village, mechanisms of reconciliation did not function. The purpose of punishments used against them, therefore, was to ensure that they would pose no further threat.

Samosud also forced peasants to defend their juridical beliefs and practices before the dominant culture. Educated Russia viewed such acts not only as violations of the criminal code but as proof of the ignorance and low level of civilization in which the rural population was immersed. Villagers rejected official law on this matter, as they did on many issues that touched their lives, and continued to behave as necessity dictated, resorting to *charivaris* or violence when necessary and accepting the risks accompanying their collective actions. Peasants were clearly aware that state law forbade *samosud* because they frequently attempted to conceal the results of their popular justice, and probably succeeded more often than we would imagine. Yet their views of justice did not draw the same delimitations as official law with regard to which crimes they could and could not punish. Infractions punished by *vozhdeniia,* for example, concerned the community alone, and outsiders had no business meddling in such affairs regardless of what their law might forbid. Similarly, official courts did not punish crimes such as horse theft as severely as peasants believed they should; and in cases of witchcraft the state had ceased to regard this serious problem (as villagers saw it) to be a crime. Official law punished crimes according to an entirely different set of criteria from those used by the peasantry — criteria that often took little account of local needs and concerns; and participants in the murder of a horse thief or a witch may have found no alternative to their own methods of justice.

Peasant juridical beliefs, like *samosud* itself, were most concerned with protecting the community from disruptive and harmful forces. Their juridical practices thus developed as a body of ideas incorporating norms of behavior, rules, and principles that could best serve to maintain and preserve the community. Through the continual assertion of its principles in juridical practice, the rural community asserted and reproduced not only its worldview but also the social, economic, sexual, and cultural relations by which this very community took on meaning. Although certain types of interaction with the dominant culture could be incorporated, transformed, or at least made manageable by the village population, other efforts to force changes on peasant views of law, crime, or justice threatened to disrupt basic mechanisms through which the reproduction of the community took place. *Samosud* was one such mechanism, and efforts to eradicate the practice highlights the larger clash between peasant and official culture. When the community's ability to preserve and reproduce itself appeared threatened by government laws or regulations, peasants resisted, rejected, or simply ignored them. No such reaction was seen when the state tampered with the township court, for its reform did not impinge on villagers' lives in significant ways. The survival of *samosud* well into the Soviet period should be viewed not merely as an indication of the tenacity of Russian peasant culture in an era of major socioeconomic change but as the continued viability of an important, local, and spontaneously generated institution designed to regulate and protect village society.

MAKING CONNECTIONS: VIOLENCE

1. Richard van Dülmen and Stephen Frank both discuss methods of punishing criminals, the former by states and judiciaries in early modern Germany, the latter by nineteenth-century Russian peasants. Compare the punishments described in the two articles. Where do you see similarities and differences in the punishments inflicted and in the motives behind them? To what extent were the Russian rituals of punishment analogous to those in Germany? In which place were punishments most severe? How did a criminal's gender affect the type of punishment received?

2. Why were the Russian peasants especially interested in certain types of crimes? Why did they, unlike early modern Germans, often find and punish some criminals rather than leave the task to the state judicial system?

3. How were the German and Russian communities involved in the punishment of wrongdoers? How did cruel punishments function to bind communities together? What qualms, if any, did the Germans and Russians have about chastising people ferociously? Do you think the cruelest punishments succeeded better than milder forms to deter the German and Russian people from crime? Why or why not?

A WOMAN'S WORLD:
DEPARTMENT STORES AND THE
EVOLUTION OF WOMEN'S
EMPLOYMENT,
1870–1920
Theresa M. McBride

A fixture of Western society today, the department store is actually a quite recent innovation. It first appeared in mid-nineteenth-century Paris and revolutionized the retail trade. Because department stores had a wide variety of products to sell and many employees, they differed greatly from traditional retail businesses. What new merchandising principles did the new stores espouse? What did the French novelist Émile Zola mean in claiming that the department store helped bring about a "new religion"? How did department stores change attitudes toward and patterns of consumption?

Theresa M. McBride, a historian of French women and the family, depicts the department store as the "world of women," of female customers and employees. McBride has consulted census lists, municipal statistics, contemporary publications, newspapers, police reports, and government records concerning workers and business in order to reconstruct the personal and work lives of female clerks. Who were the female clerks, and why did they choose to find employment in department stores, where hours were long, the pace often frenetic, the rules stifling, the threat of fines and dismissal constant, and the supervision intense? What could the clerks hope for in their careers?

Female employees today would not tolerate being locked up in dining halls, living in company apartments, and having their sexual lives the subject of department-store concern. But in the nineteenth century, department-store owners mixed capitalism with old-fashioned paternalism, combining the pursuit of profit with the enforcement of morality. The owners believed it was necessary to concern themselves with the after-work behavior of female clerks.

Theresa M. McBride, "A Woman's World: Department Stores and the Evolution of Women's Employment, 1870–1920," *French Historical Studies* 10 (fall 1978): 664–683.

The female clerks had little time to relax or to go out, but when they could, they took advantage of the independence that wage-earning offered. Thus they frequented inexpensive restaurants and enjoyed the attractions of city life. Why did other women of the same social background envy the female clerks' jobs and status? What major changes occurred by World War I that affected women's employment in department stores?

In the 1840s Aristide Boucicaut[1] took over a small retail shop for dry goods and clothing in Paris. This shop became the "Bon Marché," the world's first department store, and soon the idea was emulated by other commercial entrepreneurs throughout the world. The department store helped to create a "new religion," as Emile Zola[2] described the passion for consumption nurtured by the department stores' retailing revolution. As churches were being deserted, Zola argued, the stores were filling with crowds of women seeking to fill their empty hours and to find meaning for empty lives. The cult of the soul was replaced by a cult of the body — of beauty, of fashion. The department store was preeminently the "world of women," where women were encouraged to find their life's meaning in conspicuous consumption and where they increasingly found a role in selling. Thus, the department store played a highly significant role in the evolution both of contemporary society and of woman's place in that society.

The department stores came to dominate retail trade by introducing novel merchandising principles. Most obviously, they were much larger than traditional retail establishments and united a wide variety of goods under one roof; specialization was retained only in the *rayons* or departments into which the stores were divided. Department store entrepreneurs throughout the world evolved the techniques of retailing between the 1840s and 1860s, which included the important innovation of fixed pricing, and eliminated bargaining from a sale. Fixed pricing was a revolutionary concept because it altered the customary buyer-seller relationship, reducing the buyer to the role of passive consumer, whose only choice was to accept or reject the goods as offered at the set price. Even the buyer's desire for certain items was created through the tactics of large-scale retailing: publicity, display of goods, and low prices of items. The salesperson became a simple cog in the giant commercial mechanism; instead of representing the owner, the salesclerk became a facilitator, helping to create an atmosphere of attention and service while the merchandise "sold itself."

The low mark-up of the large stores allowed lower prices (hence the name — Bon Marché)[3] and helped to attract crowds of customers from throughout the city.

---

[1] Merchant and philanthropist (1810–1877).

[2] Novelist (1840–1902).

[3] Cheap.

The department stores could not simply depend upon the traditional bourgeois clientele of smaller shops (the upper classes ordered goods from their own suppliers) and had to attract customers from among the petite bourgeoisie.[4] By catering to the budgets and the "passion for spending" of the petite bourgeoisie, the department stores brought increasing numbers of people into contact with modern consumer society.

A significant part of the department stores' merchandising revolution was the presentation. Exhibits in the spacious galleries of the stores, large display windows, publicity through catalogs and newspaper advertising shaped illusions and stimulated the public's desires for the items offered. The salesperson was herself part of that presentation, helping to create an atmosphere of service and contributing to the seductiveness of the merchandise.

In order to attract customers and facilitate a heavy volume of sales, the department stores needed a new kind of staff. Whereas the shopkeeper could rely upon family members and a loyal assistant or two, the department store became an employer on the scale of modern industrial enterprises. In the 1880s the Bon Marché employed twenty-five hundred clerks; the Grands Magasins du Louvre . . . by 1900 had a staff of thirty-five hundred to four thousand, depending on the season. Smaller provincial stores typically employed several hundred people. The Nouvelles Galeries in Bordeaux, for example, had 554 employees in 1912, divided into sales (283), office staff (60), and stock control (211). In 1906, by comparison, more than half of all commercial enterprises in France employed no more than five people (54 per cent), and two-thirds had ten or fewer employees. The average number of employees was 2.8. With such a large number of clerks, the entrepreneur could not expect to treat them like family members nor to encourage their . . . hope that they might some day take over control of the store.

Beyond simple size, the department stores were innovators in the ways in which they recruited, trained, and treated their employees. The fixed price system and the practice of allowing customers to browse freely meant that a large percentage of the work force were simply unskilled assistants, who brought the items to the customers and took their payments to the cashiers. Costs were minimized by paying very low base salaries. But loyalty and diligence were assured by a highly graduated hierarchy in which the top ranks were achieved only through intense competition. Entrepreneurs like Boucicaut realized that in order to create the proper atmosphere in their stores they would have to reward top salespeople by the payment of commissions on sales and by allowing them to enjoy a high level of status and responsibility. The department stores formalized the system of recruitment, promotion, and rewards to create a group of employees who would espouse the interests of the firm as their own or be quickly weeded out.

Women were a crucial element in this system. In fact, although women did not form the majority of the stores' work force until after 1914, women dominated

---

[4] The lower middle class.

certain departments and came to symbolize the "world of women," as the department store was described. Women were both the clerks and the customers in this market place, for the mainstays of the new stores were fashions and dry goods. Women were scarcely new to commerce, but their role was expanding and changing in the late nineteenth century. A parliamentary investigation into the Parisian food and clothing industries found women clerks throughout those industries, and the report's conclusions insisted upon the importance of the unsalaried work of women who were *patronnes*[5] or who shared that responsibility with their husbands. Typically, several members of the family worked in family-run businesses, so that daughters also received some early work experience. Most shops could not have survived without the contributions of female family members. For the women themselves, this kind of work was both an extension of their domestic role and an important experience in the world of business. While the department stores involved women in commercial activity in a very different way, traditional commercial roles continued to be exercised by the wives and daughters of shopkeepers well into the twentieth century.

One of the best descriptions of the new store clerks emerges from the investigations of Emile Zola for his novel, *Au bonheur des dames,*[6] in which the young heroine secures employment with a large department store closely modelled after the Bon Marché and the Grands Magasins du Louvre. Zola's heroine Denise is the carefully sketched model of the female clerk: young, single, and an immigrant to Paris from a provincial store.

Denise was hired at the store after the management assured itself of her experience and her attractiveness. In the first few days, she learned to adjust to the pace of work, the supervision of older saleswomen, and to the competitiveness of the older clerks who tried to monopolize the sales. Most beginners like Denise spent much of their time arranging displays of merchandise and delivering items to customers. During peak seasons, many clerks started as temporary help "with the hope that they would eventually be permanently hired," but only a small proportion of them survived this period of "training." During the first year, beginners received little more than room and board. But if the debutante could withstand the low salaries, long hours, and often heavy-handed surveillance of other salesclerks, she had a chance to enter the ranks of the relatively well-paid saleswomen.

At the highest level of the sales hierarchy were the department heads, *chefs de rayons,* and their assistants, whose responsibilities included not only sales but also the ordering of merchandise for their own divisions and the hiring and supervision of salespersonnel. Salespeople provided information about merchandise, and once items were sold, took them to be wrapped, and delivered the payment to the cashier. Saleswomen and men were generally divided into different departments: men sold male clothing, household furnishings, and even

---

[5] Employers.

[6] *The Paradise of Women.*

women's gloves and stockings, while women handled baby clothing and women's dresses, reflecting the pattern in the industry as a whole. Significantly, men made up the majority of department heads and assistants, though a few women managed to win out against the intense competition to head departments.

Department stores employed many women who were not sales clerks. There were office staffs of women who carried on the ordering, advertising, and the mail-order business. In addition, the largest stores employed hundreds of seamstresses, who were clearly distinguished from the sales force by the designation *ouvrière*[7] (rather than "employee"). The seamstresses received none of the benefits of the employees, such as free lodging or medical care, and the market provided by the department stores for the handwork of the domestic garment-making workers kept the institution of "sweated" labor alive well into the twentieth century.

The proportion of women employed in the department stores steadily increased after a large strike by clerks in 1869. In part, employers recruited women because they represented a tractable labor force. Department stores gradually replaced some male clerks with female clerks who were more "docile" and "lacking in tradition" and who, consequently, would be less eager to strike. But there were other reasons for recruiting women clerks. Women were cheaper to hire than men and readily available because of the narrowing of other employment options for women. The spread of public education for women provided a pool of workers who were reluctant to work as seamstresses or domestics. And women workers impressed employers with their personal qualities of "politeness," "sobriety," and even a "talent for calculation."

Considering both the obvious advantages of a female work force and the important traditional role of women in commerce, it seems inevitable that women should have been hired as clerks in the new department stores. But women sales-clerks were recruited from different sources than other female workers and remained a distinctive group through the period of the First World War. Why women clerks replaced men when the occupational opportunities expanded in commerce is, then, not so simple a question.

Department store clerks were very different from the largest group of women workers in the late nineteenth century — domestic servants. The young women who came to work in the Parisian *grands magasins*[8] were recruited from the cities and towns of France, while the domestic servants came from the countryside. Over half (53 per cent) of the female clerks who lived in the Parisian suburbs in 1911 and worked in Parisian stores had been born in Paris. Zola noted that one-third of the Bon Marché's saleswomen were native Parisians and that this was a larger percentage than among the male clerks. Salesmen were undoubtedly more mobile both geographically and socially. Both male and female employees who

---

[7] Worker.

[8] Department stores.

were not native Parisians had generally moved there from some provincial city where they had completed the essential apprenticeship in another store.

Department store clerks, like other commercial employees, often came from the ranks of urban shopkeepers and artisans. Children of shopkeepers frequently worked for a time in the large stores to learn commercial skills before returning to work in the family business. Over half of the shopgirls living with parents were from employee or shopkeeping families. . . . The occupational backgrounds of French clerks were primarily the urban, skilled occupations. A few even came from possible middle-class backgrounds, having parents who were teachers or *commerçants,*[9] but these were rare. In general, a clerk was not a working-class girl working her way out of poverty but more typically a lower-middle-class girl whose father was himself commercially employed, if not a shopkeeper.

Department store clerks were young. But unlike other women workers, who might begin their working lives at eleven or twelve, store clerks were rarely under seventeen years old. The Parisian *grands magasins* selected women only after a period of training, and thus the majority of the work force were in their early twenties. . . . Domestic servants and seamstresses included a wider range of ages because women could be employed at much younger ages in those occupations and could go back to work in small shops or as charwomen or seamstresses after their families were grown.

The career of the sales clerk, however, could be very short. Apart from the attrition due to marriage, the occupation simply wore some women out. Stores rarely hired anyone over 30, and the unlucky woman who lost her job after that age might be permanently retired. Younger women were more attractive, stronger, and cheaper to employ than older, more experienced women.

The life of the department store clerk was monopolized by the store. About half of the unmarried women were housed by the stores. The Bon Marché had small rooms under the roof of the store, while the Louvre housed its employees in buildings nearby. The rooms provided by the Bon Marché for their female employees were small with low ceilings; each contained a simple bed, table, and chair. But though these rooms were unadorned and sometimes overcrowded, they were often better than the rented room a young clerk could expect to find on her own. The lodgings at the Bon Marché included social rooms, where the management provided pianos for the women and billiard tables for the men. Visitors of the opposite sex were not allowed there, not even other employees. A concièrge kept track of the employees, and her permission had to be requested in order to go out at night. Such permission was nearly always granted as long as the eleven o'clock curfew was respected. Although department store entrepreneurs were innovators in retailing practices, their attitudes toward employees retained the strong flavor of paternalism that was typical of small-scale retailing. In small

---

[9] Tradespeople.

shops, the woman employee was almost a domestic, living in and working with other members of the family in the shop. Store managers of the department stores acted "in loco parentis"[10] at times, too, by exercising strong control over the lives of their saleswomen to preserve respectable behavior and to protect the public image of their firms.

The practice of housing female employees on the premises illustrates a variety of capitalistic and paternalistic motivations. There was considerable advantage to having salesclerks housed nearby, given the long hours they were expected to work. Employers also expressed . . . concern about the kind of . . . behavior, such as drinking, which could result from a lack of supervision. Women and young male clerks were both the victims and the beneficiaries of this system; adult men were allowed much greater freedom. The offer of housing and other benefits was combined with the opportunity to more closely control the lives of salespeople. Because of the economic advantages of insuring a well-disciplined work force, department store owners prolonged the paternalism of shopkeepers long after the size of the new enterprises had destroyed most aspects of the traditional relationship.

Department store clerks were surrounded by their work. Not only housed in or near the store but also fed their meals there, the women were never allowed out of the store until after closing. The large dining halls where employees took their midday meal were an important feature of the first department stores, and one contemporary described them as follows: "At each end of the immense dining halls were the department heads and inspectors; the simple male employees were seated in the center at long tables. Only the opening out of newspapers and the low hum of voices broke the silence, and everyone was completely absorbed in eating, for all were required to finish [in an hour]. . . ." Female clerks ate in a different room, separately from the men. There were three sittings to accommodate the large number of employees, the first one beginning at 9:30 A.M. The break was closely supervised, and each employee had less than an hour, calculated from the time she left her post until she returned there. Although employees only rarely complained about the food they were served, much criticism was levelled at the conditions under which employees were forced to eat. Despite protests, women employees were never allowed to leave the store nor to return to their rooms during their breaks. At the Galeries Lafayette, they were locked into their dining hall during the meal. This kind of control indicates more strongly the "severity" than the "paternal indulgence" which managerial policy espoused.

Work rules throughout the store were very strict. Employees were dressed distinctively as a way of identifying them and making them conscious of their relationship to the store. Until after 1900, male employees were required to arrive at work wearing a derby or "melon," and the women were uniformly dressed in

---

[10] In the place of the parents.

black silk. Surveillance by inspectors and supervisors assured that employee behavior was as uniform as their dress. Employees were expected to begin work at 8 A.M., and penalties were imposed on the tardy. At the Magasins Dufayel, a clerk was fined 25 centimes for being five minutes late; if she were two hours late, she could lose an entire day's wage. The average workday lasted twelve to thirteen hours, for the department stores did not close until 8 P.M. in the winter and 9 P.M. in the summer. During special sales or while preparing displays for the new season, clerks frequently had to work overtime without any special compensation. Although clerks in small shops often worked even longer hours, work in the department stores was judged more tiring by two parliamentary investigators in 1900, who argued that the large crowds attracted to the new stores quickened the pace of work.

By 1900 the workday for most female clerks had been reduced in accordance with an 1892 law setting a ten-hour maximum for women. The length of the clerk's workday had aroused much concern about the women's health, but their situation was still . . . better than that of the thousands of seamstresses who worked in sweatshop conditions in Parisian attics for little pay. Even before the reform, the workday of the salesgirl had been the envy of domestic servants, whose freedom was much more limited and whose employers did not allow the few hours of leisure which shopgirls enjoyed.

Characteristic of the way in which reforms were effected was the campaign for Sunday closing. In the 1890s . . . the large department stores began to adopt the practice of remaining closed on Sundays, giving most of their work force a day off. Although some employees were still needed to mount special expositions, prepare for sales, or unload deliveries, Sunday closing assured virtually all the women clerks a day off per week. The campaign for Sunday closing . . . inspired the most significant level of employee organization seen in this period. Concerted pressure was exerted by the predominantly male unions who occasionally solicited the support of women clerks and at times took up issues which were specifically female ones, such as the practice of locking up the women in their dining hall. As with other reforms, the chief opponents of reform were those who were concerned about the autonomy and survival of small shops that remained open longest in order to compete with the department stores. Overall, the challenge to the department store owners' authority was slight.

The authority of the employer, evident in the rigid work rules . . . was . . . obvious in the firing policies. The threat of termination was an excellent tool for shaping docile, hard-working employees, and employers did not use it sparingly. At the Bon Marché, the new recruits were quickly sized up in terms of their suitability as Bon Marché employees; among the four hundred new employees who were hired in 1873, 37 per cent were fired in the first five years. Most firings came without warning or compensation. Commonly, employers were not required to provide their employees with advance notice of termination, and employees lived with the sense of insecurity.

In the "severe yet beneficent" approach, however, there were also sweeter inducements to employee loyalty. Entrepreneurs like Boucicaut of the Bon Marché or Cognacq[11] of the Samaritaine knew that the success of their ventures depended in large part upon the formation of loyal employees. The department stores offered numerous incentives of various kinds. Compensation was high compared to other female salaries. Though young clerks received little more than their room and board, the average salary of a top saleswoman was three hundred to four hundred francs per month around 1900. Even a single woman could live very comfortably in Paris on a salary of that level. By contrast, the average wage of a woman employed in industry in 1902 was two francs per day, and the best industrial salaries scarcely exceeded three francs. Thus, a working woman rarely achieved an income of 75 francs per month, compared to the average saleswoman's income of 75 francs per week.

Clearly the averages conceal an enormous range of salaries, since the greater part of the total was earned in commissions. All of the stores gave 1 or 2 per cent commissions on sales, . . . and, in addition, employees received discounts on merchandise purchased at the store. These incentives inspired many employees to associate their own interests with those of the firm but also to go into debt over their purchases of clothing and household items.

Long-term employees received the greatest advantages, such as the benefits from the provident fund begun by the Boucicaut family. After five years' service the store invested an annual sum on behalf of each employee. After 1886 a woman with 15 years of service could begin to draw benefits after the age of forty-five. The benefits averaged six hundred to fifteen hundred francs per year, depending on the individual's salary and length of service. . . . The fund paid death benefits to employees' families, and women clerks could draw a small sum from it when leaving the store to be married. At the Grands Magasins du Louvre, the store contributed two hundred francs per year to a similar fund. The Louvre also sponsored employee savings plans and invested in vacation homes for employees. In addition, Cognacq of the Samaritaine subsidized the building of inexpensive apartments on the outskirts of Paris, and the Boucicaut family built a hospital.

As a result, . . . department store owners earned a . . . reputation for philanthropy. . . . A parliamentary committee in 1914 reluctantly concluded that the department stores treated their employees better than family-run shops, even though the report . . . was generally hostile to large-scale retailing.

Critics of the department stores emphasized the destruction of the familial relationship between employer and employee in large-scale commerce, but store owners were scarcely indifferent to the quality of employees' family lives. Women employees received paid maternity leaves (up to six weeks at the Louvre)—an important innovation. Employers also promoted larger families by awarding gifts of two hundred francs for the birth of each child. The Samaritaine . . . ran a day nursery for the children of employees in the 1890s.

---

[11] T. E. Cognacq (1839–1928).

Employers took an interest in the employee's welfare to prevent harm to the public image of the firm. Disreputable or disruptive behavior by employees was punished by disciplinary action, including firing. Informal liaisons among employees were strongly discouraged, and upon discovery employees were forced to "regularize" their relationship or face immediate dismissal. Relationships among employees of the same store were not encouraged for fear that they would disrupt the work atmosphere. . . . In spite of such disapproval, marriages among employees were probably common. Once formalized, the relationship between two employees received the blessings of the management in the form of a monetary gift (generally one hundred francs). Whether employers induced women to retire after marriage is impossible to determine, but the percentage of married women in their work force was low.

Employer investment in employee productivity produced plans for paid sick leave, health care, and annual vacations. Most stores assured their employees of several sick days per year, and the Bon Marché employees could be admitted to the Boucicaut hospital for long-term illnesses. The Louvre sent several employees each year to a store-owned estate in the countryside for a "cure." Commercial employees were also among the first workers to receive annual paid vacations, although at first many of these so-called vacations were actually unpaid leaves during the dead seasons of January–February and August–September. . . . [P]aid holidays of several days to two weeks became common for department store employees in the early 1900s.

The combination of paternalistic motivations and publicity seeking also inspired the organized choral groups supported by the Bon Marché. The employee groups "le Choral" and "l'Harmonie" presented regular public concerts for employees, customers, and invited guests in the great galleries of the store. A winter concert could draw an audience of several thousand. Employees were also encouraged to participate in other uplifting types of leisure activities, such as the free language lessons offered in the evening hours.

In spite of these programs, employee life was scarcely ideal. What seemed like a life of ease and relative glamour often more closely resembled the hardships of other working-class women in the nineteenth century. Like domestic servants, shopgirls worked long hours and were heavily supervised. The lodgings in the "sixième étage"[12] of the department stores were . . . little better than that of the "chambres de bonnes."[13]

Commercial employees, like other Parisian working women, had levels of mortality which were strikingly high. Employees often suffered from tuberculosis and other respiratory diseases. The high level of mortality was not easy to explain, but no one disputed the fast pace of work and long hours, which could produce fatigue and reduce the employee's immunity to certain diseases. Thus, the

---

[12] The sixth floor (the seventh floor, counting the ground floor).

[13] The maids' rooms.

first protective legislation dealt directly with the problem of fatigue, requiring that a seat be provided for every female employee in the store. The legislation could not assure, however, that the clerks would actually be allowed to rest during the day. Noted an investigator in 1910:

> Among other examples, last October I saw a new salesgirl who remained standing from 8 A.M. to 7 P.M. near a sales table full of school supplies in the midst of an indescribable jostling, in a stuffy atmosphere, without stopping, often serving several customers simultaneously, accompanying them to the cashier and hurrying to return to her station; she was constantly under the threat of a reprimand from her department head, and with all of that, she had to be always smiling, amiable, even when the excessive pace of work rendered that especially difficult.

Street sales represented the worst abuse of employees, since they required a similar regimen but completely out-of-doors, even in the winter. These sales . . . were an important part of retailing, but the consequences for employees could be tragic. Several saleswomen wrote to *La Fronde*[14] in 1898: "One of our fellow workers died last winter from an illness contracted when she was required, as we ourselves are, to work outside exposed to all kinds of weather." Even once Sunday closing was secured, the long, unrelieved days of work contributed to tuberculosis, anemia, and a variety of nervous disorders. The pace of work and the crush of customers induced a level of stress which combined with the inadequate diet of most shopgirls gave rise to a variety of gastro-intestinal problems. The medical reports stress the obvious dangers in shop work of tuberculosis and other long-term disabilities, but they also asserted a connection between the physical environment and the morally degrading aspects of work for women.

Social observers in the nineteenth century often felt that female employment offered . . . too many opportunities for the sexual abuse of women. . . . The low salaries of most women made it impossible for them to support themselves without male companionship, which a girl acquired "at the price of her honor and her dignity." Some salesgirls could be seduced by wealthy customers or lecherous supervisors. . . . [T]he shopgirl was the victim of the role she had to play — an attractive amiable "doll," who was forced "to maintain an eternal smile." Whether or not she was sexually promiscuous, the salesgirl's role inspired moralists to imagine her debauchery.

A typical salesclerk was probably planning to marry a young employee or shopkeeper, and thus the suggestion of a sexual relationship might simply be a prelude to marriage. Salesgirls often came to the department stores with the hope of finding better suitors there. The inescapable fact that most salesclerks were young and single meant that their culture was that of young, urban, single people, whose attitudes and behavior were different from their middle-class employers.

---

[14] The first newspaper run entirely by women.

The single state was almost a condition of employment, as it was with domestic service. Employees complained that the practice of providing housing inhibited their freedom to marry. About two-thirds of the female employees of the
Louvre in 1895 were unmarried. In 1911, in the suburbs of Paris, only 14 per cent
of the saleswomen were married. But the clerks hoped that work "was only a temporary occupation for them" and that they would ultimately retire from the occupation upon marriage. . . .

The young single employee . . . helped to create a new urban leisure culture
in the years before the First World War. This culture included the attendance at
concerts and sporting events. Employees took up bicycling, which itself allowed
for freer sociability and a new style of courting. Employees also frequented cafés
and certain restaurants. Musical groups and organized activities at the department
stores were clearly intended to lure employees away from such public entertain-
ments, but they did not succeed. Employees continued to use more of their leisure
time in their own ways.

Women employees could expect to have the use of their Sundays and a few
evening hours . . . between closing and curfew time. Department store clerks
generally purchased their own evening meal at a restaurant, and thus they developed the habit of public dining. Whole chains of inexpensive restaurants . . . were
established to supply inexpensive meals to a new class of consumers — clerks and
office employees. Cheap but respectable, such establishments catered to the limited budgets of employees and office clerks and were located near the banks and
stores. Shop girls could also dine inexpensively in the Latin Quarter, where,
"needless to say, a woman alone is the commonest of sights and you will not hesitate to enter any of these establishments," according to the author of *A Woman's
Guide to Paris*. Unlike the working classes, who frequented cafés mainly at midday, employees, especially the male clerks, were highly visible in the evenings in
the cafés and restaurants of central Paris.

Leisure for the female clerk also included Sunday strolls in the parks, mixing
with young soldiers, servant girls, and bourgeois families. Shopgirls were said to
"shine" in their leather boots and stylish hats, which set them apart from the
other working girls. The salesgirl's dress expressed the ambiguity of her position.
On the street, employees' appearances showed a preoccupation with their public
image; most of the women tried to dress attractively in spite of the cost. "The employees seem the queens of the urban proletariat. When one encounters them in
the street, it is difficult to distinguish them from ambitious petit bourgeois: they
wear hats, gloves, and fine boots. This is a necessity, it seems, in their occupation,
but it costs them dearly." The stylish clothes of the shopgirl suggest two things
about the experience of store clerks before 1914. The salesclerk herself was affected by the retailing revolution of the department stores and seduced by the attractiveness of current fashions. But the salesclerk's behavior was also the result
of her ambiguous social position, a status which was complicated by the enormous range of salaries and benefits within the sales hierarchy. Zola suggested that
the department store clerk was "neither a worker nor a lady . . . [but] a woman
outside." Monsieur Honoré of the Louvre suggested that young clerks were re-

cruited from the working classes because they were attracted by the idea of escaping a life of manual labor. But the reality is more complex than the desire of a working-class girl to become a bourgeoise. The department stores did offer their employees an important chance for mobility — the owners of the four major department stores had started their careers as simple employees. But for most clerks, and especially for a woman, the possibility of becoming a shop owner was distant. Instead, one could hope to be promoted in the store's hierarchy, although even this kind of promotion was more difficult for women to achieve than for men.

The reality of mobility is impossible to assess precisely, but one can gain an impression of what a female salesclerk may have achieved by her experience in a department store. Most salesclerks came from the petite bourgeoisie and in particular from employee families. Moreover, the young women who found suitors most often married other employees. During the 1880s, when the city of Paris gathered data on marriages, the percentage of female clerks who married male employees was between 45 and 50 per cent. The intermarriage of clerks was the result of their associations at work and also of their desire for a respectable life. Rather than raising them into the middle class, their endogamy helped to form an independent lower middle class culture. Through marriage, employees tied their lives and their fortunes together, forming a group whose experiences and aspirations were significantly different from those above and below them.

The transition from shopkeeping to modern merchandising did not represent an easy process for employees. It was the male department store clerks who organized the first union and mounted the largest and earliest strikes of employees. Again in 1919 and 1936, department store clerks, by this time predominantly female, contributed heavily to the labor struggles of those crisis years. Employer paternalism, which had characterized the first generation of department stores, earned the employers a reputation for philanthropy, but it . . . enclosed the salesclerk in an interlocking structure of life and work that was difficult to escape.

Inevitably, fashions in clothing and in retailing changed, and the First World War accelerated the pace of those changes. The era of live-in clerks ended. Women came to predominate in the ranks of department store employees. Declining salaries and benefits during the war years were only partially restored by the wave of strikes in 1919. Female clerks gained a forty-eight hour week in 1917 but never recovered their élite status among working women.

As department store work evolved, so did the work experience of most women. By 1920 clerical work in offices as well as shops was much more common for women. Whereas in 1906 only one woman in ten worked as an employee, by 1936 one in every three was employed as a clerk. From the feminization of clerical work resulted the "deprofessionalization" of the clerk: lower salaries, the influx of unskilled labor, and declining benefits. The evolution of department store work since the 1840s has thus been an example of broader social changes. This "paradise of women," as Zola described the department store in the 1880s, became truly feminized only after the First World War, but the experience of female salesclerks in the first generation of department stores suggests much about the changing character of work and the place of women in that transformation.

MAKING CONNECTIONS: WORK

1. The Industrial Revolution was a watershed in history, increasing the number of goods produced, decreasing their price, and employing legions of workers to manufacture the goods. In the wake of the Industrial Revolution came a consumer culture that McBride explores in the nineteenth-century department store. How did the work of female clerks in department stores compare to the work women did in the previous century, as described by Hufton in Part One? In the eighteenth century, what, if anything, was comparable to the "world of women" that the department store encompassed?

2. McBride explains the rules department stores implemented to regulate both the work and social lives of female employees. Discuss whether this attempted control was something new, or whether it was simply a nineteenth-century version of the traditional paternalism that working women confronted in many fields of labor. To what extent were female clerks better off financially and socially than female domestic servants or industrial workers had been in the eighteenth century?

PART THREE

THE
TWENTIETH
CENTURY

Alistair Horne
Alex de Jonge
William J. Chase
Laura Tabili
Henry Friedlander
Philippe Ariès
Ellen Furlough
Kristina Orfali

One might argue that the twentieth century has been the worst century in the history of Western civilization. Mass murder and widespread torture, made easier by new technologies, have led us to view prior epochs as remarkably humane. Totalitarianism and genocide are two of this century's contributions to humankind, and nuclear catastrophe, now a permanent specter looming ominously offstage, may be the third. Few regions of Europe have not experienced the sequence of recent horrors that include World War I, Fascist and Communist brutalities, World War II and the Holocaust, and the terrorism that currently punctuates modern life. Ethnic cleansing and mass murder and rape in the 1990s in the former state of Yugoslavia demonstrate the power of tribalism and the cruel side of human nature that Western civilization only partially veils.

These tragedies have markedly influenced the social history of contemporary Europe, for the lives of millions have been altered dramatically in short periods of time. (The significance of long durations of time — a century or more — studied analytically by historians of medieval and early modern Europe, becomes less noticeable in the contemporary era.) Indeed, warfare in the twentieth century has become total, involving entire populations, soldiers and civilians alike.

Warfare has been an endemic disease in Europe since at least the Middle Ages, but, more than in previous centuries, wars have devastated the Continent in this one. Alistair Horne's essay re-creates the unspeakable horrors of the World War I Battle of Verdun, while Henry Friedlander explains the workings of the Nazi camps during World War II, when Germany conducted the so-called war against the Jews.

Alex de Jonge depicts vividly the hyperinflation and resulting socioeconomic disequilibrium in Germany a few years after World War I. Born in that same conflagration, the Russian Revolution promised a viable alternative to bourgeois society as well as to Fascism. In describing life in Moscow during the 1920s, William J. Chase allows us to see whether Communism did indeed bring about an egalitarian and efficient workers' society. Social inequalities existed elsewhere as well. Political democracy did not inevitably lead to social harmony, especially when a democracy had a history of imperial subjection of other peoples, as Laura Tabili demonstrates in her article on racial discrimination in England.

Because Europe in the twentieth century has become more closely knit through economic ties, travel, and communication systems, occurrences in one

242

country create ripples throughout the Continent. Local isolation and agricultural self-sufficiency are things of the past; changes in the economy very quickly affect everyone, and consumers nearly everywhere share a common culture and a higher standard of living than their ancestors had in preindustrial Europe. Who in Europe does not know of Coca-Cola and the ubiquitous McDonald's? One of the ideals of modern citizenship is keeping abreast of the news, made readily available by the mass media, because we have come to realize that individuals and society can no longer go their own way with impunity; we are all, in every aspect of our lives, affected by changes that take place far from us. The peasant in an isolated village, eking out an existence in total ignorance of the outside world, is fast becoming extinct, save perhaps in Albania and a few other remote regions. Ellen Furlough's study of Club Méditerranée and French consumer culture emphasizes the difference between today's world and the one we have lost. So does Kristina Orfali in her depiction of recent Sweden, a culture that has repudiated many of the past characteristics of Western civilization. Philippe Ariès, in his provocative interpretation of the changing attitudes toward death in the twentieth century, also emphasizes how far we have come from traditional society.

In sum, the twentieth century is like no other, but remnants from earlier centuries still survive. In some ways — in regard to life expectancy and health, for example — people are better off; in others, they may be worse off, prey to new diseases and to new applications of technology that often are used to repress, oppress, and wage war. What issues do Westerners face now that are likely to haunt us in the years to come?

THE PRICE OF GLORY:
VERDUN 1916
Alistair Horne

If war is hell, then the Battle of Verdun, from February to December 1916, was its deepest circle. The French and Germans sustained approximately one million casualties. The horrors of the battle can scarcely be imagined, but Alistair Horne manages to immerse us in the sights, smells, and feelings that Verdun, the most destructive battle in history, evoked. Historians of warfare have begun to move away from descriptions of military maneuvers and biographies of generals and heroes to reconstructions of war from the perspective of the ordinary soldier. Horne takes that approach in this powerful, moving essay, part of a trilogy of books this British historian has written on the Franco-German conflict from 1870 to 1940. Horne's re-creation of the battle's horrors is especially vivid owing to his use of veterans' letters and diaries and of conversations he had with the participants and their relatives.

What was the approach march like, and how did the battlefield appear? Horne frequently refers to colors, something that historians of warfare tend to ignore, save when discussing uniforms or flags. He also speaks of the overwhelming odors of Verdun; the living mixed promiscuously with the dead. Indeed, Verdun was an open cemetery, with ghastly and mutilated corpses of both men and animals prominent everywhere. Filth and disease contributed to the enormous suffering. Above all was the nearly constant artillery bombardment raining death on those who could do little to protect themselves from indiscriminate shells. What does Horne mean by the statement that "Verdun was the epitome of a 'soldier's battle'"? What was the fate of the wounded?

Horne considers the runners, ration parties, and stretcher-bearers to have been the greatest heroes of Verdun. How did the high probability of death or mutilation and the constant, seemingly unendurable suffering affect the soldiers physically and mentally? Does the saying that "there are no atheists in a foxhole" ring true at Verdun? One wonders, after reading this selection, whether the suf-

Alistair Horne, *The Price of Glory: Verdun 1916* (London: Macmillan, 1978), 185–210.

fering and deaths of the soldiers were meaningless, mere sacrifices on the altar of nationalism.

Although from March to the end of May the main German effort took place on the Left Bank of the Meuse, this did not mean that the Right Bank had become a "quiet sector." Far from it! Frequent vicious little attacks undertaken by both sides to make a minor tactical gain here and there regularly supplemented the long casualty lists caused by the relentless pounding of the rival artilleries. Within the first month of the battle the effect of this non-stop bombardment, by so mighty an assemblage of cannon, their fire concentrated within an area little larger than Richmond Park,[1] had already established an environment common to both sides of the Meuse that characterized the whole battle of Verdun. The horrors of trench warfare and of the slaughter without limits of the First War are by now so familiar to the modern reader that further recounting merely benumbs the mind. The Battle of Verdun, however, through its very intensity — and, later, its length — added a new dimension of horror. Even this would not in itself warrant lengthy description were it not for the fact that Verdun's peculiarly sinister environment came to leave an imprint on men's memories that stood apart from other battles of the First War; and predominantly so in France where the nightmares it inspired lingered perniciously long years after the Armistice.[2]

To a French aviator, flying sublimely over it all, the Verdun front after a rainfall resembled disgustingly the "humid skin of a monstrous toad." Another flyer, James McConnell, (an American . . .) noted after passing over "red-roofed Verdun" — which had "spots in it where no red shows and you know what has happened there" — that abruptly

> there is only that sinister brown belt, a strip of murdered nature. It seems to belong to another world. Every sign of humanity has been swept away. The woods and roads have vanished like chalk wiped from a blackboard; of the villages nothing remains but grey smears. . . . During heavy bombardments and attacks I have seen shells falling like rain. Countless towers of smoke remind one of Gustave Doré's[3] picture of the fiery tombs of the arch-heretics in Dante's "Hell." . . . Now and then monster projectiles hurtling through the air close by leave one's plane rocking violently in their wake. Aeroplanes have been cut in two by them.

. . . The first sounds heard by ground troops approaching Verdun reminded them of "a gigantic forge that ceased neither day nor night." At once they noted, and were acutely depressed by, the sombre monotones of the battle area. To some it

---

[1] In London.

[2] Of 11 November 1918, ending hostilities on the western front.

[3] French illustrator and painter (1832–1883), famous for his illustrations of books, including Dante's *Divine Comedy*.

was "yellow and flayed, without a patch of green"; to others a compound of brown, grey, and black, where the only forms were shell holes. On the few stumps that remained of Verdun's noble forests on the Right Bank, the bark either hung down in strips, or else had long since been consumed by half-starved pack-horses. As spring came, with the supreme optimism of Nature, the shattered trees pushed out a new leaf here and there, but soon these too dropped sick and wilting in the poisonous atmosphere. At night, the Verdun sky resembled a "stupendous *Aurora Borealis*," but by day the only splashes of colour that one French soldier-artist could find were the rose tints displayed by the frightful wounds of the horses lying scattered about the approach routes, lips pulled back over jaws in the hideousness of death. Heightening this achromatic gloom was the pall of smoke over Verdun most of the time, which turned the light filtering through it to an ashy grey. A French general, several times in the line at Verdun, recalled to the author that while marching through the devastated zone his soldiers never sang; "and you know French soldiers sing a lot." When they came out of it they often grew crazily rapturous simply at returning to "a world of colour, meadows and flowers and woods . . . where rain on the roofs sounds like a harmonic music."

A mile or two from the front line, troops entered the first communication trenches; though to call them this was generally both an exaggeration and an anachronism. Parapets gradually grew lower and lower until the trench became little deeper than a roadside ditch. Shells now began to fall with increasing regularity among closely packed men. In the darkness (for obvious reasons, approach marches were usually made at night) the columns trampled over the howling wounded that lay underfoot. Suddenly the trench became "nothing more than a track hardly traced out amid the shell holes." In the mud, which the shelling had now turned to a consistency of sticky butter, troops stumbled and fell repeatedly; cursing in low undertones, as if fearful of being overheard by the enemy who relentlessly pursued them with his shells at every step. Sometimes there were duckboards around the lips of the huge shell craters. But more often there were not, and heavily laden men falling into the water-filled holes remained there until they drowned, unable to crawl up the greasy sides. If a comrade paused to lend a hand, it often meant that two would drown instead of one. In the chaos of the battlefield, where all reference points had long since been obliterated, relieving detachments often got lost and wandered hopelessly all night; only to be massacred by an enemy machine-gunner as dawn betrayed them. It was not unusual for reliefs to reach the front with only half the numbers that set out, nor for this nightmare approach march to last ten hours or longer.

One of the first things that struck troops fresh to the Verdun battlefield was the fearful stench of putrefaction; "so disgusting that it almost gives a certain charm to the odour of gas shells." The British never thought their Allies were as tidy about burying their dead as they might be, but under the non-stop shelling at Verdun an attempt at burial not infrequently resulted in two more corpses to dispose of. It was safer to wrap the dead up in a canvas and simply roll them over the parapet into the largest shell-hole in the vicinity. There were few of these in which did not float some ghastly, stinking fragment of humanity. On the Right

Bank several gullies were dubbed, with good cause, *"La Ravine de la Mort"*[4] by the French. Such a one, though most of it in French hands, was enfiladed by a German machine gun at each end, which exacted a steady toll. Day after day the German heavies pounded the corpses in this gully, until they were quartered, and requartered; to one eye-witness it seemed as if it were filled with dismembered limbs that no one could or would bury. Even when buried,

> shells disinter the bodies, then reinter them, chop them to pieces, play with them as a cat plays with a mouse.

As the weather grew warmer and the numbers of dead multiplied, the horror reached new peaks. The compressed area of the battlefield became an open cemetery in which every square foot contained some decomposed piece of flesh:

> You found the dead embedded in the walls of the trenches, heads, legs, and half-bodies, just as they had been shovelled out of the way by the picks and shovels of the working party.

Once up in the front line, troops found that life had been reduced, in the words of a Beaux Arts[5] professor serving with the Territorials,[6] "to a struggle between the artillerymen and the navvy, between the cannon and the mound of earth." All day long the enemy guns worked at levelling the holes laboriously scraped out the previous night. At night, no question of sleep for the men worn out by the day's shelling (it was not unknown for men in the line to go without sleep for eleven days). As soon as darkness fell, an officer would lay out a white tape over the shell ground, and the "navvies" began to dig; feverishly, exposed, hoping not to be picked up by enemy flares and machine guns. By dawn the trench would probably be little more than eighteen inches deep, but it had to be occupied all day, while the enemy gunners resumed their work of levelling. No question of latrines under these conditions; men relieved themselves where they lay, as best they could. Dysentery became regarded as a norm of life at Verdun. Lice, made much of by combatants on other fronts, received little mention. With luck, by the second morning the trench might have reached a depth of barely three feet.

Over and again eye-witnesses at Verdun testify to the curious sensation of having been in the line twice, three times, without ever having seen an enemy infantryman. On going into the line for the first time, one second-lieutenant who was later killed at Verdun, twenty-six-year-old Raymond Jubert, recalled his Colonel giving the regiment instructions that must have been repeated a thousand times at Verdun:

---

[4] "The Ravine of Death."

[5] From the École Nationale Supérieure des Beaux-Arts in Paris.

[6] The French Territorial Army was composed of veterans and older citizens. They usually took secondary jobs, thus freeing front-line troops for combat.

You have a mission of sacrifice; here is a post of honour where they want to attack. Every day you will have casualties, because they will disturb your work. On the day they want to, they will massacre you to the last man, and it is your duty to fall.

Battalion after battalion decimated solely by the bombardment would be replaced in the line by others, until these too had all effectiveness as a fighting unit crushed out of them by the murderous shelling.[7] After nights of being drenched by icy rain in a shell-hole under non-stop shelling, a twenty-year-old French corporal wrote:

> Oh, the people who were sleeping in a bed and who tomorrow, reading their newspaper, would say joyously — "they are still holding!" Could they imagine what that simple word "hold" meant?

The sensation provoked by being under prolonged bombardment by heavy guns is something essentially personal and subjective; first-hand accounts cover a wide range of experience. To Paul Dubrulle, a thirty-four-year-old French Jesuit serving as an infantry sergeant at Verdun, whose journals are outstanding for their un-embellished realism, it seemed as follows:

> When one heard the whistle in the distance, one's whole body contracted to resist the too excessively potent vibrations of the explosion, and at each repetition it was a new attack, a new fatigue, a new suffering. Under this régime, the most solid nerves cannot resist for long; the moment arrives where the blood mounts to the head; where fever burns the body and where the nerves, exhausted, become incapable of reacting. Perhaps the best comparison is that of seasickness . . . finally one abandons one's self to it, one has no longer even the strength to cover oneself with one's pack as protection against splinters, and one scarcely still has left the strength to pray to God. . . . To die from a bullet seems to be nothing; parts of our being remain intact; but to be dismembered, torn to pieces, reduced to pulp, this is a fear that flesh cannot support and which is fundamentally the great suffering of the bombardment. . . .

. . . More than anything else, it was the apparently infinite duration of the Verdun bombardments that reduced even the strongest nerves. Sergeant-Major César Méléra, a tough adventurer, who had sailed around the world in peacetime and who appeared little affected by the horrors of war, describes his experience of Verdun shell-fire initially with an unemotional economy of words: "Filthy night, shells." Three days later he was confiding to his diary that the night bombardment made him "think of that nightmare room of Edgar Allan Poe, in which the walls

---

[7] To us this kind of futile sacrifice symbolizes the First War mentality. Yet one must always remember the dilemma facing the French at Verdun. . . . By 1916 both sides had already experimented successfully with "thinning out" the forward areas to reduce shell-fire casualties. But in the cramped space at Verdun where the loss of a hundred yards might lead to the loss of the city the risk of any such thinning out could not be taken by the French. Similarly the Germans, always attacking, could not avoid a permanent concentration of men in the forward lines. (Author's note.)

closed in one after the other." The following day: "Oh how I envy those who can charge with a bayonet instead of waiting to be buried by a shell," and, finally, the admission:

> Verdun is terrible . . . because man is fighting against material, with the sensation of striking out at empty air. . . .

. . . With the steadily increasing power of the French artillery, experiences of the infantryman on both sides became more and more similar. In June a soldier of the German 50th Division before Fort Vaux declared that "the torture of having to lie powerless and defenceless in the middle of an artillery battle" was "something for which there is nothing comparable on earth." Through this common denominator of suffering, a curious mutual compassion began to develop between the opposing infantries, with hatred reserved for the artillery in general. To Captain Cochin on the Mort Homme,[8] it seemed as if the two artilleries were playing some idiotic game with each other, to see which could cause the most damage to the two unhappy lines of infantrymen.

What the P.B.I. felt about their own gunners may be gauged from a French estimate that out of ten shells falling on a Verdun trench, "on an average two were provided by the friendly artillery." Sergeant Élie Tardivel tells how in June seven men from a neighbouring platoon had just been killed by a single French 155 shell:

> I met the company commander; I told him I had brought up some grenades and barbed-wire; I asked where I was to put them. He replied: "Wherever you wish. For two hours our own guns have been bombarding us, and if it goes on I shall take my company and bombard the gunner with these grenades!"

Emotions between the infantry and gunners resembled those sometimes held towards the heavy-bomber crews of World War II, whom the ground troops viewed as sumptuously quartered well away from the enemy, making brief sorties to spray their bombs indiscriminately over both lines. A French company commander, Charles Delvert, describes passing two naval batteries en route for Verdun:

> Not a single man on foot. Everybody in motors. The officers had a comfortable little car to themselves. . . . I looked at my poor troopers. They straggled lamentably along the road, bent in two by the weight of their packs, streaming with water, and all this to go and become mashed to pulp in muddy trenches.

Other infantrymen were irked by the impersonal casualness with which the heavy gunners crews emerged from their comfortable shelters to fire at targets they could not see, "appearing to be much less concerned than about the soup or the bucket of wine which had just been brought."

---

[8] The "Dead Man," a hill between the town of Verdun and the front line that was the scene of ferocious combat.

This picture is to some extent endorsed by the artillery themselves. Staff-Sergeant Fonsagrive, serving with a 105 mm. battery wrote in his journal during the peak of the March battle on the Right Bank, "the fine weather continues, the days lengthen; it is a pleasure to get up in the morning. . . ." Watching the planes dog-fighting overhead, there was plenty of leisure time for day-dreaming about wives and families. Later, Fonsagrive notes with some vexation:

> One day when, quietly sitting underneath an apple tree, I was writing a letter, a 130 mm. shell landed forty metres behind me, causing me a disagreeable surprise.

. . . Not all French gunners, however, were as fortunate as Sergeant Fonsagrive. When death came from the long-range German counter-battery guns, it came with frightening suddenness. A gunner sipping his soup astraddle his cannon, a group of N.C.O.s playing cards would be expunged by an unheralded salvo. In action, the field artillery particularly had even less cover than the infantry; often reduced still further by officers of the old school of that notably proud French arm, "La Reine des Batailles,"[9] who believed (and there were still many like them) that to take cover under fire was almost cowardice. Casualties among some batteries were in fact often at least as high as among the infantry. Captain Humbert, a St. Cyrien[10] of the 97th Infantry Regiment, testifies to the effect of the German artillery's systematic sweeping of the back areas, knowing that the French field batteries must all be there:

> Nobody escapes; if the guns were spared today, they will catch it tomorrow. . . . Whole batteries lie here demolished. . . .

Lieutenant Gaston Pastre, though also a heavy gunner, provides a very different picture to Fonsagrive. Arriving at Verdun in May, he found the unit he was relieving had lost forty per cent of its effectives; "If you stay here a month, which is normal," they warned him, "you will lose half of yours too." The reverse slopes up to Fort St. Michel on the Right Bank, where Pastre's battery was sited, were crammed with every calibre of gun; it was "nothing more than one immense battery, there are perhaps 500 pieces there. A wonderful target for German saturation fire — anything that falls between Fort Michel and the road is good." There were generally only two periods of calm in the day; between 4 and 6 A.M. and between 4 and 7 P.M. when, like subhuman troglodytes, the French gunners emerged from the ground to repair the damage. For the rest of the time, to move from one shelter to another — a distance of about twenty yards — required considerable courage. By night the solitary road from Verdun came under constant fire from the German gunners, certain that French munition columns must be coming up it nose to tail. It presented "a spectacle worthy of Hell," in which men not killed out-

---

[9] "The Queen of Battles."

[10] Someone who had attended St. Cyr, the principal French military academy.

right were often hurled off their gun carriages by shell blast, to be run over and crushed by their own caissons in the dark.

Next to the incessant bombardment, the stink of putrefaction, and the utter desolation of the battlefield, Verdun combatants testify again and again to the terrifying isolation, seldom experienced to the same degree in other sectors. Verdun was the epitome of a "soldier's battle." Within an hour or less of the launching of each organized attack or counter-attack, leadership over the lower echelons ceased to play any significant role. Company commanders would lose all but the most spasmodic and tenuous contact with their platoons, often for days at a time. The situation where one French machine-gun section found itself holding a hole in the front two hundred yards wide with its two machine guns for several days in complete detachment from the rest of the army, was by no means unique. To add to this demoralizing sense of isolation, the tenacious curtain of smoke from the bombardment meant that the front line frequently could not see the supporting troops behind; nor, worse still, could their rockets of supplication asking for the artillery to bring down a barrage, or cease shelling their own positions, be seen at the rear. Countless were the true heroes of Verdun, fighting small Thermopylaes[11] in the shellholes, who remained unsung and undecorated because no one witnessed their deeds.

> After twenty months of fighting, where twenty times I should have died [Raymond Jubert admitted] I have not yet seen war as I imagined it. No; none of those grand tragic tableaux, with sweeping strokes and vivid colours, where death would be a stroke, but these small painful scenes, in obscure corners, of small compass where one cannot possibly distinguish if the mud were flesh or the flesh were mud.

Of all the participants qualifying for the title of hero at Verdun, probably none deserved it more than three of the most humble categories: the runners, the ration parties, and the stretcher-bearers. As a regular lieutenant in charge of the divisional runners at Souville stated, simply: "The bravery of the man isolated in the midst of danger is the true form of courage." With telephone lines no sooner laid than torn up by shellfire, and the runner become the sole means of communication at Verdun, the most frequently heard order at any H.Q. was "send two runners." From the relative protection of their holes, the infantry watched in silent admiration at the blue caps of the runners bobbing and dodging among the plumes of exploding T.N.T. It was an almost suicidal occupation. Few paths were not sign-posted by their crumpled remains, and on the Mort Homme one regiment lost twenty-one runners in three hours.

---

[11] Thermopylae was a small mountain pass in Greece where the Persians in 480 B.C. annihilated a Spartan army to the last man.

Perhaps demanding even more courage, though, was the role of the *cuistot*,[12] *ravitailleur*,[13] or *homme-soupe*,[14] as the ration parties were variously called, in that it was played out in the solitariness of night.

> Under danger, in the dark, one feels a kind of particular horror at finding oneself alone. Courage requires to be seen [noted Jubert]. To be alone, to have nothing to think about except oneself . . . to have nothing more to do than to die without a supreme approbation! The soul abdicates quickly and the flesh abandons itself to shudders.

On account of the shelling, motor transport could approach no closer than a cross-roads nicknamed "Le Tourniquet"[15] at the end of the *Voie Sacrée*.[16] The massacre of the horses, unable to take cover upon the warning whistle of a shell, had become prohibitive. Thus all rations for the men at the front had to come up on the backs of other men. The *cuistots*, three or four to a company, were generally selected from among the elderly, the poor shots, and the poor soldiers. One of the most moving pictures printed in *L'Illustration*[17] during the war was of one of these unhappy *cuistots* crawling on his stomach to the front at Verdun, with flasks of wine lashed to his belt. Each carried a dozen of the heavy flasks, and a score of loaves of bread strung together by string, worn like a bandolier. They often made a round trip of twelve miles every night; even though, bent under their loads, at times they could barely crawl, let alone walk, in the glutinous mud. They arrived, collapsing from fatigue, only to be cursed by comrades, desperate from hunger and thirst, on finding that the flasks of precious *pinard*[18] had been punctured by shell fragments, the bread caked with filth. Frequently they never arrived. Fixed enemy guns fired a shell every two or three minutes on each of the few well-known routes with the accuracy of long practice. . . .

For all the gallantry and self-sacrifice of the *cuistots*, hunger and thirst became regular features at Verdun, adding to the sum of misery to be endured there. Twenty-two-year-old Second-Lieutenant Campana notes how he dispatched a ration party of eight men one night in March. The following morning five came back — without rations. That night another eight set out. None returned. The next night some hundred men from all companies set forth, but were literally massacred by violent gunfire. After three days without food, Campana's men were reduced to scavenging any remnants they could find upon the bodies lying near

---

[12] Cook.

[13] Carrier of supplies.

[14] Soup man.

[15] The turnstile.

[16] The "Sacred Way," the road that took the French soldiers to Verdun.

[17] A French newspaper.

[18] Wine.

their position. Many had been decomposing for several weeks. The experience was more the rule than the exception; so too, as winter sufferings gave way to a torrid summer, was this spectacle:

> I saw a man drinking avidly from a green scum-covered marsh, where lay, his black face downward in the water, a dead man lying on his stomach and swollen as if he had not stopped filling himself with water for days . . .

Worst of all was the lot of the stretcher-bearers, which usually fell — until the supply was used up — to the regimental musicians. The two-wheeled carts that comprised the principal means of transporting the wounded on other French sectors proved quite useless over the pock-ridden terrain at Verdun; the dogs used to sniff out the wounded went rabid under the shelling. Unlike the runners or the *cuistots,* when carrying a wounded man the unhappy *musiciens-brancardiers*[19] could not fling themselves to the ground each time a shell screamed overhead. Often the demands simply exceeded what human flesh could obey. Response to pleas for volunteers to carry the wounded was usually poor, and the troops at Verdun came to recognize that their chances of being picked up, let alone brought to medical succour, were extremely slim.

During the Second World War, there were cases when the morale of even veteran British Guardsmen suffered if, in the course of an action, they were aware that surgical attention might not be forthcoming for at least five hours. On most Western battlefields, it was normally a matter of an hour or two. Surgical teams and nursing sisters, copiously provided with blood plasma, sulfa-drugs, and penicillin, worked well forward in the battle area, so that a badly wounded man could be given emergency treatment without having to be removed along a bumpy road to hospital. For the more serious cases, there was air transport direct to base hospital, possibly hundreds of miles to the rear. In contrast, at Verdun a casualty — even once picked up — could reckon himself highly fortunate if he received any treatment within twenty-four hours. During the desperate days of July, the wounded lingered in the foul, dark, excrement-ridden vaults of Fort Souville for over six days before they could be evacuated.

Poorly organized as were the French medical services, demand far outstripped supply almost throughout the war, but several times at Verdun the system threatened to break down altogether. There were never enough surgeons, never enough ambulances, of course no "wonder drugs," and often no chloroform with which to perform the endless amputations of smashed limbs. If a casualty reached the clearing station, his ordeals were by no means over. Georges Duhamel, a doctor at Verdun . . . , vividly describes the chaos in one of these primitive charnel houses in *"La Vie des Martyrs."*[20] Arriving during the early stages of the battle, he noted in despair, "there is work here for a month." The station was overflowing with badly wounded who had already been waiting for treatment for several days.

---

[19] Musician–stretcher-bearers.

[20] *The Life of the Martyrs.*

In tears they beseeched to be evacuated; their one terror to be labelled "untransportable." These, not merely the hopelessly wounded, but those whose wounds were just too complicated for the frantic surgeons to waste time probing, or who looked as if they would be little use to the army again, were laid outside in the bitter cold. It was not long before German shells landed among this helpless pile, but at least this reduced the doctors' work. Inside, the surgeons, surrounded by dustbins filled with lopped-off limbs, did the best they could to patch up the ghastly wounds caused by the huge shell splinters.

Later Duhamel and his team were visited by an immaculate Inspector-General who told them they really ought to plant a few flowers around the gloomy station. As he left, Duhamel noticed that someone had traced "Vache"[21] in the dust on the brass-hat's car.

At the clearing stations the backlog of even the partially repaired mounted alarmingly as, with the constant demand of the Voie Sacrée supply route, all too few vehicles could be spared for use as ambulances. British Red Cross sections appeared on the front . . . and later American volunteers. Though the crews drove twenty-four hours at a stretch, unable to wear gasmasks because they fogged up, still there seemed to be more wounded than the ambulances could hold. Meanwhile in the overcrowded, squalid base hospitals, those who had survived so far were dying like flies, their beds immediately refilled. Clyde Balsley, an American very badly wounded with the "Lafayette Squadron," noted in contrast that

> the miracles of science after the forced butchery at Verdun . . . made a whole year and a half at the American Hospital pass more quickly than six weeks in the [French] hospital at Verdun.

The wounded in these hospitals lived in terror of the periodical decoration parades; because it had become a recognized custom to reward a man about to die with the Croix de Guerre.[22] Of slight compensation were the visits of the "professional" visitors, such as the patriotic, exquisite, "Lady in Green," described by Duhamel, who spoke inspiredly to the grands mutilés[23] of

> the enthusiastic ardour of combat! The superb anguish of bounding ahead, bayonet glittering in the sun. . . .

Equipment in these hospitals was hopelessly inadequate, but at Verdun the situation was exacerbated still further by the poisonous environment, virulently contaminated by the thousands of putrefying corpses. Even the medically more advanced Germans noted the frequency of quite minor wounds becoming fatal. Gas gangrene, for which an effective cure was not discovered till a few weeks before the Armistice, claimed an ever-increasing toll; during the April fighting on the Right Bank, one French regiment had thirty-two officers wounded of whom no

---

[21] Swine.

[22] Military Cross.

[23] Badly disabled.

fewer than nineteen died subsequently, mostly from gas gangrene. In an attempt to reduce infection of head wounds, Joffre[24] issued an order banning beards; the *poilus*[25] complained bitterly, and still the wounded died. After the war, it was estimated that, between 21 February and the end of June, 23,000 French alone had died in hospitals as a result of wounds received at Verdun. How many more died before ever reaching hospital can only be conjectured.

So much for the physical; and what of the spiritual effects of this piling of horror upon horror at Verdun? Many were affected like the young German student, highly religious and torn with doubts about the morality of war, who wrote home shortly before being killed at Verdun on 1 June:

> Here we have war, war in its most appalling form, and in our distress we realize the nearness of God.

As in every war men confronted with death who had forgotten, or never knew how, began to pray fervidly. Sergeant Dubrulle, the Jesuit priest, was revolted above all by the hideous indignities he had seen T.N.T. perpetrate upon the bodies God had created. After one terrible shelling early in the battle when human entrails were to be seen dangling in the branches of a tree and a "torso, without head, without arms, without legs, stuck to the trunk of a tree, flattened and opened," Dubrulle recalls "how I implored God to put an end to these indignities. Never have I prayed with so much heart." But, as day after day, month after month, such entreaties remained unanswered, a growing agnosticism appears in the letters from the men at Verdun. Later, on the Somme, even Dubrulle is found expressing singularly non-Catholic sentiments:

> Having despaired of living amid such horror, we begged God not to have us killed — the transition is too atrocious — but just to let us be dead. We had but one desire; the end!

At least this part of Dubrulle's prayer was answered the following year.

For every soldier whose mind dwelt on exalted thoughts, possibly three agreed with Sergeant Marc Boasson, a Jewish convert to Catholicism, killed in 1918, who noted that at Verdun "the atrocious environment corrupts the spirit, obsesses it, dissolves it."

Corruption revealed itself in the guise of brutalization. . . .

It was indeed not very exalting to watch wounded comrades-in-arms die where they lay because they could not be removed. One Divisional Chaplain, Abbé Thellier de Poncheville, recalls the spectacle of a horse, still harnessed to its wagon, struggling in the mud of a huge crater. "He had been there for two nights, sinking deeper and deeper," but the troops, obsessed by their own suffering, passed by without so much as casting a glance at the wretched beast. The fact was

---

[24] Joseph Joffre (1852–1931), French commander in chief, 1911–1916.

[25] French soldiers.

that the daily inoculation of horror had begun to make men immune to sensation. Duhamel explains:

> A short time ago death was the cruel stranger, the visitor with the flannel foot-steps . . . today, it is the mad dog in the house. . . . One eats, one drinks beside the dead, one sleeps in the midst of the dying, one laughs and one sings in the company of corpses. . . . The frequentation of death which makes life so precious also finishes, sometimes, by giving one a distaste for it, and more often, lassitude.

A period of conditioning on the Verdun battlefield manufactured a callousness towards one's own wounded, and an apathetic, morbid acceptance of mutilation that seem to us — in our comfy isolation — almost bestial. Captain Delvert, one of the more honest and unpretentious of the French war-writers, describes his shock on approaching the Verdun front for the first time, when his company filed past a man lying with his leg shattered by a shell:

> Nobody came to his assistance. One felt that men had become brutalized by the preoccupation of not leaving their company and also not delaying in a place where death was raining down.

In sharp contrast to the revolted and tortured Dubrulle, young Second-Lieutenant Campana recounts how, at the end of his third spell in the line at Verdun, he cold-bloodedly photographed the body of one of his men killed by a shell that hit his own dugout,

> laid open from the shoulders to the haunches like a quartered carcass of meat in a butcher's window.

He sent a copy of the photograph to a friend as a token of what a lucky escape he had had.

Returning from the Mort Homme, Raymond Jubert introspectively posed himself three questions:

> What sublime emotion inspires you at the moment of assault?
> I thought of nothing other than dragging my feet out of the mud encasing them.
> What did you feel after surviving the attack?
> I grumbled because I would have to remain several days more without *Pinard*.
> Is not one's first act to kneel down and thank God?
> No. One relieves oneself.

This kind of moral torpor was perhaps the commonest effect of a spell at Verdun, with even the more sensitive — like Jubert — who resisted the brutalizing tendency admitting to a congelation of all normal reactions. Jubert also recalls the man in his regiment who, returning from the front, was overjoyed to find his house on the outskirts of Verdun still intact; but, on discovering that all its contents had been methodically plundered, he simply burst into laughter.

To troops who had not yet been through the mill at Verdun, passing men whom they were about to relieve was an unnerving experience; they seemed like beings from another world. Lieutenant Georges Gaudy described watching his own regiment return from the May fighting near Douaumont[26]:

> First came the skeletons of companies occasionally led by a wounded officer, leaning on a stick. All marched, or rather advanced in small steps, zigzagging as if intoxicated. . . . It was hard to tell the colour of their faces from that of their tunics. Mud had covered everything, dried off, and then another layer had been re-applied. . . . They said nothing. They had even lost the strength to complain. . . . It seemed as if these mute faces were crying something terrible, the unbelievable horror of their martyrdom. Some Territorials who were standing near me became pensive. They had that air of sadness that comes over one when a funeral passes by, and I overheard one say: "It's no longer an army! These are corpses!" Two of the Territorials wept in silence, like women.

Most of the above accounts come from the French sources. For, compressed in their hemmed-in salient and hammered by an artillery that was always superior, maintained and succoured by organization that was always inferior, things were almost invariably just that much worse for the French. But, as time went on, the gap between the suffering of the opposing armies became narrower and narrower, until it was barely perceptible. By mid April German soldiers were complaining in letters home of the high casualties suffered by their ration parties; "many would rather endure hunger than make these dangerous expeditions for food." General von Zwehl, whose corps was to stay at Verdun, without relief, during the whole ten months the battle lasted, speaks of a special "kind of psychosis" that infected his men there. Lastly, even the blustering von Brandis, the acclaimed conqueror of Douaumont for whom war previously seems to have held nothing but raptures, is to be found eventually expressing a note of horror; nowhere, he declares, not even on the Somme, was there anything to be found worse than the "death ravines of Verdun."

---

[26] The major fortress at Verdun.

MAKING CONNECTIONS: VIOLENCE

1. Warfare has been endemic in Western civilization, but at no time more horrible than in the twentieth century. Added to the ritualized violence that Europeans had grown to expect and that Richard van Dülmen and Stephen Frank explored in Parts One and Two was the brutality of war. Warfare did not single out specific individuals, such as criminals, but aimed to kill the enemy, the "other." Twentieth-century warfare combined the commonplace of cruelty with the new weapons that modern technology contributed: the machine gun, poison gas, the submarine, more powerful armaments. Although other wars had unspeakable barbarities — one thinks of the medieval Crusades, the sixteenth- and seventeenth-century wars in southeastern Europe between Christian and Turk, the suppression of internal rebellions, the English wars against the Irish, for example — our own century has surpassed them in numbers killed, both of soldiers and of civilians. What differences do you see in the regard for human

life in the articles by van Dülmen, Frank, and Horne? How does the butchery at Verdun compare to the barbaric punishments in early modern Germany and to the summary justice peasants meted out in nineteenth-century Russia? Why was the butchery at Verdun a different type of violence?

2. Horne notes that the soldiers at Verdun became inured to the dead around them, for the dead mixed promiscuously with the living. To what extent do you think Western civilization has conditioned us to accept a constant, high level of violence? Why are we shocked only when the violence explodes beyond our acceptance threshold, as in the case of Verdun, or with the Holocaust, or with murders committed by children? How could you argue that the absence of violence has been an aberration, found only in rare times?

3. "The Price of Glory: Verdun 1916" provokes the nagging thought that the half million who died there did so for no good reason. The differences between French and German soldiers disappeared as the battle roared on. Did the deaths and other casualties become part of a ritualized form of violence that states and social groups have engaged in for millennia, as did the Germans and Russians that van Dülmen and Frank describe? Why has violence been a lynchpin of our history, a necessary evil that defines the heritage of Western civilization?

INFLATION IN WEIMAR GERMANY
Alex de Jonge

The most celebrated instance of prices spiraling out of control is the hyperinflation in Weimar Germany in 1923. At the outbreak of World War I, the dollar was worth four marks; by November 1923, a person needed four trillion marks to purchase one dollar. To put this unprecedented devaluation of Germany's currency into perspective, consider the Price Revolution of the sixteenth century. This great period of inflation began in Spain and prices rose highest there, approximately 400 percent over the course of the century. Contemporaries had difficulty understanding the causes, not to mention the effects, of that increase — significant to be sure, but small compared to the hyperinflation of 1923. Alex de Jonge, a professor of Russian and comparative literature, relies primarily on memoirs and travel accounts to re-create life in Germany during the extraordinary years of hyperinflation.

The German inflation was rapid and intense. What were the causes of the hyperinflation? The Nazis found it useful to blame the Allied powers of the First World War and the Treaty of Versailles, and many Germans came to believe the Nazi interpretation. Why would they not? After all, a man who should have known better, the director of the Reichsbank, implemented a solution for inflation that would have been laughable had it not been disastrous: the use of printing presses to churn out more and more currency.

Hyperinflation had profound effects on the German social fabric. How did hyperinflation cause social chaos and affect morality, including the Germans' sexual behavior? Why did barter become so popular? Was it a coincidence that virulent anti-Semitism appeared at this time? Alex de Jonge offers dramatic and often pitiable stories of the wreckage of lives that resulted from the economic disequilibrium. Yet some groups prospered while others suffered. What finally brought an end to the period of hyperinflation?

The year 1923 has a special and dreadful connotation in German history, for it was the year of the great inflation. If defeat, abdication and revolution had begun

---

Alex de Jonge, *The Weimar Chronicle, Prelude to Hitler* (New York: New American Library, 1978), 93–105.

to undermine the traditional values of German culture, then the inflation finished the process so completely that in the end there were no such values left. By November 1918 there were 184.8 marks to the pound. By late November 1923 there were 18,000,000,000,000. Although the mark was eventually "restored," and the period of inflation succeeded by a time of relative prosperity for many people, life for anyone who had lived through the lunatic year of 1923 could never be the same again.

Such a cataclysmic loss of a currency's value can never be ascribed to a single cause. Once confidence goes, the process of decline is a self-feeding one. By late 1923 no one would hold German money one moment longer than it was really necessary. It was essential to convert it into something, some object, within minutes of receiving it, if one were not to see it lose all value in a world in which prices were being marked up by 20 percent every day.

If we go back beyond the immediate cause of hyperinflation — beyond a total lack of confidence in a currency that would consequently never "find its floor," however undervalued it might appear — we find that passive resistance in the Ruhr[1] was a major factor. Effective loss of the entire Ruhr output weakened the mark disastrously, encouraging dealers to speculate against it, since the balance of payments was bound to show a vast deficit. Confidence in the currency could only begin to be restored when resistance ended late in 1923.

It has been the "patriotic" view that reparations were also a significant factor. Certainly they constituted a steady drain upon the nation's resources, a drain for which it got no return. But reparations alone would not have brought about hyperinflation. There were still other causes. Sefton Delmer[2] believes that the true explanation lay in Germany's financing of the war. She had done so very largely on credit, and was thereafter obliged to run a gigantic deficit. There were other more immediate causes, such as a total incomprehension of the situation on the part of Havenstein, director of the Reichsbank. Failing to understand why the currency was falling, he was content to blame it upon forces beyond his control — reparations — and attempted to deal with the situation by stepping up the money supply! . . .

By October 1923 it cost more to print a note than the note was worth. Nevertheless Havenstein mobilized all the printing resources that he could. Some of the presses of the Ullstein newspaper and publishing group were even commandeered by the mint and turned to the printing of money. Havenstein made regular announcements to the Reichstag to the effect that all was well since print capacity was increasing. By August 1923 he was able to print in a day a sum equivalent to two-thirds of the money in circulation. Needless to say, as an anti-inflationary policy, his measures failed.

. . . Certainly [inflation] had its beneficiaries as well as its victims. Anyone living on a pension or on fixed-interest investments — the small and cautious in-

---

[1] Belgian and French troops occupied the Ruhr Valley early in 1923 because the Germans had not delivered coal as the reparations agreement stipulated.

[2] A German newspaper reporter.

vestor — was wiped out. Savings disappeared overnight. Pensions, annuities, government stocks, debentures, the usual investments of a careful middle class, lost all value. In the meantime big business, and export business in particular, prospered. It was so easy to get a bank loan, use it to acquire assets, and repay the loan a few months later for a tiny proportion of the original. Factory owners and agriculturalists who had issued loan stock or raised gold mortgages on their properties saw themselves released from those obligations in the same way, paying them off with worthless currency on the principle that "mark equals mark." It would be rash to suggest . . . that the occupation of the Ruhr was planned by industrialists to create an inflation which could only be to their benefit. Yet we should remember that Stinnes,[3] the multi-millionaire, had both predicted that occupation and ended up the owner of more than 1,500 enterprises. It should also be remembered that some businessmen had a distinctly strange view of the shareholder. He was regarded by many as a burdensome nuisance, a drag upon their enterprise. He was the enemy and they were quite happy to see him wiped out to their benefit. Inflation was their chance to smash him. Witness the behavior of a banker at a shareholders' meeting at which it was suggested he should make a greater distribution of profit: "Why should I throw away my good money for the benefit of people whom I do not know?"

The ingenious businessman had many ways of turning inflation to good account. Thus employees had to pay income tax weekly. Employers paid their tax yearly upon profits which were almost impossible to assess. They would exploit the situation of a smaller businessman, obliged to offer six to eight weeks of credit to keep his customers, by insisting on payment in cash. The delay between paying for the goods and reselling them eroded any profit the small man might make, while the big supplier prospered.

Whether or not the industrialists actually caused inflation, their visible prosperity made them detested by an otherwise impoverished nation. Hugo Stinnes became an almost legendary embodiment of speculation and evil. Alec Swan[4] remembers how hungry Germans would stare at prosperous fellow countrymen in fur coats, sullenly muttering *"Fabrikbesitzer"* (factory owner) at them. The term had become an insult and an expression of envy at one and the same time.

Hyperinflation created social chaos on an extraordinary scale. As soon as one was paid, one rushed off to the shops and bought absolutely anything in exchange for paper about to become worthless. If a woman had the misfortune to have a husband working away from home and sending money through the post, the money was virtually without value by the time it arrived. Workers were paid once, then twice, then five times a week with an ever-depreciating currency. By November 1923 real wages were down 25 percent compared with 1913, and envelopes were not big enough to accommodate all the stamps needed to mail them;

[3] Hugo Stinnes, speculator.

[4] An Englishman who lived in Germany during the 1920s.

the excess stamps were stuck to separate sheets affixed to the letter. Normal commercial transactions became virtually impossible. One luckless author received a sizable advance on a work only to find that within a week it was just enough to pay the postage on the manuscript. By late 1923 it was not unusual to find 100,000 mark notes in the gutter, tossed there by contemptuous beggars at a time when $50 could buy a row of houses in Berlin's smartest street.

> A Berlin couple who were about to celebrate their golden wedding received an official letter advising them that the mayor, in accordance with Prussian custom, would call and present them with a donation of money.
>
> Next morning the mayor, accompanied by several aldermen in picturesque robes, arrived at the aged couple's house, and solemnly handed over in the name of the Prussian State 1,000,000,000,000 marks or one half-penny.

The banks were flourishing, however. They found it necessary to build annexes and would regularly advertise for more staff, especially bookkeepers "good with zeros." Alec Swan knew a girl who worked in a bank in Bonn. She told him that it eventually became impossible to count out the enormous numbers of notes required for a "modest" withdrawal, and the banks had to reconcile themselves to issuing banknotes by their weight.

By the autumn of 1923 the currency had virtually broken down. Cities and even individual businesses would print their own notes, secured by food stocks, or even the objects the money was printed on. Notes were issued on leather, porcelain, even lace, with the idea that the object itself was guarantee of the value of the "coin." It was a view of the relationship between monetary and real value that took one back five hundred years. Germany had become a barter society; the Middle Ages had returned. Shoe factories would pay their workers in bonds for shoes, which were negotiable. Theaters carried signs advertising the cheapest seats for two eggs, the most expensive for a few ounces of butter which was the most negotiable of all commodities. It was so precious that the very rich, such as Stinnes, used to take a traveling butter dish with them when they put up at Berlin's smartest hotel. A pound of butter attained "fantastic value." It could purchase a pair of boots, trousers made to measure, a portrait, a semester's schooling, or even love. A young girl stayed out late one night while her parents waited up anxiously. When she came in at four in the morning, her mother prevented her father from taking a strap to her by showing him the pound of butter that she had "earned." Boots were also highly negotiable: "The immense paper value of a pair of boots renders it hazardous for the traveler to leave them outside the door of his bedroom at his hotel."

Thieves grew more enterprising still in their search for a hedge against inflation.

> Even the mailboxes are plundered for the sake of the stamps attached to the letters. Door handles and metal facings are torn from doors; telephone and telegraph wires are stolen wholesale and the lead removed from roofs.

In Berlin all metal statues were removed from public places because they constituted too great a temptation to an ever-increasing number of thieves. One of the consequences of the soaring crime rate was a shortage of prison accommodation. Criminals given short sentences were released and told to reapply for admission in due course.

It was always possible that one might discover an unexpected source of wealth. A Munich newspaperman was going through his attic when he came upon a set of partly gold dentures, once the property of his grandmother, long since dead. He was able to live royally upon the proceeds of the sale for several weeks.

The period threw up other anomalies. Rents on old houses were fixed by law, while those on new ones were exorbitantly high. As a result in many parts of Germany housing was literally rationed. If one were fortunate enough to live in old rented property, one lived virtually free. The landlord, however, suffered dreadfully: to repair a window might cost him the equivalent of a whole month's rent. Thus yet another of the traditional modes of safe investment, renting property, proved a disaster. Hitherto well-to-do middle-class families found it necessary to take in lodgers to make ends meet. The practice was so widespread that not to do so attracted unfavorable attention suggesting that one was a profiteer. . . . Real property lost its value like everything else. . . . More telling is a famous song of inflation:

We are drinking away our grandma's
Little capital
And her first and second mortgage too.

As noted in the famous and highly intelligent paper the *Weltbühne*,[5] the song picked out the difference between the "old" generation of grandparents who had scraped and saved carefully in order to acquire the security of a house, and the "new generation" for whom there could be no security any more, who "raided capital" or what was left of it, and were prepared to go to any lengths to enjoy themselves. Where their parents' lives had been structured with certainties, the only certainty that they possessed was that saving was a form of madness.

Not all Germans suffered, of course. Late in 1923 Hugo Stinnes did what he could to alleviate the misery of his fellow countrymen by the magnanimous decision to double his tipping rate in view of the inflation. Along with rents, rail fares were also fixed and did not go up in proportion to inflation. Consequently, travel appeared absurdly cheap. Alec Swan recalls crossing Germany in the greatest style for a handful of copper coins. Yet even this was beyond the means of most Germans. A German train in 1923 would consist of several first-class carriages occupied entirely by comfortable foreigners, and a series of rundown third-class carriages crammed to bursting with impoverished and wretched Germans.

Although the shops were full of food, no one could afford it except foreigners. Germans often had to be content with food not normally thought of as fit for human consumption. In Hamburg there were riots when it was discovered that

---

[5] The *World Arena*, a left-wing journal.

the local canning factory was using cats and rats for its preserved meats. Sausage factories also made much use of cat and horse meat. Moreover, . . . some of the most famous mass murderers of the age used to preserve and sell the meat of their victims in a combination of savagery and an almost sexual obsession with food that mythologizes much of the darkness and the violence that were latent in the mood of Weimar.

If 1923 was a bad year for the Germans it was an *annus mirabilis*[6] for foreigners. Inflation restored the sinking morale of the army of occupation; small wonder when every private found himself a rich man overnight. In Cologne an English girl took lessons from the *prima donna* of the opera for sixpence a lesson. When she insisted that in future she pay a shilling, the *prima donna* wept with delight. Shopping became a way of life: "All through that autumn and winter whenever we felt hipped we went out and bought something. It was a relaxation limited at home, unlimited in the Rhineland."

Germany was suddenly infested with foreigners. It has been suggested that the English actually sent their unemployed out and put them up in hotels because it was cheaper than paying out the dole. Alec Swan stayed with his family in a pension in Bonn. They had moved to Germany because life was so much cheaper there. . . .

To find oneself suddenly wealthy in the midst of tremendous hardship proved rather unsettling. Inflation corrupted foreigners almost as much as the Germans. The English in Cologne could think of nothing else.

> They talked with sparkling eyes and a heightened color, in the banks, the streets, the shops, the restaurants, any public place, with Germans standing around gazing at them.
>
> Scruples were on the whole overwhelmed by the sudden onslaught of wealth and purchasing power beyond one's dreams.

As Alec Swan put it:

> You felt yourself superior to the others, and at the same time you realized that it was not quite justified. When we went to Bellingshausen, which was a sort of wine place near Königswinter, we would start drinking in the afternoon. I would always order champagne and my Dutch friend would shake his head in disapproval. We'd have two ice buckets: he with some Rhine wine and me with German champagne. It was really rather ridiculous for a chap of my age to drink champagne on his own.
>
> Being as wealthy as that was an extraordinary feeling, although there were many things you couldn't get in Germany. It was impossible to buy a decent hat, for instance. But you could have any food you wanted if you could pay for it. I haven't eaten anything like as well as that in my life. I used to go to the Königshalle (that was the big café in Bonn) at eleven o'clock in the morning for

---

[6] Extraordinary year.

a *Frühschoppen*[7] and a *Bergmann's Stückchen,* a large piece of toast with fresh shrimps and mayonnaise. For a German that would have been quite impossible.

I paid two million marks for a glass of beer. You changed as little money as you could every day. No, one did not feel guilty, one felt it was perfectly normal, a gift from the gods. Of course there was hatred in the air, and I dare say a lot of resentment against foreigners, but we never noticed it. They were still beaten, you see, a bit under and occupied.

My mother did buy meat for three or four German families. I remember I bought an air gun, and, when I grew tired of it, I gave it to my German teacher's son, with some pellets. Some time later the woman came to me in tears saying the boy had run out of pellets, and they could not afford to buy any more.

On another occasion Swan, all of twenty-two at the time, took the head of the Leipzig book fair out for a meal and looked on incredulously as the elderly and eminent bookseller cast dignity to the winds and started to eat as if he had not had a meal in months.

Stories of money changing and currency speculation are legion. *Bureaux de change*[8] were to be found in every shop, apartment block, hairdresser's, tobacconist's. An Englishman named Sandford Griffith remembers having to visit a number of cities in the Ruhr which had local currencies. He stopped at a dealer's to change some money, but when he produced a pound note the dealer was so overcome by such wealth that he simply waved a hand at his stock of currency and invited the astonished Englishman to help himself. Foreigners acquired antiques and *objets de valeur*[9] at rock-bottom prices. A favorite trick was to buy in the morning with a down payment, saying that one would fetch the rest of the money from the bank. By waiting until the new exchange rate had come out at noon before changing one's money into marks, an extra profit could be made on the amount that the mark had fallen since the day before.

The population responded to the foreign onslaught with a double pricing system. Shops would mark their prices up for foreigners. It would cost a tourist 200 marks to visit Potsdam, when it cost a German 25. Some shops simply declined to sell to foreigners at all. In Berlin a . . . tax on gluttony was appended to all meals taken in luxury restaurants.

Foreign embassies were also major beneficiaries of inflation, giving lavish banquets for virtually nothing. Indeed the *Weltbühne* noted with great resentment the presence of foreign legations of nations so insignificant that they would never hitherto have dreamed of being represented in Germany. The spectacle of foreigners of all nations, living grotesquely well and eating beyond their fill in the middle of an impoverished and starving Germany did not encourage the Germans to rally to the causes of pacifism and internationalism. The apparent reason for their inflation was there for all to see, occupying the Ruhr.

---

[7] Pint of beer.

[8] Foreign exchange offices.

[9] Valuables.

The surface manifestations of inflation were unnerving enough, but its effect upon behavior, values and morals were to reach very deep indeed, persisting for years after the stabilization of the mark, right up to the moment when Hitler came to power. The middle class — civil servants, professional men, academics — which had stood for stability, social respectability, cultural continuity, and constituted a conservative and restraining influence was wiped out. A French author met a threadbare and dignified old couple in spotless but well-worn prewar clothes in a café. They ordered two clear soups and one beer, eating as if they were famished. He struck up a conversation with the man, who spoke excellent French and had known Paris before the war. "Monsieur," the man replied, when asked his profession, "I used to be a retired professor, but we are beggars now."

There was a general feeling that an old and decent society was being destroyed. If the year 1918 had removed that society's political traditions and its national pride, 1923 was disposing of its financial substructure. In response, people grew either listless or hysterical. A German woman told Pearl Buck[10] that a whole generation simply lost its taste for life — a taste that would only be restored to them by the Nazis. Family bonds melted away. A friend of Swan, a most respectable German whose father was a civil servant on the railways, simply left home and roamed the country with a band. It was a typical 1923 case history. Young men born between 1900 and 1905 who had grown up expecting to inherit a place in the sun from their well-to-do parents suddenly found they had nothing. From imperial officer to bank clerk became a "normal" progression. Such disinherited young men naturally gravitated toward the illegal right-wing organizations and other extremist groups. Inflation had destroyed savings, self-assurance, a belief in the value of hard work, morality and sheer human decency. Young people felt that they had no prospects and no hope. All around them they could see nothing but worried faces. "When they are crying even a gay laughter seems impossible . . . and all around it was the same . . . quite different from the days of revolution when we had hoped things would be better."

Traditional middle-class morality disappeared overnight. People of good family co-habited and had illegitimate children. The impossibility of making a marriage economically secure apparently led to a disappearance of marriage itself. Germany in 1923 was a hundred years away from those stable middle-class values that Thomas Mann[11] depicted in *The Magic Mountain,* set in a period scarcely ten years before. Pearl Buck wrote that "Love was old-fashioned, sex was modern. It was the Nazis who restored the 'right to love' in their propaganda."

Paradoxically, the inflation that destroyed traditional German values was also largely responsible for the creation of that new, decadent and dissolute generation that put Berlin on the cosmopolitan pleasure seeker's map, and has kept it or its image there ever since. It was no coincidence that 1923 was the year that the Hotel

---

[10] An American writer (1892–1973).

[11] German author (1875–1955) and winner of the Nobel Prize in literature in 1929.

Adlon first hired gigolos, professional male dancers, to entertain lady clients at so much per dance. It was also a period when prostitution boomed. A Frenchman accustomed enough to the spectacle of Montmartre[12] was unable to believe his eyes when he beheld the open corruption of Berlin's Friedrichstrasse. Klaus Mann[13] remembers:

> Some of them looked like fierce Amazons strutting in high boots made of green glossy leather. One of them brandished a supple cane and leered at me as I passed by. "Good evening, madame" I said. She whispered in my ear: "Want to be my slave? Costs only six billion and a cigarette. A bargain. Come along, honey."
> . . . Some of those who looked most handsome and elegant were actually boys in disguise. It seemed incredible considering the sovereign grace with which they displayed their saucy coats and hats. I wondered if they might be wearing little silks under their exquisite gowns; must look funny I thought . . . a boy's body with pink lace-trimmed skirt.

Commercial sex in Berlin was not well organized and was considered by connoisseurs to be inferior to that of Budapest, which had the best red-light district in Europe. But in Berlin there was no longer any clear-cut distinction between the red-light district and the rest of town, between professional and amateur. The booted Amazons were streetwalkers who jostled for business in competition with school children. . . .

> Along the entire Kurfürstendamm powdered and rouged young men sauntered, and they were not all professionals; every schoolboy wanted to earn some money, and in the dimly lit bars one might see government officials and men of the world of finance tenderly courting drunken sailors without shame. . . .
> At the pervert balls of Berlin, hundreds of men dressed as women, and hundreds of women as men danced under the benevolent eyes of the police. . . . Young girls bragged proudly of their perversion. To be sixteen and still under suspicion of virginity would have been considered a disgrace in any school in Berlin at the time.

Another visitor was struck by what he referred to as Berlin's "pathological" mood:

> Nowhere in Europe was the disease of sex so violent as in Germany. A sense of decency and hypocrisy made the rest of Europe suppress or hide its more uncommon manifestations. But the Germans, with their vitality and their lack of a sense of form, let their emotions run riot. Sex was one of the few pleasures left to them. . . .
> In the East End of Berlin there was a large *Diele* (dancing café) in which from 9 P.M. to 1 A.M. you could watch shopkeepers, clerks and policemen of mature age dance together. They treated one another with an affectionate mateyness; the

---

[12] District in Paris.

[13] German writer (1906–1949).

evening brought them their only recreation among congenial people. Politically most of them were conservative; with the exception of sex they subscribed to all the conventions of their caste. In fact, they almost represented the normal element of German sex life.

. . . There was a well-known *Diele* frequented almost entirely by foreigners of both sexes. The entertainment was provided by native boys between 14 and 18. Often a boy would depart with one of the guests and return alone a couple of hours later. Most of the boys looked undernourished. . . . Many of them had to spend the rest of the night in a railway station, a public park, or under the arch of a bridge.

Inflation made Germany break with her past by wiping out the local equivalent of the Forsytes.[14] It also reinforced the postwar generation's appetite for invention, innovation and compulsive pleasure seeking, while making them bitterly aware of their own rootlessness. It is not surprising that cocaine was very much in vogue in those years. The drug was peddled openly in restaurants by the hat-check girls, and formed an integral part of the social life of Berlin.

Inflation was also taken as evidence that the old order was morally and practically bankrupt. Capitalism had failed to guarantee the security of its citizens. It had benefited speculators, hustlers, con men and factory owners. It had spawned Hugo Stinnes, but had done nothing for the common good. The need for an alternative system appeared universally self-evident, and until one came along the thing to do was to enjoy oneself, drink away grandma's capital, or exchange one's clothes for cocaine: a dinner jacket got you four grams, a morning coat eight.

Inflation and the despair that it created also acted as the catalyst of aggression. It was at this time that anti-Semitism began to appear in Berlin. An attractive German lady remembers walking through a prosperous suburb with a Jewish friend when someone called to her in the street, "Why do you go around with a Jew? Get yourself a good German man." In one sense she found it understandable. The ordinary German was very slow to adjust to the special situation of inflation, and in 1923 anyone who was not very quick on their feet soon went under. Jews were better at economic survival in such situations than were other Germans — so much so, she says, that by the end of inflation they had become terribly conspicuous. All the expensive restaurants, all the best theater seats, appeared to be filled by Jews who had survived or even improved their position.

One can imagine that Germans who had lost their own status might have resented the spectacle. One old conservative I spoke to added a second reason for the rise of anti-Semitism in a Prussian society which had traditionally been quite free of it. The arguments advanced are his own, and tell us something of his prejudices. He believes that the Weimar Republic was too liberal with regard to immigration from the East, admitting thousands of Jews from Galicia and the old Pale of settlement,[15] persons who, in his words, were "Asiatics, not Jews." They

---

[14] A prosperous bourgeois family in novels by John Galsworthy (1867–1933).

[15] The Pale was an area where Jews were permitted to live in Russia.

found themselves in a strange anonymous town, free of all the ethical restraints imposed by life in a small community where their families had lived for several generations. They tended therefore to abandon all morality as they stepped out of their own homes, morality being strictly a family affair. They would sail as close to the wind as the law would allow, for they had no good will, no neighborly esteem to lose. The gentleman in question is convinced that their mode of doing business during the inflation did a great deal to create or aggravate more generalized anti-Semitic feelings.

Yet precisely these immigrants were to prove a mainstay of the republic. An old Berlin Jew who had spent some time in prewar Auschwitz told me that it was just these Eastern Jews who offered the most active and effective resistance to National Socialism. They were activists where native Berliners, Jew and Gentile alike, were more inclined to remain on the sidelines.

Certainly the period saw a rise in pro-National Socialist feelings. The first Nazi that Professor Reiff[16] knew personally was a schoolboy in his last year. The young man's father, a small civil servant, had just lost everything through inflation, and as a result his son joined the party. Pearl Buck records the views of an anti-monarchical businessman worried by inflation, who said of the Nazis: "They are still young men and act foolishly, but they will grow up. If they will only drop Ludendorff[17] and his kind, maybe someday I'll give them a chance."

For many people, who felt that they had lost all zest for a life rendered colorless by war and poverty, who could see that they lived in a world in which *Schieber*[18] won and decent folk lost, a new ideology combining patriotism and socialist anticapitalism seemed to be the only viable alternative to a totally unacceptable state of financial chaos and capitalist *laissez-faire*. The shock of inflation had made people mistrustful of the past, immensely suspicious of the present, and pathetically ready to have hopes for the future. It was perfectly clear to them that new solutions were needed, equally clear that until such solutions should appear they could put their trust in nothing except the validity of their own sensations.

The mood of the inflationary period . . . endured well beyond inflation itself to become the mood of the Weimar age, a blend of pleasure seeking, sexual and political extremism, and a yearning for strange gods.

It was an epoch of high ecstasy and ugly scheming, a singular mixture of unrest and fanaticism. Every extravagant idea that was not subject to regulation reaped a golden harvest: theosophy, occultism, yogism and Paracelcism.[19] Anything that gave hope of newer and greater thrills, anything in the way of narcotics, mor-

---

[16] Professor of economics who lived in Berlin during the Weimar period.

[17] Erich Ludendorff (1865–1937), German general in World War I who helped direct the war effort. He later joined the Nazi party.

[18] Profiteers.

[19] Doctrines associated with the Swiss physician and alchemist Paracelsus (1493–1541).

phine, cocaine, heroin found a tremendous market; on the stage incest and parricide, in politics communism and fascism constituted the most favored themes.

It was indeed a time for the revaluation of all (devalued) values.

The mood of 1923 persisted long after inflation ended, which is why the manner of its ending is offered here as a postscript, for nothing was restored but the currency.

Restoration of confidence was only possible when passive resistance in the Ruhr ended in the autumn of 1923. At the same time, the Reichsbank appointed Hjalmar Schacht to deal with inflation. He was an extremely able man with a clear grasp of essentials. He realized that his main problem was to restore confidence both within and without Germany, and to try to prevent people from spending money as soon as it came into their hands. He established a new currency, based on the notional sum total of Germany's agricultural wealth, the *Roggen-Mark* (rye mark). This had the effect of restoring psychological confidence in the currency. He combined the move with a gigantic bear trap laid by the Reichsbank to catch the speculators who would regularly build up huge short positions in marks, in the almost certain expectation that the mark would continue to fall against the dollar: i.e., they sold marks they hadn't got, knowing that they could buy them for a fraction of their present value when the time came to meet the demand. When the mark stopped falling, thanks to the Reichsbank's engineering, they had to rush to close their positions, and were forced to buy marks which had actually begun to go up. Many speculators lost the entire fortunes which they had built up over the year.

Schacht's measures sufficed to stop the rot, but in the period between the ordinance declaring the new currency and the appearance of the first notes, there was an interim of pure chaos in which . . . "four kinds of paper money and five kinds of stable value currency were in use. On November 20, 1923, 1 dollar = 4.2 gold marks = 4.2 trillion paper marks. But by December the currency was stable." The last November issue of the weekly *Berliner Illustrirter Zeitung*[20] cost a billion marks, the first December issue 20 pfennigs. Confidence seemed to have been restored overnight. Germany could breathe again. . . .

---

[20] *Berlin Illustrated Newspaper.*

DAILY LIFE IN MOSCOW, 1921–1929
William J. Chase

Bolsheviks (Communists) intended the Russian Revolution of 1917 to usher in a society of, by, and for the workers. Civil war and foreign invasions delayed the establishment of a proletarian system, but soon the socialist Russian state became the worldwide model for many who favored social equality and an end to the oppression of the weak by the strong. But William Chase, a specialist in Soviet history and urbanization at the University of Pittsburgh, shows that all was not well in paradise. Contemporary newspapers and journals, police records, census and other statistical data, interviews of workers, and government reports reveal that daily life in Moscow in the 1920s was often nasty and brutish.

Chase examines in turn the standard of living, housing, family life, and relations between workers and their neighbors. Where do you see the realities of daily life falling below workers' expectations, and how do you account for the frustrations and problems that workers faced? To what extent did the government contribute to or alleviate the discomforts and indignities that so frequently beset workers? Enduring low wages, overcrowding, lack of privacy, and poor sanitation, workers sought the causes of their discontent. Whom did they blame for Moscow's problems?

If thousands of Moscow residents (Muscovites) endured substandard housing conditions, thousands more searched continuously for a place to live. Many workers and homeless took refuge in factory barracks or in overnight barracks. Because crime was also a great problem, the barracks became breeding grounds for criminality, including gangs, prostitution, and drug addiction. What was daily life like in the barracks?

Socialism preached social equality, even between men and women; the law enshrined gender equality. However, the weight of tradition bore heavily on women, as did overcrowding and the scarcity of household conveniences. Chase shows that even minor problems, such as apartment buildings having only one doorbell, eroded family and neighborly relations. Divorces as well as fights between neighbors illustrate the tensions and anxieties the deplorable living conditions fostered.

William J. Chase, *Workers, Society, and the Soviet State: Labor and Life in Moscow, 1918–1929* (Urbana, IL: University of Illinois Press, 1987), 173–191, 193–199, 204.

On the one hand, this essay does not elicit envy or admiration for the impoverished lives of the overwhelming majority of Muscovites in the 1920s, although one might admire their perseverance under deplorable conditions. On the other hand, perhaps urban life in Moscow was no worse than that in other European cities in previous centuries. What developments in the lives of Muscovites do you attribute specifically to the government, the first Communist state in Western civilization?

On the Bolshevik revolution's tenth anniversary, *Trud*[1] published an article entitled "Moscow after ten years," which noted with justifiable pride the Soviet state's many accomplishments — lower death and infant mortality rates, fewer deaths from infectious diseases and tuberculosis, easily accessible medical care, the rising standard of living, and improved working conditions. Few could argue with these successes and the ways in which they ameliorated life in Moscow. But the capital was far from problem free. Annually, deepening unemployment and housing crises engulfed the city. Its apartments were overcrowded and rife with tensions; thousands were homeless. Shortages of consumer goods and municipal services complicated many residents', especially women's, lives. Life's daily problems and strains seemed minor compared to those of the 1918 to 1921 period, but they were no less real and no less irritating. In fact, precisely because the economic recovery and improvements raised hopes and expectations, some workers found the enduring problems particularly troublesome and frustrating. More important, solutions to these problems remained beyond the control of workers and, given the NEP's[2] fiscal strictures, that of the city soviet.

Because deepening problems and mounting frustrations continually undermined improvements and successes, a ubiquitous yet rather amorphous dissatisfaction and anger tempered workers' hopes and aspirations. Outside the factories, they expressed these emotions most concretely in their complaints about housing. While they frequently criticized the city soviet for its failures and inability to overcome the shortage and poor quality of housing, workers more often vented their wrath on their well-to-do neighbors — nepmen,[3] professionals, speculators, specialists — whom they believed prospered at their expense and who enjoyed creature comforts of which workers could only dream. The steady stream of press articles which criticized these groups' behavior and activities and the official campaigns against them heightened and legitimized workers' prejudices, attitudes and behavior. When the agricultural crisis struck in 1928, workers' standard of living began to plummet. Fear of a return to the deprivations of the

---

[1] Labor union newspaper.

[2] New Economic Policy, instituted in 1921 to revive the Russian economy.

[3] Speculators and merchants who profited from the New Economic Policy.

1918–1922 period heightened worker anger and made many receptive to the party's campaign against society's "bourgeois" elements — specialists, nepmen, and kulaks.[4]

While many issues divided the proletariat, the experiences of daily life outside the factory worked to unite them around common grievances and against common enemies. By examining workers' daily experiences and frustrations, we can refine our understanding of that class' attitudes and behavior. This [essay] focuses on the most important of these daily realities — the standard of living, housing, family life, and relations between workers and their neighbors. . . .

After years of economic collapse and deprivation, raising the workers' living standard proved to be a slow and uneven process. Until 1924, workers' standard of living improved at times and declined at others. There were several reasons for this fluctuation. One was the abandonment of natural wages[5] at a time of hyperinflation.[6] In late 1920, natural wages accounted for 95 percent of the average worker's pay; the next year the proportion fell to 85 percent. During 1922, the transition to money wages intensified. By mid-1924, wages in kind[7] accounted for only 7 percent of the average paycheck. Late that year, they were abandoned entirely. Despite the steady rise in workers' nominal wages,[8] inflation often reduced their value thereby subjecting the rise in real wages[9] to periodic reversals. Reliance on the expensive private market for many essential commodities further sapped workers' buying power.

Delayed wage payments also undermined workers' real wages. Delaying wage payments was a common practice during the early 1920s. The currency depreciation placed factory administrators in extremely awkward positions — by law their expenditures could not exceed their income, and they had to pay their workers on time. In heavy industrial enterprises that were slow to recover, the cash flow problem and shortage of capital were especially severe and intensified with the transition to cash wages. Either for lack of money or for bookkeeping purposes, many factory administrators delayed paying wages. Given the inflation rate, even a few days delay reduced workers' purchasing power. Understandably, the practice also contributed to widespread worker unrest. Nationally in 1922–1923, wage issues accounted for half of the strikes and two-thirds of the strikers. The figures for Moscow were comparable. During the summer of 1923, industrial unrest reached a peak and rumors of a general strike appear to have had some basis in fact. Most strikes were wildcat strikes organized around wage issues without the knowledge or support of the unions. . . .

---

[4] Wealthy peasants unwilling to join collective farms.

[5] The portion of output allocated to workers paid in the form of the goods produced.

[6] Rapid, uncontrolled inflation.

[7] Wages paid in the form of the goods produced.

[8] Wages defined as the face value of the money paid.

[9] Wages defined as the value of the goods and services that nominal wages can buy.

For these reasons, calculating the extent to which workers' standard of living rose between 1921 and 1924 is difficult. Contemporary officials were equally as confounded. At the Thirteenth Party Conference in January 1924, Tomskii, the trade union boss, claimed that real wages had risen during the previous year, but several delegates challenged his claim. According to one calculation, average real wages in Moscow in October 1922 stood at more than 60 percent of the 1913 level. But according to *Trud,* workers' average real wages nationwide were less than 40 percent of the 1913 wage.

After 1924, steadily rising nominal wages and the relatively stable currency and prices quickly raised workers' living standard. For all workers, the nominal wage hikes were significant. Between early 1925 and late 1928, the average Moscow worker's wage rose by about one-third. There was, however, considerable disparity from industry to industry — textile workers' wages increased by 50 percent; for printers, the figure was less than 20 percent. . . . Wages also varied with skill levels and production experience. For example, unskilled workers in 1927 earned about 70 percent of the average worker's wage, whereas older, experienced, skilled workers could earn twice the average wage. . . .

Real wages also rose steadily. In 1926, average real wages reached the prewar level. During the next two years, they increased significantly: in 1926/27, they exceeded the 1913 level by 15 percent; in 1927/28, they were more than 20 percent higher. Even for many of those whose real wages fell below the average, their standard of living after 1926 was better than before the revolution. The free social insurance system, low-cost housing, transportation and admission to social and cultural events, and, in some cases, free education translated into greater economic security and real wages than in pre-revolutionary times. The years 1925–1928 were indeed the "good years" of the NEP. But the onset of the agricultural crisis in 1928 suddenly undid these gains — food prices in the private markets soared from 100 to 200 percent higher than those in state markets and in 1929 rationing was re-introduced.

Even during the heyday, however, many working-class families found it difficult to make ends meet unless more than one member worked or they had other sources of income. In 1926, approximately one-quarter of Moscow's proletarian families had two or more members working. Factory workers' families had the highest proportion of multiple wage earners. In families where the primary wage earner was unskilled or semiskilled and hence generally earned less than the average wage, the financial pressure to have family members work was greatest. Given the unemployment rate, securing work was often difficult and hence many workers' relatives engaged in petty trade, part-time and seasonal work, and occasionally speculation. Such activities were most common among low-paid workers' families.

While workers' living standard rose until 1928, that of their bosses and many nepmen was much higher and rose more rapidly. In early 1925, the average worker's monthly wage was 64 rubles and that of the average employee was 108 rubles; by late 1928, the figures were approximately 95 and 150 rubles respectively. . . . But these averages conceal the very high salaries earned by some employees. Factory directors, engineers, and technical specialists were among the highest paid employees, and, in 1928, they earned average monthly salaries of 220 rubles. Some within this group of administrators earned much more, upward of 600 rubles in the case of "bourgeois" (as opposed to Communist) factory directors. It was these personnel who implemented unpopular labor policies and productivity campaigns in the factory. While workers labored harder with each passing year, their wages declined relative to those of their bosses. Many nepmen also earned more than workers. In 1925/26, the average monthly income of a "bourgeois" entrepreneur (a factory owner or successful trader) was 420 rubles, while that of a "semi-capitalist entrepreneur" (a small scale producer or trader) was 100 rubles.

As a class, workers earned less than any of the city's major occupational groups, significantly less in some cases. While they struggled daily to make ends meet, such "bourgeois" elements, who had been pariahs after the revolution, prospered. Their good fortune galled workers. Envy, anger, frustration, these emotions provided the backdrop against which workers and their "bourgeois" neighbors interacted. . . .

Workers' families devoted slightly less than half of their income to food. The 1922 figures reflect the expenditures for December only and are not representative of the annual average. Because of the 1921–1922 famine, until the 1922 harvest Muscovites reportedly spent upward of 95 percent of their income on food. In that year, food and rationing were the main topics of factory meeting discussions, and newspapers ran regular columns devoted to the famine and its consequences. But even after the famine, regular newspaper articles on available food supplies underscored Muscovites' and officials' ongoing concern with food.

The proportion of workers' wages spent on food varied with one's income. Throughout the 1920s, the lowest paid workers spent more than half and the highest paid workers only one-quarter of their earnings on food. As real wages rose, so too did the amount of food purchased. The quality of food consumed also improved and workers' diets became increasingly well balanced as the years passed. Among working-class families surveyed in December 1922, animal products (meat, fish, and dairy products) accounted for only 9 percent of the food consumed, grains (rye, wheat, and grits) for 47 percent, and vegetables and potatoes for 42 percent. Their average caloric intake was 3,409 calories, most of which came from bread and potatoes. Two years later, the diets had changed markedly. Meat and dairy products accounted for one-fifth of the food consumed; vegetables and potatoes for one-third. Grains remained the major staple, accounting for 43 percent of their diet. But the types of grain consumed changed somewhat. Those surveyed in 1924 ate three times more wheat and 40 percent less rye than their counterparts in 1922. Because of the reduced intake of grains and potatoes, the average worker in 1924 consumed 3,250 calories. This improved diet, which provided more protein and vitamins, remained the norm until 1928. Not everyone, however, ate such balanced diets, which obviously varied with income and personal preferences.

In the early 1920s, workers received food from three sources — rations, state stores and cooperatives, and private markets. Although rationing continued until 1924, the size of rations declined sharply after 1922. Workers purchased 60 percent of their food in September 1923 at private markets; three years later, the proportion had declined to 38 percent. Given the low cost, increased quantity and improved variety of foodstuffs in state stores, workers were able to purchase more food there per ruble with each passing year and thereby to improve their diets. Then in 1927, a war scare gripped Russia. Peasants, especially kulaks, responded to the scare and the worsening market situation by holding back their produce. Moscow quickly felt the effects. Food prices rose rapidly in 1928 and rationing was reintroduced early the next year. By late 1929, cereals, sugar, tea, butter, oil, herring, soap, eggs, meat, potatoes were rationed. After several years of steady improvement, suddenly there was less food on the workers' tables. Once again, Muscovites were forced to turn to the private market where prices went as high as the market would bear, two to three times those in state markets. Rationing and the renewed dependence on the high priced, black market triggered memories of the Civil War.[10] Justifiably fearful of a return to those days, many urban workers endorsed the party's collectivization and antikulak campaigns in hopes that they would alleviate the new crisis. Clearly, the food situation during the 1920s was a mercurial one. The uncertainty of the early 1920s gave way to several years of steady improvement; but in 1928–1929, fear and anxiety once again punctuated workers' daily lives.

After food, the average working-class family devoted the next largest proportion of their income — more than one-fifth — to clothing. Although this marked a substantial improvement over pre-revolutionary times, workers were not necessarily better dressed. The limited availability and shoddy quality of some clothing combined to restrict the upgrading of most workers' wardrobes. The presence of more than 1,900 used clothes and junk dealers in Moscow in 1926 testifies to the considerable demand for used clothing.

Prior to the revolution, rent and utilities consumed more than one-fifth of the average worker's income. In Russia in 1910, wages were lower and rents higher than anywhere in western Europe; Moscow had the country's highest rents. For this reason, many workers lived in barracks and small, overcrowded apartments. After 1917, housing costs dropped dramatically, and during the 1920s, workers' rents remained very low. Several factors determined an occupant's rent, the most important being his occupation. Workers received preferential treatment; their rents could not exceed 10 percent of their income. The 1928 rental scale used to determine rents in publicly owned housing fixed rents according to occupations. All other factors being equal, employees were to pay 28 percent more in rent than did workers, artisans/craftsmen (private operators) 175 percent more, profes-

---

[10] Struggle for control of Russia, 1918–1922, among Bolsheviks, monarchists, and liberal democrats; complicated by the armed intervention of Great Britain, France, and the United States.

sionals 324 percent more, and nonworking elements (e.g., proprietors) 934 percent more. The dwelling's size and the presence (or absence) of running water, electricity, and/or sewer connections also affected the rent. But the extent to which occupation-based rental scales actually determined rents is unclear. As we shall see, many workers believed that they did not. . . .

Until 1922, the state prohibited the sale of liquor, a policy initiated during World War I. Despite prohibition and the authorities' sustained struggle to curtail the number of boot-leggers (samogonshchiki), illegal samogon (home-brewed vodka, generally 25 proof) was easy to find. In 1922, the state legalized the sale of beer and wine; two years later, it did the same for hard liquor. As the availability of liquor and the number of rural migrants increased, the problem of alcohol abuse in the city became very serious. The increasing death toll there due to drunkenness testifies to the problem's dimensions. In 1923, when the production and sale of vodka were still forbidden, 16 deaths were attributed to drunkenness; in 1926, the figure soared to 144. During the 1926 Christmas holiday alone, 30 people died from excessive alcohol consumption. The proportion of patients in Moscow psychiatric clinics who received treatment for alcohol-related disorders rose from 6 percent in 1924 to 25 percent in 1925. Clearly, excessive drinking was a severe problem. . . .

On the other hand, the small proportion of income spent on entertainment and culture masked a considerable gain. In pre-revolutionary times, many cultural activities were beyond workers' financial means. Social pressure and barriers further reduced the number of workers who attended the opera, ballet, symphony, museums, galleries and even films. After the revolution, admission prices to such cultural events were very cheap and workers and their families were encouraged to attend. Post-revolutionary Moscow also bustled with amateur and avant-garde theatrical performances in neighborhood and factory club theaters, sporting events, and the circus. How many workers actually attended such affairs is difficult to estimate. When they did go out for entertainment, movies, sporting events, the circus, and local taverns appear to have been the more popular affairs. But these are impressions; a thorough study of working-class culture(s) remains to be done.

One establishment that the party and unions hoped would be a center of proletarian social and cultural life was the workers' clubs. But during the 1920s, these clubs had limited popularity. In Moscow city and guberniia[11] in late 1923, there were 481 clubs with approximately 150,000 members; in 1927, the city's 181 clubs had some 100,000 members. The membership figures must be viewed with caution since many members rarely frequented the clubs or participated in their activities. Low attendance resulted from several factors — poorly defined and organized activities, poor organization, and a rowdy clientele.

----

[11] Provincial soviet.

In the early 1920s, the clubs' poorly organized activities resulted from a shortage of competent club officials and a strident debate between Proletkul't[12] and the party over the nature of club activities. Proletkul't envisioned the clubs as "forges of the new culture" and devoted its energies to organizing various types of cultural activities such as music, art and drama. The party and unions sought to focus club activities along more utilitarian lines and sponsored lectures on hygiene and politics, literacy circles, and other practical activities that might appeal to workers and serve official policy.

Younger workers (under thirty) who participated in Proletkul't cultural activities appear to have dominated the clubs' regular patrons. But many of them engaged in rowdy, disruptive behavior, and, on occasion, young "hooligans" damaged the clubs thereby forcing factory committees to form guard teams to defend their property. Rather than endure the rowdyism and antagonism of younger workers, many older workers preferred to frequent local taverns where they could socialize and drink with their peers. Considering the atmosphere at many clubs and their refusal to sell alcohol, the taverns' popularity is understandable. . . .

Housing was justifiably the proletariat's most chronic grievance. They bore the brunt of the city's ever-deepening housing crisis. Their experience during the NEP stands in stark contrast to that during the Civil War when they were the chief beneficiaries of the massive housing redistribution. Squalid though they became as a consequence of the 1918–1921 economic collapse, the confiscated apartments into which workers moved represented a dramatic improvement over the barracks and basement dwellings which they had previously inhabited. Ironically, while the quality of their housing was poor, workers had more living space per capita in 1920 than they ever had or would again for several decades. Because the 1920s witnessed a reversal of the 1918–1921 experience, worker frustration became all the more intense.

As the city's population mushroomed after 1920, the amount of living space per person declined steadily and the competition for housing intensified. On the tenth anniversary of the revolution, many workers, especially those who moved to the city after 1921, lived in dwellings that more closely resembled those of pre-revolutionary times than those that they believed the revolution had promised. Although the need for housing became more acute with each passing year, until 1925 economic policy dictated that industrial restoration received the majority of available capital. Consequently, throughout the decade, housing construction and repair lagged far behind the rate of population increase. Between 1921 and 1926 the number of inhabitable apartments increased by 38 percent, but the city's population practically doubled.

Worker discontent with their housing surfaced early. In May 1922, A. Rosenberg, a member of the Khamovnicheskii *raion*[13] soviet, reported that the housing

---

[12] An organized movement to produce art and culture relevant to proletarian interests.

[13] A political subdivision comparable to a county.

shortage had already become critical. Workers were fully justified, he stated, to demand the repair of their present dwellings and the construction of new ones. Unless these demands, endorsed by factory committees, *raion* soviets and party organizations, were met, workers' living conditions would continue to deteriorate. But four months later, the editor of *Rabochaia Moskva*,[14] Boris Volin, wrote that the city soviet had too few resources to meet the demand for housing construction and repair. He agreed that the situation was very poor, but counseled workers to be patient. Workers paid little heed and their complaints mounted. In October, the city soviet responded to their criticisms and demands by creating an Extraordinary Housing Commission. The commission's first act was to order that 10 percent of the city's living space be made available to housing associations . . . which were organized at the workplace. This "new" living space was to be distributed to those in need of housing on a priority basis: workers and employees without adequate housing were the first priority; the registered unemployed, the second priority.

Many residents were reluctant to give up part of their dwellings. For example, the Uritskii factory's housing association encountered resistance from two recalcitrant apartment dwellers. One was a professional who lived with his wife and fourteen-year-old daughter in a five-room apartment; the other, a nepman whose three member family also occupied five rooms. The association dismissed both protests and allocated one of the professional's large rooms to three workers and their spouses. By November 1, the Extraordinary Commission announced that the 10 percent levy had resulted in 11,341 "new" rooms which were occupied by some 21,000 people. Unfortunately, the levy did little to reduce the growing demand for housing. What it did do was expose some of the housing inequities that existed. While three workers' families shared one subdivided room, the professional's family lavished in four rooms. This case was no exception.

By 1924, there was public discussion of "the housing hunger, the housing catastrophe." The next year, a trade union official lamented that Moscow's living space was filled "to the point of overflowing." . . . These were not exaggerations. With each passing year, the amount of living space per person declined — from 9.3 square meters in 1920 to 5.5 square meters in 1927 — and the average number of inhabitants per apartment increased — from five in 1920 to nine in 1926. As the demand for housing outstripped construction, the populations of factory barracks swelled, apartments were subdivided with increasing frequency, the renting of corners became more common, and many homeless people were forced to sleep in corridors, storerooms, sheds, kitchens, bathhouses, and even asphalt cauldrons. For those who refused to live in such conditions, the only alternative was to live outside the city and commute as much as fifteen kilometers to work.

While rapid population growth and inadequate construction were the prime reasons for Moscow's housing crisis, they were not the only reasons. In fact, the

---

[14] *Worker's Moscow.*

city's population in 1923 was 25 percent smaller than in 1917; yet the number of apartments had diminished by only 18 percent. True, much of that housing was in disrepair and of substandard quality. But what made the crisis worse was the city soviet's desire to place workers in decent apartments and not have to reopen the accursed barracks that had housed so many before the revolution. . . . [A]t least until 1923 the soviet's housing policy produced some success. The average amount of living space per person that year was slightly greater than in 1912. Nonetheless, overcrowded housing remained a reality of Moscow life. In 1923, more than one-half of the residents lived in apartments with two occupants per room; another third lived in apartments with three to five people per room. Less than 10 percent had the luxury of having a room to themselves.

But the success of the soviet's policy was limited. Although many Moscow workers had more living space than they did before 1917, as a class they had the least amount of living space. That inequity remained true throughout the decade. In 1927, the average amount of living space per person (in square meters) was: workers — 5.6; artisans — 5.9; employees — 7.0; professionals — 7.1. The types of dwellings in which workers lived varied widely. The 1918–1921 redistribution primarily benefited those workers who resided in Moscow during those years. The 10 percent levy benefited those workers who returned to Moscow in 1921–1922. After that, the number of workers forced to live in factory barracks, corners of apartments, sheds and other substandard dwellings grew annually. Everything was different, but little had changed in the area of housing.

To illustrate how crowded Moscow housing was during the 1920s, consider the following examples. But first, a word of caution. Relative to most workers, especially the most recent arrivals, the housing described below was comfortable, even spacious. In 1922, warehouseman V. lived in a one-room apartment in an old wooden house with his wife, two daughters, and, for at least part of the year, his mother-in-law. The apartment had 13 square meters of living space and one window. The furnishings were meager: a bed, a couple of tables and stools, and a kerosene primus stove. Late the next year, the family moved to a newly renovated apartment, which also had one room (18.6 square meters) and one window. The parents slept in the bed and the children slept on the floor.

During the first half of 1924, textile worker O., her husband, and two children lived in a one-room apartment in a two-story house shared by four families. Their apartment had only 7.7 square meters of living space and one window. The family had two cots; the mother and daughter slept in one, the father and son in the other. They moved in 1925 to a somewhat larger and cleaner one-room apartment. The room was large enough for both O. and her husband to have their own corners. Two chairs, stools, and tables were the only furniture in the apartment. . . .

To fit such cramped conditions, it follows that most families' furniture was quite simple. That of workers V. and O.'s discussed above was typical. Stools were more common than chairs and beds were scarce. Surveys conducted in 1923 and 1924 found an average of three people per bed in Moscow. Those without beds slept on the floor, tables or makeshift plank beds. It was common for very young children to sleep in open drawers. Such conditions inspired the following popular little tune:

> *In Moscow we live as freely,*
> *as a corpse in his coffin.*
> *I sleep with my wife in the dresser,*
> *My mother-in-law sleeps in the sink. . . .*

During the early 1920s, workers also demanded an improvement in the quality of their housing. The deterioration of dwellings during the Civil War had turned many apartments into spawning areas for infections and epidemic diseases. To identify and cleanse such dwellings, in 1921 the city soviet organized volunteer health sections and public clean-up campaigns. Some 2,500 such sections existed by 1923 and their activity proved to be crucial in the struggle against epidemics. But cleaning dilapidated, substandard housing and repairing and improving that housing were two different activities. The latter proceeded extremely slowly.

The slow rate of repairs resulted from two factors — the lackadaisical attitude of some residents toward housing maintenance, and the shortage of capital. . . . The fact that housing was very cheap (rent free until 1922) and did not belong to the occupants "has killed the economic interest of the dwellers" who often mistreated their dwellings or failed to maintain them. In 1922, the Petrograd soviet lamented "the insuperable difficulties in fighting the psychology of the man in the street (*obyvatel'*) who looks upon national property as belonging to nobody and therefore at times aimlessly destroys it." Surely the same problem existed in Moscow.

The disrepair of housing in the early 1920s testifies to the consequences of years of neglect. At factory meetings and in the press, workers constantly complained about overcrowding and the need to repair walls, windows, floors, stairs, ceilings, and water and heating systems. They recognized that the lack of capital hampered the repair process, but that in no way lessened the stridency of their demands. Frustrated by the slow pace, some workers stole factory goods and supplies with which to repair their apartments. Although discontent over the disrepair diminished somewhat after 1925, complaints continued to appear in the press.

Even if residents had adhered to the letter of the law, overcoming their housing's disrepair was beyond their financial means. Unfortunately, it was also beyond the city soviet's means. Until 1924, the inflation rate placed severe fiscal strictures on the soviet, which, in accordance with national policy, gave priority to industrial recovery and the restoration of municipal utilities. Funds for housing repair were simply insufficient to meet the demand. In 1923, the city soviet allocated less than one-tenth of the amount spent in 1913 for housing repair. This meager sum barely made a dent in the problem.

Nor was the soviet in a position to build enough new housing. No large scale housing construction took place in Moscow before 1923 and few housing units were built in 1924. Of the new housing built in 1923/24, 60 percent was built by private investors and cooperatives. Until the establishment in 1925 of a bank to finance municipal housing, the city lacked access to the credit necessary to construct the requisite new housing. The bank's creation marked a turning point in municipal housing construction. After 1925, the city soviet and state agencies built more than 80 percent of all new housing. Still, insufficient capital limited new construction. . . .

Not only was the amount of housing construction during the NEP inadequate, but what was built was often of inferior quality. A 1927 city soviet investigation of newly constructed housing revealed a host of problems. Many floors, doors, and windows were made from unseasoned wood and poor quality materials, and within a short time they warped or split, often rendering them useless. So poorly designed were many buildings that some rooms were accessible only through other rooms, making their use as individual apartments difficult and annoying to the residents. Other problems among the long "series of shortcomings" included unnecessarily congested stairwells, inadequate insulation from street noise, the absence of sufficient baths and ventilation systems, and the construction of excessively large rooms that had to be subdivided. For lack of funds, the construction of creches,[15] day-care centers, and rooms for collective use in apartment buildings had to be deferred.

Given that demand far outstripped housing construction and renovation, many workers turned to their factories in search of a place to live. Many of the city's larger factories, such as Dinamo, AMO, Trekhgornaia and Serp i molot, owned reasonably decent apartment buildings. But factory administrators often preferred to use these dwellings to attract skilled workers and *spetsy*.[16] Those apartments available to other workers were quickly filled in the early 1920s. To their newest workers, the factories offered only a place in their barracks. Precisely what proportion of the city's proletariat lived in factory barracks is unclear. Two facts appear certain: the number grew with each passing year, and the majority of them were new workers from the villages.

Despite attempts by factory and union activists to maintain certain standards of quality and cleanliness in the barracks, the conditions there were reminiscent of those in pre-revolutionary times. In 1928, *Trud* described one barracks:

> The long narrow room has only one window, which cannot be opened. Some of the panes are broken and the holes plugged with dirty rags. Near the doorway is an oven which serves not only for heating but for cooking as well. The chimney spans the entire length of the room from the doorway to the window. The smell of fumes, of socks hung to dry, fills the room. It is impossible to breathe in the closeness of the air. Along the walls are crude beds covered with dirty straw ticks and rags, alive with lice and bugs. The beds have almost no space between

---

[15] Day nurseries.

[16] Specialists.

them. The floor is strewn with cigarette butts and rubbish. About two hundred workers are housed here, men and women, married and single, old and young — all herded together. There are no partitions, and the most intimate acts are performed under the very eyes of other inhabitants. Each family has one bed. On one bed a man, a wife and three children live, a baby occupies the "second floor" — a cot hanging over the bed. The same toilet is used by men and women.

Living in these overcrowded and unsanitary barracks affected workers in many ways. They got less sleep and became ill more often than those who had better dwellings. Consequently, they had higher absenteeism rates and were less productive than the average worker. . . .

As much as workers who resided in apartments or barracks had reason to complain, they enjoyed a privilege not shared by all residents — they had a place to live. For thousands of Muscovites, the search for housing was a daily ordeal. As early as September 1922, a letter to the editor of *Rabochaia Moskva* stated that "masses of people pass the night on the streets." In view of the approaching winter, the author proposed the construction of overnight lodgings. . . .

As the number of homeless Muscovites increased, so too did the number of overnight barracks. By 1929, the city operated eight such dwellings. . . .

The conditions in overnight barracks were worse than those in factory barracks. Despite regulations which stipulated that they meet certain sanitary requirements and possess certain amenities of life, the shortage of capital and uncaring attitudes of the temporary tenants meant that these ideals were rarely met. Some barracks lacked separate facilities for men and women, and most were extremely overcrowded, dirty and lacked hot water, laundry facilities, and litter baskets. The dining areas were especially unsanitary and often strewn with garbage. The food and dining conditions were often so horrible that few tenants ate there. At one lodging only four of the 120 tenants ate in the dining hall.

So large was the city's homeless population that the increasing number of night lodgings were unable to accommodate them. When the weather permitted, many people slept in parks, public gardens, cemeteries, streets, and along the river banks. During the winter months, they sought shelter in abandoned or partially constructed buildings, train stations, sheds, bathhouses, and even asphalt cauldrons. The unemployed, *besprizorniki* (homeless orphans), and recent migrants comprised the vast majority of the homeless population, although some permanent workers also populated their ranks.

From this group came the largest number of criminals. Leaving aside professional criminals, evidence of whose nefarious activities is too sparse to allow for discussion, the most visible of the city's criminals were the *besprizorniki,* the orphaned and runaway children for whom criminality was both a game and means of survival. . . .

Left to their own devices, they formed gangs that offered them protection and enhanced their criminal activities. The boys specialized in theft; the girls, in theft and prostitution. The gangs created their own communal organizations and systems for the division of their spoils. They lived where they could — in sheds, asphalt cauldrons, parks, abandoned buildings or boats, or, if they had some money, in night shelters. . . . In their social milieu, the use of drugs (especially cocaine) and alcohol were everyday occurrences, and children as young as five indulged and stole so that they could purchase more.

Orphaned girls frequently turned to prostitution. In 1927, more than one-quarter of the prostitutes arrested in Moscow were under eighteen years of age, some were as young as twelve. While some became prostitutes to sustain themselves, others did so to support their drug habit. Almost three-quarters of those arrested in 1924 regularly used cocaine, opium, or morphine. Many other women also became prostitutes. While some did so for personal reasons that will forever remain secret, many resorted to prostitution in order to survive. Unemployment, the lack of financial support, and the need to sustain their families left them no choice. Women of the street practiced their trade quite openly in several parts of town, Tverskaia and Trubny squares being the best known. In the former, the sidewalks swarmed with teenage prostitutes; in the latter, the trade was less brisk and males in search of whores had to frequent one of several large tenements, in the corridors of which hung the sweet smell of opium and where next to the doors were tacked photographs of the "fair occupant in the scantiest of costume." Those who operated out of these shabby tenements had a distinct advantage over their competitors — they had a bed. The housing shortage forced the others to ply their trade in hallways, alleys, backyards, and on park lawns and benches.

Despite the efforts of the police, party, and state agencies to eliminate crime, prostitution, and drug use and to reduce the number of *besprizorniki,* all remained common features of Moscow life. Considering the deepening housing and unemployment crises, this is hardly surprising. But the conspicuous presence of criminals, prostitutes, and drug users adversely affected the quality of life there. Because most thefts, robberies, muggings, and rapes occurred at night, men and women alike worried about venturing out alone after dark. The large numbers of homeless who passed the night in public places only heightened these anxieties. Parents were also greatly concerned for their children. This was particularly true of the parents of unemployed juveniles, who out of idleness or for want of excitement fell in with *besprizorniki* gangs and took to drinking and drug use.

Workers' relatively low wages and their overcrowded living conditions imposed severe strains on them and their families and adversely affected their lives. While daily frustrations, anxieties, and uncertainties punctuated the lives of all family members, women often bore the heaviest burden. The most obvious example of this was their role in the division of family labor.

Legally, men and women were equal. But at home, as on the job, traditional, patriarchal attitudes held sway. Shopping, cleaning, cooking, and child-care were, according to most Russian males, women's work. That many women also held full-time jobs turned most days into an exhausting experience. The scarcity of household conveniences, municipal services, electricity, refrigeration, and running water forced women to devote long hours each day to household chores. For want of refrigeration, women had to shop virtually every day, an exercise that often required traveling from store to store and waiting in queues.[17] Because cooking on portable primus stoves turns even a simple meal into a long ordeal, cooking also consumed much time. So too did cleaning the apartment and washing clothes. Less than one-fifth of the city's apartments had running water, and hence water for cleaning and cooking had to be carried from communal taps, pumps (usually located outside), or from the river or open canals. According to time-budget studies conducted in 1931, women who worked full-time jobs spent an additional five hours a day on domestic chores and child-care. This left two or three hours a day at most for personal sanitation, politics, or self-improvement. Males, on the other hand, devoted only two hours a day to domestic chores and child-care.

The personal and social costs engendered by overcrowded housing conditions and the demands of daily life are difficult to estimate, but data on crime in Moscow suggest that they were substantial. Between 1923 and 1927, the crime rate among females rose more rapidly than did that of males. While males were more likely to commit crimes of property or hooliganism (often associated with drunkenness), females were more commonly arrested for attacks on people. During those years, the number of women arrested for assault and battery increased by five times; those arrested for murder and "shocks, blows, and attacks on individuals" by six times. As a proportion of all crimes, those against people soared from 10 to 40 percent. People who lived in one room or less and those without permanent residences were the most apt to commit crimes. Spouses, relatives, and neighbors were their most common victims.

Of the 202 cases of hooliganism that came before Moscow's Peoples' Courts in the mid-1920s, 25 percent of them were directly attributed to the acute housing problem. Many of those convicted were housewives, mostly workers' wives, who were found guilty of starting fights over an apartment or kitchen. Petty though the issues may seem, they provide a measure of the frustration and hostility that the strains of daily life induced.

Crime statistics measure only people's most dramatic reactions to their conditions. A host of minor problems also eroded their patience and civility. For example, consider the problems caused by so simple a device as a doorbell. Because they were formerly one-family residences, many of Moscow's apartment buildings had only one doorbell for all of the residents. So as to avoid confusion, each apartment was assigned a doorbell code usually determined by the number of rings. It goes without saying that such a system is fraught with the potential for error and, in some cases, mistakes or misuse precipitated fights and arguments.

Daily frustrations and hardships could not help but affect the stability of workers' families. Judging from the city's divorce rate, the impact was significant. Unfortunately, the nature of the data prohibits identifying the reasons for divorce and that rate among workers. But so steeply did the city's divorce rate rise that it seems inconceivable that the strains and quarrels of daily life did not contribute

---

[17] Lines.

to its increase. In 1921, there were 5,790 divorces; in 1927, 19,421 divorces; and in 1929, 23,745 divorces.

The 1920s remains the decade of the easy divorce. After 1926, the "postcard divorce" made the dissolution of marriage especially easy. The "postcard divorce" operated in the following manner. If either spouse wished to divorce the other, that person simply went to the ZAGS office (*Zapiski aktov grazhdanskogo sostoianiia,* which registered all marriages and divorces) and filled out a postcard announcing that the marriage had been terminated. The divorced, and possibly unwitting, spouse received the announcement in the mail several days later.

But divorce did not always end a couple's relationship. Because of the housing shortage, many divorced couples were forced to remain room-mates. When one of them remarried or took a lover, the situation could become extremely awkward. Indeed, just such a situation formed the basis of the popular contemporary film "Bed and Sofa" in which two workers contend for the love of one's wife and the right to her bed. Then there was the case of a ballerina who surprised her husband by bringing home a new husband after divorcing the former husband in the morning. Since he could find no other housing, the rejected male had to occupy a corner in his former wife's "honeymoon suite."

Economic insecurity and overcrowded housing affected even the happily married. Nowhere is this more graphically illustrated than in the city's rising abortion rate. In 1920, the Soviet government legalized abortions performed by trained doctors in approved hospitals and clinics. During the 1920s, more and more women elected to have abortions. The number of registered abortions per 100 births rose from 19.6 in 1923, to 31.4 in 1925, to 55.7 in 1926. While some women chose abortion to terminate an unwanted pregnancy or for medical reasons, more than half of those who received abortions did so because they lacked the financial resources to support a child. Low wages, unemployment, and the shortage of housing space were major considerations for women who sought abortions.

While some party members regarded the rising abortion rate as "massive" and "horrifying," others accepted it and argued that the women's reasons for electing the operation were real and justifiable. On one fact, all agreed. The abortion law marked a significant improvement over the pre-revolutionary situation, when abortions were illegal and untrained doctors, midwives, and nurses clandestinely performed them in unsanitary conditions, situations that often resulted in infection, permanent bodily injury, or death. During the 1920s, the number of women who died from abortions, contracted postoperative ailments, or reported to hospitals with incomplete abortions contracted steadily.

The lowest average wages of the city's major occupational groups, the least amount of housing space per person, a rapidly rising crime rate directly attributable to these conditions, and the personal frustrations and anxieties that accompanied these depressing phenomena, these were the realities with which the Moscow working class struggled daily. To be sure, these were not items on that class's revolutionary agenda. What made the experiences especially galling was that their bosses and other well-to-do residents did not endure such hardships.

On the contrary, they prospered and frolicked during the NEP. Their success and happiness only further angered workers. . . .

There was no quintessential working-class experience during these years. Skilled and experienced urban workers earned higher wages and generally had better apartments than did new workers whose recent arrival and lack of skills and experience translated into lower wages and factory barracks housing. But the differences between workers paled in comparison to those between workers and nepmen, "speculators, professionals, etc." When it came to wages, housing, and the other daily realities that defined their lives beyond the factory gates, workers were far more united than they were divided.

WOMEN "OF A VERY LOW TYPE": CROSSING RACIAL BOUNDARIES IN IMPERIAL BRITAIN

Laura Tabili

When gender is analyzed within the history of imperialism, it illuminates the British perceptions of colonial peoples. Laura Tabili, a historian at the University of Arizona who specializes in modern British racial and ethnic diversity and working-class culture, investigates here the experiences of white and black women in British seaports during the 1920s, 1930s, and 1940s. Tabili focuses especially on the women who crossed racial boundaries to marry or to socialize and the prejudice they faced. Tabili's sources include newspapers, correspondence, investigative reports, contemporary books and journals, and government documents (of the Board of Trade, for example).

How did the environment of dockside settlements in port cities and a sailor's occupation affect interracial marriages and family life? How did these interracial settlements undermine the notion of "imperial manhood" as well as threaten British respectability and the idea of an "imperial race"? Tabili makes clear that imperialism mandated the control of people from British colonies, of female sexuality, and of racial boundaries. Elite prejudice against working-class people joined with narrow-mindedness toward race, gender, and sexuality. In Britain itself, such intolerance and bigotry came together in privileged white attitudes toward interracial matches, no matter how hard-working, civil, or British these couples were. Linked to these prejudices were centuries-old attitudes toward the poor that connected poverty to sin and faulted those who lacked employment or the means to be self-sufficient. That is, many of the elite did not consider the socioeconomic causes of unemployment, poverty, and destitution. Thus, interracial couples suffered not only from the economic problems peculiar to port cities, maritime occupations, and working-class life but also from racial stigmatization. The situation was worse for black women, who suffered, as Tabili shows, from "the triple oppressions of race, class, and gender." Nevertheless, Tabili ar-

Laura Tabili, "Women 'of a Very Low Type': Crossing Racial Boundaries in Imperial Britain," in *Gender and Class in Modern Europe,* ed. Laura L. Frader and Sonya O. Rose (Ithaca: Cornell University Press, 1996), 165–190.

gues that both white and black women, despite their hardships, contributed to the survival and cohesion of Britain's interracial seaport settlements. What types of discrimination did "women of a very low type" and their families face? Why did the problems seem not to deter interracial marriages?

One comes away from this essay realizing that imperialism cannot be separated from the oppression both of people ruled in lands far away and of groups in the home country as well. By definition, imperialism assumed a hierarchy of power wherein elite whites discriminated against women, the poor, and the racially different. Tabili emphasizes that imperialistic attitudes are still evident in some contemporary British social practices and views. No doubt the legacy of imperialism also exists in other Western states that divided much of the world among themselves in the nineteenth and twentieth centuries.

T aboos on sexual activity have been fundamental to state formation and to social stratification. In the 1920s, '30s, and '40s, at the height of Britain's imperial power, interracial marriage was deplored as a threat to racial boundaries and as a catalyst for racial conflict. White women who consorted with Black workingmen were denounced in gendered and class-specific terms as disruptive, deficient, "of a very low type." Investigating the conditions of Black and white women's lives in Britain's interracial neighborhoods not only shows how imperial race, class, and gender imperatives converged to constrain them but suggests that by transgressing racial boundaries women could strengthen as easily as fragment social solidarities, belying the rhetoric that defamed them. It also illustrates the interdependence of racism, classism, and sexism in upholding the imperial system, and the genuine threat these women posed by refusing to conform.

Early twentieth-century observers frequently attributed racial conflict to sexual competition — competition among Black and white men for white women. The *Daily Mail* of June 13, 1919, under the headline "Black Men and White Girls," reported a "race feud in Cardiff between the white population and the blacks" caused by "hostility towards the blacks mainly because of their association with white girls and women." The *Western Mail* titillated readers with images of race and gender disorder, alleging the recently paid-off Black seaman ashore would "proceed to spend money freely in arraying himself in the 'swankiest' garb he could obtain. Then, with a flashily dressed white girl, it was his delight to parade the streets and visit houses of entertainment." But in the eyes of the press, police, and other observers, Black men were less culpable than imprudent white women — "the Dulcineas[1] of Liverpool and Cardiff," who exacerbated "primordial" "racial antipathy." Scolded *Reynolds Newspaper*, "A foolish woman and a Negro may easily cause a serious riot, for the white man will not put up with it."

---

[1] Girlfriends of easy virtue; from the Spaniard Miguel de Cervantes's (1547–1616) satirical novel *Don Quixote* (1605).

Such responses reflected a common view of women and of racial or cultural "others" as disruptive to the solidarity of an otherwise homogeneous and unproblematically unified society. Journalists, social workers, employers, and civil authorities denounced white women who married Black workingmen as deviant, overlooked Black women, and deprecated interracial children as a social menace. Women in interracial neighborhoods were defamed as sources of racial and sexual disorder defined in class and gendered terms. In much of the literature on British race relations, similarly, if women have appeared at all, it has been as objects of contention who, when not entirely passive, acted only to aggravate "primordial" hostility between men of two mutually exclusive and ineluctably hostile racial groups. Such interpretations leave unchallenged a normative view of class and national identity as uniformly white and male, in relation to which racial and gender differences appear anomalous and divisive.

Reading through these hostile sources to reconstruct the daily lives of white and Black women in Britain's racially diverse seaport neighborhoods reveals that gender, race, and class identities were actually fluid and complex. Racial groups were fissured by class, gender, and age, while boundaries between racial categories were shifting, permeable, unstable, and cross-cut by gender relations and family ties. In addition, racial distinctions imported from Britain's overseas colonies reacted in unpredictable ways with domestic class and gender processes.

In Britain as in the colonies, the groups called "Black" and "white" were far from internally homogeneous, mutually exclusive, or mutually hostile. The epithet "black," or the polite term "coloured," described Africans and West Indians, South Asians, Arabs, and other colonized people. This diverse population shared neither physiognomy nor culture; they were united by a political and historical relationship of colonial subordination. Thus "Black" was a political status rather than a physical description: the boundary between Black and white was structured not simply by natural attributes but by power relations, changing over time and continually contested. In the course of several decades this flexible category shifted and broadened to encompass new groups. Racial definitions were further complicated by racially mixed children. Examining Black and white women's experiences in Britain's interracial neighborhoods can thus enhance our understanding of how global processes of class, race, and gender formation were negotiated in the everyday lives of ordinary people.

Imperial processes both shaped the Black presence in Britain and rendered it problematic. Most Black working people in interwar Britain were to be found in seaport settlements, formed in the late nineteenth century as the merchant shipping industry began to recruit cheaper labor in the colonies. A single industry but an economically, politically, and culturally critical one, the merchant navy was deeply implicated in Britain's rise to and fall from global dominance, and in the reconstitution in Britain of imperial racial hierarchies.

The pejorative images of women who transgressed racial boundaries accompanied a maritime division of labor that reproduced colonized people's subordination aboard ship. The wage structure and the labor market in British merchant shipping were designed to take advantage of the pay differentials between Britain and the colonies. Employers hired tens of thousands of colonized seamen — approximately one-fourth of their workforce — on long-term contracts beginning and terminating in colonial ports, paying one-third to one-fifth as much as white and Black seamen who operated in the relatively free European labor market. Employers reserved the better jobs for white workers, another colonial practice. Borrowing racialized gender representation from the colonies, employers demeaned Black seamen as less than men — "natives" or "boys," physically inferior, emotionally unstable, bestially hypersexual — to deny them men's wages as well as masculine prerogatives such as autonomy and authority. The British state and the National Union of Seamen, Britain's major maritime union, supported these racial hierarchies through legal and contractual mechanisms such as the National Maritime Board,[2] immigration regulation, and ruthless policing.

In spite of or perhaps because of these structural inequalities and impediments, in the early decades of the twentieth century, thousands of men left ships in British ports to seek jobs under union-mandated conditions, with improved working conditions, wages, rations, shipboard quarters, and chances of surviving a voyage. Apart from the illegality of jumping ship in mid-contract, as British colonial subjects they were fully entitled to live and work in Britain. Settling in dockside neighborhoods, they formed social networks, established religious, political, and fraternal organizations and institutions, and married into local families. The largest interracial settlement, numbering several thousand, was Bute Town in Cardiff, notorious worldwide as Tiger Bay, but settlements numbering in the hundreds existed in several other ports, including Toxteth in Liverpool; Holborn in South Shields; Salford, the port of Manchester; Kingston-upon-Hull; Limehouse, Stepney, and Poplar in London; and Newport and Barry on the Bristol Channel.

Among Black as well as white seamen, seafaring was a kin- and community-based occupation. In Britain's dockland neighborhoods, colonized men clustered in geographically specific enclaves, linked or defined by kinship, language, religion, or other bonds, and analogous to the Little Italies or Chinatowns found in American cities. In 1932, for example, the social investigator David Caradog Jones[3] identified several "racial colonies" in Liverpool's cosmopolitan dockside postal district 8, also known as Toxteth. These included "Chinese in Pitt Street" and larger enclaves of "negroes" in Pitt Street and Upper Canning Street; local settlement workers reported that "Arabs and [Indian] Lascars"[4] also lived nearby. Social life was supported by shops, cafés, clubs, and boardinghouses run by fellow countrymen. But because Black women were scarce, most men were compelled to seek wives among the local white population. Of 285 West African and West Indian men surveyed in Liverpool in 1919, for example, forty were married, eight

---

[2] Government agency created in 1919 to negotiate pay and working conditions for the British shipping industry.

[3] Social investigator (1895–1974).

[4] East Indian sailors.

to Black women. Of these eight Black or "coloured" women, only three lived in Liverpool.

Far from disruptive, Black women in small numbers and white women in larger numbers sustained Britain's interracial settlements. The practical support of wives and families ashore was critical to men absent at sea, and their importance was reflected in women's inclusion as nonvoting members in the National African Firemen's and Sailors' Union, a short-lived labor organization. Wives, more likely literate in English and conversant with British institutions and cultural practices, might assist their husbands in public sphere activities usually reserved to men. . . . In 1935 a defense committee composed of "Malays, Arabs, Somalies, West Indians and Africans," formed to resist the British Shipping Assistance Act, which effectively barred Black seamen from state-subsidized ships, boasted of "the unanimous support of the women as well as the men." Women were also active in the ethnic service sector, assisting in cafés, acting as shills or informal agents for boardinghouses, and operating cafés, brothels, and other businesses. In the 1940s Stepney's "West Indian club" was managed by a white woman.

But marriage itself brought concrete and direct benefits. Although the emotional and practical rewards of marriage were no doubt the principal incentive, marriage or cohabitation with either a Black or a white woman incidentally thwarted official efforts to preserve the geographical and economic disparities between colonizer and colonized by returning a man to the colonies. In spite of their presumptive British nationality, the authorities treated single Black men as transients, refusing to relieve[5] them, and instead viewing applications for relief as opportunities to deport them. Some even called unmarried or undocumented Black sailors "removable men."

But a man who founded a household established domicile in the United Kingdom. Households' eligibility for relief and other social services rendered him less vulnerable to employers' and immigration authorities' control. He was freed to seek work either ashore or at sea, and to bargain over the price of his labor in the same market as white seamen. In Britain he could also claim other rights, such as union membership, restricted in the colonies. Householders' implied responsibility for and control over dependents signified respectable manhood, as it legitimated claims on the state. The authorities, moreover, were reluctant to deport married men, less out of respect for the conjugal bond than out of fear that, deprived of their breadwinners, wives and children would require relief. An employer's efforts to keep West African crewmen "under control," for example, were frustrated by "the disinclination of the Home Office to insist upon the removal of men who, though without British passports, have married white women in Liverpool, or are living with white women and have children by them." Marriage might also integrate a man into a local family, giving him resources when unemployed and eroding the social barriers reinforcing racial divisions at work. . . .

---

[5] Grant assistance via the poor law.

Interracial settlements thus threatened to undermine the very imperial processes of racial subordination and exploitation that had formed them. Interracial couples' depiction as a problem or "pathology" reflected their subversion of the racially hierarchized labor system that underpinned the shipping industry's profitability — indeed, the imperial system. Held together by bonds of kinship and personal obligation, interracial families and settlements proved relatively impermeable by employers, the union, and the state. British maritime employers frankly pursued race segregation ashore to dampen militancy aboard ship. In the words of Captain Brett of the Shipping Federation, an employers' cartel, "The more [Black seamen] mix with Europeans, the more ambitious they become to obtain European wages and European conditions." Although nearly all seafarers were men, employers and their allies recognized women in port populations as threats to shipboard racial inequalities. Since marriage with either a Black or a white woman conferred relative immunity to official actions, the authorities not surprisingly frowned on Black men's relations with local women. In 1933 the immigration officer P. N. Davies commented in frustration: "Unless the men are held in prison, several would set about establishing domicile by formal and informal marriages." Officials reinforced overt constraints with gendered and racialized imagery stressing the perils of interracial marriage. In January 1926, for example, the Liverpool immigration officer E. N. Cooper reported that his colleague "Mr. Fudge, who has now acquired a very intimate knowledge of the native mind [sic], assures me that the height of ambition of the native West African is to get a white woman, preferably with children, to live with him and to qualify for the dole.[6] These women are generally prostitutes of a very low type." As references to "the native mind" suggest, hostility to interracial couples reflected not only the imperatives of imperial profitmaking but the interdependence of colonial and metropolitan race, class, and gender practices and representations.

For metropolitan social relations themselves were shaped by imperial ambitions. Turn-of-the-century efforts to rehabilitate the working class by regimenting youth and exerting pronatalist[7] pressure on women were intended to facilitate the reproduction of an "imperial race." Less obviously, definitions of gender, race, and class were reconstructed in relation to one another. A redefinition of masculinity — "imperial manhood" — was grasped as the remedy for British decline, and infused with racist, jingoistic, and class-specific content. Working-class men's imputed "loafing," "irregular habits," and "hooliganism" were seen as symptoms of insufficient manhood. From the late nineteenth century through the 1940s, families were defined as "rough" rather than "respectable" if they failed to meet class-specific expectations that wives remain in the home, dependent on a skilled breadwinning husband. This "rough" stereotype of woman as a "carnal mag-

[6] Payments to the unemployed.

[7] One who believes that government social and tax policies should be designed so as to encourage a high birthrate.

dalen"[8] resonated with a longstanding albeit evolving tradition, in which all women, together with colonized and working people generally, as well as animals and the natural world, were sexualized, feared, and repressed as sources of disorder, sensuality, and pollution. Conversely, colonized men were defamed as unfit for political or economic power by denial of their manhood, even their humanity, in gendered as well as racial terms: "effete," "unmanly," "sedentary . . . delicate . . . languid," "children," "savages." Thus class differences themselves carried racial connotations, and were gender-specific. Interracial settlements and interracial couples, by transgressing these boundaries and inverting the hierarchies, problematized and threatened the multiple inequalities on which the imperial system rested.

In the 1920s and 1930s social observers, social workers, and state officials continued to depict interracial couples as a menace. . . . [I]nterracial families were disparaged in the 1930s in eugenic language, in the 1940s in the language of social deviance. Yet this language of pathology was also gendered. White women who married or lived with Black workingmen were denounced as unwomanly — unfit mothers and wanton wives — while their husbands were deprecated as less than men. These gendered images were infused with assumptions about race and class derived from colonial and metropolitan practices alike.

For in addition to jeopardizing workplace racial inequalities, white women who married Black workingmen fell afoul of dominant expectations about sexual conduct and feminine respectability. In addition to sexual probity, the promoters of an "imperial race" enjoined "maternalism" and "respectability" on women in the metropole. Definitions of "respectability" were themselves gendered and class-specific. The class-based ideal of a breadwinning husband and dependent wife and children was simply economically unfeasible for most working people. Because many workingmen earned less than an adequate wage, the conditions of working-class women's lives demanded work outside the home and other public-sphere activities, such as neighborliness, which were incompatible with middle-class definitions of respectability. Prescribed standards of proper maternal care demanded adequate nourishing food, good-quality clothing, abundant water, fuel, and soap, and other resources beyond the reach of most poor women. Observers denounced women unable to meet these unrealistic demands as "ignorant," responsible for their families' poverty; deficiencies in their maternal qualities, indeed, were blamed for the deterioration of the British racial stock, imperiling the empire.

The pejorative view of interracial couples assumed the absence of respectable women and manly men. Black men might be seen as unmanly because they earned less than a living wage and might depend on women in other ways to negotiate the treacherous terrain of life ashore. Black men's frequent underemployment and underpayment and the lack of job prospects for interracial children were

---

[8] Referring to Mary Magdalene, a reformed prostitute whom Jesus forgave in Luke 7:37–50.

the source of interracial families' exceptional poverty. Many Black men earned even less than white workingmen, impugning their masculinity and thereby their wives' respectability, as women were compelled into waged labor and even into casual prostitution to supplement household incomes. Wives' exceptional public visibility and their families' "low standard of life" were thus due to race discrimination. Yet to many outsiders they simply constituted evidence that these women were not womanly: they were negligent mothers and wanton wives. A 1930 report on "the colour problem in Liverpool" depicted white women who went with Black men as "unreliable and of a poor type"; women "of a somewhat better type" were redeemed only if they expressed remorse for having "brought these coloured children into the world handicapped by their colour." A report on wartime Stepney depicted white women who married Black men as amoral, stupid slatterns whose fecklessness accounted for their families' problems. . . .

Even Nancie Hare, an otherwise sympathetic observer for the London-based League of Coloured Peoples, criticized white mothers for keeping their children out of school to work. "Coloured men have not the judgment of Englishmen concerning the white women they meet, so that a coloured man may marry a woman . . . whom he afterwards finds to have lower standards of cleanliness, general attainments, and ambitions for the children than he himself has." Yet poor white parents too often removed children from school because they needed their wages desperately. Hare acknowledged that since working-class wives were most often in charge of family budgets, of which their husbands remained blissfully ignorant, and also in charge of "speaking for" children with employers, this painful decision was usually theirs. If there were indeed disagreements about children's education, they may have reflected differences in orientation between upwardly mobile migrant men and their proletarian wives, "the children of docks." Mothers' fears that ambitious children might be rejected suggest their own experiences with British class relations.

An aggravating factor was the distinctive pattern of gender relations in maritime districts, which elite observers found particularly abhorrent. In the late nineteenth century "the loose sex relationships of sailor-town" had included de facto polygamy — "'sailors' women' who maintained stable relations with a series of seamen and lived with them periodically when they came into port." Vestiges of this pattern apparently persisted in some ports in the 1930s: some wives of Black men, reported the social worker Muriel Fletcher,[9] "go to other men's houses while their own husbands are at sea." In her view, many were not professional prostitutes, but had turned to casual prostitution "in order to eke out their scanty income . . . because of the fact that they are living with a coloured man" — that is, because Black men's wages were inadequate and unreliable, and their claims on British rights and resources tenuous. But in addition, the epithet "prostitute" was

---

[9] Social worker in Liverpool during the 1930s.

often invoked spuriously to control, intimidate, or disparage women who deviated from prescribed norms — through public activity such as work outside the home, through having multiple partners, or, in this instance, simply through marrying or living with particular men. When such arrangements transgressed racial boundaries, they were especially disturbing, for in Britain as in the colonies, the dominant "norm" of racial endogamy was rooted in power relations.

In the colonies, control of white women and their sexuality had become a means to enforce racial boundaries, ensuring the perpetuation of a substratum of disfranchised and superexploitable workers with no claims of kinship or solidarity on European colonizers. White women in interwar British ports too were made responsible for maintaining racial endogamy and other sexual norms, thereby safeguarding both maritime profits and imperial hierarchies.

Perhaps this explains observers' preoccupation with interracial sexuality, reflected in views of colonized people and working-class women as pathologically hypersexual. Muriel Fletcher asserted that women became involved in interracial unions because they were already demoralized and devalued through sexual misconduct: if not prostitutes or former prostitutes, they were disgraced by illegitimate children. The men, conversely, unrestrained in the British context by "tribal discipline," became promiscuous, brutal, and "contemptuous" of women: "able to speak but little English," they shared "little but the physical bond" with their consorts. Like the Liverpool Committee for the Protection of Half-Caste Children, Fletcher stressed the at once narcotic and insatiable quality of Black men's sexual passion, which rendered white women "unable to break away," and the chief constable of Cardiff reported with disapproval that "certain women court the favour of the coloured races." A 1942 report on Stepney alleged that "the vast majority" of the white women there "have come into the district with the deliberate intention of trading on the coloured men; . . . women who, having failed to achieve real satisfaction in life, have tried to find it through sex and the easy acquisition of material things." These women were deficient in the inward and outward attributes of respectability and civility: "They have gradually lost all moral sense. Almost all of these women are below normal intelligence, and, according to officials who have dealt with them, oversexed."

Thus the rhetoric that defamed women in Britain's interracial neighborhoods incorporated elements from discourses of class, race, gender, and sexuality derived from the domestic as well as the colonial experience. Mistrust of poor and working women as unreliable upholders of racial or national solidarities perhaps reflected the recognition that their stake in the imperial order was diminished by their subordinate position within it. From the late nineteenth century onward, working-class women had been denounced for subverting the imperial project through their failure to attain the gendered ideals of dependent wife and domesticated mother, thus to bring forth an "imperial race." To disrupt the racial stratification on which the empire rested, to assist colonized men in attaining the prerogatives of British manhood — the role of breadwinner and householder — and to problematize racial categories by bringing forth children who did not fit within them to place claims on the state and on British resources was to compound this failure.

Distasteful as much of this material is, it supports the prevalent view that interracial families were viewed with intense hostility and defamed in the familiar language of race, class, gender, and sexual repression. But whose view this was demands careful specification. Undermining the notion of either an endemically racist "tradition of intolerance" or a racially enlightened consensus in British society, investigation suggests there was no consensus, hostile or otherwise, toward interracial families; we find, rather, a variety of voices.

Privileged white women as well as white men defamed interracial couples in class-based terms reminiscent of sometimes embittered relations between the middle-class home visitor — the much-resented "lady from the West End come to do good" — and beleaguered working-class wives and mothers. The eugenically minded Liverpool Association for the Welfare of Half-Caste Children, for example, was founded by Miss Rachel Fleming[10] of University College Aberystwyth, and commissioned the hostile and now notorious report by Miss Muriel E. Fletcher. Women were also prominent among authors of the Stepney survey, as were two Black clergymen: the Reverend E. A. Ejesa-Osora, assistant priest of St. Mary-le-Bow, and Imam S. D. Khan, Jamiab-ul-Muslimin,[11] suggesting that racial affinities, when cross-cut by class or status difference, were no more durable than gender affinities.

Some of these investigators seemed at the same time to identify with the white wives; perhaps that is why they ignored Black women. Fletcher described them as "hopeless and embittered, resentful of approach, yet anxious to confide in someone once their confidence had been won." Yet class-specific definitions of womanly respectability prompted harsh judgments of these "fallen women." . . . [E]ven social workers and investigators, of whom we might expect homogeneity of opinion, were far from unanimous. True, Constance King[12] of the Liverpool Settlement shared the view of "the early founders of the Settlement movement" that poverty was the result of personal defects: "essential poverty of mind, body, and spirit." But David Caradog Jones attributed poverty in Liverpool to "economic conditions and . . . the failure of nations." . . .

Interracial couples themselves reported that their problems stemmed not from individual race or gender pathology but from socioeconomic deprivation common to their working-class neighbors, compounded by race discrimination in the market and by the state. Black and interracial couples did face real obstacles in interwar Britain. Largely ghettoized in historically disreputable dockside neighborhoods, they paid more than white couples for cramped, inferior housing.

---

[10] Sociologist and advocate of higher education for women.

[11] Spiritual leader of a Muslim community.

[12] Social worker in Liverpool.

Husbands suffered longer periods of unemployment. Their children were disadvantaged at school and in the job market. Fletcher found most Black-headed families in Liverpool living "below the poverty line," in part because the largest employer of West Africans, the Elder Dempster Steamship Lines, systematically underpaid African seamen with state and union sanction. Cardiff authorities paid reduced relief to Black-headed households: "The excuse is made that the needs of coloured men are less."

Yet these social and economic penalties were insufficient to deter intermarriage, which continued throughout the twentieth century. In contrast to lurid reports by Fletcher and the Stepney team, Nancie Hare reported interracial marriages "often quite as happy as is marriage between British people of the same standard of life." Black husbands and fathers compared favorably with white men of the same class, occupation, and district, reputedly spending more time and money on their wives and children and less in the pubs. "Race" riots in 1919 were allegedly provoked in part by consorts of Black men "boasting to the other women of the superior qualities of the negroes as compared with those of the white men." One of Hare's informants amused her by exclaiming, "I wouldn't change my husband for fifty white men!" The flexibility of racial identities, indeed, was reflected in Hare's report that many white wives identified with their husbands' social networks: "They take sides with them; they include themselves in the category 'coloured' and talk of 'we,'" and they joined social organizations such as the "Universal Negro Movement Association."[13] . . .

The discrepancies among these various accounts suggest that the view of interracial couples as pathological and of white wives as women "of a very low type" was far from universal. Maritime communities formulated their own definitions of the "elusive and shifting" divide between "rough" and "respectable," only partly coincident with those of middle-class outsiders. Working people may well have had norms of sexual propriety and of race and gender order that differed from those elites promoted. In the terms of the working class as we understand them, it would be invalid categorically to apply the label "rough" to interracial families. If they were defined as "rough," we would expect to see strong links within the neighborhood, for "less respectable survival strategies were more heavily neighborhood based." Conversely, families defined as "rough" should have provoked complaints about "pub visits and public drunkenness," "apronless women," undisciplined children running "wild," and other infringements of "respectable" codes. True, Fletcher reported, "other women in the house take it in turns to look after the children on the nights on which the mother is absent." Yet schoolteachers and other observers reported children of Black fathers more warmly dressed than other local children, and Caradog Jones commented on harmonious if distant relations with white neighbors.

---

[13] Confused reference to the Jamaican Marcus Garvey's Universal Negro Improvement Association, founded in 1914 to increase pride among African Americans.

Interracial settlements apparently applied norms similar to those found in the larger working-class community. In postwar Tyneside a woman's status in the interracial community was elevated by her "ability to organize and manage her home, and . . . the control and training of her children," and damaged by "intimacy with another man during her husband's absence, or . . . frequent visits to public houses." Mothers vetted prospective sons-in-law not merely on the basis of their race but on their relative status in the locality and community. Thus there is little evidence to support elite assumptions that wives of Black men were uniformly women "of a very low type," or were so defined by their neighbors. Instead they were apparently little different from other women in these maritime neighborhoods, many of whom might have failed to attain prescribed standards of womanly respectability.

Thus the evidence suggests that white women promoted cohesion rather than division in interracial neighborhoods. In contrast to common images of disorder and pathology, women and interracial families were sources of order and stability, bridging and thereby blurring the racial boundaries dividing white and Black working people. Outsiders may have disparaged them precisely because, in offering colonized workingmen the prerogatives of British manhood, they destabilized the racial inequalities supporting imperial power. Indeed, the hostile rhetoric suggests that interracial couples undermined more than racial hierarchies, for it drew on existing discourses of class, gender, and sexuality, both domestic and colonial, to impugn their manliness and womanliness. In transgressing racial boundaries, interracial couples threatened to disarrange class and gender hierarchies as well, destabilizing the multiple structures of inequality sustaining imperial power. Yet this defamation and the hostility it expressed were not universal. Rather, critics of interracial marriages may have borrowed from received race, class, and gender discourses in an effort to build a racially exclusive consensus that did not yet exist in the 1920s and 1930s, if it ever did.

But not all the women in these neighborhoods were white. Outsiders focused on racially mixed couples because they threatened the race and gender barriers upholding British imperial power. For this reason, information about Black women is fragmentary and obscure. Yet Black women lived in these settlements, and, as in other racially mixed societies, Black and white men also married them when they were present. Recovering their story is critical to an accurate understanding of racial and social dynamics in Britain and in the empire.

Black women's importance to this reconstructed narrative did not inhere in their numbers, which were undoubtedly small. Their erasure from popular consciousness and historical memory, however, went hand in hand with white wives' depiction as sociopaths. Ignoring the fact that Black men also married Black or interracial women when they were available reinforced the view that interracial unions were the products of a pathological attraction between white women and Black men, rather than of the more mundane desire to establish a home and family. Restoring Black women to the historical record, then, repudiates the stress on Black and white men competing only for white women, racist in its view of Black women as less desirable and of Black men as sexually incontinent, and sexist in its view of white women either as agents of disruption or as passive objects of male contention.

What we discover supports the hypothesis that Black women in Britain lived out their lives subject to the triple oppressions of race, class, and gender. They shared a disadvantaged and exploited class position with their white neighbors; they shared race oppression with their families and communities; and both of these disadvantages were compounded by sex and race discrimination in the labor market, and race bias in the marriage market, to which working-class women turned to supplement their inadequate wages. These women's experiences also suggest that the boundary between Black and white could shift from generation to generation, and that Black and white working people could be as bound together by kinship as divided by race.

Women of color in interwar Britain were as ethnically disparate as their menfolk. In 1919, a partial census of African and West Indian seafarers and their families included a Jamaican and a Liverpool-born Black wife. Fletcher found many adult women who were daughters of mixed couples, and David Caradog Jones found six British-born "half-caste" women over forty-five years of age in his 1939 survey. In Stepney in 1942 the survey team enumerated twelve "coloured" women, including Malays, West Africans, and two of mixed race, including a "half-caste Indian." Indeed, the most visible and well-documented women of color were the racially ambiguous daughters of interracial couples.

Like interracial marriages themselves, these children embodied a blurring of racial categories that threatened the interdependent hierarchies sustaining British imperial power. Because interwar Britain lacked the codified racial categories of the Jim Crow American South or of Nazi Germany, children who were neither Black nor white provoked disquiet. They did not fit — a prima facie problem reflected in the pejorative term "half-caste." Only in the course of growing from children to adults did their position become clear. . . .

Observers were far from unanimous in deploring a "half-caste pathology." The Liverpool Settlement worker Constance King, to be sure, drew on eugenic and on class and race discourses, concluding, "Their mixed parentage is in the modern industrial world a handicap comparable to physical deformity." Fathers with "a lower standard of civilization" and mothers "often of a poor type," King reported, produced children "as a rule of poor stamina, physically and morally." . . .

But Nancie Sharpe reported, "Children of a coloured father are usually well dressed for the area they live in." She reported, in contrast to Fletcher, that all but a small "minority" of white wives appeared genuinely fond of both their husbands and their children. The Stepney team, while denouncing white mothers as negligent harlots, acknowledged that the typical Black father "instinctively [sic] loves children, will spoil them . . . and do his best for them in every way." Caradog Jones found in 1939 that the mean child mortality rate for interracial families was substantially lower (at 0.2 deaths per family) than among whites (at 1.3). Caradog Jones, Hare, and Fletcher found the children bright and popular in school: several had won scholarships to "central and technical schools." Nancie Hare reported them "little different" from other neighborhood children: "They go to the same schools, their mothers are English and their upbringing is little different . . . they are gay and witty . . . often popular at school . . . and of course, in many cases, the coloured children are related to the white." The Stepney team concurred: "The years they spend at school are probably among the happiest of their lives. They have not yet become really conscious of their colour."

Yet as they matured, teenagers began to meet discrimination. Scholarship students in secondary schools were snubbed by white children unaccustomed to the racial diversity common in dockland schools. Nonetheless, one Black boy became captain of his school's football squad. But, like their neighbors, few interracial couples could afford to keep their children in school beyond the minimum leaving age, and "once in the labour market they have to face the prejudice against colour."

Caradog Jones, echoing Fletcher, asserted in 1932 that "the Anglo-negroid when grown up do not easily get work or mix with the ordinary population." George Brown,[14] visiting Cardiff in 1935 on behalf of the League of Coloured Peoples, found "the responsible grooves of the general social order" barred to them: "Secondary education and industrial employment are practically closed to them . . . no coloured boy or girl can procure a job in any office no matter how qualified he or she may be. . . . No engineering works will employ them and apart from shipping they have no other outlet." Yet in 1934 the Liverpool Education Committee and the Juvenile Employment Bureau had concluded that "the employment position of half-castes, while . . . considerably worse than that of white children . . . was not entirely hopeless." . . .

But as gender differences intensified in the teen years, disabilities attached to womanhood compounded those of class and race in both the labor market and the marriage market, the latter so critical to working-class women's economic survival. The Liverpool Association for the Welfare of Half-Caste Children reported that "the majority of Anglo-negroid girls" were unable "to secure work either in domestic service or in factories," and so perpetuated imputed social pathology and sexual disorder, evidenced in "the number of prostitutes and the number of illegitimate children, born with a definitely bad heredity and exposed to a definitely bad environment." George Brown reported that in Cardiff, "opposition to receiving the girls as menials in domestic service, forces them to positions where they are physically and financially exploited." Hare corroborated his observation: "There is very little work even for white girls and coloured girls find it almost impossible." While most found work in local cafés and lodging houses, a few worked as servants or in ships, and two girls were distinguished by their success in obtaining work in a local cigar factory. In wartime Stepney, too, the color bar in employment allegedly enhanced girls' "temptation to . . . drift into promiscuous living with coloured men." These young women were thus handicapped not by

---

[14] An American expatriate who studied at the London School of Economics in the 1930s and married a British woman.

imagined eugenic deficiencies but by the disadvantages of their class position compounded by those attached to racial difference and to womanhood.

The dearth of "respectable" work for the girls may have caused them problems in the marriage market, although on this issue the sources are wildly at odds. Although investigators in both Liverpool and Tyneside reported cases of young "half-caste" women who married white men, Sharpe reported: "Coloured girls especially are in difficulties, as . . . when the time for 'walking-out' comes, the boys of the neighbourhood will not marry them. . . . The boys have not the same difficulty, as there does not seem to be such an objection to them on the part of the white girls, and there is a bigger choice of occupation for them." Yet both Fletcher and a postwar survey found these women married very young. Fletcher attributed this finding to their poor job prospects, but Sidney Collins[15] reported that "Anglo-coloured" wives were in high demand because of their relative scarcity, especially within the Islamic community.

This discussion has been meant to suggest that considering women's position challenges the notion of race and gender as inevitably divisive of otherwise unproblematic class and national solidarities. Not simply aggravating conflicts among workingmen, white and Black women were integral to the survival of Britain's interracial seaport settlements. Black men in Britain were not transients, as outsiders portrayed them, for they had wives and kin ashore in Britain. Black men married Black women when they were available, countering colonialist myths about their lustful threats to white womanhood. Interracial neighborhoods were not enclaves of isolated socially deviant mixed couples, but were sustained by interracial kin networks in which Black and white women played a critical role.

These settlements took shape in a structural context of labor market stratification and central and local state hostility, both shaped in turn by imperial imperatives. The attack on women and children in Britain's interracial neighborhoods appears to have been an effort to control and recolonize Black men, specifically the labor force of a strategic and powerful industry, by discrediting and marginalizing their families. Interracial families and settlements threatened to subvert the economic hierarchies that made imperialism profitable for influential sections of the British elite. The ample material reasons for opposing interracial marriage were reinforced by notions of racial inferiority adapted from the colonial experience and by fears of physical degeneracy and gender disorder derived from British class relations. The defamation of white women and the erasure of Black women, however spurious, acknowledged women's critical role in the survival of Britain's interracial settlements. The intensity of outsiders' hostility was a measure of the threat interracial marriages posed to a particular vision and practice of domestic and imperial order.

For hostility to interracial sex relations in British seaports was far from isolated: a similar and explicitly gendered discourse of pathology appeared in Euro-

---

[15] Sociologist during the 1950s.

pean colonies during the same decades. Black men's status as householders implied not only patriarchal control over white women and their sexuality but other prerogatives of British "manhood," threatening imperial race and gender hierarchies that defined colonized men as feminized, childlike, and bestial — less than men. White women who married or lived with Black men were denounced as gender outlaws, contributing to imperial decline through their failure to maintain racial boundaries as well as their deviation from class-based norms of womanly respectability: they were defamed in gendered terms as bad mothers and unchaste wives. Norms of respectable manhood and womanhood were racially contingent, less because "whiteness" was a constitutive element in a static and monolithic definition of class identity — or of "Britishness" — than because employers, by denying Black men a man's wage and by refusing employment to "half-caste" children, forced their wives and daughters to transgress class-based norms of womanhood by engaging in waged labor outside the home and even in casual prostitution. Slippage among discourses of womanliness, racial purity, and respectability suggests an effort to construct a rationale for racial exclusivity out of received class and gender assumptions. In addition, it reflected the recognition, in the words of Sidney Collins, that "the coloured immigrant and the prostitute [or, simply, the "unrespectable" working-class wife] share the common experience of marginality to the society."

For class, race, and gender divisions and sexual control were mutually reinforcing facets of the same oppressive hierarchy. The dominant vision of race and gender order was class-specific: among their working-class families and neighbors such women found a measure of acceptance and support. Yet neither Black nor white women nor their racially mixed daughters could escape the disabilities attached to race, class, and gender that permeated interracial neighborhoods as they permeated the larger society and indeed the imperial system in which these settlements were embedded. Britain's "colour problem" was not an isolated anomaly confined to the ports: the hostile rhetoric as well as the material practices that disadvantaged interracial families and communities were shaped by intertwined race, class, and gender processes that were not marginal but integral to British society, indeed to the imperial project. Still, British race relations did not simply mirror colonial ones, but were refracted by domestic class and gender relations.

Although stigmatized as sites of gender and sexual disorder and of racial conflict, interracial families and dockside schools and neighborhoods provided temporary shelter to children of mixed race. As the experiences of British girls and women of mixed race demonstrate, kin ties could cut across racial boundaries from generation to generation, confounding reified definitions of racial difference and their attendant disabilities. Racial positioning could shift in an individual's life course, shaped by age, gender, family, and economic relations. Black and white women were critical agents in this destabilizing process. Understanding the British working class as plural, fluid, and global rather than monolithic, static, and parochial should prompt rethinking of essentialist explanations for racial conflict and disadvantage.

In the subsequent half century, as women as well as men have migrated from Britain's colonies and former colonies, gender anxiety has been displaced onto the more numerous and visible Black women in Britain. Black and interracial families and neighborhoods are still depicted as deviant, their deviance now attributed to cultural practices. The focus of gender and sexual repression has shifted, too: harassment of women who join their menfolk in Britain has taken the form of callous and humiliating "virginity testing" and more recently DNA testing. This practice, along with such others as forcing Islamic schoolgirls to bare their legs for physical training classes, suggests lingering prurience about Black families and their cultural and sexual practices. The still insufficiently documented story of white and Black women in Britain's interracial neighborhoods reveals that the disabilities attached to race were not biological, hereditary, eugenic, or cultural, but instead economic, political, historical, imperial, and gendered.

MAKING CONNECTIONS: WOMEN AND THE FAMILY

1. Many in the United States today revere England for its history of constitutional development, parliamentary democracy, and rule of law. Great Britain, however, also has a legacy of imperialist aggression and arrogant superiority fueled by its early industrial might and the self-confirming mind set of Social Darwinism. Focusing on racially mixed marriages and attachments in British seaports during the first half of the twentieth century, Tabili analyzes British racism and its impact on families that had violated sexual and cultural boundaries intended to separate the races. To what extent were these racially mixed unions more loving or caring than the marriages Jacques Gélis characterizes in Part One and Anna Clark in Part Two? Both Clark and Tabili describe marriages and families in England a century apart, Clark being interested in the working class and Tabili in sailors, also part of the working class. Compare marriage and family life in the articles by Clark and Tabili. To what do you ascribe the differences between them? How do issues of race, occupation, and imperialism help to differentiate Clark's plebeian marriages from Tabili's racially mixed ones?

2. Where were women better off, in seventeenth-century France, early industrial England, or in the marriages that Tabili portrays? Give evidence to support your view.

THE NAZI CAMPS
Henry Friedlander

The Nazi death camps by themselves are sufficient to differentiate the twentieth century from all earlier historical periods. The Germans murdered, with a callous equanimity that makes one shudder, approximately eleven million people. This figure does not include those killed in warfare, or even the masses of civilian victims of airplane bombardments or of German reprisal executions. Historians use the term *Holocaust* to refer to the systematic extermination of the Jews, the primary target of Nazi barbarity. Of the eleven million killed in the German effort to "purify" Western civilization, between five and six million were Jews and one million of those were children. Various groups, in addition to the Jews, went to the Nazi camps.

Henry Friedlander, a Holocaust survivor and a historian specializing in Judaic studies, explains that the camps before 1939, heinous though they were, did not match in numbers or brutality those after 1939, and especially those functioning after 1942. Notice how World War II affected the development of the Nazi camps. Who ran the camps, and how were they organized? What was life like for the prisoners at the camps? What was the relationship between the camps and German industries? How did the camps in western Europe differ from those in eastern Europe?

Why did the Nazis, after experimenting with various methods of exterminating masses of people, reach the conclusion that the killing centers provided the most effective means of attaining "the final solution"? The Germans experimented with and came to prefer specific methods of murder at the death camps. How did Auschwitz, the best known of the camps, earn its infamous reputation?

The Nazis established camps for their political and ideological opponents as soon as they seized power in 1933, and they retained them as an integral part of the Third Reich until their defeat in 1945. During the 1930s, these concentration

---

Henry Friedlander, "The Nazi Camps," in *Genocide: Critical Issues of the Holocaust*, ed. Alex Grobman and David Landes (Los Angeles: Simon Wiesenthal Center, 1983), 222–232.

camps were at first intended for political enemies, but later also included professional criminals, social misfits, other undesirables, and Jews.

During World War II, the number of camps expanded greatly and the number of prisoners increased enormously. Opponents from all occupied countries entered the camps, and the camps were transformed into an empire for the exploitation of slave labor. Late in 1941 and early in 1942, the Nazis established extermination camps to kill the Jews, and also Russian POWs and Gypsies. These camps had only one function: the extermination of large numbers of human beings in specially designed gas chambers. The largest Nazi camp, Auschwitz-Birkenau, combined the functions of extermination and concentration camp; there, healthy Jews were selected for labor and, thus, temporarily saved from the gas chambers. In this way, small numbers of Jews survived in Auschwitz and other Eastern camps. In 1944–1945, as the need for labor increased, surviving Jews were introduced into all camps, including those located in Germany proper.

In the United States, the term "death camp" has frequently been used to describe both concentration and extermination camps. It has been applied to camps like Auschwitz and Treblinka — killing centers where human beings were exterminated on the assembly line. But it has also been applied without distinction to camps like Dachau and Belsen — concentration camps without gas chambers, where the prisoners were killed by abuse, starvation, and disease.

Six Nazi concentration camps existed on German soil before World War II: Dachau, near Munich; Sachsenhausen, in Oranienburg near Berlin; Buchenwald, on the Ettersberg overlooking Weimar; Flossenbürg, in northern Bavaria; Mauthausen, near Linz in Austria; and the women's camp Ravensbrück, north of Berlin. Other camps like Esterwegen, Oranienburg, or Columbia Haus had existed for a few years, but only the permanent six had survived; they had replaced all other camps. Dachau opened in 1933, Sachsenhausen in 1936, Buchenwald in 1937, Flossenbürg and Mauthausen in 1938, and Ravensbrück in 1939.

These camps, officially designated *Konzentrationslager* or KL, and popularly known as Kazet or KZ, were originally designed to hold actual or potential political opponents of the regime. A special decree had removed the constitutional prohibition against arbitrary arrest and detention, permitting the political police — the Gestapo — to impose "protective custody" (*Schutzhaft*) without trial or appeal. The protective custody prisoners — mostly Communists and Socialists, but sometimes also liberals and conservatives — were committed to the camps for an indefinite period. The camps, removed from the control of the regular prison authorities, were not run by the Gestapo; instead, they were administered and guarded by the Death Head Units of the black-shirted SS (*Schutzstaffel*),[1] a private Nazi party army fulfilling an official state function.

Reich Leader of the SS Heinrich Himmler appointed Theodore Eicke as Inspector of the Concentration Camps and Commander of the Death Head Units.

---

[1] Elite guard.

Eicke had been Commandant of Dachau; he had built it into the "model camp." Eliminating unauthorized private murders and brutalities, he had systematized terror and inhumanity, training his SS staff and guards to be disciplined and without compassion. From the prisoners, Eicke demanded discipline, obedience, hard labor, and "manliness"; conversion to Nazi ideology was neither expected nor desired. Eicke issued rules that regulated every area of camp life and that imposed severe punishments for the least infraction. His petty rules were a perversion of the draconic training system of the Prussian army. This system accounted for the endless roll calls (the *Appell*), the introduction of corporeal punishment (the *Pruegelstrafe*), and the long hours of enforced calisthenics. The SS added special refinements to this torture: suspending prisoners from trees, starving them in the camp prison (the *Bunker*), and shooting them while "trying to escape." In this system, labor was only another form of torture.

When Eicke became Inspector, he imposed the Dachau system on all concentration camps. Every camp had the same structure; every camp was divided into the following six departments:

1. The *Kommandantur.* This was the office of the commandant, a senior SS officer (usually a colonel or lieutenant-colonel and sometimes even a brigadier general) assisted by the office of the adjutant. He commanded the entire camp, including all staff, guards, and inmates.

2. The Administration. The administrative offices were charged with overseeing the camp's economic and bureaucratic affairs. Junior SS officers directed various subdepartments, such as those for supply, construction, or inmate properties.

3. The Camp Physician. This office was headed by the garrison physician and included SS medical officers and SS medical orderlies. The camp physician served the medical needs of the SS staff and guards; he also supervised medical treatment and sanitary conditions for the inmates.

4. The Political Department. This office was staffed by SS police officers (not members of the Death Head Units), who were assigned to the camps to compile the dossiers of the prisoners and to investigate escapes and conspiracies. They took their orders from both the commandant and the Gestapo.

5. The Guard Troops. These were the military units assigned to guard the camp. Quartered in barracks and trained for combat, they served under their own SS officers. They manned the watch towers and the outer camp perimeter. Officially, they had contact with the prisoners only when they accompanied labor brigades as guards.

6. The *Schutzhaftlager.* The protective custody camp was the actual camp for the prisoners; surrounded by electrified barbed wire, it occupied only a small fraction of the entire camp territory. It was headed by a junior SS officer (captain or major) as protective custody camp leader. He was assisted by the senior SS noncommissioned officer; this roll call leader (*Rapportführer*) supervised the day-by-day running of the camp. Under him, various SS men served

as block leaders in charge of individual prisoner barracks and as commando leaders in charge of individual labor brigades.

The SS hierarchy of the protective custody camp was duplicated by appointed inmate functionaries. But while the SS were always called "leader" (*Führer*), the inmate functionaries were called "elders" (*Aeltester*). The chief inmate functionary, for example, was the camp elder, corresponding to the SS roll call leader. The functionary corresponding to the block leader was the block elder, who was in charge of a single barrack. He was assisted by room orderlies, the so-called *Stubendienst*. The functionary corresponding to the commando leader was the *kapo* in charge of a single labor brigade. He was assisted by prisoner foremen, the *Vorarbeiter*. In large labor brigades with several *kapos,* the SS also appointed a supervising *kapo* (*Oberkapo*). (The unusual title *kapo*, or *capo*, meaning head, was probably introduced into Dachau by Italian workers employed in Bavaria for road construction during the 1930s. During World War II popular camp language, especially as spoken by non-German inmates, transformed *kapo* into a generic term for all inmate functionaries.) In addition, inmate clerks, known as *Schreiber,* performed a crucial task. The camp clerk assisted the roll call leader and supervised the preparation of all reports and orders. Clerks also served in labor brigades, the inmate infirmary, and various SS offices.

Until 1936–1937, the prisoners in the concentration camps were mostly political "protective custody prisoners" committed to the camps by the Gestapo. At that time, the category of "preventive arrest" . . . was added to that of "protective custody." The Criminal Police, the Kripo, and not the Gestapo, thereafter sent large numbers of "preventive arrest prisoners" to the camps. These included the so-called professional criminals. . . . They were rounded up on the basis of lists previously prepared; later, the police simply transferred persons who had been convicted of serious crimes to the camps after they had served their regular prison terms. The Gestapo and Kripo also used preventive and protective arrest to incarcerate the so-called asocials, a group that included Gypsies, vagabonds, shirkers, prostitutes, and any person the police thought unfit for civilian society. Finally, the Gestapo sent to the camps those whose failure to conform posed a possible threat to national unity; this included homosexuals as well as Jehovah's Witnesses.

In the concentration camps, the inmates lost all individuality and were known only by their number. Shorn of their hair and dressed in prison stripes, they wore their number stitched to their outer garment (during the war in Auschwitz non-German prisoners usually had this number tattooed on their forearm). In addition, the arrest category of each prisoner was represented under his number by a color-coded triangle. The most common were: red for political prisoners, green for professional criminals, black for asocials, pink for homosexuals, and purple for Jehovah's Witnesses. Inmate functionaries wore armbands designating their office. The SS used mostly "greens" for the important offices, but during the war the "reds" often replaced them and in some camps even non-German inmates were appointed *kapos* and block elders.

Before 1938, Jews usually entered the camps only if they also belonged to one of the affected categories. In the aftermath of the *Kristallnacht*[2] in November, 1938, the police rounded up the first large wave of Jewish men. Approximately 35,000 Jews thus entered the camp system, but most were released when their families were able to produce valid immigration papers for them.

In 1938, after the roundups of criminals, asocials, Jews, and Jehovah's Witnesses, and after the waves of arrests in Austria and the Sudetenland, the camp population reached its highest point for the prewar years. But after the release of large numbers, it sank again to approximately 25,000 by the summer of 1939.

World War II brought substantial changes to the Nazi concentration camp system. Large numbers of prisoners flooded the camps from all occupied countries of Europe. Often entire groups were committed to the camps; for example, members of the Polish professional classes were rounded up as part of the "General Pacification Operation" and members of the resistance were rounded up throughout western Europe under the "Night and Fog Decree."[3] To accommodate these prisoners, new camps were established: in 1940, Auschwitz in Upper Silesia and Neuengamme in Hamburg; in 1941, Natzweiler in Alsace and Gross-Rosen in Lower Silesia; in 1942, Stutthof near Danzig; in 1943, Lublin-Maidanek in eastern Poland and Vught in Holland; in 1944, Dora-Mittelbau in Saxony and Bergen-Belsen near Hanover.

By 1942, the concentration camp system had begun to develop into a massive slave labor empire. Already in 1939, the SS had established its own industries in the concentration camps. These included the quarries at Mauthausen, the Gustloff armament works at Buchenwald, and a textile factory at Ravensbrück. During the war this trend continued; every camp had SS enterprises attached to it: forging money and testing shoes at Sachsenhausen, growing plants and breeding fish at Auschwitz, and producing fur coats at Maidanek. In addition, the SS rented out prisoners for use as slave labor by German industries. The prisoners were worked to death on meagre rations while the SS pocketed their wages: Both SS and industry profited. I. G. Farben established factories in Auschwitz for the production of synthetic oil and rubber; Dora-Mittelbau was established to serve the subterranean factories of central Germany. However, the largest expansion came with the creation of numerous subsidiary camps, the *Aussenkommandos*. For example, Dachau eventually had 168 and Buchenwald 133 subsidiary camps. Some of these — like Mauthausen's Gusen — became as infamous as their mother camp. The growing economic importance of the camps forced a reorganization. Early in 1942, the Inspectorate of the Concentration Camps, previously an independent SS agency, was absorbed by the agency directing the SS economic empire. It became Department D of the SS Central Office for Economy and Admin-

---

[2] "Night of the Broken Glass," Nazi anti-Jewish riots, 10 November 1938.

[3] Order issued 7 December 1941 to seize "persons endangering German security."

istration (*SS Wirtschafts-Verwaltungshauptamt,* or WVHA); chief of WVHA Oswald Pohl became the actual master of the camps.

After 1939, the concentration camps were no longer the only camps for the administrative incarceration of the enemies of the regime. They lost their exclusivity to a variety of new institutions: ghettos, transit camps, and different types of labor camps. In eastern Europe, the German administration resurrected the medieval ghetto, forcing the Jews to live and work behind barbed wire in specially designated city districts. These ghettos served as temporary reservations for the exploitation of Jewish labor; eventually everyone was deported and most were immediately killed.

The Germans did not establish ghettos in central or western Europe, but a variety of camps existed in most occupied countries of the West. In France, camps appeared even before the German conquest. There the French government incarcerated Spanish Republican refugees and members of the International Brigade.[4] After the declaration of war, these camps received large numbers of other aliens: Jewish and non-Jewish anti-Nazi German and Austrian refugees; Polish and Russian Jews; Gypsies and "vagabonds." The largest of these camps was Gurs, in the foothills of the Pyrenees; others included Compiègne, Les Milles, Le Vernet, Pithiviers, Rivesaltes, and St. Cyprien. After the German conquest, these camps were maintained by the French and the inmates were eventually deported to Germany or Poland.

Most Jews from western Europe went through transit camps that served as staging areas for the deportations to the East: Drancy in France, Malines (Mechelen) in Belgium, and Westerbork in Holland. Theresienstadt, established in the Protectorate of Bohemia and Moravia, served the dual function of transit camp and "model" ghetto.

Captured Allied soldiers found their way into POW camps: the Oflags for officers and the Stalags for the ranks. Their treatment depended in part on the status of their nation in the Nazi racial scheme. Allied soldiers captured in the West, even Jews, were treated more or less as provided by the Geneva Convention.[5] Allied soldiers captured in the East, however, did not receive any protection from international agreements. Camps for Red Army POWs were simply cages where millions died of malnutrition and exposure. Prisoners identified as supporters of the Soviet system — commissars, party members, intellectuals, and all Jews — were turned over by the *Wehrmacht*[6] to the SS Security Police, who either shot them or sent them to concentration camps.

---

[4] Foreigners who fought under the auspices of the Soviet Union for the Republicans during the Spanish Civil War.

[5] A series of treaties signed in Geneva between 1864 and 1949 that provide for humane treatment of soldiers and civilians.

[6] The German army.

Labor camps had appeared immediately after the start of the war. Hinzert in the Rhineland was opened for German workers and was later transformed into a Buchenwald subsidiary for former German members of the French Foreign Legion. Similar camps appeared in Germany for workers imported from the East (*Ostarbeiter*) and in most European countries for a variety of indentured workers, such as those for Jews in Hungary.

Most important were the Forced Labor Camps for Jews in the East. Hundreds of these camps, ranging from the very small to the very large, were established in Poland, the Baltic states, and the occupied territories of the Soviet Union. These forced labor camps were not part of the concentration camp system, and they were not supervised by WVHA. Instead, they were operated by the local SS and Police Leaders, Himmler's representatives in the occupied territories. While executive authority rested with the SS Security Police, the camps could be run by any German national: police officers, military officers, or civilian foremen. Although the supervisors were always German, the guards were usually non-German troops. Some of these were racial Germans (*Volksdeutsche*), but most were Ukrainians, Latvians, and other eastern European nationals recruited as SS auxiliaries.

Conditions varied from labor camp to labor camp. Some were tolerable and others resembled the worst concentration camps. Like the Jews in the ghettos, those in the labor camps were eventually deported and killed; some labor camps, like Janowska in Lemberg, also served as places for mass executions. Only a few camps, economically valuable for the SS, remained in operation. In late 1943, WVHA seized them from the SS and Police Leaders and turned them into regular concentration camps: Plaszow near Cracow in Poland, Kovno in Lithuania, Riga-Kaiserwald in Latvia, Klooga and Vaivara in Estonia; other camps, like Radom, became subsidiaries of these or older concentration camps.

World War II also changed the function of the concentration camp system. On the one hand, it became a large empire of slave labor, but on the other, it became the arena for mass murder. During the war, persons sentenced to death without the benefit of judicial proceedings were taken to the nearest concentration camp and shot. Large numbers of inmates no longer able to work were killed through gas or lethal injections. Thousands of Russian POWs were killed in the concentration camps, while millions of Jews were systematically gassed in Auschwitz and Maidanek.

In 1943 and 1944, large numbers of Jews entered the concentration camp system. Many had been selected for labor upon arrival at Auschwitz; others had been prisoners in labor camps and ghettos that were transformed into concentration camps. These Jewish prisoners were retained only in the East. Germany itself was to remain free of Jews, and this included the camps located on German soil. But as the front lines advanced upon the Reich and the need for labor increased, Jewish prisoners were introduced into all camps, including those located in Germany proper. Eventually, Jews made up a large proportion of inmates in all concentration camps.

The end of the war brought the collapse of the concentration camp system. The approach of the Allied armies during the winter of 1944–1945 forced the evacuation of exposed camps. The SS transported all prisoners into the interior of the Reich, creating vast overcrowding. On January 15, 1945, the camp population exceeded 700,000. Unable to kill all the inmates, the SS evacuated them almost in sight of the advancing Allies. Inmates suffered and died during the long journeys in overcrowded cattle cars; without provisions and exposed to the cold, many arrived at their destination without the strength necessary to survive. Others were marched through the snow; those who collapsed were shot and left on the side of the road.

As the Russians approached from the East and the Anglo-Americans from the West, cattle cars and marching columns crisscrossed the shrinking territory of the Third Reich. The forced evacuations often became death marches; they took a terrible toll in human lives, killing perhaps one-third of all inmates before the end. Even camps like Bergen-Belsen, not intended for extermination, became a death trap for thousands of inmates. Thus, the Allies found mountains of corpses when they liberated the surviving inmates in April and May, 1945.

In 1941, Hitler decided to kill the European Jews and ordered the SS to implement this decision. After the invasion of Russia, special SS operational units, the *Einsatzgruppen,* killed Communist functionaries, Gypsies, and all Jews. These mobile killing units roamed through the countryside in the occupied territories of the Soviet Union, rounding up their victims, executing them, and burying them in mass graves. The units consisted of members of the Security Police and of the SS Security Service, recruited for this purpose by Reinhard Heydrich and his Central Office for Reich Security (*Reichsicherheitshauptamt,* or RSHA). They were supported by units of the German uniformed police and they used native troops whenever possible; local Lithuanian, Latvian, Estonian, and Ukrainian units participated in these massacres whenever possible. To increase efficiency, the Technical Department of RSHA developed a mobile gas van, which was used to kill Jewish women and children in Russia and Serbia. But the troops did not like these vans; they often broke down on muddy roads.

The *Einsatzgruppen* killings were too public. Soldiers and civilians watched the executions, took photographs, and often turned these massacres into public spectacles. The killings also demanded too much from the SS troops. They found the job of shooting thousands of men, women, and children too bloody. Some were brutalized; some had nervous breakdowns. To maintain secrecy and discipline, the SS leaders searched for a better way. They found the perfect solution in the extermination camps, where gas chambers were used to kill the victims. These killing centers were installations established for the sole purpose of mass murder; they were factories for the killing of human beings.

Murder by gas chamber was first introduced in the so-called Euthanasia program. Late in 1939, Hitler ordered the killing of the supposedly incurably ill. The program was administered by the Führer Chancellery, which established for this purpose the Utilitarian Foundation for Institutional Care, whose headquarters was located in Berlin at Tiergartenstrasse 4 and was known as T4. The victims (the mentally ill, the retarded, the deformed, the senile, and at times also those with diseases then considered incurable), chosen by boards of psychiatrists on the basis of questionnaires, were transferred to six institutions — Bernburg, Brandenburg, Grafeneck, Hadamar, Hartheim, and Sonnenstein — where specially constructed gas chambers were used to kill the patients. This radical ideological experiment in murder involved German nationals, and public protests forced the Nazi leadership to abort it in 1941. However, the program continued for adults and particularly for children on a smaller scale throughout the war, especially for the murder of ill concentration camp prisoners under the code designation 14f13.

Killing centers using gas chambers appeared late in 1941. In western Poland, the governor of the annexed area known as the Wartheland established a small but highly efficient killing center at Kulmhof (Chelmno) for the extermination of the Lodz Jews. A special SS commando, formerly occupied with killing mental patients in East Prussia, operated the installation. Using gas vans and burning the bodies, the commando killed at least 150,000 persons. In eastern Poland, the Lublin SS and Police Leader Odilo Globocnik headed the enterprise known as Operation Reinhard. Its object was to concentrate, pillage, deport, and kill the Jews of occupied Poland. He established three extermination camps: Belzec, Sobibor, and Treblinka. To operate these killing centers, he requested the services of the T4 operatives. A number of these, including the Kripo officer Christian Wirth,[7] traveled to Lublin to apply their know-how to the murder of the Jews. Augmented by SS and police recruits with backgrounds similar to those of the T4 personnel, and aided by Ukrainian auxiliaries serving as guards, they staffed the extermination camps and, under the overall direction of Wirth, ran them with unbelievable efficiency.

Belzec opened in March, 1942, and closed in January, 1943. More than 600,000 persons were killed there. Sobibor opened in May, 1942, and closed one day after the rebellion of the inmates on October 14, 1943. At least 250,000 persons were killed there. Treblinka, the largest of the three killing centers, opened in July, 1942. A revolt of the inmates on August 2, 1943, destroyed most of the camp, and it finally closed in November, 1943. Between 700,000 and 900,000 persons were killed there. These three camps of Operation Reinhard served only the purpose of mass murder. Every man, woman, and child arriving there was killed. Most were Jews, but a few were Gypsies. A few young men and women were not immediately killed. Used to service the camp, they sorted the belongings of those murdered and burned the bodies in open air pits. Eventually they, too, were killed. Very few survived. Kulmhof and Belzec had only a handful of survivors. Sobibor and Treblinka, where the above-mentioned revolts permitted some to escape, had about thirty to forty survivors.

The method of murder was the same in all three camps (and similar in Kulmhof). The victims arrived in cattle wagons and the men were separated from the women and children. Forced to undress, they had to hand over all their valuables. Naked, they were driven towards the gas chambers, which were disguised as

---

[7] SS Major (1885–1944) who carried out gassings on incurably insane Germans in 1939.

shower rooms and used carbon monoxide from a motor to kill the victims. The bodies were burned after their gold teeth had been extracted. The massive work of mass murder was accomplished by unusually small staffs. Figures differ (approximately 100 Germans and 500 Ukrainians in the three camps of Operation Reinhard), but all agreed that very few killed multitudes.

Thus, mass murder was first instituted in camps operated outside the concentration camp system by local SS leaders. But the concentration camps soon entered the field of mass murder, eventually surpassing all others in speed and size. The largest killing operation took place in Auschwitz, a regular concentration camp administered by WVHA. There Auschwitz Commandant Rudolf Hoess improved the method used by Christian Wirth, substituting crystalized prussic acid — known by the trade name Zyklon B — for carbon monoxide. In September, 1941, an experimental gassing, killing about 250 ill prisoners and about 600 Russian POWs, proved the value of Zyklon B. In January, 1942, systematic killing operations, using Zyklon B, commenced with the arrival of Jewish transports from Upper Silesia. These were soon followed without interruption by transports of Jews from all occupied countries of Europe.

The Auschwitz killing center was the most modern of its kind. The SS built the camp at Birkenau, also known as Auschwitz II. There, they murdered their victims in newly constructed gas chambers, and burned their bodies in crematoria constructed for this purpose. A postwar court described the killing process:

> Prussic acid fumes developed as soon as Zyklon B pellets seeped through the opening into the gas chamber and came into contact with the air. Within a few minutes, these fumes agonizingly asphyxiated the human beings in the gas chamber. During these minutes horrible scenes took place. The people who now realized that they were to die an agonizing death screamed and raged and beat their fists against the locked doors and against the walls. Since the gas spread from the floor of the gas chamber upward, small and weakly people were the first to die. The others, in their death agony, climbed on top of the dead bodies on the floor, in order to get a little more air before they too painfully choked to death.

More than two million victims were killed in this fashion in Auschwitz-Birkenau. Most of them were Jews, but others also died in its gas chambers: Gypsies, Russian POWs, and ill prisoners of all nationalities.

Unlike the killing centers operated by Globocnik and Wirth, Auschwitz combined murder and slave labor. RSHA ran the deportations and ordered the killings; WVHA ran the killing installations and chose the workers. From the transports of arriving Jews, SS physicians "selected" those young and strong enough to be used for forced labor. They were temporarily saved.

Those chosen for forced labor were first quarantined in Birkenau and then sent to the I. G. Farben[8] complex Buna-Monowitz, also known as Auschwitz III, or to one of its many subsidiary camps. Periodically, those too weak to work were

---

[8] The huge German chemical and dye trust.

sent to Birkenau for gassing from every camp in the Auschwitz complex; they were simply replaced by new and stronger prisoners.

A similar system was applied in Lublin-Maidanek, another WVHA concentration camp with a killing operation. But it closed much earlier than Auschwitz; it was liberated by the Red Army in the summer of 1944. Auschwitz continued to operate even after all other extermination camps had ceased to function. But when the war appeared lost, Himmler ordered the gassings stopped in November, 1944. Only a few hundred thousand Jews survived as slave laborers in Auschwitz and other concentration camps. Those who survived the evacuation marches of early 1945 were liberated by the Allied armies.

FORBIDDEN DEATH
Philippe Ariès

During the Romantic era of the late-eighteenth and nineteenth centuries, death represented a sudden rupture between the dying person and the immediate family. The same development of sentiment and affection that saw people marrying more frequently for love had a similarly profound effect on society's attitude toward death. Family members seemed more anxious about the final departure of spouses and offspring than about their own deaths; overburdened with grief, they left us evidence of their intense bereavement in literature, diaries, and lachrymose funerary monuments.

Ariès argues that this Romantic view gave way in the twentieth century to a death revolution, in which death became something shameful and forbidden. What exactly does he mean, and how has society interdicted death? What role has the hospital played in the death revolution? What innovations have appeared in funeral rites and ceremonies? According to Ariès, what constitutes an acceptable death?

What does it mean to say that death has replaced sex as a taboo and has become the new pornography? This development has important implications for society. Where is this taboo more prevalent, in the United States or in other Western countries?

Professionally an agronomic researcher, the late Philippe Ariès turned to history for his avocation. He was most interested in the evolution of social attitudes, including those concerning childhood, the family, and private life. With his books, *Western Attitudes toward Death: From the Middle Ages to the Present* and *The Hour of Our Death,* Ariès opened up a new subject for study, the history of attitudes toward death. Now, no one would deny the importance of a society's collective feelings toward this last event in life. It is interesting to speculate about why historians virtually ignored the history of death for so long. Ariès's remarks about death help us understand the twentieth-century world and the process of social change.

Philippe Ariès, *Western Attitudes toward Death: From the Middle Ages to the Present* (Baltimore: Johns Hopkins University Press, 1974), 85–103.

During the long period . . . from the Early Middle Ages until the mid-nineteenth century, the attitude toward death changed, but so slowly that contemporaries did not even notice. In our day, in approximately a third of a century, we have witnessed a brutal revolution in traditional ideas and feelings, a revolution so brutal that social observers have not failed to be struck by it. It is really an absolutely unheard-of phenomenon. Death, so omnipresent in the past that it was familiar, would be effaced, would disappear. It would become shameful and forbidden.

. . . It . . . seems that this revolution began in the United States and spread to England, to the Netherlands, to industrialized Europe; and we can see it today, before our very eyes, reaching France and leaving oil smudges wherever the wave passes.

At its beginning doubtlessly lies a sentiment already expressed during the second half of the nineteenth century: those surrounding the dying person had a tendency to spare him and to hide from him the gravity of his condition. Yet they admitted that this dissimulation could not last too long, except in such extraordinary cases as those described by Mark Twain in 1902 in "Was it Heaven or Hell?" The dying person must one day know, but the relatives no longer had the cruel courage to tell the truth themselves.

In short, at this point the truth was beginning to be challenged.

The first motivation for the lie was the desire to spare the sick person, to assume the burden of his ordeal. But this sentiment, whose origin we know (the intolerance of another's death and the confidence shown by the dying person in those about him) very rapidly was covered over by a different sentiment, a new sentiment characteristic of modernity: one must avoid — no longer for the sake of the dying person, but for society's sake, for the sake of those close to the dying person — the disturbance and the overly strong and unbearable emotion caused by the ugliness of dying and by the very presence of death in the midst of a happy life, for it is henceforth given that life is always happy or should always seem to be so. Nothing had yet changed in the rituals of death, which were preserved at least in appearance, and no one had yet had the idea of changing them. But people had already begun to empty them of their dramatic impact; the procedure of hushing-up had begun. . . .

Between 1930 and 1950 the evolution accelerated markedly. This was due to an important physical phenomenon: the displacement of the site of death. One no longer died at home in the bosom of one's family, but in the hospital, alone.

One dies in the hospital because the hospital has become the place to receive care which can no longer be given at home. Previously the hospital had been a shelter for the poor, for pilgrims; then it became a medical center where people were healed, where one struggled against death. It still has that curative function, but people are also beginning to consider a certain type of hospital as the designated spot for dying. One dies in the hospital because the doctor did not succeed in healing. One no longer goes to or will go to the hospital to be healed, but for the specific purpose of dying. American sociologists have observed that there are today two types of seriously ill persons to be found in hospitals. The most archaic are recent immigrants who are still attached to the traditions of death, who try to snatch the dying person from the hospital so he can die at home, *more majorum;*[1] the others are those more involved in modernity who come to die in the hospital because it has become inconvenient to die at home.

Death in the hospital is no longer the occasion of a ritual ceremony, over which the dying person presides amidst his assembled relatives and friends. Death is a technical phenomenon obtained by a cessation of care, a cessation determined in a more or less avowed way by a decision of the doctor and the hospital team. Indeed, in the majority of cases the dying person has already lost consciousness. Death has been dissected, cut to bits by a series of little steps, which finally makes it impossible to know which step was the real death, the one in which consciousness was lost, or the one in which breathing stopped. All these little silent deaths have replaced and erased the great dramatic act of death, and no one any longer has the strength or patience to wait over a period of weeks for a moment which has lost a part of its meaning.

From the end of the eighteenth century we had been impressed by a sentimental landslide which was causing the initiative to pass from the dying man himself to his family — a family in which henceforth he would have complete confidence. Today the initiative has passed from the family, as much an outsider as the dying person, to the doctor and the hospital team. They are the masters of death — of the moment as well as of the circumstances of death — and it has been observed that they try to obtain from their patient "an acceptable style of living while dying." The accent has been placed on "acceptable." An acceptable death is a death which can be accepted or tolerated by the survivors. It has its antithesis: "the embarrassingly graceless dying," which embarrasses the survivors because it causes too strong an emotion to burst forth; and emotions must be avoided both in the hospital and everywhere in society. One does not have the right to become emotional other than in private, that is to say, secretly. Here, then, is what has happened to the great death scene, which had changed so little over the centuries, if not the millennia.

The funeral rites have also been modified. Let us put aside for a moment the American case. In England and northwestern Europe, they are trying to reduce to a decent minimum the inevitable operations necessary to dispose of the body. It is above all essential that society — the neighbors, friends, colleagues, and children — notice to the least possible degree that death has occurred. If a few formalities are maintained, and if a ceremony still marks the departure, it must remain discreet and must avoid emotion. Thus the family reception line for receiving condolences at the end of the funeral service has now been suppressed. The outward manifestations of mourning are repugned and are disappearing. Dark clothes are no longer worn; one no longer dresses differently than on any other day.

Too evident sorrow does not inspire pity but repugnance, it is the sign of mental instability or of bad manners: it is *morbid.* Within the family circle one also hes-

---

[1] According to the custom of the great ("social betters").

itates to let himself go for fear of upsetting the children. One only has the right to cry if no one else can see or hear. Solitary and shameful mourning is the only recourse, like a sort of masturbation. . . .

In countries in which the death revolution has been radical, once the dead person has been evacuated, his tomb is no longer visited. In England for example, cremation has become the dominant manner of burial. When cremation occurs, sometimes with dispersal of the ashes, the cause is more than a desire to break with Christian tradition; it is a manifestation of enlightenment, of modernity. The deep motivation is that cremation is the most radical means of getting rid of the body and of forgetting it, of nullifying it, of being "too final." Despite the efforts of cemetery offices, people rarely visit the urns today, though they may still visit gravesides. Cremation excludes a pilgrimage.

We would be committing an error if we entirely attributed this flight from death to an indifference toward the dead person. In reality the contrary is true. In the old society, the panoply of mourning scarcely concealed a rapid resignation. How many widowers remarried a few short months after the death of their wives! On the contrary, today, where mourning is forbidden, it has been noted that the mortality rate of widows or widowers during the year following the spouse's death is much higher than that of the control group of the same age.

The point has even been reached at which . . . the choking back of sorrow, the forbidding of its public manifestation, the obligation to suffer alone and secretly, has aggravated the trauma stemming from the loss of a dear one. In a family in which sentiment is given an important place and in which premature death is becoming increasingly rare (save in the event of an automobile accident), the death of a near relative is always deeply felt, as it was in the Romantic era.[2]

A single person is missing for you, and the whole world is empty. But one no longer has the right to say so aloud.

The combination of phenomena which we have just analyzed is nothing other than the imposition of an interdict. What was once required is henceforth forbidden.

The merit of having been the first to define this unwritten law of our civilization goes to the English sociologist, Geoffrey Gorer. He has shown clearly how death has become a taboo and how in the twentieth century it has replaced sex as the principal forbidden subject. Formerly children were told that they were brought by the stork, but they were admitted to the great farewell scene about the bed of the dying person. Today they are initiated in their early years to the physiology of love; but when they no longer see their grandfather and express astonishment, they are told that he is resting in a beautiful garden among the flowers. Such is "The Pornography of Death" — the title of a pioneering article by Gorer, published in 1955 — and the more society was liberated from the Victorian constraints concerning sex, the more it rejected things having to do with death. Along

---

[2] The late-eighteenth and nineteenth centuries.

with the interdict appears the transgression: the mixture of eroticism and death so sought after from the sixteenth to the eighteenth century reappears in our sadistic literature and in violent death in our daily life.

This establishment of an interdict has profound meaning. It is already difficult to isolate the meaning of the interdict on sex which was precipitated by the Christian confusion between sin and sexuality (though, as in the nineteenth century, this interdict was never imposed). But the interdict on death suddenly follows upon the heels of a very long period — several centuries — in which death was a public spectacle from which no one would have thought of hiding and which was even sought after at times.

The cause of the interdict is at once apparent: the need for happiness — the moral duty and the social obligation to contribute to the collective happiness by avoiding any cause for sadness or boredom, by appearing to be always happy, even if in the depths of despair. By showing the least sign of sadness, one sins against happiness, threatens it, and society then risks losing its *raison d'être*.[3] . . .

The idea of happiness brings us back to the United States, and it is now appropriate to attempt to understand the relationships between American civilization and the modern attitude toward death.

It seems that the modern attitude toward death, that is to say the interdiction of death in order to preserve happiness, was born in the United States around the beginning of the twentieth century. However, on its native soil the interdict was not carried to its ultimate extremes. In American society it encountered a braking influence which it did not encounter in Europe. Thus the American attitude toward death today appears as a strange compromise between trends which are pulling it in two nearly opposite directions. . . .

. . . In America, during the eighteenth and the first half of the nineteenth centuries, and even later, burials conformed to tradition, especially in the countryside: the carpenter made the coffin (the coffin, not yet the "casket"); the family and friends saw to its transport and to the procession itself; and the pastor and gravedigger carried out the service. In the early nineteenth century the grave was still sometimes dug on the family property — which is a modern act, copied from the Ancients, and which was unknown in Europe before the mid-eighteenth century and with few exceptions was rapidly abandoned. In villages and small towns the cemetery most frequently lay adjacent to the church. In the cities, once again paralleling Europe, the cemetery had in about 1830 been situated outside the city but was encompassed by urban growth and abandoned toward 1870 for a new site. It soon fell into ruin. . . .

The old cemeteries were church property, as they had been in Europe and still are in England. The new cemeteries belonged to private associations. . . . In Europe cemeteries became municipal, that is to say public, property and were never left to private initiative.

---

[3] Reason for being.

In the growing cities of the nineteenth century, old carpenters or gravediggers, or owners of carts and horses, became "undertakers," and the manipulation of the dead became a profession. Here history is still completely comparable to that in Europe, at least in that part of Europe which remained faithful to the eighteenth-century canons of simplicity and which remained outside the pale of Romantic bombast.

Things seem to have changed during the period of the Civil War. Today's "morticians," whose letters-patent go back to that period, give as ancestor a quack doctor expelled from the school of medicine, Dr. Holmes, who had a passion for dissection and cadavers. He would offer his services to the victim's family and embalmed, it is said, 4,000 cadavers unaided in four years. . . . Why such recourse to embalming? Had it been practiced previously? Is there an American tradition going back to the eighteenth century, a period in which throughout Europe there was a craze for embalming? Yet this technique was abandoned in nineteenth-century Europe, and the wars did not resurrect it. It is noteworthy that embalming became a career in the United States before the end of the century, even if it was not yet very widespread. . . . We know that it has today become a very widespread method of preparing the dead, a practice almost unknown in Europe and characteristic of the American way of death.

One cannot help thinking that this long-accepted and avowed preference for embalming has a meaning, even if it is difficult to interpret.

This meaning could indeed be that of a certain refusal to accept death, either as a familiar end to which one is resigned, or as a dramatic sign in the Romantic manner. And this meaning became even more obvious when death became an object of commerce and of profit. It is not easy to sell something which has no value because it is too familiar and common, or something which is frightening, horrible, or painful. In order to sell death, it had to be made friendly. But we may assume that "funeral directors" — since 1885 a new name for undertakers — would not have met with success if public opinion had not cooperated. They presented themselves not as simple sellers of services, but as "doctors of grief" who have a mission, as do doctors and priests; and this mission, from the beginning of this century, consists in aiding the mourning survivors to return to normalcy. The new funeral director ("new" because he has replaced the simple undertaker) is a "doctor of grief," an "expert at returning abnormal minds to normal in the shortest possible time." They are "members of an exalted, almost sacred calling."

Thus mourning is no longer a necessary period imposed by society; it has become a *morbid state* which must be treated, shortened, erased by the "doctor of grief."

Through a series of little steps we can see the birth and development of the ideas which would end in the present-day interdict, built upon the ruins of Puritanism, in an urbanized culture which is dominated by rapid economic growth and by the search for happiness linked to the search for profit.

This process should normally result in the situation of England today . . . : the almost total suppression of everything reminding us of death.

But, and this is what is unique about the American attitude, American mores have not gone to such an extreme; they stopped along the way. Americans are very willing to transform death, to put make-up on it, to sublimate it, but they do not want to make it disappear. Obviously, this would also mark the end of profit, but the money earned by funeral merchants would not be tolerated if they did not meet a profound need. The wake, increasingly avoided in industrial Europe, persists in the United States: it exists as "viewing the remains," the "visitation." "They don't *view* bodies in England."

The visit to the cemetery and a certain veneration in regard to the tomb also persist. That is why public opinion — and funeral directors — finds cremation distasteful, for it gets rid of the remains too quickly and too radically.

Burials are not shameful and they are not hidden. With that very characteristic mixture of commerce and idealism, they are the object of showy publicity, like any other consumer's item, be it soap or religion. Seen for example in the buses of New York City in 1965 was the following ad, purchased by one of the city's leading morticians: "The dignity and integrity of a Gawler. Funeral costs no more. . . . Easy access, private parking for over 100 cars." Such publicity would be unthinkable in Europe, first of all because it would repel the customer rather than attract him.

Thus we must admit that a traditional resistance has kept alive certain rituals of death which had been abandoned or are being abandoned in industrialized Europe, especially among the middle classes.

Nevertheless, though these rituals have been continued, they have also been transformed. The American way of death is the synthesis of two tendencies: one traditional, the other euphoric.

Thus during the wakes or farewell "visitations" which have been preserved, the visitors come without shame or repugnance. This is because in reality they are not visiting a dead person, as they traditionally have, but an almost-living one who, thanks to embalming, is still present, as if he were awaiting you to greet you or to take you off on a walk. The definitive nature of the rupture has been blurred. Sadness and mourning have been banished from this calming reunion.

Perhaps because American society has not totally accepted the interdict, it can more easily challenge it; but this interdict is spreading in the Old World, where the cult of the dead would seem more deeply rooted.

During the last ten years in American publications an increasing number of sociologists and psychologists have been studying the conditions of death in contemporary society and especially in hospitals. . . . [T]he authors have been struck by the manner of dying, by the inhumanity, the cruelty of solitary death in hospitals and in a society where death has lost the prominent place which custom had granted it over the millennia, a society where the interdiction of death paralyzes and inhibits the reactions of the medical staff and family involved. These publications are also preoccupied with the fact that death has become the object of a voluntary decision by the doctors and the family, a decision which today is made shamefacedly, clandestinely. And this para-medical literature, for which, as far as

I know, there is no equivalent in Europe, is bringing death back into the dialogue from which it had been excluded. Death is once again becoming something one can talk about. Thus the interdict is threatened, but only in the place where it was born and where it encountered limitations. Elsewhere, in the other industrialized societies, it is maintaining or extending its empire. . . .

MAKING CONNECTIONS: DISEASE AND DEATH

1. Ariès's discussion of forbidden death is more theoretical than the selections concerning death by McManners and Evans in Parts One and Two. Ariès asserts that only in the twentieth century has the discussion of death become forbidden, and death pornographic and impersonal. Ariès maintains that the topic of death (unlike that of sex) previously had been discussed openly and that the dying ended their days publicly, with friends and family in attendance. Do McManners's discussion of "death's arbitrary empire" and Evans's explanation of the challenge of cholera in eighteenth-century Hamburg support Ariès's claims? Give evidence to support your view.

2. During the past three centuries, what role have technology, physicians and hospitals, and the state played in regard to the way people cope with their own and others' deaths? How have funerals and the rituals surrounding death changed to reflect societies' changing attitudes toward death?

PACKAGING PLEASURES:
CLUB MÉDITERANÉE AND FRENCH
CONSUMER CULTURE, 1950–1968
Ellen Furlough

In the generations following World War II, Western societies, benefiting from improved technologies, increasing prosperity, and relative international peace, have given more attention and monies to leisure time than ever before. In a seemingly relentless pursuit of pleasure outside of work, people have flocked to new organizations and businesses that purport to convert spare time into happiness.

Ellen Furlough, who teaches at Kenyon College, examines how one such business, Club Med, aimed to provide an "antidote to civilization" for French people. Using Club Med's own publications as well as other contemporary works, Furlough notes the paradoxes she sees in Club Med's endeavor to furnish an escape from modern consumer society. What does she see as the social appeal of Club Med?

What were the Club Med "formula" and the "Club spirit"? What were the living conditions and the atmosphere at Club Med vacation spots? Certainly, the Polynesian and Tahitian themes affected the dress, behavior, and goals of the vacationers. What were the roles of the "congenial organizers," the GOs, and why did Club Med permit them to fraternize with the "congenial members," the GMs? What rituals did the villages perform, and how did those rituals function to close the GMs off from the outside world? One wonders whether the GMs discovered their natural selves.

Club Med emphasized social and behavioral roles in leisure activities that it believed to be antithetical to everyday French society. Furlough describes some interesting examples of such role-playing. There was a major emphasis on beautiful, naturally enhanced bodies, proudly adorned, and quintessentially erotic, and on exercise and hearty eating. The stress on comeliness and forthright sexuality represented a reaction to French civilization.

Ellen Furlough, "Packaging Pleasures: Club Méditerranée and French Consumer Culture, 1950–1968," *French Historical Studies* 18, no. 1 (spring 1993): 65–81.

The author sees incongruities in Club Med's strategies and does not believe that it was successful in providing an escape from consumer society. Some types of people took Club Med vacations and other social groups resisted the alluring appeal of Club Med's paradise vacations. Did the Club Med program bear a relationship to Western imperialism and colonization? Perhaps the little Gardens of Eden the Club intended to establish were doomed to be pale reflections of certain aspects of the dominant French culture.

In the midst of the French revolution of May 1968, a crowd of student radicals targeted and shattered the glass windows of the Parisian headquarters of Club Méditerranée. Club Med epitomized all they rejected about French consumer society — huge meals, idle bronzed bodies, abundance in the midst of underdeveloped countries, and a commitment to narcissistic, apolitical hedonism. Club Med officials responded by offering some of the students free visits to Club Med vacation villages, insisting that the students would realize that Club Med was an "antidote to civilization," set apart from the values and experiences of French consumer culture.

The students' critique and Club Med's response raise the question that I will address in this article: to what extent was it possible for Club Med to be an "antidote to civilization" and to what extent was its representation in those terms the key to its consumer appeal? I will argue that Club Med was not an antithesis to "civilization"; rather, Club Med was central to and indeed helped to construct French consumer culture and consumer capitalism — the very "civilization" that it claimed to counteract. A second and related concern will be to explore the social bases for Club Med's appeal. Here I will argue that Club Med's "formula" expressed, and helped consolidate, the orienting practices, attitudes, and values of the "new" French middle class during what has been termed the "postwar regime of accumulation."

Gérard Blitz founded Club Med in the spring of 1950. Blitz had grown up in Belgium, where his father was a socialist Jewish diamond cutter with a passion for, what was called at the time, "physical culture." In 1945 the Belgian government offered Gérard Blitz, who was with the Belgian intelligence service during the war, the job of operating a center for the rehabilitation of concentration-camp survivors. Blitz spent the immediate postwar years thus engaged at a hotel in the Haute-Savoie region of France. Meanwhile, his sister Didy and his father operated a vacation club for people who shared a love of sports and a desire to break with wartime memories. As Didy later recalled, people "wanted to live/be alive after those dark times." While visiting this club, Blitz was struck by the similarities with his project in the Haute-Savoie and by the recuperative power of relaxation, play, and the sun. Unlike previous tourist enterprises which stressed moral self-improvement, education, public service, health and fitness, Blitz stressed self-indulgent physical pleasure and a break from habitual social relations. The goal was to remake the self, an especially appealing ethos for people who had lived through the sacrifices and bodily harms of the war.

On 27 April 1950, Blitz deposited the statutes for "Club Méditerranée" and placed a modest notice in the Paris metro showing the sun, the sea, and his telephone number. In the summer of 1950, some twenty-five hundred people spent two weeks at his first Club Med village, situated on the Bay of Alcudia on the Spanish island of Majorca. Socially, most in this first group were urban and middle class — primarily students and young cadres; others were secretaries, lawyers, and doctors. They hailed primarily from France and Belgium, but also from Holland, England, Switzerland, Norway, and Denmark. There was not a single building; people lived in U.S. Army surplus tents and slept on allied army cots. Blitz provided a small orchestra and sports equipment and presided with his wife Claudine, who had lived in Tahiti and regularly dressed in a Polynesian sarong. People swam, played sports, ate at tables for eight, and were entertained at night by flamenco dancers. Yet, after various troubles, including a hurricane, people demanded their money back. Blitz averted disaster by addressing the assembled guests as *gentils membres* (congenial members, hereafter GMs) and guaranteeing satisfaction or money back. Apparently, most were satisfied in the end. At regular reunions in Paris, GMs shared summer photos and danced in grass skirts and bathing suits until dawn. They also received copies of the Club's bulletin, the *Trident,* which contained news of the Club's off-season activities and of marriages and births of new GMs (children of members were, for a while in the 1950s, given free memberships), and which served as a kind of "wish book" for the upcoming summer activities. Club Med villages proliferated.

What Club Med administrators, managers, employees (*gentils organisateurs* or congenial organizers, hereafter GOs), and the GMs would soon label the *esprit du Club*[1] was being created, and it was this "esprit" that served as the basis for the Club's self-representation as an "antidote to civilization." The crucial element of this "esprit" was that it was to be diametrically different from everyday life and provide "mental and physical detoxification." Villages were seen as "closed" spaces, isolated from their surroundings and from other tourists, places where people could "rediscover the needs that urban reality repressed." The indigenous society was portrayed as a perturbation or perhaps a curiosity that one might visit later on an organized excursion. Inside, the village represented personalized and more intimate relations, intensity of life, liberty of choice, a place where people would be limited only by their capacities. Closure within the villages was not seen as a limit, but a condition of liberty. Within the villages was thus to be realized the utopian society of abundance and ease, and the operative logic inside the villages was to each his or her desires.

By the early 1950s the explicit model for this "counter-society" was a mythologized Polynesia, and this "Polynesian" theme informed the rhetoric and practices

---

[1] Club spirit.

of the Club. There were poems in the *Trident* about how the GMs, or "Polyne-sians," dreamed of "the arch of the beach, the Polynesian huts under the palms, and dug-out canoes, men pushing their canoe into the foam of the surf, chasing young girls wearing flowers, and fishing all day." As the army surplus tents began wearing out, they were replaced by Polynesian huts, and the costume of choice at Club Med villages became the flowered Tahitian sarong. Worn by both women and men, the sarong signified the "liberated" body and nativism, and the *Trident* obligingly provided full-page illustrations on the various ways to tie one (using "Tahitian-looking" models). By 1953 Claudine Blitz arranged for groups of Tahi-tian students from Paris to introduce GMs at the village on Corfu to Tahitian music and dances. Then, in 1955, Club Med established a village on Tahiti and advertised it as a "pilgrimage to the source . . . an earthly paradise." Here Club Med constructed an alternative landscape for French people confronting the im-plications of military defeats along with an emerging technocratic order. Repre-sentations of the "Primitive" can offer "a model of alternative social organization in which psychological integrity is a birthright, rooted in one's body and sexual-ity, and in which a full range of ambivalences and doubts can be confronted and defused through the culture's rituals, customs, and play."

Because villages were to be distinct from everyday life, there evolved elabo-rate welcoming and leaving rituals so that people would both symbolically and physically enter and leave its "closed" world. For example, GOs in sarongs greeted new arrivals with a trumpet fanfare and placed flowers around their necks. Once inside the village, physical accommodations and social activities were calculated to remind GMs that they had entered a space devoted to a "total rupture with daily habits, a period of return to the forgotten rhythms of nature." The architecture, whether the tents of the early 1950s, "Polynesian" huts from the mid-50s, or the later buildings built in "local styles," emphasized its opposition to urbanism and materialism and its connection to "nature."

More important, however, was the stated objective of erasing social barriers and distinctions. This process entailed abolishing the most visible signs of social distinction, in essence peeling away social conventions to reveal people's "au-thentic" selves. It was the convention in all villages for people to address each other in the familiar "tu"[2] form and to call each other by their first names. All dis-cussions about one's occupation within "civilization" were discouraged. One of the "rules of the game" most closely attended to was a different mode of dress. Spend-ing several weeks wearing bikinis and sarongs was seen as a "rupture with daily life," and one of the most common phrases heard in a village was that "there are no social differences when everyone is in a bathing suit." Another strategy that Club executives argued muted external signs of status was the practice of replac-ing cash with colored beads. In order to have a drink at the bar, for example, peo-

---

[2] "You."

ple detached some of the colored beads that they wore around their necks or ankles. A journalist joked, "It's so hard to carry real money in sarongs." The *Trident* called this the "disappearance of money," a revealing formulation that acknowledges the way this practice rendered invisible the cash nexus of the enterprise.

Another area in which Club Med positioned itself as different from "civilization" was in its emphasis on play rather than work. Even the labor of the GOs was constructed so that they would not appear to be working. A Club Med village was instead said to be a "leisure society" wherein people would rediscover their natural selves, rhythms, and desires. Sports and ludic activities were uppermost in Club Med's definition of leisure. Every village had a wide range of available sports, and there were often lessons from Olympic champions. Opportunities for play in the villages were also to be found in the nightly "animations." A favorite prank was to have a male GM lie on the floor as a squalling baby. A woman GM would change his diapers and powder his fly. The ability to participate in such playful, one might say ridiculous, activities was to demonstrate not only one's willingness to change the rules, but the ability to refuse superiority, rediscover childhood playfulness, and demonstrate that seriousness was a convention of another time and place. Ridicule was cast as a form of relaxation.

Club Med vacations were also characterized by ease rather than effort. Unlike most forms of tourism, Club Med advertising assured people that everything would be taken care of. It emphasized the convenience of the single-price format, the ease of comfortable transport, and the generally well organized nature of villages run by "specialists." Although everything was foreseen, little within the village was programmed; people could choose whether or not to participate in the village's activities. Time was to become "indefinite." Club literature deployed a language of individual choice, insisting that "how you fill your time is your business."

The result of the village's closed and controlled environment and its available experiences was to be the physical and mental well-being of the individual body. Club Med was ultimately packaging the care of the self and its recuperation through play, relaxation, and pleasure. Physical health and physical beauty were central to this vision. Outward appearance was the mark of one's personality, discipline, and inner essence. These corporeal preoccupations were shot through all aspects of Club Med, and I will only mention four aspects here. First, the Club's press constantly created a discourse of bodily description, in essence creating images of ideal — and ultimately normative — physical shapes. Club literature routinely published pictures of the managers of villages and described their bodies. And, because most managers were male, this particular discourse constructed ideal masculine bodies. Here is one description: "André Baheux, 41 years old, . . . height 1 m77, weight 60kg, spread . . . 1 m80; biceps, thighs, and calves fully formed."

A second ongoing theme concerned the making of beautiful bodies. Club literature constantly emphasized that "thanks to the numerous physical activities that we offer, you will refind, at whatever age, your shapely figure." Exercise was the dominant issue here — there was no mention of dieting. Although there were

some discussions of women's bodies and exercise, the creation of beautiful feminine bodies tended to be portrayed in terms of various means of adornment that
were not unlike similar discussions within other aspects of French consumer culture. There were articles in the *Trident* on "How to be Beautiful in the Village" with
advice about appropriate fashions and makeup. Club Med publications encouraged women to bring beauty products with them — suntan lotion, hand cream,
deodorant, indelible eye makeup, and cream to protect the skin and brown it
lightly while waiting for a tan. Women's "natural" beauty was to be enhanced
with beauty products and proper clothing.

A third kind of discussion about the body was overtly narcissistic and self-
congratulatory. A striking example of this was the poem "Creed" published in the
Trident in 1952. The poem has four stanzas, and the first three begin: "I love my
arms," "I love my legs," and "I love my torso." These are followed by paeans to the
body part in question, for example within the "I love my arms" stanza: "rippling
deltoids, . . . flesh furrowed with veins which swell forth during vigorous play."
The final stanza reads:

> I love my body where so many forces rest in order to rise up at my command. /
> I love its colors and I love its shapes as eternal things. / I love the "gay science"[3]
> as I love healthy life. / I love to train as I love to study. / I love competitions as I
> love books. / I love races as I love my poems. / I love joy as one loves a friend. /
> I love struggle as one loves a woman. / I love all that which is Effort and Life. / I
> love my body as my soul. /

And a final theme, more muted in the printed literature but central to all the
others, was that of the erotic/libidinal body. An erotically charged climate was central to the "pleasures" that Club Med promised. The sexuality valorized at Club
Med was predominately heterosexual, casual, spontaneous, and blurred the edges
of definitions of propriety. One could, in this sense, speak of Club Med as a site
for performing an expanded repertoire of sexualities and playful (and perhaps
even transgressive) desires. For women, this could at once defy . . . the "highly
rigid regulatory frame" of gender and sexuality and remind them of the risks involved in an era when both birth control and abortion were illegal in France.[4]
Whether one chooses to interpret this erotically charged climate as "liberating" or
not, it is certain that for people at the time, a Club Med vacation signified a loos-
ening of the rules regarding sexuality. Club Med villages came to have a reputation as places with "an erotic morality" involving many "brief encounters," despite
Blitz's insistence that there was "no more and no less libertinage than on any
other kind of seaside holiday." Though unmarried GMs were housed in single-sex

---

[3] Ellen Furlough states that the subtext of the penis is obvious here and that the phrase "gay science," difficult to translate, probably refers to the German philosopher Friedrich Nietzsche's
(1844–1900) *The Gay Science.*

[4] In 1967 the Neuwirth Law authorized the sale of contraceptives, and in 1974 the law forbidding abortions was repealed. (Author's note.)

arrangements, Club conventions were that a towel folded over the outside door meant "do not disturb." A male GO boasted: "I knew the taste of all the suntan oil in the village." These four discussions were not distinct, but formed a discursive web that placed the beautiful, healthy body at its center. As the village manager in Tahiti, which had the reputation of being the village with the most emphasis on physical beauty and "liberated" sexuality, asserted: "the Club was the revenge of the beautiful on the intelligent."

Despite the Club's self-representation as the "antidote to civilization," Club Med was squarely within, and constitutive of, French consumer culture and consumer capitalism. This is not to say, however, that Club Med's self-representation as the "antidote to civilization" was a kind of false advertising, but rather that the seeming contradiction between Club Med's self-representation and its realization were part of its essence and indeed crucial for its success.

Club Med's ethos as an isolated and recuperative Eden was as carefully packaged as any other consumer commodity. Club Med was, and is, a large, multinational corporation and an important player in the tourism and leisure industry. Like other institutions that construct sites for consumption, Club Med created integrated environments promising predictable pleasures. Although Club Med was originally founded in 1950 as a nonprofit association, in 1957 it was legally reconstituted as a commercial organization. . . . From the early 1960s, a significant proportion of Club Med was owned by the Rothschild bank, and its business decisions were within an economic logic that was not unlike any other consumer industry. By 1958 Club Med's business strategies were increasingly under the purview of Gilbert Trigano, a former communist who had become involved with Club Med through his family's camping supply business. After joining the Club in 1954 and moving rapidly up its hierarchy, Trigano decided that the Club needed to move into "mass" tourism, sharpen its business aspects, and attend to such issues as market segmentation. Plans for and decisions about villages were, like any other consumer commodity's design and execution, created in Parisian corporate offices and replicated in selected environments. By 1967 the club operated 31 villages in Europe and did about 20 million dollars worth of business. It had a rapidly expanding membership of over four hundred thousand, and there were around two thousand employees at the height of the summer tourist season. The Club was the largest civilian customer of the Italian State Railways and the largest short-haul charterer of Air France planes. Its expansion was further aided in 1968 by an agreement with American Express. This not only provided an important infusion of capital but guaranteed promotion of Club Med's programs throughout American Express's extensive network of travel agencies.

Like other aspects of consumer culture, and despite the Club's rhetoric, the villages were not utopian worlds without social hierarchies. In the 1950s and 1960s, Club Med was an experience constructed by and for white, economically advantaged Europeans, and later for Americans. There was no "class erosion" at work, although there may have been some mild shaking up of conventions. GMs were young (67 percent under 30 in 1961), and the largest group was drawn from middle-class salaried sectors. The largest proportions were teachers, secretaries (predominantly women), and technicians, but GMs also included cadres, people from the liberal professions (mainly doctors) and commerce, students, and a small group of workers (mostly from the relatively well-paid trades of metallurgy and printing).

The social composition of Club Med consumers drew heavily from the social group that Pierre Bourdieu[5] and others have termed the "new middle class," a group seen as a "new petit bourgeoisie"[6] of service people and technicians and the "new bourgeoisie" of cadres and "dynamic executives." It was the ethos of this new middle class that provided a template for the "esprit" of Club Med. Bourdieu argues that the "new" or renovated bourgeoisie and the "new" petit bourgeoisie "collaborated enthusiastically in imposing the new ethical norms (especially as regards consumption) and the corresponding needs." He points especially to new notions of pleasure and new perceptions of the body. In a passage strikingly similar to the ethos of Club Med, Bourdieu states that these new formulations of pleasure and the body

> make it a failure, a threat to self-esteem, not to "have fun," . . . pleasure is not only permitted but demanded. . . . The fear of not getting enough pleasure, the logical outcome of the effort to overcome the fear of pleasure, is combined with the search for self-expression and "bodily expression" and for communication with others (relating — échange), even immersion in others (considered not as a group but as subjectivities in search of their identity); and the old personal ethic is thus rejected for a cult of personal health and psychological therapy.

He adds that this group's conception of bodily exercise aimed "to substitute relaxation for tension, pleasure for effort, 'creativity' and 'freedom' for discipline, communication for solitude." It worked toward a "a body which has to be 'unknotted,' liberated, or more simply rediscovered and accepted." In Luc Boltanski's[7] analysis of the "cadres" (a group he argues typified the new middle class), he agrees that there was a strong link between the formation and consolidation of this new middle class and a new "lifestyle." Boltanski characterizes this lifestyle as an "easy-going American style simplicity, . . . a new, relaxed way of being bourgeois, a new way of life, . . . and a new system of values." Among those values was a "cult of the waistline and devotion to the physique." I am not arguing here that Club Med was reducible to a class phenomenon, but rather that it provided an ideal space to act out this new culture and thereby contributed to its formation. This was, in short, space for redrawing social and cultural boundaries and hierarchies rather than abolishing them. Despite such stories as the one involving GMs who struck up a friendship only to discover later that one of them was a director and the other a nightwatchman at the same factory, Club Med instead offered and

[5] French social theorist (b. 1930).

[6] The lower-middle class.

[7] Author of *The Making of a Class: Cadres in French Society.*

helped consolidate another kind of cultural capital to be traded as a shared experience among privileged vacationers.

Club Med also reinforced, and in some cases reinvented, social hierarchies and boundaries between people in the villages and in host countries. Club executives saw the geographical locations for Club Med villages as culinary resources and inspirational guides for ersatz architecture (that is, "Moorish bungalows in Morocco"), populated by people who were potentially objects for the excursions and the "tourist gaze." Club Med was, in this sense, a reconfigured colonialist adventure that could be purchased. In this period of French decolonization, Club Med vacationers could continue to partake of colonialist "exoticism" even if their country no longer controlled the region politically. One journalist who went to a Club Med village in Morocco in the mid-1960s observed an excursion to "the Club's own Moroccan village." He delineated the "modern" playful vacationers from the "natives" by describing the way the Club's beach property was carefully roped off; while the Club's vacationers were cavorting on the beach and working to tan their white bikini-clad bodies, Moroccans guarding the areas "spent most of their time inside straw beehives, in which they avoid the sun that the members have come so far to find." Like other aspects of consumer society, Club Med created and sustained hierarchies privileging those who were economically advantaged, physically vigorous, "attractive," and "modern."

Club Med's claim to be an "antidote to civilization," devoid of work, preoccupations with time, seriousness, or effort can also be seen as reinforcing the very issues from which it claimed to be separate. For example, for its employees, the villages were hardly leaving behind "work"; rather, their work environments were at the forefront of the growth and proliferation of consumer service industries where . . . "the social composition of . . . those who are serving in the front line, may be a part of what is in fact 'sold' to the customer." . . . Such services "require what can loosely be called 'emotional work' such as smiling and making people feel comfortable." This can be seen as a proliferation of "feminized" work, whether women do the majority of this labor or not, and it will tend to be low paid — a characteristic aspect of the salaries of GOs. The fantasy that Club Med was creating was one where workers did not really work and where "natives" were not really oppressed — a fantasy that masked and thus helped perpetuate power relationships. Further, to "experience" the loss of a mentality of time, seriousness, and effort means one must experience their ongoing realization "outside" the vacation experience. In other words, one kind of experience (vacations) depends on and helps perpetuate its supposed opposite (everyday life).

Another way that Club Med was constructing aspects of the "civilization" that it supposedly repudiated was that its "naturalness" always depended on certain material props. Consumers bought vacations at villages containing hair salons, sophisticated sports equipment, and stores on the premises. Not only was "materialism" never absent, but Club Med fostered a key element of tourist culture — that of the souvenir. Club Med villages regularly scheduled shopping expeditions to local markets. There one could buy souvenirs — material witnesses to the commercialized "experience" of a Club Med vacation. One's transformed body could also be seen as a souvenir — returning from vacation with a tan, for example, signified physical beauty, eroticism, and a "successful" vacation.

The materialism and the consumerist theme of abundance was especially evident regarding food, an element that figured prominently in the ambiance and imaginary of the Club. Food and wine in the villages were unlimited and included in the basic cost, and both were universally said to be excellent. Club Med also fostered materialist consumer culture in the realm of clothing. From 1959, it had its own mail-order catalogue uniquely for GMs who were registered for a village for the next summer. Tahitian sarongs figured prominently in the selection.

Finally, the Club was also involved in constructing a cultural pastiche that placed it squarely within, and helped to create, other aspects of consumer (and postmodernist) culture. Not only did Club Med evoke the "natural" in the midst of a carefully packaged environment, but cultural productions were carefully utilized to create an ambiance mixing elements of "high" and "mass" culture. For example, in 1963 Club Med introduced "The Forum" into its villages. These were cast as "occasions to follow a spectacle, to participate in it, to discuss, to understand the givens of new problems, . . . to make vacations not only a rest for the nerves and the body but also an enrichment of the spirit and of the imagination." Forum discussions included Hellenism, Italian geniuses of the Quattrocento,[8] heart surgery, and the mysteries of the universe. From the mid-1960s, there were taped concerts of classical music that included a commentary in French so "no one need wonder what to think of the music." (Here again we can see Club Med attending to cultural capital.) The Club's ambiance also incorporated aspects of popular culture. One account of a British woman's journey to Club Med noted that on the journey they "twisted into the early hours of the morning." At one village, a participant described lazing in the sun next to the bar, where "the hi-fi pipes out Jacques Brel[9] and Pete Seeger."[10] Like advertising, which is, of course, another constituent element of consumer culture, Club Med promoted a "pastiche or collage effect in which the breadth and depth of cultural values can be ransacked to achieve a desired effect."

In conclusion, Club Med emerged at a particularly promising historical moment. Culturally . . . even if the reality for French people of the 1960s was more nuanced, by the late 1960s "the imaginary had changed: consumer society was in people's heads." . . . This consumer society had its symbols (the TV, the auto, the washing machine), its privileged moments (prime time, the weekend, vacations), and its recognized places (the salon, the supermarket, beach, or camping). It fostered values of abundance, comfort, and youth, and an ideology of individual choice. Club Med was all of these things, a symbol, a place, and a set of values, and its meanings were those of the larger consumer society of which it was a part.

---

[8] Fifteenth century.

[9] Belgian singer and composer (1929–1978).

[10] American folk singer and composer (b. 1919).

A central tenet of Club Med was that it proclaimed the body as a vehicle for pleasure. Club Med celebrated, permitted, promoted, and commodified, the fitness, beauty, energy, and health of the libidinal "natural" body. Club Med participants were to pay, in all senses, attention to the self, and part of the grammar of pleasure that Club Med helped create was a heightened concern with the "care of the self." One's body, in essence, was one's text to be endowed with meaning. Crucial to this project was (and is) the endless longing and impossibility of attaining and retaining a youthful, healthy, playful, sexy body. One could, by definition, never be satisfied. What is particularly interesting about Club Med was the way this dynamic interplay between longing and lacking was initially played out within an inventive cultural landscape laced with the "primitive" Polynesian. Here we can read the longing for a culture where one could be at one with nature and find sexual pleasure along with mental and physical health, . . . using the primitive within a "rhetoric of desire." And yet, Club Med fostered the notion that people could count on having easy access to a beauty parlor, mixed drinks, and piped music. Here again we see the ways in which Club Med's utilization of what might seem to be contradictory messages and strategies was indeed crucial for its success.

This raises questions about the relationship between the social management of pleasure for profit and the consumers themselves. Is this yet another instance of a Foucaultian[11] institution controlling and regulating a set of disciplines on the individual body? Or, do we need to analyze Club Med in terms of the ways in which people understood, enjoyed, created, and perhaps subverted those "experiences"? How can we understand and theorize the historical roles and experiences of pleasure as they adhere to consumption, and how do we differentiate . . . between "real pleasure and mere diversion"? Although answering these questions is beyond the scope of this article, it is certain that the "care of the self" was closely aligned with consumer culture's message of individualist self-determination and expression. The language of the self and of individual pleasure was crucial for the cultural consolidation of a new middle class, and it obviated a language of class linked to an oppositional spirit or an ongoing political struggle. The notion of the "new middle class" was itself politically important in the 1950s and 1960s, a time heralded by some as a new social order whose social center of gravity would be the middle class. This new middle class was portrayed as "a vast group of people leading comfortable lives, sharing similar values, and employed by large organizations — individualists governed by the competitive spirit and the drive to achieve." . . . [T]he new class would support the "end of ideology" and "alleviate class tensions" through a "more equitable distribution of consumer goods and education." Bourdieu offers another way to look at this group's "new ethic of liberation" — it could supply the economy with "the perfect consumers" who were

---

[11] Referring to the philosopher-historian Michel Foucault (1926–1984) who saw institutions such as the prison and the asylum as modern developments whose functions were to discipline and punish.

"isolated . . . and therefore free (or forced) to confront in extended order the separate markets . . . of the new economic order . . . untrammelled by the constraints
and brakes imposed by collective memories and expectations."

Club Med in particular, and tourism in general, were at the forefront of con-
sumerism's culture of distraction, fantasy, and desire. Club Med accented, packaged, and marketed key components of an emergent consumer culture: a rhetoric
of longing and desire, the elevation of the autonomous, healthy and pleasurable
body, a (post) modern reliance on pastiche, and a belief in (and commodification
of) the recuperative necessity of non-workplace touristic "experiences." Modern
"mass" tourism has been a crucial engine — both culturally and economically —
for modern consumer societies. While one could argue that both Club Med and
French students of 1968 were questioning disciplinary boundaries and structures, it can also be argued that to accept and experience the values, definitions,
and "pleasures" that Club Med offered was to believe that the system of consumer
capitalism giving rise to Club Med worked.

MAKING CONNECTIONS: WORK

1. In Part One, Olwen Hufton elucidates an eighteenth-century world where working
   women seemed to have little leisure time and little wealth, unable to think beyond saving for marriage or working to help the family survive. In Part Two, Theresa McBride
   describes the monotonous world of female store clerks who did, however, have time
   set aside for leisure and who helped to usher in the modern consumer culture. Ellen
   Furlough depicts what we might consider the epitome of consumer culture, the world
   of Club Med, whose goal was to jet men and women away from the humdrum work
   environment to a fantasy world of copious food, sex, and relaxation. What different
   attitudes toward work do you see when comparing the articles by Hufton, McBride,
   and Furlough? Compare as well any different attitudes toward women described in
   these articles. How has work itself changed in the last three centuries? Do you think
   the Club Med program helped women in ways that eighteenth-century Europe and the
   nineteenth-century department store could not and did not?

2. Club Med intended to provide happiness through escape. To what extent did it succeed? Have the possibility of adult Disney Worlds (such as Club Med and Las Vegas),
   welfare systems, and the lure of early retirement signaled the demise of a working culture, where people throughout the history of Western civilization had expected to
   work from an early age to as long as they were physically able to do so? The contemporary West holds that workers can look forward to purposeful leisure served by
   specific businesses and industries and to retirement upon completion of their working lives. What indication is there in Hufton's essay that female workers could not retire? How does McBride show that leisure and retirement were possible for female department store clerks? The modern welfare system — Social Security, pension plans,
   and health insurance — has enabled many workers to free themselves from the
   chronic insecurity that Hufton describes. At the same time, leisure industries exem-
   plified by Club Med have accustomed workers to expect more from life than hard
   work, drudgery, and a hand-to-mouth existence. To what extent has leisure rather
   than work become a preoccupation in the twentieth century?

THE RISE AND FALL OF THE
SWEDISH MODEL
Kristina Orfali

In the years since World War II, many have viewed Sweden as a paradise, a culture worthy of emulation and envy, because of its open, progressive society and its concern for the welfare of all its citizens. With the demise of the Soviet Union — which had before provided a model society for Eastern European states, for some individuals and political parties in the West, and certainly for many Third World countries — Sweden may now provide the only viable alternative to the creeping Americanization of Europe.

A sociologist at a research institute in Paris devoted to the study of the social sciences, Kristina Orfali relies on newspapers, magazines, books, and government documents to present a nuanced overview of Swedish society. She points out that Sweden has been at the forefront of progressive legislation. What are the goals of Swedish legislation? What does Orfali mean by the "antisecrecy model"? To what extent are children, minorities, and immigrants better off in the Swedish system?

Sweden has a reputation for being open sexually. How have changing mores as well as laws affected marital relations, homosexual culture, prostitution, and the distribution of sexually explicit materials?

Free access to official documents, the computerization of society, collective decision making, and the right of the state to intervene in family life (to prevent corporal punishment, for example) have made Swedish society open and transparent. Where then do Swedes find privacy? What tensions exist between communitarian impulses and individualism? Orfali makes clear that Swedish society is less than perfect, even if it is admired; problems still exist in spite of Swedish social engineering.

Kristina Orfali, "The Rise and Fall of the Swedish Model" in *A History of Private Life,* vol. 5, ed. Philippe Ariès and Georges Duby, trans. Arthur Goldhammer (Cambridge: Belknap Press of Harvard University Press, 1991), 417–449.

Sweden is a country that has long fascinated many parts of the world. In the 1960s a whole generation grew up on clichés of blondness and liberation, on fantasies of a sexual El Dorado filled with shapely Ekbergs[1] and sirenic Garbos[2] — but also with Bergman's[3] anguished heroines. Little by little, however, this fantasy-land metamorphosed into a dark country inhabited by bores, morbid minds, and would-be suicides, a nation of "disintegrated families," "disoriented sex," and "liberated lovers in search of love" — in short, a "paradise lost." The Swedish ideal, once the object of extravagant praise and extravagant denunciation, ultimately was converted into a hyperborean[4] mirage. The idyll was gone. The welfare state, recast in the role of meddling nuisance, no longer was a country to be imitated. Yesterday's middle way (between communism and capitalism) had become a utopian dream. Today it is fashionable on the part of many people to denounce Sweden as a "benign dictatorship" or "kid-glove totalitarianism."

There is nothing fortuitous about either the initial enthusiasm or the subsequent disillusionment. The Swedish model — in part economic and political but primarily societal — did indeed exist (and to some extent still does). The very word *model* (not, it is worth noting, of Swedish coinage) is revealing. People are apt to speak of the "Americanization of a society," of the "American myth" (that "everyone can become rich"), or even of "American values," but when they speak of a Swedish model they conjure up the image of an exemplary society. Swedish society is endowed not just with material or political content but with philosophical or even moral significance, with "the good life." As long ago as 1950 Emmanuel Mounier[5] asked himself, "What is a happy man?" The Swedes, he answered, "were the first to have known the happy city."

More than may meet the eye the Swedish model is a model of social ethics. Insofar as Sweden is a nation above suspicion, a nation that aspires to universality (in the form of pacifism, aid to the Third World, social solidarity, and respect for the rights of man), and a nation whose ideological underpinnings are consensus and transparency, it can perhaps be seen as the forerunner of a new social order. In this respect the distinction between public and private in Sweden is highly significant. Hostility to secrecy, deprivatization, public administration of the private sphere — in all these areas Sweden has shifted the boundary between public and private in noteworthy ways. But the ethos of absolute transparency in social relations and the ideal of perfect communication, both characteristic of Swedish society, are seen in many parts of today's world as violations of individ-

---

[1] Anita Ekberg, Swedish film actress (b. 1931).

[2] Greta Garbo (1905–1990), Swedish film actress, noted for her beauty and her passion for privacy.

[3] Ingmar Bergman (b. 1918), Swedish film director, famous for his complex depiction of morality and faith.

[4] The extreme north of the earth.

[5] French philosopher (1905–1950).

ual privacy. The antisecrecy model has come to be seen as an intolerable form of imperialism.

The antisecrecy model affects all areas of social life down to the most private. In Sweden, perhaps more than anywhere else, the private is exposed to public scrutiny. The communitarian, social-democratic ethos involves an obsession with achieving total transparency in all social relations and all aspects of social life.

In Sweden money is not a confidential matter. Just as in the United States, material success is highly valued and ostentatiously exhibited. Transparency does not end there. Tax returns are public documents. Anyone can consult the *taxering kalender,* a document published annually by the finance ministry that lists the name, address, date of birth, and declared annual income of each taxpayer. Turning in tax cheats is virtually an institutionalized practice. While the fiscal authorities state publicly (in the press, for example) that informing on cheats is morally reprehensible, they admit that such information is frequently used. Even in the ethical sphere the imperative of transparency takes precedence.

Another illustration of the imperative is the principle of "free access to official documents" *(Offentlighets Principen).* Under the free-access law, which derives in large part from a 1766 law on freedom of the press, every citizen has the right to examine official documents, including all documents received, drafted, or dispatched by any agency of local or national government. The law allows for examination of documents in government offices as well as for having copies made or ordering official copies from the agency in return for payment of a fee. Any person denied access to public information may immediately file a claim with the courts. In practice the right of access is limited by the provisions of the secrecy act, which excludes documents in certain sensitive areas such as national security, defense, and confidential economic information. Nevertheless, the rule is that "when in doubt, the general principle [of free access] should prevail over secrecy."

As a result of the free-access principle the Swedish bureaucracy has been exceptionally open. For a long time Sweden has been an "information society," one in which information circulates freely. Computerization has accentuated this characteristic by facilitating the exchange of large quantities of information, in particular between the private sector and government agencies. There are few other countries in which the computers of several insurance companies are closely linked to those of the vital records office. Private automobile dealers may be electronically linked to vehicle registration records; a state agency may make use of a private company's credit records. Since 1974 information stored in computers has been treated just like other public documents and thus made subject to free access.

Sweden was the first European country to establish a central Bureau of Statistics (in 1756). It was also the first to issue citizen identification numbers. Comparison of different databases has been facilitated by this assignment of a personal identification number to each citizen. The practice was begun in 1946, and the numbers were used by state agencies before being incorporated into electronic databases. They are now widely used in public and private records.

If computers make individuals transparent to the state, the machines themselves must be made transparent to individuals. The computer security act of
1973 (amended in 1982) was the first of its kind in the West. It established the
office of Inspector General for Computing Machinery with the authority to grant
authorization to establish a database, to monitor the use of databases, and to act
on complaints relative to such use. While authorization to establish a database is
usually a mere formality, it is much more difficult to obtain when the data to be
gathered includes information considered to be "private." Encompassed under this
head are medical and health records, records of official actions by social welfare
agencies, criminal records, military records, and so on. Only government agencies required by law to acquire such information are authorized to maintain these
sensitive files. Finally, any person on whom information is gathered has the right
to obtain, once a year at any time, a transcript of all pertinent information.

Some view this computerization of society as a highly effective, not to say dangerous, instrument of social control. Many foreign observers have seen it as marking an evolution toward a police state in which all aspects of private life, from
health to income to jobs, are subject to shadowy manipulation. Interestingly, computerization has aroused virtually no protest within Sweden. Everyone seems convinced that it will be used only for the citizen's benefit and never to his detriment.
The consensus reveals a deep-seated confidence in the government (or, rather, in
the community as a whole, which is ultimately responsible for control of the
information-gathering apparatus). To Swedes, the whole system — private individuals and government agencies alike — is governed by one collective morality.

We must guard against the simplistic notion that Swedish society is a kind of
Orwellian[6] universe, a world of soulless statistics. Paradoxically, this society of
numbered, catalogued, faceless individuals is also a society of individualized faces.
Every daily newspaper in the country publishes a half-page of photos to mark
readers' birthdays, anniversaries, and deaths. Society notes take up at least a full
page, and the absence of social discrimination is striking. One obituary recounts
the career of a Mr. Andersson, *Verkställande dirktör* (plant manager), while another
is devoted to a Mr. Svensson, *Taxichaufför* (taxi driver). Every birthday — especially the fiftieth, to which great importance is attached — is commonly marked
by several lines in the paper and by time off work. This mixture of a modern, com-
puterized society with still vital ancient customs is a unique aspect of Swedish society.

Transparency is also the rule in collective decisionmaking. The ombudsman
is one Swedish institution that is well-known abroad. The parliamentary ombudsman, oldest of all (dating back to 1809), handles disputes over the boundary between public and private and is especially responsible for protecting the individual's "right to secrecy." He hears complaints, takes action when the law is
violated, and offers advice to government agencies. Less well known, perhaps, but

---

[6] Referring to the totalitarian future described by the English writer George Orwell (1903–1950)
in his novel *1984* (1948).

just as important is the procedure of public investigation. Before any major law is enacted, an investigative committee is appointed to consider pertinent issues. The committee includes representatives of different political parties, important interest groups, and various experts such as economists and sociologists. After hearings, surveys, and perhaps on-the-spot investigation, the committee transmits its report to the legislative department of the relevant ministry, which then makes public recommendations. Any citizen may also submit advice to the ministry. Thus the most "private" subjects such as homosexuality, prostitution, violence, and the like become the focus of major public debates, on an equal footing with such "public" issues as price controls, the regulation of television, the Swedish book of psalms, or the country's energy policy.

This uniquely Swedish procedure plays an important role in the elaboration of policy decisions and in the achievement of consensus. Its existence demonstrates not only how the most apparently "private" subjects are dealt with by institutions but also how individuals can take part in the various phases of the decisionmaking process. Two key ethical imperatives are highlighted: transparency of the decision process and consensus concerning the results.

Many people are unaware that Lutheranism is the state religion of Sweden and that the Lutheran Church is the established church. (Contrast this with Italy, where Catholicism is no longer the established religion.) It was in 1523, at the beginning of the Reformation, that the Lutheran Church began to function as an integral part of the governmental apparatus. The church played an instrumental role in the political unification of Sweden, since participation in religious services was then considered to be a civic obligation. The strength of the bond between church and state is illustrated by the fact that until 1860 Swedes were not permitted to quit the church — and even then they were required to become members of another Christian community. This requirement was not eliminated until 1951. Any child born a citizen of Sweden automatically becomes a member of the Church of Sweden if either its father or its mother is a member. Thus 95 percent of the Swedish population nominally belongs to the official church.

Sweden therefore remains one of the most officially Christian of states, but it is also one of the most secular. The church is controlled by the government, which appoints bishops and some clergymen, fixes their salary, collects religious taxes, and so on. (A citizen who does not belong to the Church of Sweden still must pay at least 30 percent of the religious tax because of the secular services performed by the church.) The church is responsible for recording vital statistics, managing cemeteries, and other public functions. Thus, every Swedish citizen is inscribed on the register of some parish. The pastor who performs religious marriages is also an official of the state, so a religious marriage also serves as a civil marriage.

The institutional character of the Church of Sweden is reflected in public participation in religious ceremonies. Roughly 65 percent of all couples choose to be married in church. More than 80 percent of children are baptized and confirmed in the Lutheran Church. Some members of the official state church also belong to one of the "free," or dissident, Protestant churches that derive from the Lutheran evangelical wing of the religious awakening movement (*Väckelse rörelser*), most active in the early nineteenth century. Taken together, the free churches claim a higher proportion of the religious population in Sweden than in other Scandinavian countries.

Nevertheless, this formal presence of ecclesiastical institutions cannot hide the widespread disaffection with religion among Swedes. Fewer than 20 percent claim to be active churchgoers. In contrast, a tenacious, almost metaphysical anxiety is a profound trait of the Swedish temperament. Swedes may not believe in hell, but they surely believe in the supernatural. To convince oneself of this one need only glance at the half-pagan, half-religious festivals that fill the Swedish calendar or recall the importance of trolls and the fantastic in Swedish literature, folklore, and films. Or consider a writer as profoundly Swedish as Nobel prize winner Pär Lagerkvist, author of *Barabbas* and *The Death of Ahasuerus*, whose work is one long, anguished religious interrogation. André Gide,[7] another tormented conscience, wrote of *Barabbas* that Lagerkvist had pulled off "the tour de force of walking the tightrope across the dark stretch between the real world and the world of faith."

The reconciliation of the real with the spiritual is thus more tenuous than it may first appear. The collective religious morality of the past has been transformed into a new morality, still collective but now secular, while literature and film continue to reflect the spiritual world, the metaphysical anguish and tenacious guilt that have left such a deep imprint on the Swedish imagination.

The degree to which the private sphere is open to the public is clearly visible in the evolution of family structure. There is nothing new about the fact that in a modern state "functions" once left to the family have been taken over by the government or community. In Sweden, however, this deprivatization of the family has taken on a rather specific aspect. The point is not merely to intervene in private life but to make the private sphere totally transparent, to eliminate all secrecy about what goes on there. If, for example, an unwed or divorced mother applies to the government for financial assistance, or if a child is born in circumstances where the paternity is dubious, a thorough investigation is made to identify the father. Any man who, according to the woman or her friends, has had relations with the mother can be summoned to testify. Putative fathers may be required to undergo blood tests. If necessary the courts will decide. Once paternity is established, the father is required to provide for the child's upkeep.

The justification for such a procedure is not so much economic as ethical: every child has a right to know its true father. Clearly, however, acting on such a principle may yield paradoxical results. A single woman who wants to have a child and then raise it alone forfeits her social assistance if she refuses to cooperate with the paternity investigation. Although the 1975 abortion law grants women the right to control their own bodies, they do not have the right "to give birth with-

---

[7] French author (1869–1951) and winner of the Nobel Prize in literature in 1947.

out providing the name of the father." The child's rights take precedence over all others; even if the mother refuses social assistance, all available means (including the courts) will be used to force her to reveal the father's identity, on the grounds that the question is fundamental and that the child will wish to know. In paternity, therefore, there is no secrecy. Kinship is supposed to be transparent and clearly determined. The notion of legitimacy thus sidesteps the family, and the institution of marriage rests on public information, which is guaranteed by law.

Recent Swedish legislation on artificial insemination is also based on the requirement of transparency. Göron Ewerlöf, judge and secretary of the Commission on Artificial Insemination, put it this way: "It is to be hoped that future artificial inseminations will be more candid and open than they have been until now. The objective should be to ensure that birth by insemination is not unthinkable and indeed no more unusual than adoption. In matters of adoption Sweden has long since abandoned secrecy and mystery. According to specialists in adoption, this has helped to make adoptive children happier." Sweden was the first country in the world to adopt a comprehensive law governing artificial insemination (March 1, 1985). Previously, artificial insemination involving a donor had been shrouded as far as possible in secrecy. All information concerning the donor was kept hidden (or destroyed). The chief innovation of the new law — and incidentally an excellent illustration of the antisecrecy model — was to eliminate anonymity for donors. Every child now has the right to know who his biological father is and may even examine all hospital data concerning the individual. (Not even adoptive parents have access to this information.) In the past attention was focused on preventing the child from learning how it was conceived. Today it is the opposite: the primary objective is to protect the child's interest, which means not blocking access to any available information about the identity of its biological father. The commission underscored the importance of a frank and open attitude toward the child on the part of the parents. In particular, it recommended (although the law does not prescribe) that at the appropriate moment parents tell the child how it was conceived. The interest of the child was again invoked to justify the decision not to authorize artificial insemination except for married couples or couples living together as though married. It is not authorized for single women or lesbian couples. Thus the image of the standard family — father, mother, and children — has been maintained, even though the number of single-parent families in Sweden has been on the rise. Various psychological and psychiatric studies were invoked in support of this decision. The primary goal is to ensure the child's optimal development. Adoption laws are even more restrictive, and adoption is limited in most cases to married couples.

The status of the child in Sweden tells us a great deal about Swedish culture and ethics. Children are regarded both as full citizens, and as defenseless individuals to be protected in almost the same manner as other minority groups such as Laplanders and immigrants. The changing status of children is the clearest sign of deprivatization of the family. Since 1973 Sweden has had a children's ombudsman, whose role is to act as a spokesperson for children and to educate the public about children's needs and rights. The ombudsman has no legal authority to intervene in particular cases. He can, however, apply pressure to government agencies and political representatives, suggest ways to improve the condition of children, instruct adults about their responsibilities toward children, and, thanks to a twenty-four-hour telephone hot-line, offer support to individual children in distress. Thus children in Sweden enjoy specific rights and an institution whose purpose is to defend them. The objective is, while respecting the individuality of children, to make sure that they will be integrated as harmoniously as possible into the society.

The same ethic prevails in regard to immigrant children, who are entitled to receive instruction in their native language. Since 1979 the state has allocated funds to provide language lessons for immigrant children of preschool age, and nursery schools increasingly group children by native tongue. Everything possible is done to make sure that immigrant children have the tools they need to learn their mother tongue and preserve their culture by maintaining bilingual competence. Results have not always kept pace with ambitions, however. Many children have a hard time adapting to one culture or the other and a hard time mastering one of the two languages. Integration is envisioned, but respect for the immigrant's native culture is considered imperative.

Immigrants in Sweden enjoy many rights: they can vote in municipal and cantonal elections and are eligible to hold office; they are not confined to ghettos but scattered throughout the society in order to encourage integration; they receive free instruction in Swedish; and they receive the same social benefits as natives. Nevertheless, Sweden has not really been able to achieve a fusion of cultures, a melting pot in the manner of the United States.

The autonomy of the child vis-à-vis familial and parental authority is reflected in the law prohibiting corporal punishment. Since July 1979 the law governing parent-child relations has prohibited all forms of corporal punishment, including spankings, as well as mental cruelty and oppressive treatment. Examples explicitly mentioned in the law include shutting a child in a closet, threatening or frightening, neglect, and overt ridicule. Admittedly, no specific penalties for violation of these provisions have been set, except in cases of physical injury. Nevertheless, any child who is struck may file a complaint, and the person responsible cannot protest that he believed he had the right to administer a spanking. This once private right, covert yet in a sense symbolic of parental authority, no longer exists.

In various ways the political sphere controls more and more of what used to be private space. The family no longer bears exclusive responsibility for the child. The child's rights are determined not by the family but by the entire national community in the form of legal and social protections. The child therefore spends more time outside the private realm and is increasingly socialized outside the family. Parent-child relations are no longer a strictly private matter; they are governed by the public. The society as a whole is responsible for *all* its children.

This way of thinking is illustrated by the so-called parental education reform of 1980. All prospective parents were invited to participate in voluntary discussion and training groups during gestation and the first year after birth. (Those who attended these groups during working hours were entitled to compensation under the parents' insurance program.) The goal of parental training was to "help improve the situation of children and families in the society": "The community and its institutions should not themselves assume responsibility for children but should try instead to give parents the means to do the job." Interestingly, this parental training, usually administered outside the home to groups of parents, was also a way of encouraging group experience, a way of fostering solidarity among individuals faced with similar problems. Individuals were drawn into group activities, and most who began with a prenatal group continued with a postnatal one. The social reforms helped to reinforce the highly communal nature of Swedish society by emphasizing all the ways in which the individual or family cell is integrated into the larger group or society.

Because the Swedish child is considered to be a full citizen, he or she may, at an appropriate age, take legal action to alter unsatisfactory conditions. This principle applies in particular to disputes arising out of divorce. The child may be a party to hearings to determine custody and visiting rights and is entitled to legal representation. Small children may even be represented by a proxy appointed by the court. In case of separation the child may choose which of its parents it wishes to stay with, even contesting the amicable settlement reached by the parents (although visiting rights are not subject to challenge). In short, the child's opinion may be expressed and defended in exactly the same manner as that of any other citizen.

If family life is largely open to public scrutiny, so is the life of the couple. Since 1965 sexual offenses such as marital rape have been subject to criminal prosecution. Since 1981 battered women have not been required to appear in person to accuse their husband or partner; a declaration by a third party is sufficient to initiate proceedings. Of course homosexuality is no longer a crime in Sweden; criminal penalties were abolished as long ago as 1944. In 1970, following a period in which a wave of sexual liberation spread over the country, homosexuals founded the National Organization for Equality of Sexual Rights, or RFSL (Riksförbundet för Sexuellt Likaberättigande).

In 1980 the government conducted a sweeping investigation into the possibility of reforming legislation concerning homosexuals so as to prevent discrimination. The investigative commission not only proposed a series of laws guaranteeing complete equality between heterosexuals and homosexuals but also advocated active support for homosexual culture and organizations. The possibility of institutionalized cohabitation of homosexual couples conferring the same benefits as marriage was also discussed. These proposals stemmed from an official investigative commission.

Paradoxically, the proposal encountered vigorous opposition on the part of certain lesbian groups, which contended that the new laws would have the effect of forcing lesbians to accept the outmoded institution of the family, which deserved no additional support from the government. They insisted that the law concern itself not with couples, whether homosexual or heterosexual, but with individuals, regardless of their relationship. The upshot was that homosexual marriage is still legally impossible in Sweden.

Well before the sexual revolution of the 1960s sexuality had lost something of its totally private character owing to the introduction of sex-education classes in the schools. In 1933 the National Association for Sexual Information, or RFSU (Riksförbundet för Sexuellt Upplysning) was founded. The goal of this nonprofit organization was to "promote a society without prejudice, tolerant and open to the problems of sexuality and to the life of the couple." At the time the chief concern was not so much to liberalize sexuality as to combat venereal disease and abortion. Nevertheless, the effort to make sexual information widely available gradually broke down a series of taboos. In 1938 a new law on contraception and abortion struck down the ban that had existed since 1910 on distributing information about or selling contraceptives. The rules governing abortion were also modified. Abortion was authorized for three reasons: physical disability; pregnancy resulting from rape; and the possibility of serious congenital defects.

In 1942 optional sex education was made available in the schools, and in 1955 it became compulsory. Such instruction initially was quite conservative; students were told that the sole purpose of sexual relations was procreation in marriage. Soon, however, students as young as seven were studying sexuality, or what *Le Monde*[8] in a December 1973 headline called *"la vie à deux."*[9] It was stressed that "the act of love should be based on reciprocal affection and mutual respect." Nevertheless, matters as intimate as "masturbation, frigidity, homosexuality, contraception, venereal disease, and even pleasure" were discussed. By 1946 the law required pharmacies to stock contraceptives, and in 1959 the sale of contraceptives outside pharmacies was authorized.

At last sexuality was out in the open, in a quite literal sense. Finally, in 1964, advertising for contraceptives (sponsored by the RFSU) began to appear in newspapers and magazines. This advertising was meant to be informative, even technical, but frequently it adopted a playful and engaging tone, because its purpose was not only to inform but also to sell. Before long, advertising went far beyond condoms and diaphragms to include all sorts of sex-related products.

The demystification of sexuality, which initially grew out of a concern to stamp out disease, misery, and ignorance, in the 1960s came to be associated with debate about censorship. In 1951 the Swedish film *Hon dansade en sommar (She Only Danced One Summer)* caused a scandal because in it Folke Sundquist and Ulla Jacobsson, both stripped to the waist, are shown embracing. The film helped establish Sweden's reputation as a sexually liberated country. In 1963 the Bureau of Censorship passed Ingmar Bergman's *The Silence* despite numerous provocative scenes; but it prohibited screening of Vilgot Sjöman's *"491"* (1966) until a scene in which youths force a woman to have sexual relations with a dog had been cut. This act of censorship gave rise to an impassioned debate, until ultimately the

---

[8] *The World,* France's leading newspaper.

[9] "Life for two" or "conjugal existence."

uncut version of the film was allowed to be shown. Homosexual scenes began to appear on the screen in 1965.

Finally, in 1967, another Sjöman film, *I am Curious: Blue,* eliminated the last cinematic taboos. It gave rise to a polemic that resulted in its being banned for viewing by children, but the film was not cut. At this point several commissions were appointed to recommend changes in laws that were clearly outmoded. Documentaries on various sexual subjects were issued, including *The Language of Love,* which dealt with female sexual pleasure, and later, in 1971, *More on the Language of Love,* which, among other things, dealt with male homosexuality and the sexuality of the handicapped. That same year censorship of films was permanently abolished (except for scenes of excessive violence).

Pornography was to the sexual revolution of the 1960s and 1970s what sex education was to the 1940s and 1950s. Pornography is perhaps the most immediate manifestation of sexuality since, unlike eroticism, it places no mediator between the spectator and the object of desire. Nothing is suggested or even unveiled; everything is exhibited. It is interesting to note that the Swedish literary tradition contains virtually no erotic novel, no *Justine*[10] or *Histoire d'O,*[11] no equivalent to the works of Bataille,[12] the Marquis de Sade, or even Diderot in *Les Bijoux indiscrets.*[13] Sweden's only frivolous, libertine literature dates from the eighteenth century when the country was considered the "France of the North." Otherwise Swedish literature, particularly in works dealing with sex, is not much given to understatement, suggestion, or indirection. It is either overtly pornographic or resolutely didactic.

The sexual revolution seemed to sweep away the last taboos. Once the right to sexual information was established, the right to sexual pleasure was next to be proclaimed. No one was to be left out — equality for all: from homosexuality to voyeurism and zoophilia, all sexual practices were equally legitimate. The very notion of a "crime against nature" disappeared from the law and was replaced by that of "sexual offense" (*sedlighets brotten*).

A reaction was not long coming, however. Indeed, when examined closely, the sexual revolution of the 1960s and 1970s turns out to have been partly illusory. Formal taboos were eliminated, but traditional patterns remained largely untouched. At least that is the view of Swedish feminists, who vigorously attacked the portrayal of male-female relations in pornographic literature. One anecdote is worth recounting. The magazine *Expedition 66,* intended to be a female equivalent of *Playboy,* first appeared in 1964. It ceased publication fairly quickly, partly for

---

[10] Pornographic novel (1791) by the Marquis de Sade (1740–1814), author of many licentious works.

[11] *Story of O,* pornographic novel (1954) by Pauline Réage (pseudonym).

[12] Henri Bataille (1872–1922), French poet and author of psychological dramas.

[13] *The Indiscreet Jewels* (1748) is a pornographic story by Denis Diderot (1713–1784), a leading thinker of the French Enlightenment.

lack of readers but even more for lack of models. (In a gesture typical of Swedish honesty, the magazine's editor, Nina Estin, refused to use photographs from the files of homosexual magazines.) Subsequently almost all pornography was directed toward men.

An excellent illustration of the reaction against sexual liberation, and in particular of the role played by institutions in that reaction, can be found in prostitution. Rather paradoxically, it was in the early 1970s — at a time when sex ostensibly had ceased to constitute a transgression — that prostitution in Sweden increased sharply. At the peak of this phenomenon (1970–1972) more than a hundred "massage parlors" and "photographic studios" were operating in the Stockholm area alone. At the same time various voices were raised in favor of greater freedom and openness for prostitutes. . . .

In 1976 a commission was appointed to study the prostitution question, and a plan for retraining prostitutes was developed in 1980. The commission's report was extremely detailed and analyzed all aspects of the trade: prostitute, client, and procurer. It gave rise to a polemic between those who favored repression (most notably feminist groups) and those who feared that treating prostitutes as criminals would not eliminate the problem but would, by forcing it underground, render control impossible. The commission demonstrated in particular that prostitution in Sweden was closely associated with illicit drugs. Those who championed prostitution in the 1960s have therefore been forced to ask themselves whether it was truly "liberating." Finally, the commission noted that prostitution served exclusively as a means of satisfying male sexual needs. Here too the sexual revolution had not truly "liberated" women.

In the wake of this report, a series of restrictive measures was adopted. Although the new laws did not punish the client (except in cases involving sexual relations with a minor), they did provide for the prosecution of any person owning property used for the purpose of prostitution. Combined with an effective program for retraining prostitutes, the new laws have led to a marked decline in prostitution since 1980.

Laws were also passed against sexual activities involving violence, a common subject in pornographic publications. Peep shows were outlawed in 1982. The commission found that most of the patrons were older men, especially foreign businessmen, and concluded that "this was one part of the Swedish cultural heritage not really worth preserving." And so a specialty for which the country was internationally renowned came to an end. In fact, the whole flood of pornography that poured from the presses in the 1960s and 1970s has been, if not stopped, then at least channeled. Debate once focused on sex has been refocused on violence in all its forms, including sexual violence.

For all the transparency of Swedish society, certain opaque areas remain. Some things are prohibited, and because their number is small they are all the more fiercely protected. Violence, though uniformly condemned and prosecuted everywhere, is still present. Alcoholism is probably the area in which consensus is most tenuous and social control most vigorously challenged. Certain places are jealously guarded and kept strictly private: some exist in geographical space —

the home, the boat, the island — while others exist only in poetry or the imagination.

The passions are soft-pedaled in Sweden. If violence is not significantly more prevalent than in other countries, when it does occur it is much more shocking. Accordingly it is sternly proscribed, even in private, as in the ban on spanking. Sometimes the obsession with preventing violence can seem rather silly. Since 1979, for example, Sweden has prohibited the sale of war toys. In 1978 an exposition on the theme "Violence Breeds Violence" lumped together allegedly violent comic books, estimates of the number of children killed annually in automobile accidents, and statistics on drug use.

The goal is not just to prohibit violence but to prevent it. The government considers open, public violence as the culmination of violence born in private, including at home and on the playing field. At a deeper level, violence, whether internal or external, private or public, constitutes a threat to order and consensus. It remains one of the last areas of Swedish life outside public control.

Another area yet to be brought under control is alcoholism. To consume alcohol in Sweden is not an innocuous act. Feelings of guilt weigh on those who drink — not just the inveterate drunkards but the average Swedes who line up furtively at the *Systembolaget* (state liquor store) and sneak away with a few bottles carefully hidden away among their other parcels. Regulations governing the sale of alcohol are very strict. Temperance is officially praised, drunkenness publicly condemned. People rarely drink in public, not only because prices are high but even more because the community quietly but firmly disapproves. Drinking is permissible — and even valued — only on specific occasions, at holidays such as Midsummer's Night or the mid-August crayfish festival; at such times one drinks in order to get drunk. According to the official morality, it is just as inappropriate to drink at home in private and for no "social" reason — that is, without a justifying ritual of communication — as it is to drink in public. A daily apéritif or glass of wine can become a reprehensible secret act, something that can produce feelings of guilt.

Swedish laws on alcohol are extremely harsh. There are heavy penalties for drunk driving, which is defined as operating a motor vehicle with a blood level of more than 0.5 grams of alcohol. Alcohol cannot be purchased by anyone under the age of twenty-one, even though the age of legal majority is eighteen. This severity is hard to understand in terms of statistics alone. Alcohol consumption in Sweden in 1979 amounted to 7.1 liters per person, compared with 17 liters for France. Sweden ranks roughly twenty-fifth in the world in per-capita alcohol consumption.

The severity of the law can be understood only in terms of history. The manufacture and sale of alcoholic beverages were regulated long before the turn of the century, but it was around then that the temperance movement, having gained a powerful position in the Swedish Parliament, won adoption of a law unparalleled elsewhere in the world — the so-called Bratt System, under which anyone who wished to purchase alcohol had to present a ration book. Even today, no issue unleashes passions as strong as those connected with the alcohol problem, largely owing to members of temperance societies, whose influence in Parliament is out of proportion with their numbers in the population. Not so very long ago one deputy in three belonged to a temperance organization, and anti-alcohol societies have traditionally been a fertile breeding ground for politicians.

Nevertheless, alcohol seems to be one area in which breakdown of consensus is possible. Swedish unanimity in opposition to alcohol is more apparent than real, for in private Swedes readily violate the ban and boast, like people everywhere, of their ability to "hold their liquor."

There is a much more solid consensus in opposition to drugs. Since 1968 laws against narcotics abuse have become stricter. Serious infractions of the narcotics laws incur one of the stiffest penalties in Swedish law: ten years in prison. Furthermore, the law does not distinguish between "soft drugs" and "hard drugs." Compared with alcoholism, however, drug abuse is quantitatively a minor problem.

Violence, alcoholism, drugs: these are the principal forms of deviant behavior in Swedish society, the last areas not entirely controlled by the political sphere, the last transgressions in a society liberated from the taboos of the past.

In such a highly communitarian society, so tightly controlled by the "public," where can the individual find a private refuge? In his home, his rustic frame *sommarstuga*[14] lost in the forest or tucked away on some lake shore. The individual home is like an island, private space par excellence, cut off and personalized. In "Scandinavian Notes" Emmanuel Mounier remarked that "the most collectivist nations — Russia, Germany, Sweden — are those in which housing is most solitary."

The dream of every Swede is essentially an individualistic one, expressed through the appreciation of primitive solitude, of the vast reaches of unspoiled nature. Often built without running water and with the most rudimentary facilities, the *stuga* enables its owner to return to his rural roots and to commune intimately with nature. Virtually no Swede will travel abroad during that beautiful time in May and June when nature, at last emerged from the interminable sleep of winter, bursts forth with a dazzling and liberating light and Sweden once again becomes the land of 24,000 islands and 96,000 lakes! The small cabin lost in the country or forest thus remains, along with the island, the archipelago, and the sailboat (of which there are more than 70,000 in the Stockholm area alone), the last refuge of individualism in a highly communitarian society.

The themes of isolation, nature, and archipelago are omnipresent in Swedish literature and film. The novel entitled *The People of Hemsö* figures as a moment of illumination in Strindberg's otherwise somber oeuvre. The beautiful film *Summer Paradise* starring Gunnel Lindblom takes place entirely in the enchanting setting of a wonderful lakeside house. Though a genuine refuge, this private space can in certain situations become a tragic trap in which individuals seek desperately to recover some lost primitive state of communication, some original purity.

---

[14] House in the woods.

. . . Crimes of passion are rare in Sweden (when one does occur, it is headline news). People almost never raise their voices and rarely gesticulate; usually they keep silent. Curiously in this society, where all sorts of things are said out loud and with unaccustomed frankness, people have difficulty conversing. Although workplace relations are simple, direct, and devoid of hierarchy and everyone addresses everyone else familiarly, dinner invitations are stiffly formal and prissy, something that constantly surprises foreign visitors. It does not make conversation any easier. In Swedes, Mounier saw "the diffuse mysticism and poetry of lonely men: the Swedish people remain, in a sense, incapable of expression."

This truly private side of a self that manifests itself not so much in action as in imagination is a good starting point for exploring Swedish society and attempting to grasp its paradoxes and contradictions. How else can we understand the coexistence of such highly communitarian and public feeling with such intensely inward individualism? The solitude of that world of silence, the Great North, the intimate communion with nature — therein lies the source of Scandinavian individualism. Primitive solitude compensates for community in all its forms — organization, group study, celebration. Everything, from holidays to laws, is directed toward breaking down solitude, allowing each person a say, maintaining the traditional community intact as a necessary condition of physical survival in the harsh world of the past and of moral survival in the harsh world of the present. What else could account for the incredible popularity of the ancient pagan festivals, generally associated with rural life but now transformed into Christian holidays? Walpurgis Night celebrates spring, Saint Lucy's Night the winter solstice, Saint John's Night the middle of summer (*Midsommar*), to name only a few of the holidays that dot an unchanging calendar. For one night everyone forgets hierarchy, social class, differences, and enmities and, in togetherness and unanimity, recreates the perfectly egalitarian, perfectly consensual utopian community. During one unbridled *Midsommar* Miss Julie in Strindberg's[15] play talks, drinks, sleeps, and plans a future with her father's valet. Then morning comes and restores social difference, the impossibility of communication, and rebellion. A night's folly ends in death. How can one possibly understand the Swedish imagination if one sees this as nothing more than an insipid story of impossible love between a countess and a valet?

The Swedish model can be interpreted as a "total" or "totalizing" society. It depends on a perfectly consensual communitarian ethic, which in turn depends on absolute insistence on transparency in social relations (from the old ritual known as *nattfrieri*[16] to the child's right to know the identity of his father today). Private life cannot escape the influence of the dominant ethos. The Swedish model combines yesterday's communitarian morality with the modern social-democratic ethos.

---

[15] August Strindberg (1849–1912), Swedish novelist, poet, and playwright.

[16] "Night courting," the practice whereby a man courted his sweetheart secretly at her farm on summer evenings.

In the 1930s Marquis Childs[17] referred to "Sweden, the middle way," thus characterizing the country in a manner that would influence first his fellow Americans and, later, others. Sweden's material prosperity, which as early as 1928 included "a telephone in every hotel room, a plentiful supply of electricity, model hospitals, [and] broad, clean streets," along with an almost flawless social organization, lent credence in the 1930s to the notion of a Swedish model. European countries suddenly took a lively interest in the country, hoping to unearth the secret of its astonishing material success.

Spared the ravages of the Second World War, Sweden maintained its productive apparatus intact. To much of postwar Europe it seemed utopia incarnate, and Swedes became "the Americans of Europe." In many respects Sweden was seen as a more attractive model of social organization than the United States because inequality in Sweden was less pronounced. As Queffélec[18] pointed out in 1948, the Swedes "question all this natural prosperity." Also, the country's "moral health" enabled it to "avoid the dreadful consequences of Americanization." Mounier delightedly recounted the comment of one Swedish observer who was quite appreciative of American civilization: "The Swede, however, is actually much more attached to the individual than is the American."

In the 1940s and 1950s some in the West saw the typical Swedish woman as one who was "beautiful, athletic, and healthy." While "the legendary freedom of Scandinavian morals" was taken for granted, "to the traveler these young people seem distant and not very emotional. Couples dance quite properly" (*Action*, September 1946). Louis-Charles Royer wrote in *Lumières du Nord* (*Northern Lights*, 1939): "It is extremely difficult to court women in this country, because they always treat you as a pal." In 1954 François-Régis Bastide in his book *Suède* (Sweden) asked: "What should you say to a young Swedish woman?" His answer: "Whatever you do, it is extremely dangerous to mention the well-known reputation that Swedish women have . . . That is certain to chill things off."

The Swedish woman's reputation was no doubt associated with the campaign to provide sexual information, which since 1933 had done so much to break down sexual taboos. Sweden had provided sex education in the schools since 1942, at a time no other country had gone to such lengths. The West had confused sexual information with sexual freedom, creating an image of Sweden as sexual paradise.

In 1964 French Prime Minister Georges Pompidou visited "this strange socialist monarchy" and in a famous phrase characterized his social and political ideal as "Sweden with a bit more sun." Thus attention was once again focused on the Swedish ideal, which would attain the peak of its glory in the 1970s. During this period Sweden was in vogue; whenever it was mentioned, it was held up as an example.

---

[17] American newspaperman (1903–1990) and author of *Sweden: The Middle Way*.

[18] Henri Queffélec, French novelist, essayist, and poet (b. 1910).

Everywhere Sweden was exalted and glorified. Some had dreamed the American dream; others had idealized the Soviet Union or China or Cuba. Now the "Swedish model," the image of a just compromise, seduced Europe. Sweden became a journalistic cliché. The sexual revolution of the 1960s reinforced the myth. A cover story on "Free Love" appeared in 1965, and one French magazine devoted a special issue to Sweden. . . . Sweden was the wave of the future: the press said it, television showed it, books explained it. The "Swedish case" was analyzed and dissected. People also began to ask questions.

By 1975 articles criticizing Sweden had begun to appear. Headlines such as "Women Not Totally Free" and "The Disintegrating Family" were read. Roland Huntford launched a vigorous attack on social-democratic Sweden in his book *The New Totalitarians* (1972). The defeat of the social democrats in 1976, after more than forty-four years in power, raised questions about the political stability of Sweden. . . . Sweden was portrayed in France as a perverse model, a highly coercive society. This "prodigiously permissive" society was said to have engendered its own destruction. "Sweden: Liberated Lovers in Search of Love," was trumpeted in 1980. That same year one could read: "The Swedish mirror, much admired abroad, is broken. Something is amiss in the world's most unusual system." One headline asked, "Sweden — paradise lost?"

The Swedish model had not lived up to its promise. Racism, xenophobia, suicide, and alcoholism all existed there too. The countermodel was now at its height, even if traces of the old paradise remained. In 1984 *Le Point*[19] asked students at France's leading institutions of higher education what country best corresponded to their idea of the good society. Switzerland led the list, followed by the United States; Sweden came in fifth, behind France.

If the Swedish model had lost its appeal, it was because the country had slipped badly. Claude Sarraute[20] wrote of "incessant investigations by the tax and welfare authorities, unreasonable, Orwellian interventions in people's lives. The government keeps tabs on incomes and individuals. The meddlesome welfare state sticks its nose everywhere, even into the way you bring up your children. It encourages children to turn in 'deviant' parents." Much of the West decided it wanted no part of this "revolution in private life." Though the Swedish model may still exist, the Swedish myth is dead as a doornail.

---

[19] The French weekly newsmagazine, *The Point*.

[20] Journalist at *Le Monde* and author of numerous books (b. 1927).

ACKNOWLEDGMENTS

Richard van Dülmen, "Rituals of Execution: From Purification to Deterrence" from *Theatre of Horror: Crime and Punishment in Early Modern Germany,* translated by Elisabeth Neu. Copyright © 1985 by C. H. Beck'sche Verlagsbuchhandlung (Oscar Beck). Translation copyright © 1990 by Polity Press. Reprinted with the permission of C. H. Beck Verlag.

Christopher R. Friedrichs, "Poverty and Marginality" from *The Early Modern City 1450–1750.* Copyright © 1995 Longman Group Limited. Reprinted with the permission of the publisher.

Jacques Gélis, "The Experience of Pregnancy" from *History of Childbirth: Fertility, Pregnancy and Birth in Early Modern Europe,* translated by Rosemary Morris. Copyright © 1984 by Librairie Arthème Fayard. Translation copyright © 1991 by Polity Press. Reprinted with the permission of Blackwell Publishers.

John McManners, "Death's Arbitrary Empire" from *Death and Enlightenment.* Copyright © 1981 by John Mc-Manners. Reprinted with the permission of Oxford University Press, Ltd.

Robert Darnton, "Workers' Revolt: The Great Cat Massacre of the Rue Saint-Séverin" from *The Great Cat Massacre and Other Episodes in French Cultural History.* Copyright © 1984 by Basic Books, Inc. Reprinted with the permission of BasicBooks, Inc., a subsidiary of Perseus Books Group, LLC.

Olwen Hufton, "Women, Work, and Family" from Natalie Zemon Davis and Arlette Farge, eds., *A History of Women in the West, Volume III: Renaissance and Enlightenment Paradoxes.* Copyright © 1991 by Gius. Laterza & Figli Spa. Copyright © 1993 by the Presidents and Fellows of Harvard College. Reprinted with the permission of The Belknap Press of Harvard University Press.

Albert Soboul, "The Sans-Culottes" from *The Sans-Culottes,* translated by Remy I. Hall. Copyright © 1965 by Éditions du Seuil. Translation copyright © 1972 by Doubleday & Co. Reprinted with the permission of Georges Borchardt, Inc.

Keith Wrightson, "Infanticide in European History" from *Criminal Justice History: An International Annual* 3 (1982). Copyright © 1982 by the Crime and Justice History Group, Inc. Reprinted with the permission of the Greenwood Publishing Group, Inc.

Anna K. Clark, "The Struggle for the Breeches: Plebeian Marriage" from *The Struggle for the Breeches: Gender and the Making of the British Working Class.* Copyright © 1995 by the Regents of the University of California. Reprinted with the permission of the University of California Press.

Sidney Pollard, "Factory Discipline in the Industrial Revolution" from *Economic History Review* 16 (December 1963). Copyright © 1963. Reprinted with the permission of Sidney Pollard.

K. H. Connell, "The Potato in Ireland" from *Past and Present: A Journal of Historical Studies* 23 (November 1962). Copyright © 1962. Reprinted with the permission of the Past and Present Society and Mrs. K. H. Connell.

F. M. L. Thompson, "Victorian England: The Horse-Drawn Society" from a lecture at Bedford College/University of London (October 20, 1970). Copyright © 1970, 1991, 1996 by F. M. L. Thompson. Reprinted with the permission of the author.

Richard J. Evans, "Matters of Life and Death" from *Death in Hamburg: Society and Politics in the Cholera Years, 1830–1910.* Copyright © 1987 by Oxford University Press. Reprinted with the permission of the publishers.

Eugen Weber, "Is God French?" adapted from "Dieu: Est-Il Français?" in *Peasants into Frenchmen: The Modernization of Rural France 1870–1914.* Copyright © 1976 by the Board of Trustees of the Leland Stanford Junior University. Reprinted with the permission of Stanford University Press.

Alain Corbin, "The Perfumes of Intimacy" from *The Foul and the Fragrant: Odor and the French Social Imagination.* Copyright © 1986 by the President and Fellows of Harvard College and Berg Publishers, Ltd. Reprinted with the permission of Harvard University Press.

Stephen P. Frank, "Popular Justice, Community and Culture among the Russian Peasantry, 1870–1900" from Ben Eklof and Stephen Frank, eds., *The World of the Russian Peasant: Post-Emancipation Culture and Society.* Copyright © 1990. Reprinted with the permission of HarperCollins Publishers, Ltd.

Theresa M. McBride, "A Woman's World: Department Stores and the Evolution of Women's Employment

1870–1920" from *French Historical Studies* X (Fall 1978). Copyright © 1978 by the Society for French Historical Studies. Reprinted with permission.

Alistair Horne, "The Price of Glory: Verdun 1916" from *The Price of Glory: Verdun 1916* (London: Macmillan Publishers, 1978). Copyright © 1978 by Alistair Horne. Reprinted with the permission of The Peters Fraser and Dunlop Group Limited.

Alex de Jonge, "Inflation in Weimar Germany" from *The Weimar Chronicle, Prelude to Hitler,* New American Library, pp. 93–105. Copyright © 1978 by Alex de Jonge. Reprinted with permission of the author.

William J. Chase, "Daily Life in Moscow, 1921–1929" from *Workers, Society and the Soviet State: Labor and Life in Moscow, 1918–1929.* Copyright © 1987 by the Board of Trustees of the University of Illinois. Reprinted with the permission of the University of Illinois Press.

Laura Tabili, "Women 'of a Very Low Type': Crossing Racial Boundaries in Imperial Britain" from Laura L. Frader and Sonya O. Rose (eds.), *Gender and Class in Modern Europe.* Copyright © 1996 by Cornell University. Reprinted with the permission of Cornell University Press.

Henry Friedlander, "The Nazi Camps" from A. Grobman and D. Landes, eds., *Genocide: Critical Issues of the Holocaust.* Copyright © 1983 by the Simon Wiesenthal Center. Reprinted with the permission of the Simon Wiesenthal Center.

Philippe Ariès, "Forbidden Death" from *Western Attitudes toward Death: Middle Ages to the Present.* Copyright © 1974 by The Johns Hopkins University Press. Reprinted with the permission of the publishers.

Ellen Furlough, "Packaging Pleasures: Club Méditerranée and French Consumer Culture, 1950–1968" from *French Historical Studies,* vol. 18, no. 1 (Spring 1993). Copyright © 1993 by the Society for French Historical Studies. Reprinted with the permission of Ellen Furlough.

Kristina Orfali, "The Rise and Fall of the Swedish Model" from Philippe Ariès and Georges Duby, eds., *A History of Private Life, Volume V: Riddles of Identity in Modern Times,* translated by Arthur Goldhammer. Copyright © 1991 by the President and Fellows of Harvard College. Reprinted with the permission of The Belknap Press of Harvard University Press.